ACTIO SPECTA LE CINEMA

A S nd Sound Reader

Edited by José Arroyo

bfi Publishing

Te!

First published in 2000 by the
British Film Institute
21 Stephen Street, London W1P 2LN

The British Film Institute is the UK national agency with
responsibility for encouraging the arts of film and television
and conserving them in the national interest.

Cover image: John Travolta in *Face/Off* (John Woo, 1997)
Set by Ketchup
Printed in Great Britain by St Edmundsbury Press,
Bury St Edmunds, Suffolk

British Library Cataloguing-in-Publication Data
A catalogue record for this book is available from the British Library

ISBN 0–85170–757–2 (paperback)
ISBN 0–85170–756–4 (hardback)

Contents

Preface

This volume was originally conceived as a collection of essays on action cinema based on texts published in *Sight and Sound* over the last ten years. But the process of selection changed my notion of what the volume could/should be about. *Sight and Sound* is a monthly publication. Its writers, an eclectic bunch of academics, practitioners and journalists, are afforded enough time to allow for reflection but must still write to a deadline. Thus I was reading some of the best and most informed writers on film offering a considered response to their object of analysis in the immediate context. Reading ten years' worth of such material gives one a pretty good overview of debates, issues and interests. In the process, the volume exploded from the restrictions of genre.

Part of the reason is that the concept became less and less useful when applied to contemporary Hollywood cinema. The observant reader may notice the slippage here between contemporary Hollywood cinema, action/spectacle, high concept and the blockbuster. This is not sloppiness – though each of the terms refers to something different, the meanings overlap substantially. For instance, films as diverse as *Armageddon* and *The Mask of Zorro* (both 1998) easily fit into all four categories. Richard Schickle has argued that all genres have merged into two metacategories: action/adventure and comedy. (Schatz, 1993, p. 33.) While I hesitate to agree, I understand what he means: this volume fits easily within his action/adventure metacategory.

The volume developed into action/spectacle almost organically. The best articles on action tended to have a broader scope. The essays on spectacle tended to enrich those on action. The juxtaposition and ordering of the essays resulted in an argument for a type of cinema that cannot quite constitute a mode but which exceeds the boundaries of a genre.

The essays are divided into eight sections. Each begins with an introduction and I will thus not linger long here on contextualising individual articles. The section 'The Big Loud Action Movie' provides a historical context for action/spectacle, explores the representation of gunfire and action in cinema and offers a case study that explores the aesthetics of the category. Arnold Schwarzenegger was chosen as the subject for a case study because he is action/spectacle's most representative star. John Woo's Hong Kong action films had a great influence on Hollywood cinema and he now makes Hollywood movies. This trajectory raised issues of genre and mode across culture that made him an irresistible choice for a director's case study. The section titled 'The Influence of the Facile' explores how theme parks, comic books, television and other areas of popular culture have influenced contemporary action/spectacle. The sections 'Indie Pulp' and 'Serial Killer' provide a partial limit and connected counterpoint to action/spectacle. The penultimate section, 'Critical Perspectives on a Mode', contains essays on films ranging from *Romeo and Juliet* to *Jurassic Park*, implicitly arguing that characteristics previously associated with high-concept action movies have now become characteristic of big-budget Hollywood in general. Finally, the last section is a collection of reviews. The rationale for these choices was initially to expand the range of films discussed. But the criteria eventually transformed into that of reviews that offered insight into both action/spectacle and the individual film.

Describing some of the failings of film studies, Richard Dyer has written: 'Time and again we are not told why Westerns are exciting, why horror films horrify, why weepies make us cry, but instead are told that, while they are exciting, horrifying or tearjerking, the films also deal with history, society, psychology gender roles, indeed, the meaning of life.' (1992, p. 3.) The essays in this volume, if they don't fully answer why action/spectacle thrills, awes and amuses, certainly offer an interesting and entertaining account of how it does so and why this might be valuable.

Introduction

Action and spectacle have been an integral part of the cinema since its inception. While historians have made much of the differences between Georges Méliès' fantastic productions and the Lumière Brothers' documenting of the life that surrounded them, we should remember that the Lumière Brothers' success was founded on the fact that the mere showing of images in motion was unusual and thrilling. What today seems innocuous – a shot of some workers coming out of a factory, say – then seemed magical, a spectacular demonstration of the miracles of science more exciting than the bullet photography in *The Matrix* is for us today.

Every generation has defined what constitutes action and spectacle differently. Sound, colour, widescreen – once sensational – are no longer special attractions. While watching Cagney is always exciting, the fight scenes in his gangster films now seem quaint and unrealistic. It is easy to see the continuities in what makes the chase scenes in *Stagecoach* (1939), *Bullit* (1968) and the pre-credits sequence of *The World Is Not Enough* (1999) spectacular (extraordinary stunts performed at high speed and edited to create variations in narrative tension), but the differences are equally distinctive: Bond has to chase on ground, air and water for a greater length of time through a greater number of explosions to thrill. Whether these constitute simple differences of degree or more substantial differences in kind is a question we will return to.

Action in Hollywood cinema has functioned as spectacle in its own right, associated with, if not quite relegated to, particular genres: the gangster film, westerns, action/adventure. But the spectacular was never restricted to action – stars were regularly presented as spectacle and narrative tended to linger on sensational sets and costumes or come to a full stop to show armies of extras or Fred and Ginger dancing. The spectacular, too, is associated with particular genres: the musical, the epic, the costume drama, science fiction. Both sets of genres were produced to be entertainments and were mainly received as such. As 'only entertainment' – their potential disturbances on the whole managed by censorship and the profit-making motive – they were regarded as the opposite of serious works of art designed to change perceptions, push aesthetic boundaries and challenge our views.

Contemporary action/spectacle is less easily associated with genre. Certainly films as diverse as *Titanic, Men in Black* and *Jurassic Park: The Lost World*, all from 1997, fit a similar production profile (high-budget, lavishly produced potential blockbusters that anchor a studio's seasonal release schedule), answer to shared expectations of content (funny, scary, laden with action and special effects) and to some extent have a similar narrative structure (equilibrium, disruption, a quest for resolution against deadline interspersed with set pieces, the restoration of equilibrium and the impression of closure). One can link each film to historical genres: *Titanic* to the women's film, melodrama and disaster movies; *Men in Black* to action/adventure, comedy and sci-fi; *The Lost World* to children's films, comedy and horror. Yet it is difficult to detect a shared iconography, style or thematic concern.

The problems of applying traditional concepts of genre to contemporary action/spectacle become evident when one looks at the sequels that have become so ubiquitously successful over the past quarter century. As with genre, the expectation of a sequel is that it will be the same but different: that it will produce the same characters in a similar setting and story told in roughly the same way so audiences may experience a repetition, and ideally an intensification, of the pleasures of the original. Yet a look at a series like the *Alien* films demonstrates that a sequel can successfully deliver on its inherent promise with relative disregard for genre. *Alien* can be described as a horror film, *Aliens* as action/adventure and *Alien³* as an existential Aids allegory in art-film mode (though, as with *Alien Resurrection,* a too radical departure from expectations was blamed for the film's relative box-office failure).

This volume was conceived with the rationale that while action/spectacle has become such a popular type of Hollywood cinema as to be almost synonymous with it, such films have not yet received the critical attention one might expect. Perhaps this is because, as R. L. Rutsky and Justin Wyatt suggest in 'Serious Pleasures: Cinematic Pleasure and the Notion of Fun', 'film criticism's academic legitimacy has always been based on the distinctions between serious pleasure and mere diversion (the repeated attempts to separate "high" from "mass" culture, art from "mere" commodity).' (1990, p. 4.) It may also be, as Jim Collins suggests in 'Genericity in the Nineties', that 'contemporary film criticism has been utterly unable to come to terms with [the] very profound changes in the nature of entertainment because [these films'] hyperconscious eclecticism is measured against 19th Century notions of classical narrative and realist representation.' (1993, p. 250.) Or, as Jon Belton suggests, that 'The films themselves set up a deliberate resistance: they are so insistently not serious, so knowing about their own escapist fantasy and pure entertainment nature, and they consistently invite the audience's complicity in this.' (1996, p. 205.) Of course, there has been a substantial amount of important work in the area – for instance, Collins, Radner and Collins, 1993; Lewis, 1998; Maltby and Craven, 1995; Neale and Smith, 1998; Tasker, 1993; Wyatt, 1994, Wasko, 1994. Yet this seems insufficient when one considers that its subject is a quarter-century of one of the most influential and successful imperial cinemas, so critically derided as to be blamed for the decline and, occasionally, the death of cinema itself, and so different from 'classic' cinema that the application of traditional methods of analysis is often inadequate. Reading through the last decade of *Sight and Sound* to choose the articles that make up this volume made vivid the scope, complexity and richness of this area of film; each article selected offers insights into individual films, directors and cycles, while as a whole the collection raises further questions that to my knowledge have yet to be answered.

Contempt for the contemporary

In 1977 the American Film Institute's list of the 50 greatest American films sent Louise Brooks into a rage. 'The two Disneys on the AFI list [*Fantasia* and *Snow White and the Seven Dwarfs*] give away the plot,' she wrote to a friend. 'The voters grew up on TV comic strips: no attention is necessary to follow. My friend in the building, Avram

Phelosof, 26, Syracuse University – he picked *Kane, Strangelove, The General, Godfather, 2001.* Under my fiendish glare he was afraid to pick *Star Wars*, which he knows frame by frame.' (Paris, 1989, p. 500.) *Star Wars* (1977) privileged an imaginary world over a 'real' one, action over characterisation, spectacle over depth; as with television and comic books, the idea that it could have any aesthetic value was to Brooks beneath contempt. Her self-described fiendish glare was clearly intended to prevent the barbarians from being welcomed through the gates.

Had Brooks been alive 20 years later she might have been further enraged to find that *Star Wars* had accrued enough critical stock to make it to number 15 on the AFI's 1998 list (http://www.racecentral.com/afi.html). But the list, in fact a successful marketing ploy disguised as a populist attempt at canon formation, should not distract us from observing that Brooks' views on *Star Wars* find wide echo in relation to action/spectacle. Robin Wood has argued that the 80s, when action/spectacle became established as the dominant mode, was 'the most impoverished, the most cynical, the most reactionary, the emptiest [era], in the entire history of Hollywood.' (1985, p. 5) Writing in 1996, Susan Sontag claimed that the cinema of the previous decade demonstrated an 'ignominious, irreversible decline' with commercial cinema settling for 'a policy of bloated, derivative film-making' which produces films made purely for entertainment that are 'astonishingly witless'. (1996, p. 27.)

Hollywood cinema as exemplified by the action/spectacle mode of the last two decades is widely seen as mass culture at its most crudely capitalistic: the selling of lowest-denominator highest-impact sensation with no other purpose than to facilitate the exchange of affect for cash. Richard Schickle, for instance, has written that 'Hollywood seems to have lost or abandoned the art of narrative. [Film-makers] are generally not refining stories at all, they are spicing up concepts, refining gimmicks, making sure there are no complexities to fur our tongues when it comes time to spread the word of mouth.' (Schatz, 1993, p. 33.) According to Jean Douchet, '[Today], cinema has given up the purpose and the thinking behind individual shots [and narrative], in favour of images – rootless, textureless images – designed to violently impress by constantly inflating their spectacular qualities.' (Buckland, 1999, p. 178.) From this perspective, discussing such films in terms of aesthetics might appear ludicrous: as James Schamus has written, for such films 'the budget is the aesthetic'. (Maltby and Craven, 1995, p. 24.) But is this really so? In 'The Work of Art in the Age of Mechanical Reproduction' Walter Benjamin argued that, earlier, 'much futile thought had been devoted to the question of whether photography is an art. The primary question – whether the very invention of photography had not transformed the entire nature of art – was not raised.' (1968, p. 227.) In a related way, it would be useful to ask not whether action/spectacle cinema fits traditional notions of cinematic art, but how the very existence of such cinema might require a rethink of what film art is and can be. This question is one that has informed the selection and ordering of the articles in this volume and one on which the articles themselves provoke further questioning.

The argument that Hollywood cinema is characterised by pseudo-individuation, an advertising aesthetic, standardisation, conservatism and passive consumption is one Adorno and Horkheimer made in *The Dialectic of Enlightenment* in relation to the 'classic' cinema so beloved of those who now speak of Hollywood's decline. One could even claim that their analysis is as broadly valid for the cinema of that period as it is applicable to Hollywood today. But I would also venture that their argument is fundamentally incorrect. Instead of looking at what Hollywood cinema was and could be, they evaluated it negatively in accordance with aesthetic criteria developed for high culture, giving short shrift to its utopian dimension, both aesthetically and socially. Likewise, one can argue that much of the opprobrium heaped on contemporary Hollywood cinema today stems not so much from an analysis of what it is (which could use further exploration on all levels: economic, technological, aesthetic, theoretical) than from what it is not ('classic' Hollywood). The point here is not to argue against historical contextualisation but to resist the nostalgic notion of a golden age and ideal reference point, particularly if that era coincides with the cinema of one's youth. As Peter Kramer reminds us, 'Juvenilisation, the technological renewal of the cinematic experience, the trend towards big event pictures, and the displacement of narrative by spectacle had all been the subject of critical debate in the 1950s long before the new breed of blockbusters in the 1970s and 1980s provoked strong critical reactions along these lines.' (1998, p. 303.)

The issues that inform the essays in this volume are in many ways those of traditional film criticism: authorship, genre, style, aesthetics, socio-cultural and historical significance and, unavoidably, value. Where they differ is in not taking the object of their analysis for granted: questioning rather than assuming what cinema is and what are the appropriate modes of perception and/or consumption. In other words, these essays were written with the conscious intention of understanding and explaining their object of analysis – as if Brooks had brought her celebrated critical insights and considerable writing talent to explore what someone as intelligent and educated as her neighbour might have found in *Star Wars*. But perhaps it's understandable: *Star Wars* was as different from Pabst or Von Sternberg as *The Matrix* is from the films Altman or Coppola made in the 70s.

Death and difference

Pronouncements on the death of cinema used to strike me as bewildering. How can cinema be dying when customers still line up at the multiplexes and attendance figures and box-office revenues are rising? When Hollywood cinema is available in more places and in more formats than ever before? The notion that cinema is dead or dying makes sense only if one concludes that the cinema we see at the multiplex is so different from what was traditionally defined as cinema as to constitute something else. According to Pauline Kael, 'Although there is a fear on the part of some people in the press that movies are dying, the medium itself is still exciting to schoolkids – maybe more exciting than ever. It's the art of film as we used to talk about it that is probably metamorphosing into something else – into the show, which is what it started as.' (Sawhill, 1998, p. 93.)

A comparison between the top ten box-office hits of 1976 – the year between the releases of *Jaws* and *Star Wars* – and the top ten of 1996 is a powerful indication of the extent to which Hollywood cinema has changed. According to Cobbett Steinberg in *Reel Facts*, the top ten hits of 1976 were (in decreasing order of domestic rentals): *One Flew*

Over the Cuckoo's Nest, All the President's Men, The Omen, The Bad News Bears, Silent Movie, Midway, Dog Day Afternoon, Murder by Death, Jaws (reissue) and *Blazing Saddles* (reissue). (1981, p. 445.) According to Box Office Statistics, the top ten hits of 1996 were *Independence Day, Twister, Mission Impossible, Jerry McGuire, Ransom, 101 Dalmatians, The Rock, The Nutty Professor, The Birdcage* and *A Time to Kill* (htpp://www.vex.net/~odin/Gross/). A cursory glance indicates that the 1976 films are more diverse, place greater emphasis on characterisation and social commentary, contain relatively little action and spectacle, use music more sparingly, have fewer special effects, are less glossy and loud, and are more sober and reflective. But a closer look reveals more fundamental differences, to the extent that it can be argued that the two groups of films belong to distinct modes of production.

Historians always urge attention to continuities as well as to rupture. But the differences between contemporary Hollywood cinema and the cinema of the 70s need to be underlined. Though the names of the major film-production companies have remained largely stable in the last half of the twentieth century (Warners, Paramount, Disney, Universal, United Artists, MGM), the way they are composed is substantially different. According to Tino Balio, 'The quintessential sixties conglomerate was Gulf + Western. The parent company of Paramount Pictures as of 1966, Gulf + Western owned or had interests in a range of unrelated industries such as sugar, zinc, fertiliser, wire and cable, musical instruments, real estate and a score of others.' (1998, p. 61.) The mergers of the 80s, on the other hand, were characterised by vertical and horizontal integration so a company could maximise the synergy of controlling production, distribution and exhibition across a range of outlets. Disney, for instance, not only owns film-production companies such as Touchstone, Hollywood Pictures and Miramax, but also theme parks, ABC Television, the Walt Disney Channel, ESPN, publishing companies, record labels and radio stations, stores selling merchandising and a substantial stake in internet company Starwave and the Infoseek search engine. Thus Disney produced *Home Improvement*, one of 1994's highest-rated television shows, for the ABC network it owns. It then produced *The Santa Clause* (1994), a huge hit with *Home Improvement* star Tim Allen. It also published Allen's autobiography *Don't Stand Too Close to a Naked Man* through its trade book-publishing company Hyperion. All these products cross-promoted each other to Disney's profit. 'It was a classic example of the multiplier effect from true synergy,' writes Michael Eisner, Disney CEO. (1998, p. 341)

If the composition of the conglomerates that produce Hollywood films has changed, so has the market they produce for. Ostensibly referring to Reaganomics and deregulation, the 1989 Time Warner annual report stated, 'In the Eighties we witnessed the most profound political and economic changes since the end of the Second World War. As these changes unfolded, Time, Inc., and Warner Communications, Inc., came independently to the same fundamental conclusion: globalization was rapidly evolving from a prophesy to a fact of life. No serious competitor could hope for any long term success unless, building on a secure home base, it achieved a major presence in all of the world's important markets.' (Lewis, 1998, p. 98) In relation to film, this meant that the choice of subject matter, stars and style had to be made with an international audience in mind. This might help explain the prevalence of action/spectacle, for, as Maltby and Craven point out, action does better internationally than movies that rely on dialogue. 'More than any other movie star,' they write, 'Schwarzenegger personifies contemporary Hollywood's orientation toward a global market.' (1995, p. 71.)

The ways Hollywood films are advertised and distributed have also changed. According to Thomas Schatz, the 1975 release of *Jaws* – promoted through a $2.5 million media blitz with saturation advertising on television and released on a wide number of screens – can be seen as a consolidation of previous distribution and marketing practices and a precursor to contemporary trends. (1993, p. 18.) Justin Wyatt notes, 'Whereas in the past, this type of opening had been reserved for films which the studio judged to have little playability, the opening of *Jaws* signified the adoption of this release and marketing pattern for high-quality studio pictures.' (1994, p. 111.) This expensive pattern of release and marketing partly accounts for blockbuster films in that a film is expected to earn the majority of its theatrical revenues in its first weeks of release.

But the overall period within which a film generates revenue is now much longer and encompasses different media. In the early 70s a film was expected to garner most of its revenue from its theatrical release and network television. But today a film's economic lifespan is virtually limitless. The usual distribution pattern involves first a theatrical release, then video (rental and sell-through), pay television, network television and ancillary markets at home and abroad. This has substantially increased films' earning potential. In fact, in the US, video is now a greater source of revenue than theatrical box office. According to Janet Wasko, 'in 1990, consumers spent $14.9 billion renting or buying video cassettes, outpacing theatrical box office revenues by nearly $10 billion.' (1994, p. 114.) However, a film's theatrical release remains important in that box office is an indicator of how a film will do in ancillary markets and thus helps determine prices charged for exhibition in subsequent media.

Such an economic and industrial infrastructure obviously affects what types of films are made and how, accounting in part for the prevalence of what has come to be called high-concept cinema. Though people as diverse as Michael Eisner and Jon Peters claim credit for the idea, the term is popularly associated with Don Simpson, co-producer with Jerry Bruckheimer of such examples of the genre as *Flashdance* (1983), *Top Gun* (1986) and the *Beverly Hills Cop* films (1986 and after). The idea basically refers to films whose story premise can be told in twenty-five words or less to allow for saturation marketing that will permit the widest possible release. For instance, 'Arnold Schwarzenegger and Danny De Vito in *Twins*' basically tells the story of the film. Moreover, as Justin Wyatt explains in his important book on the subject, 'high-concept can be identified through the surface appearance of the films' high tech visual style and production design which are self-conscious to the extent that the physical perfection of the film's visuals sometimes "freezes" the narrative in its tracks.' (1994, p. 25.) The simplification of character and narrative is accompanied by an excessive use of music, often to accompany montages or set pieces that are overplayed in relation to the narrative information they convey and whose primary purpose seems to be to sell the soundtrack. A logo and stars help to identify, communicate and sell the concept. Wyatt notes that 'the look of the images, the marketing hooks, and the reduced narratives form the cornerstones of High Concept.' (1994, p. 22.)

The economic infrastructure within which films are made, the variety of formats in which they are viewed and the increasing importance of marketing have obviously had an effect on aesthetics. But developments in film-production technology have also changed what can be shown and how. Special effects are ubiquitous in action/spectacle not only because they are possible, but also, at least for big-budget films, because they are affordable (as well as working as a form of product differentiation). Of the many technological changes that affect the way films look and sound, I here want to mention two: the Steadicam and computer-generated imagery (CGI).

The Steadicam is now so ubiquitous it is difficult to believe it was not introduced until 1976. According to Jean-Pierre Geuens, the Steadicam has 'significantly altered the visual look of films.' (1993–4, p. 8.) It combines the ease of operation and range of a handheld camera with smooth, jitter-free movements. Geuens sees its attributes as speed, flexibility, mobility and responsiveness but finds its overall effect negative since its very ease often excludes consideration of composition and point of view. Geuens also argues that the Steadicam depersonifies and dematerialises perspective (p. 16). Whether or not one agrees, the very ubiquity and distinctiveness of the device has left a mark on contemporary film aesthetics that needs to be explored.

The effects of CGI on the aesthetics of contemporary action/spectacle are more clearly evident and it has become one of the key characteristics of the mode. It can be used both to create realistic effects and to draw attention to itself as actively constructing an imaginary hyperreal. According to Michele Pierson, science-fiction films of the early to mid 90s utilised special effects as both an element of narrative and a distinct form of technological spectacle. Pierson argues that though 'the aesthetic project governing the production of CGI effects for science-fiction films is frequently presented as being geared towards simulation, this period of special effects production also marks the emergence of a popular, techno-futurist aesthetic that foregrounds the synthetic properties of electronic imagery.' (1999, p. 158.) Special effects in action/spectacle often draw attention to themselves, asking the viewer to share the joke, pretend s/he is fooled or simply marvel at what technology and imagination are capable of. In all instances the spectacular use of CGI tends to slow the narrative and distract from the story.

When considering the aesthetics of contemporary Hollywood cinema it is necessary to think about what film today might be. Certainly a movie like *Batman* (1989) is very different from 70s cinema. In '"Holy commodity fetish, Batman!"; the political economy of a commercial intertext' Eileen Meehan suggests the film 'is best understood as a multimedia multi-sales campaign' (1991, p. 52) and describes how its initial budget was not only for the film's production but constituted the capital outlay for a range of cultural products including two soundtracks, animated videos, comic books and a vast array of merchandising. Each product helped sell the others and the consumption of each required an intertextual awareness of the others. (Without an understanding of the origins of Batman as described in the comic books, for instance, parts of the film such as the robbery at the beginning which fools the viewer into thinking it is Bruce Wayne's parents who are going to be killed, become incomprehensible.) The investment in the film was also an investment in a concept, style and look that could be recycled in sequels. Watching the movie can thus be seen as not merely a privileged but a prismatic view into a matrix of signification, a view enlarged by the different experiences offered by the various Batman products, which always remain partial and incomplete.

Such a film evidently requires a different mode of viewing. The spectator has to be an adept interpreter of intertextual references, since popular films, as Janet Wasko notes, not only make self-conscious use of parody but 'often initiate or continue an endless chain of other cultural products.' (1994, p. 4.) Justin Wyatt describes the viewing of high concept as follows: 'In place of identification with narrative, the viewer becomes sewn into the "surface" of the film, contemplating the style of the narrative and the production. The excess created through such channels as the production design, stars, music, and promotional apparatus enhances this appreciation of the film's surface quality.' (1994, p. 60.) Michele Pierson's description of the spectator of sci-fi films also hints at a distracted contemplation: 'the mode of arts-and-effects direction characteristic of science-fiction cinema in the early 1990s is very much directed towards establishing a spectatorial relation to its computer-generated special effects that is wondering and even contemplative.' (1999, p. 169.) Thus we are invited to view Hollywood cinema as spectators who are knowledgeable, contemplative and appreciative of surface, and open to narrative distractions.

We have established that contemporary Hollywood cinema, as represented by action/spectacle, is substantially different from Hollywood cinema of the 70s in terms of its industrial infrastructure, economics and aesthetics. Individually, each of these might constitute only a difference in degree, but cumulatively they suggest a difference in kind. What Hollywood cinema is, where we see it and how we see it has changed. As the essays in this volume demonstrate, action/spectacle is a case in point. Rather than dismiss it, we should develop methods to explain, categorise, differentiate and evaluate without stooping to populism or patronising its audience.

References

Adorno, Theodor and Max Horkheimer, *The Dialectic of Enlightenment* (London: Verso, 1979).

Balio, Tino, '"A major presence in all of the world's important markets"; the globalization of Hollywood in the 1990s', in Neale and Smith (eds), *Contemporary Hollywood Cinema*, pp. 58–73.

Belton, John, 'Papering the Cracks: Fantasy and Ideology in the Reagan Era', in John Belton (ed.), *Movies and Mass Culture* (London: The Athlone Press, 1996), pp. 203–31.

Benjamin, Walter, 'The Work of Art in the Age of Mechanical Reproduction', *Illuminations* (New York: Schoken Books, 1968), pp. 217–52.

Buckland, Warren, 'Between science fact and science fiction', *Screen*, vol. 40 no. 2, Summer 1999, pp. 177–91.

Collins, Jim, 'Genericity in the Nineties: Eclectic Irony and the New Sincerity', in Collins, Radner and Preacher Collins (eds), *Film Theory Goes to the Movies*, pp. 242–63.

Collins, Jim, Hilary Radner and Ava Preacher Collins (eds), *Film Theory Goes to the Movies* (London: Routledge, 1993).

Dyer, Richard, 'Introduction', *Only Entertainment* (London: Routledge, 1992), pp. 1–9.

Eisner, Michael (with Tony Scwaratz), in Michael Eisner, work in progress (London: Penguin).

Geuens, Jean-Pierre, 'Visuality and Power: The Work of the Steadicam', *Film Quarterly*, vol 47 no. 2, Winter 1993–4, pp. 8–17.

Hill, John and Pamela Church Gibson, *The Oxford Guide to Film Studies* (Oxford: Oxford University Press, 1998).

Kramer, Peter, 'Post-classical Hollywood', in Hill and Church Gibson, *The Oxford Guide to Film Studies*.

Lewis, Jon, 'Money Matters: Hollywood in the Corporate Era', in Jon Lewis (ed.), *The New American Cinema* (Durham, NC: Duke University Press, 1998), pp. 87–121.

Maltby, Richard and Ian Craven, *Hollywood Cinema* (Oxford: Blackwell, 1995).

Neale, Steve and Murray Smith (eds.), *Contemporary Hollywood Cinema* (London: Routledge, 1998).

Paris, Barry, *Louise Brooks* (London: Hamish Hamilton, 1989).

Pierson, Michele, 'CGI effects in Hollywood science-fiction cinema 1989–1995: the wonder years', *Screen*, 1999, pp. 158–76.

Rutsky, R. L. and Justin Wyatt, 'Serious Pleasures: Cinematic Pleasure and the Notion of Fun', *Cinema Journal*, vol. 30 no. 1, Fall 1990, pp. 3–19.

Sawhill, Ray, 'A Talk with Pauline Kael', *Newsweek Extra*, Summer 1998, pp. 93–4.

Schatz, Thomas, 'The New Hollywood' in Collins, Radner and Preacher Collins (eds.), *Film Theory Goes to the Movies*, pp. 8–37.

Sontag, Susan, 'The Strongest Experience', *The Guardian*, 2 March 1996, p. 27.

Steinberg, Cobbett, *Reel Facts* (New York: Penguin Books, 1981).

Tasker, Yvonne, *Spectacular Bodies: Gender, Genre and the Action Cinema* (London: Routledge, 1993).

Wasko, Janet, *Hollywood in the Information Age* (Cambridge: Polity Press, 1994).

Wood Robin, '80s Hollywood: Dominant Tendencies', *CineAction*, no. 1, Spring 1985, pp. 3–5.

Wyatt Justin, *High Concept: Movies and Marketing in Hollywood* (Austin: University of Texas Press, 1994).

Mission Impossible (Brian De Palma, 1996)

Section I:
The Big Loud Action Movie

For close to a quarter-century action/spectacle has been the most popular and most critically derided mode of film-making in Hollywood. The following introductory section provides a valuable description of a spectacularly hybrid cinema, one not easily contained within strictly defined categories of genre, as well as a historical context for it. This is accompanied by an inquiry into the representations and uses of gunfire and action, two interrelated but distinct staples of the mode. The section concludes with a case study that explores the aesthetics of action/spectacle and indicates a mode of evaluation, issues which whether overtly raised or merely imbricated in the very praxis of criticism, recur throughout the volume.

Larry Gross writes about what he calls 'The Big Loud Action Movie' as the movie-as-Theme Park, the movie-as-giant-Comic-Book and the movie-as-Ride. He dates the mode of film-making from around 1977 to *Star Wars* and *Close Encounters of the Third Kind*, films which 'mark a new moment in thinking successfully (and in newly marketable terms) about making visually spectacular cinema'. Gross finds antecedents in the Bond films after *From Russia with Love*, the cinema of Irwin Allen and *2001: A Space Odyssey*. Gross also outlines four chararacteristics: a) the elaborate and expensively produced elevation of B Movie genre plots; b) a reduction of narrative complexity; c) the Cinematic, the Image and Technology dominate the narrative experience; and d) self-deprecating humour.

Jason Jacobs follows this by an exploration of the conventions of representing gunfire. Jacobs sees *The Wild Bunch* as an early example of the gradual transformation of modern Hollywood cinema into a pure thrill machine, offering sensation over story, the cause-effect narrative engine becoming subordinate to the spectacle. Jacob notes that popular knowledge of weaponry and its effects increased as a result of the Vietnam War and the assassination of JFK and, thus, gunfire had to be represented as more visceral and out of control in order to be seen as realistic. Jacobs also notes that gunfire sequences are a highly stylised spectacle in which 'genuine dramas of mastery and loss' are played out and that these sequences are of particular pleasure to men.

Richard Dyer takes up some of the issues raised by Gross and Jacobs arguing that 'the celebration of sensational movement, that we respond to in some still unclear sense "as if real", for many people *is* the movies'. Dyer explores how in contemporary cinema it is largely the action film that delivers speed, generally in the sense of the movie as action with next to no plot. Dyer also explores how this type of relation to movement and speed involves a gendered and racialised view of being in the world.

Dyer argues that, 'Action movies, as the most common contemporary form of the cinema of sensation, ally the speed they offer with white male characters.'

In the final article of this section, José Arroyo agrees that the 'popcorn' movie (what Gross calls the 'Big Loud Action Movie') is the dominant mode of Hollywood filmmaking (and, as such, needs to be taken seriously), but notes that it doesn't fit easily into traditional discourses of aesthetics. These films seem to lack coherence, balance, internal consistency and depth but, in their attempt to provide 'The Ride', they can be seen to belong to a long history of the 'cinema of attractions'. Here the pleasures on offer, as well as much of the films' value, lie in the set pieces which function somewhat like numbers in a musical. Their function as spectacle exceeds their function as narrative. The aim of the action set piece is often the evocation of horror and dread usually associated with the sublime. Arroyo argues that critical attention to the representation of speed and movement through the *mise en scène* of framing, camera movement, design, colour, music and even the line of the body might lead to a different appreciation of this type of film. For Arroyo, the degree to which action/spectacle cinema succeeds in orchestrating an expressive use of non-representational signs for aesthetic and visceral effects (and what these might be) is a more important criterion of value than analyses of plot, character or an application of crude notions of realism.

BIG AND LOUD

Larry Gross

Batman Forever grosses $53 million in its first weekend. *Waterworld* will do whatever it will do. *Die Hard with a Vengeance* has performed, *Judge Dredd* is presumed to be so bad that it won't, but *Congo* has eluded the worst reviews imaginable, so you can't figure. Whatever you call this genre – the movie-as-Theme-Park, the movie-as-Giant-Comic-Book, the movie-as-Ride – I call it simply the Big Loud Action Movie. For better or worse it has been a central economic fact, structuring all life, thought and practice in Hollywood at least since the late 70s. This will not change soon.

The Big Loud Action Movie may seem like the size of the American Government, too big and wasteful to win anyone's intellectual assent or moral approval, and also too big to reform itself or go away. Challenges to this way of making films are routinely voiced. Condemnations of the content of such pictures (and the lack thereof) are routinely offered. But the fact remains, simple, pristine, inescapable: Big Loud Action Pictures make up an enormous percentage of those films that gross over $200 million in the United States, and go on to make five times that in foreign and ancillary markets.

With numbers like that Hollywood will never stop making these films.

The genre we're living with today I date as commencing in the Year of our Lord 1977, the year of *Star Wars* and *Close Encounters of the Third Kind.* For me these films mark a new moment in thinking successfully (and in newly marketable terms) about making visually spectacular cinema. But commercial film was arguably itself born through spectacle, and spectacular action, with *The Birth of a Nation* in 1915. The moment there was sound, film-makers recorded the voice of *King Kong* (1933) and the airplane machine-guns that would shoot him down, to give huge audiences cheap thrills.

Indeed, the reason that a simple knee-jerk condemnation of the Big Loud Action Movie of today is unsound is that some of the greatest films in cinema history – from Abel Gance's *Napoléon* to *2001* – overlap and interweave in their aspirations and in their formal procedures with the Big Loud Action Movies – this corporatised crap – that Hollywood makes today. Our scorn for this degradation of epic cinema needs to be modified by awareness that the serpent tail of grandiosity is as much to be found in the so-called sophisticated members of the film audience as in the thrill-junkies, presumed brainless, who live off the current crop.

Hollywood has been pragmatically schizoid about the status of Action in its narratives from the beginning. Serial pulp fiction, as far back as Pearl White and Fairbanks and their adventure flicks, has been churned out by Hollywood: low-budget sci-fi, westerns, thrillers, all things B for many decades. But at the same time the claim of epic special effects, action and imagery has always attracted whoever was on Hollywood's

A List. *Wings*, directed by William Wellman, was the Action movie of its day (1927) and won the first prestigious Academy Award. A classic prestige picture from mid-30s Hollywood, such as W. S. Van Dyke's *San Francisco*, tells a fairly ordinary-scale romantic soap opera story, but gets its audiences juiced with ten minutes of huge special effects and unremitting action when the city itself succumbs to an earthquake. Even in so tame a picture, the shrilling shock of scale is part of the commercial package. David Selznick ingeniously applied scale to every detail of *Gone with the Wind*, and turned it into the most popular American film of all time, still. Although it does not rely on wall-to-wall violence, everything in it, even the floral prints on Scarlett O'Hara's dresses, is big. Selznick is also one of the precursors of the Big Loud Action Movie because he was involved in marketing his film in a new way. *Gone with the Wind* is the prototype of the Event Picture that *Batman Returns* represents today. Total saturation of every adjacent media outlet is used to pound consumers with 'awareness' of the film. This procedure Selznick invented.

Lean to Bond

So we acknowledge that serious artists have always tried to make 'big' pictures, throughout film history. Griffith and Gance have already been mentioned, but probably the prototype of the serious big-scale Action director working within the commercial system, in the pre-*Star Wars* world, is David Lean. To understand where we are and what we've given up along the way, consider *The Bridge on the River Kwai* and *Lawrence of Arabia*. These films share a number of vulgar commercial aspirations with the Big Loud Action Movie. They are blatantly in love with their own technology. They are loud and violent epics trying rigorously to reduce most dramatic situations to issues of extreme physical jeopardy. They are expansions of a Kipling-esque adolescent boys' adventure universe.

But what Lean retained are two realities that, since *Star Wars*, Big Loud Action Movies have managed to repress, eliminate or overcome: psychological complexity, and the registration of accurate social and historical detail. Even though Lean's films take place in a world of Action heroics, his protagonists (Alec Guinness in *Kwai*, Peter O'Toole in *Lawrence*) are capable of inwardness, of a conflicted self-questioning element that few 80s or 90s action heroes in a big expensive film are allowed time for. And the patterns of action do not, in Lean's films, entirely obliterate tangible lived social reality (specifically the facts of ethnic difference, between English and Japanese in *Kwai*, between English and Arab in *Lawrence*). Lean is a God to today's Big Loud Action Movie-Makers. Along with Akira Kurosawa he set a standard (for the time) of big-action, big-budget film-making that nonetheless managed to contain genuine seriousness. The Serious Action Epic was something Hollywood remained committed to throughout the 60s and 70s, in such projects as *Ben-Hur* and *Cleopatra*, in projects like *The Wild Bunch*, and finally in such Vietnam films as Cimino's *The Deer Hunter* and Coppola's *Apocalypse Now*. The moment these last two films came out, 1978–79, was a strange, sad one in Hollywood: it did contain these instances of higher studio seriousness (in addition, there was Terry Malick's *Days of Heaven*), but these now seem poignantly dinosaurish in their ambition to combine commercial scale and seriousness. Subsequent attempts at this that were serious, such as *Empire of the Sun* or

Heaven's Gate, have been deemed misfires or have been pragmatically chopped down into smaller, neater thematic packages so as to resemble the Big Loud Action Movie they actually want to surpass – sometimes such a modest expansion of ambition-in-disguise works fairly well as in *The Hunt for Red October* or *Clear and Present Danger*, movies with a whiff of nostalgia for the psychological and political complexities of the Lean/Kurosawa type of action movie.

I've associated Big Loud Action Movies with the phenomenal success and influence of George Lucas and Steven Spielberg, but before describing these directors' impact more specifically I want to point to three forces in the film-making of the late 60s and 70s that prepared us (warmed us up, if you will) for the effect that Lucas and Spielberg were to have.

1. *James Bond after 'From Russia with Love' gives up spying for what?* For an entirely new super-kinetic cartoon-type action movie, that's what. In the Bond series, from *Goldfinger* on, espionage and plot mechanics disappear almost entirely. Pure-action set pieces, large in scale, take over, moving the series ever more towards science fiction without claiming to go forward in time (not literally, anyway). And an industry never entirely absent from the Hollywood action cinema gets fully underway: the quip industry. James Bond never dispatches villains without an appropriate witty one-liner. That has become the mode of speech of the protagonist of every Big Loud Action Movie ever since.

The Bond films were very important for other reasons. Technology, not only behind the screen, but as subject matter, as object of pleasurable consumption, becomes central. Goldfinger's lasers, Bond and his super-outfitted Aston Martin, these point to the marriage of Big Action and Science Fiction, the sense that the new hero must be a Superhero, *ergo* a technically enhanced one. My favourite instance of this in a full-fledged Big Loud Action Movie is Sigourney Weaver's big-and-tall loading machine in *Aliens*. Some twenty years have elapsed, but conceptually it's only a blink. It is also interesting that George Lucas said that he conceived of Indiana Jones exactly in opposition to James Bond, as a hero with a whip and a hat instead of machinery; but it is important to realise that (inevitably, oedipally) we always borrow a good deal from what we oppose. Indiana Jones' quipping urbanity owes a lot to Bond. Why else cast Sean Connery as his father?

2. *That Master Without Honour: the Cinema of Irwin Allen.* Here's an unreported fact about American cinema in the mid-70s. While Hollywood was at its post-war artiest, with people named Robert Altman, Hal Ashby and Bob Rafelson getting a majority of critical ink, Irwin Allen was busy making shitloads of money with *The Poseidon Adventure* and *The Towering Inferno*. The cruelly interpersonal action-adventure violence we're now used to was in low supply in these films: nonetheless gut-churning jeopardy fuelled every minute of their narrative structure. No dramatic experience other than imminent death was ever allowed on-screen, and they were films utterly involved in the romance of spectacular technology. They were films as engineering problems, something that men like Jim Cameron and John McTiernan have subsequently shown enormous interest in. The first two *Alien* movies and the first two *Die Hard* movies are, in one important sense, simply Irwin Allen movies, though much better directed and much more intricately produced. An implacable killing force/situation is unleashed in an isolated space and on a small group of people, resulting in one spectacular disas-

ter/death after another, until the force/situation is either subdued or escaped. This is one of the basic formulas of the current Big Loud Action Movie.

3. *2001: A Space Odyssey*. Dare I suggest that this lofty, metaphysical and deep film, ratified by volumes of informed and serious critical speculation, is organically linked in film history to the big-scale junk the studios are churning out today? You bet.

Firstly, there is not, in fact, really a single facet of the Big Loud Action Movie, good and bad, that doesn't partly have this film as its source.

Secondly, action is everything in *2001*. Everything. Whether it's apes tossing bones, futuristic flight attendants picking up dropped pens or Keir Dullea as Astronaut Bowman in multicoloured close-up smashing through the time-space continuum, everything in *2001* is a sensory-action feat. Everything is a blast, a sensation, a thrill. Words are of next to no significance (except perhaps as illustration of the bad faith of relying on words). Psychology is next to nothing. Character interaction is next to nothing. To say that the film foregrounds a love of technology that mobilises audience attention, deriding all interest in narrative anecdote, is to put it mildly. And finally there's that chief pesky plot situation (when one finally does show up): the protagonists must undo the murderous work of a super-talented machine that isn't too fond of human beings. Don't you hear Jim Cameron's and Ridley Scott's wheels turning? I know I do.

Thirdly, Kubrick's subsequent extensive critical discussions of his movie – in their articulateness, confidence and overall hipness – became gospel to a nascent film-school generation. Cinema, in Kubrick's view, was to bypass literature completely, to work entirely through the purely cinematic, to fuse image and sound in some graphically absolute fashion that would enable it also to bypass old logics, thereby reaching straight to a (presumably young, hip) audience's central nervous system. Which was utopian late 60s thinking. (The movie was, you may remember, a huge, huge hit, and this pretty much without journalistic critics supporting it.) Perhaps every great revolutionary should work out what the perversion of his doctrine is going to be before he puts it forward – even when he enacts it as brilliantly as Kubrick did, both in theory and in practice. But that's not the way the historical cookie crumbles. Kubrick helped partly articulate the cultural excuse for Big Loud Action Movies.

Last summer, in the *New Yorker*, Anthony Lane invoked Kubrick's theology about action-oriented visual cinema when he compared Jan De Bont's *Speed* with the 'pure cinema' of Bresson and Tarkovsky. He didn't stupidly or literally insist that the Keanu Reeves vehicle was as significant or as complex; he merely suggested that, at the level of cinema logic, they were not so very different. Which is either a subtle type of ideological apologetics or some genuine personal expression of enthusiasm. It also (along with high grosses) lets highly skilled practitioners of Big Loud Action Movies look at themselves in the mirror, or sleep at night. Kubrick, in a peculiar, roundabout way, established the groundwork for elevating intellectually debased genre material to significance through the focus on form-for-its-own-sake as a mark of artistic seriousness. In this sense he made it possible for men like George Lucas and Steven Spielberg to turn in the direction they did.

Formula repackaged

All of which brings us back to the year 1977, and *Close Encounters* and *Star Wars*. To say cinema has never quite been the same (some would say it's never recovered) would be to slight the confirming impact of their collaboration four years later on, *Raiders of the Lost Ark*. Lucas and Spielberg absorbed, at every level, everything so far mentioned and repackaged it all to formulate commercial cinema's discourse as we inhabit it today. To sum up:

1. *Spielberg's and Lucas' elaborate and expensively produced elevation of B Movie genre plots.* In *Close Encounters* you have the same ordinary-man-meets-Martians format that fuelled countless bad 50s sci-fi films. Lucas went further back, to *Buck Rogers* serials and early comic books, for his sources. The pair simply and powerfully refused to imagine that this kind of trash was an inferior basis for movies, and they took their student awareness of genre cinema – from Ford and Hawks through to Kubrick – as their rationale.

2. *There's a reduction of Narrative Complexity. Star Wars* is organised as four chases: Luke evades Imperial Guards; Luke chases after Princess Leia; Luke and pals are chased off the Death Star; Luke is pursued by Darth Vader as he attempts to drop his bomb package. A chase, a chase, a chase, and a chase. The Big Loud Action Movie has proved its absorption of this doctrine over and over and over and over again: chase, explode, etc. By the time they made *Raiders* together, the two had the chase structure down to such precise levels of control that they got ten or twelve into the film (with sub-chases within some chases). The concept of the Ride is now fully in place. Such narrative austerity has proven to be so popular that it has inspired much rhetorical gymnastics to accommodate it: such narrative construction is referred to as 'mythic'. But it would be more accurate to call it comic-book narrative. I personally see nothing wrong with Comic Books. The first *Star Wars* is, in my opinion,- superb comic-book film-making. But however much we'd like it to be, *Beowulf,* Wagner's *Ring Saga*, *The Waste Land* or Stravinsky's *Rite of Spring* it just ain't.

3. *The Cinematic, the Image and Technology dominate the narrative experience.* Seeing spaceships entering and leaving the frame brought cheers from Lucas' first audiences. Narratively speaking, they had no idea what they were cheering for, but their senses were deeply gratified. When Luke and Han and the others went into hyperspace, well, people came in their seats. Equally boldly on Spielberg's part, the last 15 minutes of *Close Encounters* was people watching people watching. A big lighted thing came on the screen, and the audience said it was good. This ability to make the visual sensation answer all questions of meaning and value is what makes Lucas and Spielberg the filmmakers that a subsequent generation of directors of Big Loud Action Movies have wanted to be. Following Kubrick's example, food for the eyes (some would say candy) wins audience assent. And not just images: sound too plays its part. The sounds that exploded off the screen in the first gunfight in *Indiana Jones* were no mere handguns (I know because Joel Silver and Walter Hill later hired the sound effects of specialist Steve Flick to bring off similar effects for the gunfire in *48 Hrs*). Lucas was so passionate about making sound a component to reach into the audience's consciousness that he decided to invent sound technology of his own.

4. *Of crucial importance to these films and their commercial poise is self-deprecating humour.*

Han Solo, Indiana Jones and cute droids tell us that the film-maker is comedically self-conscious; this makes the movie's violence into fun, brings more kids into the theatre and successfully insulates the films from critical contempt. You can't insist the films are silly if the film-makers half-admit it ahead of you. The tension between action that is sensorially overwhelming and humour that permits you to breathe back away from it is the organising rhythm of all subsequent Big Loud Action Movies. Bond's one-liners were key here (as in a slightly different way were Eastwood's in the Leone pictures), but with Spielberg and Lucas the hint of self-parody becomes a tactic for winning and keeping critics' respect.

What will forever dignify what Spielberg and Lucas accomplished (aside from the profits) is that they were the first to bring all these elements together with that degree of personal purpose that so much subsequent formula product has lacked. Lucas peddled *Star Wars* to the studios for half a decade before making it on a very modest budget. Spielberg did a quiet survey of how many people believed in UFOs, making the assumption that this was the modest audience he could count on to justify the cost of making his film. The much-vaster-than-anticipated success of these films has forever dispelled the relative innocence and authenticity with which they were undertaken.

Since 1981, the institutionalisation of the Big Loud Action Movie has proceeded apace. It has realigned the creative atmosphere in Hollywood, shaping the release slates of all the major studios and virtually crushing European art cinema. I don't think that it is either particularly necessary or particularly edifying to savage the worst of these movies. They tend to disappear from our minds and memories with merciful speed. Some of us are in the process of forgetting while still sitting in the theatre. I'd like to consider two of the best, and speculate on what makes them a little bit different. Both Jim Cameron's *Aliens* and Andy Davis' *The Fugitive* take the relentless jeopardy structure and chase aspect and the spectacular scale imagery of the Big Loud Action Movie, and organise them with unusual coherence and an unusual component of emotional sincerity.

Neither film deviates from the norm of this kind of movie. They don't have real relationships, but both skilfully refer to the feeling of those relationships that their story structure must preclude. Sigourney Weaver, running and shooting her way through *Aliens*, is always hungering for the material relationship to little Newt that there's no time for within the movie's structure; Harrison Ford palpably agonises over the loss of material happiness imposed by the plot he's trapped in. In a sense the audience feels the impact of these drastically oversimplified jeopardy situations more deeply in both films than in other Big Loud Action Movies. So they succeed in having it both ways – comic-book simplicity of situation and emotional power.

Both films also cleverly vary the monotony of the pure action-hero-in-jeopardy format, by introducing, with speed and precision, a group of lively subordinate characters. Weaver's fellow alien-killing marines and Tommy Lee Jones' team of scared-but-sleepy detectives take us out of the exclusive narcissistic focus-at-all-costs on the hero. Thus we are getting judicious injections of a few elements from the older, more serious Action movies into today's Big Loud Action Movie format. Both *Aliens* and *The Fugitive* are interestingly melancholy films. They obliquely allude to our contemporary feeling of powerlessness. The heroes do not win so much as endure, or survive, while 'humour' feels like a legitimate expression of an outlet for anxiety rather than a knee-jerk reminder that none of this should be taken that seriously.

Region of retreat

This year's model, *Batman Forever*, is clearly critic proof. This format, which is hyperbolising our anxiety about urban crime while kidding our dream of easily overcoming it, has simply (as the saying goes) 'caught on'. *Die Hard with a Vengeance* is skilful status quo. *Johnny Mnemonic* has had, I think, a bit of a bad rap: it strives to incorporate *Alphaville* as much as *Total Recall*. The guy I feel a little badly for is Kevin Reynolds. A decade ago he made a movie called *The Beast* (about Russian soldiers lost in a desperate and senseless mission in the Afghanistan desert). It was as determined and lucid a serious Action Epic as any in the last fifteen years. It was roundly ignored by audiences and critics. He has retreated, for career health reasons, into the region of the Big Loud Action Movie, and *Waterworld*. I'm not sure he will get out alive.

GUNFIRE

Jason Jacobs

The cinematic transition from the bloodless death to the crimson ballets of the slo-mo bullet-fest is generally dated, however casually, to the release of *The Wild Bunch* in 1969. Its opening and closing gun battles paid attention to the detail of bullet impacts in a sustained and stylistic manner rarely seen before. Death was no longer simply about Right shooting Wrong, Good triumphing over Bad: in *The Wild Bunch* it is spectacular, empty and nihilistic. Everyone loses. The pleasure is in witnessing the process of losing.

Gunfire battles *were* sometimes spectacular and excessive before this point; indeed, to a certain extent cinema and gunfire had *always* been intertwined. Guns and movies have been twin obsessions of American culture in the twentieth century, and both have mythic status. The movies represented glamour and excess, guns represented the Law and its democratic aspirations; as the Wild West proverb has it, 'God created men, but Samuel Colt made them equal.' Since the outlaw Barnes fired his Colt Peacemaker at the audience in *The Great Train Robbery* (1903), gunfire in films has continued apace, through the final shoot-outs of Howard Hawks' *Scarface* (1932), the gunfights of the western, the casual gun-toting of film noir, right up to Peckinpah, De Palma, Tarantino and Woo.

Perhaps cinema and guns were made for each other. In both, the apparatus is mechanical, chemical, rhythmic. They share some terminology (the shot, the magazine), a point-and-shoot rationale and a historical moment: in the late nineteenth century, the development of the fully automatic Maxim gun (mounted on a tripod) coincided with the first showing of the Lumières' films. If Hollywood cinema is fundamentally built around the drive of causal relations (this happened because that did) the gun also embodied a cause-effect apparatus (he bleeds because I shot him). It is precisely the rationality of this causal momentum which seems to disintegrate at the end of *The Wild Bunch* and in other modern gunfire sequences, such as those of *Bonnie and Clyde*, *The Godfather*, *The Getaway*, *Dillinger*, *Magnum Force*, *Taxi Driver*, *Assault on Precinct 13*, *The Long Riders*, *Blade Runner*, *Scarface*, *The Terminator*, *The Year of the Dragon*, *Full Metal Jacket*, *Lethal Weapon*, *Die Hard*, *State of Grace*, *Nikita* and *Reservoir Dogs*. In various ways in each of these films (if sometimes very different ways) the shooting is no longer a means to an end but an end in itself.

Obviously there needs to be some qualification here. Modern gunfire should not be equated with everything Peckinpah did after *The Wild Bunch*, nor should one pretend that there have not been films since in which the gunfire remains subordinate to character and plot development. I'm talking about an influential stylistic *tendency* which emerged during the 60s, which may indeed have been a culmination of earlier styles and forms (such as those of spaghetti westerns or the new forms of realism that European art cinema provided). But it is also clear that *The Wild Bunch* marks a departure from what came before, a change in the conventions of movie gunfire (just as the conventions of the car chase and the sex scene changed). The 60s ushered in a greater realism in the depictions of death and injury. In part, a more liberal climate was a factor. But gunfire sequences also reflected and incorporated anxieties produced by the assassination of President Kennedy and the Vietnam War, events which provided a newly graphic and realist context.

The assassination of JFK brought a new immediacy to issues of bullet injury. The ballistic puzzle of JFK's death raised issues of range, calibre and entrance and exit wounds to the level of national importance: if the assassin was shooting from behind, why was Kennedy's head thrown back? The idea that bullets did not necessarily travel in a straight-line trajectory entered popular currency: a slug could travel in and out of the body, bend, expand, ricochet. According to weapon and type of bullet, bigger or smaller wounds could result. The Zapruder footage, screened on US national television in 1975, graphically showed the spectacular difference a frangible bullet could make compared to a regular one. One second Kennedy is shot in the neck but still together, the next his head is peeled open in a mist of brain and gore.

The Vietnam War had a different impact. The television reporting of firefights in the jungles of Indochina regularly noted the sense of confusion and frustration that US soldiers felt at the absence of a clearly identifiable target. Who is the enemy? What are we shooting at? Why? Such second-wave Vietnam movies as *Platoon* and *Full Metal Jacket* regularly stage this confusion in their gunfire sequences.

With these two events, the representation of gunfire was required to become both more visceral and out of control to be realistic. A wincing gunfighter nursing a flesh wound on his shoulder is no longer realism: life is messier than that. *The Wild Bunch*, its final holocaust especially, aimed to show you what it was *really* like to get shot.

However, its realism operates not despite its heavy stylisation but largely because of it. Peckinpah used every cinematic technique in the book for its famous ending. Fast cutting between firing and bullet impact, snap zooms (sometimes into unfocused abstracts of red on white), crosscutting between the slow-motion, bullet-ripped, blood-squirting leaps of Mexican soldiers, and Warren Oates as Lyle psychotically spinning the Browning machine gun around and firing. Close-ups of blood exploding from flesh, close-ups of roaring guns, close-ups of faces screwed tight in agony, and all the time the symphony of bullet report and men screaming. Peckinpah keeps the screen ferociously busy with the dynamics of explosion (walls, bodies, guns) with a cutting rate more rapid than MTV. It is the founding bullet-fest, a heavily mediated *mise en scène* of industrial barbarism. And yet it captured – more precisely than anything before – the reality of gunfire as an excessive and bloody confusion, in which it is increasingly unclear who is shooting at whom and where the bullets are coming from.

This confusion is also achieved technically. Peckinpah uses a vast variety of camera angles, and lenses with long focal lengths to give a flattened perspective to the carnage, suggesting a suffocating proximity between the combatants. Blood, bullets, Mexicans and bandits appear to shoot and die almost on top of each other. Like Kennedy's death, bullets come from nowhere and without reason, and like the battlefields of Indochina, a desperate and crowded confusion prevails. Hence it is the *active mediation* of gunfire and bullet impact in this movie which supplies the meaning of the sequence, even if that meaning is painfully nihilistic.

However disturbing, the sequence is also exhilarating. Aside from the ferocious stylistic fireworks, exactly where the pleasure in the witnessing of such agony originates is difficult to identify – but a few notions suggest themselves. The first is that the sequence is an early example of the gradual transformation of modern Hollywood cinema into a pure thrill machine, offering sensation before story, the cause-effect narrative engine becoming (at significant points, in various ways and to varying degrees) subordinate to the spectacle. Seduction by spectacle, providing sensuous and visceral pleasures, is now considered characteristic of many contemporary Hollywood films (though some critics regard it as an infantile characteristic).

In gunfire sequences, what constitutes the spectacle is not simply the amount of gunfire released, but the visible impact on the body. The special-effects bullet-impact squib has a dynamic of its own, an attraction as the spectacle of visible injury. Sometimes it seems that a pumping artery lies just beneath the material of the victim's clothing, and the bullet operates like a lance to a boil. Alternatively, there is a more messy and explosive form where the 'boil' itself detonates outwards in wild and runny rivulets of blood and stringy gobs of gore. The 'Odessa steps' ending of De Palma's *The Untouchables* offers some designer versions of these squibs: where each slo-mo detonation has a shiny liquid texture, as if Armani himself had sewn them, as accessories, into the fabric.

It is the cumulative effect of such spectacles – the sustained provision of visual and kinetic motion – which makes good gunfire sequences so enjoyable. John Woo's Hong Kong action movies are exemplary in this respect. Woo has said that he choreographs his gun battles with the precision of musical numbers: a Peckinpah on an inspired drug-bender, Woo uses every technique and every type of squib to deliver some of the most sustained and unlikely gunfire sequences on film. At the end of *Hard-Boiled* the two cop heroes, Chow Yun-Fat and Tony Leung, are working their way through some hospital corridors, leaving a war-crime's worth of dead bad guys in their wake. Their squib-soaked progress is filmed and choreographed with a steadicam in one take: sometimes the sound and action groan into slow motion (usually to extend a wounding frenzy), then groan back up to normal speed; the two even get into a lift and start cleaning out the *next* floor before we get a cut. Some dislike Woo's extended and bloody depiction of cops shooting bad guys, bad guys shooting cops, cops shooting cops, usually point blank with a gun in each hand and few grenades to spare. As with those who hate techno music, the fundamental misunderstanding is that it's all the same, just banal repetition: once you've seen one guy shot, why show the other twelve dozen? Those who like both Orbital and John Woo know that more *is* more, that repetition is part of a cumulative dynamic, that no part is ever the same as that preceding it: it is the constant and unbelievable accumulation of impact and firepower that makes a Woo film like *The Killer* akin to an all-night blood-and-bullets rave.

As my adoration of Woo might suggest, the pleasure of gunfire is also somewhat gender-specific, which leads to my second suggestion for the origin of such pleasures. Gunfire sequences offer particular pleasures for men, pleasures which often cannot be found elsewhere. Just as important as the shooting in this *Hard-Boiled* sequence is the emotional relationship between the two cops; indeed, such relationships are often fundamentally bound up with the gunfire itself. In Woo's *A Better Tomorrow II* one character can only stop weeping and win Chow Yun-Fat's respect and love when he finally picks up a gun and starts shooting at something. Many men find the end of *The Wild Bunch* an exhilarating sequence, but it is also a tender one. Somehow the pain and agony of gunfire legitimates a kind of male intimacy usually outlawed in the Hollywood film, or else awkwardly displaced onto dramas of male camaraderie (as with much of Hawks). With Lyle and Tector (Ben Johnson) dead, their leader Pike Bishop (William Holden) finally succumbs to the amount of lead drilled into his bleeding body. Dutch (Ernest Borgnine) clambers over the carnage towards him, weeping, 'Pike! Pike!' – and then dies next to his friend. It is a tender moment because one feels that Dutch was about to express his love for his friend, to hold him tight and tell him, 'It's OK, we'll die together.' It's corny, but after all the four of them *have* been wearing their wounds like fluid brooches: they've earned the right to cry out, to scream, to weep, even if the price of that expression is terminal. Such intimacy and close physical contact between wounded men carries a powerful cultural message: it's OK to touch me *now* – I'm bleeding, I'm, dying. Would Mr White (Harvey Keitel) tenderly comb Mr Orange's (Tim Roth) hair in *Reservoir Dogs* if Orange wasn't bleeding to death?

But this is only part of a broader pleasure, a pleasure which I think is less gender specific and more universal than it might at first seem (and this is my third suggestion for such pleasure's origins). It is connected with a modern fascination, centred on the body as a site of both perfection and decay. On the one hand we are told that our bodies are 'at risk' from disease, viruses, smoking, junk food and ageing; on the other, and in response, we are encouraged to 'take care of ourselves', to eat healthy food, to exercise, to give up smoking and aspire to the perfect body. If the responsibility for this is ours, so is the anxiety. A hitherto healthy body riddled by gunfire graphically reproduces this anxiety; what's more, it celebrates the abdication of responsibility for the body itself. So the pleasure gained from watching gunfire sequences is bound up with issues of control and its loss. This is strikingly illustrated in the standard shot routines of these sequences. Mastery and power (the cool handling of high-tech weapons) are directly contrasted with the loss of control over the body, the messy exit of blood and the involuntary convulsions. For example, in *Reservoir Dogs*, Mr White shoots two cops in their car. We are given a shot of White, cool, collected, powerful, firing a Smith and Wesson 645 in each hand; in the next shot we are given a chaos of injury, exploding glass and flesh and shrieking cops. This quick transition between mastery and vulnerability is certainly the characteristic trajectory of male orgasm, and there are further correspondences: a 'powerful weapon' is brandished, its contents released; there's an analogous cause-effect chain, in that the beating spurt of orgasm has its equivalent in the gushing of the bullet impact and consequent involuntary body movement. But one should be wary of the cliché which equates all specific cinema thrills to sexual pleasures: because control and its loss has a far more significant meaning in the real world.

This is best illustrated by those gunfire sequences in which the shooter is also the wounded. In *The Wild Bunch*, as noted above, a shot and bleeding Lyle screams as he spins with the machine gun, spraying destruction indiscriminately. One gets the acute sense that the gun is controlling *him*, that he couldn't let go if he wanted to. The technology has overwhelmed its user. Similarly, at the end of *Taxi Driver*, Travis Bickle (Robert De Niro) is also shot and bleeding, but the logic of his on-board arsenal propels him to continue the killing until he runs out of ammo. Again, the gun becomes the agency of control to the extent that Iris's (Jodie Foster) cry, 'Don't shoot him!' becomes an impossible request: Travis evacuates the brains of the brothel keeper over the wall. In *Reservoir Dogs*, Mr Orange, lying in a lake of his own blood, empties his entire weapon into Mr Blonde, but continues pointing it even when it's empty, as if the gun itself was urging him to continue. Automatic gunfire creates automatic people.

But even this explanation doesn't give the entire picture. More than just the technology powers these characters. They have a heroic quality too. Tim Roth's blood-soaked Orange defiantly shooting and Warren Oates' Lyle swinging on the machine gun have something iconic about them, something which recalls the paintings of the Crucifixion or of St Sebastian. The fifteenth-century painter Andrea Mantegna's powerful paintings of Sebastian depict him as shot through with arrows, bleeding, and looking heavenwards for redemption beyond the agony of the material world. But neither Orange nor Lyle have any such recourse. They can only turn to their guns and fire back.

And herein lies the profoundest desire and deepest pleasure in these gunfire sequences: in the will to fight back, to gain mastery over one's life even in circumstances so desperate and agonised. They give us a highly stylised spectacle in which are played out genuine dramas of mastery and loss. If these do reflect male pleasures and anxieties, this is because in a patriarchal world men have more to lose. The passivity and weakness associated with women are a direct reflection of the systematic way they have been denied access to that power. But there is nothing positive about passivity, no strength in lying back to wait for the next bullet.

Society continually offers us examples of how we cannot do anything about our situation: famine, disease, war, interest rates, inflation and job security. We seem to have less and less control over what happens to us, however often we are told to take responsibility for it. It is because most of us know what it's like to be under fire (if only metaphorically), and what the yearning to shoot back feels like, that it feels so damn good to watch gunfire in these films. The desire to shoot back is positive, and even subversive, at a time when our first instinct might be to keep our heads down and not make trouble. Marx argued that the fight against capitalism begins with 'the weapon of criticism and the criticism of weapons'. That is, in critically and actively fighting back, even as the odds and guns are ranged against us. Pleasure in gunfire sequences simultaneously reflects our recognition of our vulnerability and our desire to fight back. As the screenwriter Charles Higson explained in his recent 'Obsession' (*S&S*, August 1995), after his first youthful viewing of the end of *The Wild Bunch*, 'I wanted to go out in a blaze of glory, I wanted a Gatling gun, I wanted to be pierced by a hundred bullets.'

* * *

The Godfather

In the early 70s, special make-up effects pioneer Dick Smith invented the 'mole', a means of placing a squib under a mock layer of skin: it was first used here in *The Godfather* (Smith later worked on the ending of *Taxi Driver*). The bullet bursting in skin is not only more realistic, but more visibly painful, more surgical. Sonny Corleone (James Caan) is ambushed by a Thompson-toting brigade of mobsters. Sonny stays alive for an unfeasibly long time – long enough to show the sustained brutality the bullets subject his body to. The extended spectacle of his death, culminating in a superfluous close-range shooting and a kick in the head (cut from television versions), shows us the violent end of a man (it also sells the film). In life Sonny was explosive material, a testosterone-fuelled grenade. His death is equally overblown.

Scarface

'Say hello to my little friend.' Tony Montana (Al Pacino) launches a rocket grenade at the South American hit squad. Spectacle overcomes realism. His M16 is fitted with a flash suppressor, but it acts like a flame-thrower. Gunfire must be visible. In Hawks' 1932 original, Paul Muni begs the cops not to shoot him. In De Palma's, Montana, powered by rage,  coke and bloody-minded refusal, repeatedly riddled by gunfire, screams for more. 'I'm still standing, come on! Is this the best you can do?'

Terminator 2: Judgment Day

This gunfire sequence is one of the most spectacular: Arnie fires a big gun, and the environment explodes – cars, shrubs, the ground. Cops scatter for cover. Then a moment of comic disbelief as the Terminator's electronic scan notes 'Human casualties: 0.0'. A surgical strike. The film was released in 1991, during the Gulf War, when the myth of the 'smart' techno-weapon was in fashion: those weapons that achieved their objectives without killing people. However spectacular, this sequence resonates with such claims. The new paternal Terminator represents the US, narrowly protective of its interests and justifying the most elaborate violence as harmless. He uses a Vulcan mini-gun, designed for use on helicopter gunships – used by the US to 'police' the Somali capital Mogadishu in 1993. 'Human casualties (estimated): 4000.0'.

The Getaway

The pump-action shotgun holds a special place in gunfire sequences: noisy, messy and indiscriminate, with the added aural bonus of the re-cocking action every shot. Doc McCoy (Steve McQueen), a bank robber on the run, is 'made' by a shop-owner who calls the cops. In response, McCoy walks next door to the gunshop: 'I want a shotgun, 12-gauge. Pump... That's fine,

wrap it up.' But instead of blowing the cops away, he blasts their car. Which updates the scriptwriting maxim that a gun seen in the first reel should be used in the last, except the eventual use of the weapon we've been teased with is only this. The car's chassis tears and buckles, gruesome inklings of its effect on the human body.

Full Metal Jacket

Sniper fire should be accurate and deadly; the film technique used here is. This sequence (several soldiers wounded by a Vietcong sniper) is shocking, but mainly because it tries so hard, using graphic and excessive simulation of bullet impact. The squib detonations are filmed in slow motion from a low angle, giving a scientific precision, unpleasant without being engaging. The solemnity and the refusal to acknowledge the cinematic pleasure of carnage (however disturbing that recognition is) leaves the viewer cold.

Hard-Boiled

By the mid-80s a long barrel and a big
impact seemed passé, even sexist. For the
'new gun' era, high capacity – staying
power – was more important than size. In
1985 the US army adopted the Beretta 92,
a high capacity (16 rounds) semi-auto-
matic handgun, and Hollywood became
awash with them: *Lethal Weapon*, *Die
Hard*, the John Woo films. High capacity

autos fire many bullets, quickly. Who needs a revolver, however awesome, when you
can 'spray and pray' with a Beretta 92 or a Glock 19? An automatic pistol offers the
rapid movement of the slide, the spinning egress of cartridges. As Woo's films have
demonstrated, with more bullets and a faster firing-rate, the gunfire spectacle can be
endlessly extended.

Taxi Driver

Different bullets and guns have
different impacts on the body.
The rise of the gun as star, the
damage as co-star, can be dated
to *Dirty Harry* in 1971: 'This is a
.44 Magnum, the most powerful
handgun in the world. And it
could blow your head clean off.'
Larger calibres and longer barrels became fashionable, their
disturbing association with
machismo played up. In Peckinpah's *The Getaway* Rudy (Al
Lettieri) carries an eight-inch
Colt Python .357 Magnum with
a ventilated cooling rib on the
barrel, which is regularly
stroked by his girlfriend. In *Taxi
Driver* Travis buys a .44 Magnum
because he's been told of its
power by a satanic fare, played
by Scorsese himself. The connection with sexual violence is

made horribly explicit: 'You ever see what a .44 Magnum pistol can do to a woman's
face? Fucking destroy it. Just blow it right apart. Ever see what it could do to a woman's
pussy, now that you should see. You must think I'm pretty sick, right?'

ACTION!

Richard Dyer

It must have been the way I was saying it. When people have asked me if I've seen any good films lately, I've replied, 'Oh yes, *Speed*,' and they've looked startled. It's as if I wasn't saying the title of a film but lapsing into some ill-understood subcultural jargon: 'Yeah, man – speed.' Perhaps I lengthened the vowel or arched my body involuntarily, because they weren't entirely wrong. *Speed* is, like, speed.

In all truth, it isn't as much of a trip as one could imagine it being. There's nothing in it like the camera hanging out of the jeep in *Hatari!*, or skimming over Julie Andrews in *The Sound of Music*, or the hand-held prowling in *Wolfen*, none of the magnificent shock cuts and zooms of Hammer horror or the likes of Mario Bava and Dario Agento, let alone the thrillingly torrential cutting of the 'Odessa Steps' sequence in *The Battleship Potemkin* or the eponymous tempest in *Storm Over Asia*. Nor is there the gross-out factor in *Speed* that might elevate it to late-night and video-cult status, none of the gore of even a mainstream movie such as *Under Siege* (kitchen knives in skulls, fingers in eyeballs), to say nothing of the I-can't-believe-I'm-seeing-this climaxes of films such as *Basket Case* or *The Re-animator* (but don't bother to check this out on the British release videos). Indeed, *Speed* teasingly draws back from delivering such an experience, even when it titillates us with the promise that it's about to show us a white, middle-class mother and baby smashed to smithereens.

Speed gets its rush from a sheer squandering of sensational situations. Keanu Reeves is a cop who has to deal with three desperate predicaments: a plummeting lift, a bus primed to explode if it drops to below 50 mph and an out-of-control subway train. One situation follows straight after the other, set in motion by an obscurely vengeful ex-cop (Dennis Hopper) with a genius for deadly remote-control technology. Any one of these variations of velocity would have been enough for most movies. *Speed* is like Sylvester Stallone dangling over the ravine at the start of *Cliffhanger* plus the office explosion in *Lethal Weapon 3* plus the train crash in *The Fugitive* plus the chase along the sunken canal in *Terminator 2*, all put end to end with no boring bits in between. No dodgy politics. No naff attempts at psychologising the villain: he's a nutcase. No mushy buddiness: the film barely pauses when Keanu's partner is blown to bits through his (Keanu's) lack of foresight. No elaborate excuses to get the camera to linger on the star's muscles: Keanu's not that kind of boy. And no love interest to send the kids into frenzies of squabbling and going to the loo: there is a girl (Sandra Bullock on fine form) and Keanu does get her, but it's all done on the run with only a quick clinch at the end. This is the movie as rollercoaster: all action and next to no plot.

The cinema has always had the potential to be like this. Whether or not it is true that the first audiences for the Lumière brothers' film of a train entering a station ducked in terror as it advanced towards them, the idea that they did has often seemed to be emblematic of what film is about. The Lumières ushered in a new technology that has become ever more elaborate, revelling in both showing and creating the sensation of movement. *Train Arriving at a Station* and *Speed* belong to a distinguished lineage. It includes all those celebrations of movement so prized by earlier commentators on film: the simple documentary dwelling on movement, be it vast or tiny, train crashes or water fleas (to take oft-cited early examples); such staged delights as the Keystone Cops, cowboys and Indians, Fred and Ginger, climaxes *à la* Griffith; and all those attempts to make cinema move analogously to music, as in animated abstract ballets or 'symphonies' of the great modern cities. The lineage also includes, however, *This is Cinerama*, Imax cinema presentations and now (in Portrush, Northern Ireland, at Granada Studios in Manchester, at the Trocadero in London's Piccadilly) the Showscan Dynamic Motion Simulator, a 'magic chair' that promises to deliver 'the ultimate fantasy: Reality'. The celebration of sensational movement, that we respond to in some still unclear sense 'as if real', for many people *is* the movies.

I would not want to erect this into an absolute aesthetic principle, as some theorists have done. The stasis of film-makers such as Ozu, Duras and Akerman is just as authentically cinematic as the movement of Murnau, Minnelli or, indeed, Jan De Bont, the director of *Speed*. Yet stillness and contemplation are rare in popular cinema. The triumph of the word 'movie' over the more static 'pictures' or evocative 'flicks' is not just a product of US cultural imperialism; it also catches something of the sensation we expect when we go to the cinema.

It seems, though, that we seldom want the sense of movement and excitement, the speed, by itself. How many times does one want to visit the Imax or, probably, a Showscan Dynamic Motion Simulator? We generally want the exhilaration and rush embedded in a fiction. Such fictions situate the thrills. They refer us to the world. They do not usually pretend to show us the world as it really is, but they point to that world. They offer us thrills and elations we might seldom have, might think it impossible really to have, but they relate such imaginings of elation to the human co-ordinates of the real world: the environments we live in, the social categories in which we have our being. In the process, they propose and legitimate kinds of thrills, and who gets them and who pays the price.

In contemporary cinema, it is the action film that most characteristically delivers speed in a story. One has only to think of the stars of such films – Schwarzenegger, Stallone, Bruce Willis, Harrison Ford, Steven Seagal, Jean-Claude Van Damme and now Keanu Reeves – to have an indication of whose thrills are being legitimated: straight white men. This doesn't mean that no one else can possibly imagine having the thrills alongside Arnie or Keanu, but it does contribute to the reproduction of a masculine structure of feeling. Extreme sensation is represented as experienced, not within the body, but in the body's contact with the world, its rush, its expansiveness, its physical stress and challenge. There is nothing wrong with such feelings of extreme and, as it were, worldly sensation, but the movies tie them to male characters and male environments, suggesting they are really only appropriate to men. This is not a matter of saying that I want – let alone my wanting women to want – to have quite this kind of sensational experience, but that there is a deeper, underlying pattern of feeling, to do with freedom of movement, confidence in the body, engagement with the material world, that is coded as male (and straight and white, too) but to which all humans need access.

In *Speed*, as in most action films of the past fifteen or more years, it is not quite true to say that *only* straight white men get the thrills. We now have a well-established pattern, whereby the hero is accompanied by white women and men of colour (rarely women of colour) who are also exposed to the dangers that bring the thrills. Though the screaming heroine or cringing black man do still crop up, women and men of colour are nowadays more likely to be allowed to be tough and brave, to be able to handle themselves and often to have skills the white hero doesn't possess. Even if they don't start out that way, they eventually make the grade. The figure of the black police chief or crack platoon leader who provides back-up at crucial moments is a staple of the genre, as is the moment when the heroine finally has to kill, deliberately and efficiently, to save the cornered hero.

Speed loses its potential black helper, the bus driver in the central segment, early on, leaving Keanu and his white helper to save the busload of mainly non-white passengers. The helper, though, is a woman (Sandra Bullock). Unlike her (literally) poor fellow commuters, she's travelling by bus only because she has had her driving licence taken away for speeding (the film is not without a sense of humour). She has to take charge of the bus when the driver is incapacitated and performs brilliantly, managing sharp corners and interweaving across busy traffic lanes, all at top speed, with splendid aplomb and verve mixed with terror. She does get the thrills of extreme physical danger and the exultation of mastery of a machine. Yet *Speed* still conforms to the pattern of contemporary action films by constituting her as helper. She's not the main man. Conan (in the Schwarzenegger films) and Indiana Jones are two of the many heroes who now do their thing with women and black people in tow, but never quite as equals, never with quite the same access to the speed of worldly sensation.

Worldly thrills are seldom bought at no price. In the classic western and jungle adventure film, to take relatively easy targets, it is the native people who pay the biggest price for the white man's exhilaration. With Rambo or a film like *Under Siege*, it's anyone who gets in the way, which generally means other males – many action films are indeed mainly affairs between men. *Speed* largely avoids giving us time to note death: there are innocent bystanders knocked off and some police, but by and large the film is oddly benign. Old ladies petrified to leap from lifts, babies in prams, poor commuters of colour on the unstoppable bus, such people are safe in *Speed*, not expendable as they might be in many other films. The price is elsewhere, in things. It is the transport system itself that is smashed about: cars, lorries, barriers, planes and even the roadway in a final eruption of a subway train from below. It is an orgy of destruction of one of the great frustrations of modern urban living – getting about.

It is not impossible to imagine action movies otherwise. They don't have to be about the destruction of subject peoples and the natural environment, they don't have to centre forever on straight white men. The shifts in gender and race roles I've already suggested indicate the possibility of change. The problem with *Passenger 57* (which in any case was no worse than *Under Siege*, say, or *Die Hard 2*) was not that its hero was a black man, and certainly not Wesley Snipes' inadequacy as a star, but dull plotting and direction. There are many precedents for the woman as hero of adventure, notably Leni Riefenstahl's mountain films, Fearless Nadia (the Indian star celebrated in the wonderful recent film *Fearless: The Hunterwali Story*), Sigourney Weaver in the *Alien* films, and the 'women warriors' discussed by Yvonne Tasker in her recent book *Spectacular Bodies*.

Yet I would not want to underestimate how difficult it will be to make it normal

and unremarkable to have people of colour and women as subjects of worldly sensation. Experience of space has race and gender dimensions which set limits to how
plausible or exceptional one may find a representation. Colour ghettoisation, for
instance, instils assumptions about space that are hard to shake. White people often
say they are fearful of going into black ghettos, but seldom stop to consider that such
ghettos are themselves surrounded on all sides by the powerful white ghetto. Entering and being in white space can be profoundly intimidating, however at ease Wesley
Snipes or Danny Glover may appear in it on screen. Even more fundamentally, perhaps, much cross-cultural research suggests that we start learning our relation to our
environment from the moment of cradling, and that we learn it differently according
to gender. To feel it is OK to be unrestrained, to kick against what surrounds you, to
thrust out into the world is what boys learn, not girls. To see women strain against the
world may be inspirational, but also at some psychic level unbelievable. Heroes of
action who are other than male and white (and straight and able-bodied) are still going
to feel exceptional for some time to come.

Action movies as the most common contemporary form of the cinema of sensation
ally the speed they offer with white male characters. Women and people of colour
may be let in on the action, but either in secondary roles or with a sense of their excep-
tionality. Yet the experience action movies offer is in another way not so traditionally
masculine at all.

To go to an action movie is to sink back in the seat and say, 'show me a good time'.
Maybe we also cringe, shield our eyes, convulse our bodies – maybe we are often not
so much more sophisticated than those putative Lumière audiences – but mentally
we abandon ourselves to the illusion. Many have seen this as the essence of nearly all
film experience, no matter what the genre; it underlies the notion of 'classical cinema'
that has become so entrenched in film studies.

Such surrender to pleasure has greatly worried cultural, and not just film, criticism.
Perhaps the image that most famously captures this intellectual worry about movies as
sensation is that of the feelies in Aldous Huxley's *Brave New World*: the masses hooked
up to a wash of sensations as part of an enforced passivity that keeps them mindlessly
turning the cogs of capitalism. There is a point here. Passivity in life, in politics, is problematic: it means acquiescing to a status quo that damages people along class, gender,
racial, sexual and other lines; for many women lying back within heterosexual sex has
not always meant enjoying it; and there are besides always others who pay the real price
for the megabuck sensations of the world's well-to-do minority. Yet it is hard not to see
in Huxley's hatred something else: a libidinal fear of passivity itself.

Modern discussion of cultural pleasures tends to take sexuality as the founding form
of all enjoyment, as the appetite *par excellence*. (I look forward to a return to theory and
criticism which takes eating as its primary metaphor for understanding enjoyment.)
Pleasures that are approved or disapproved of get mapped on to ideas of what sex is like.
The notions of active and passive have been made to do a great deal of muddled but suggestive work, ineluctably correlated with gender roles within heterosexuality. On the
one hand, proper gender identity has seemed to be realised in the performance of active
male and passive female coital roles. On the other hand, a phantasm of sex as assault
has haunted the minds of heterosexual male intellectuals. As a result, when they have

imagined passivity in sex they have imagined something terrifying. Passivity is thus both demeaning for a man, because it makes him like a woman, and frightening too. So it is with all delectation – since sex provides the measure of all pleasures. The worst thing imaginable is to go to the cinema to lie back and enjoy it. Which suggests another terror, lurking beneath the fear of being like, and being treated like, a woman. For what kind of a man is it who lies back and enjoys it? A queer, of course. Queers of every sex know that passivity need not be alarming, but then that's queers for you, not a palatable message for chaps hell-bent on being straight.

In relation to adventure movies, there is a delicious paradox here. Such movies promote an active engagement with the world, going out into it, doing to the environment; yet enjoyment of them means allowing them to come to you, take you over, do you. When Jean-Claude Van Damme kicks his way out of trouble, when Harrison Ford leaps into the torrent in *The Fugitive*, when Keanu lies on his back under the careering bus in *Speed*, we may identify with them, imagine the rush of excitement as we brace ourselves against, and master, the world; but we're also letting ourselves be carried along, going with the flow of the movie, ecstatically manipulated.

The favoured position of hardcore fans for watching action movies in the cinema is slumped in the seat with legs slung over the seat in front. This is an excellent position for anal sex as well as for cunnilingus and fellatio. Come to think of it, for the male viewer action movies have a lot in common with being fellated. At the level of cultural imagery, the fellatee is considered the butch one – perhaps because he supplies the phallus, perhaps because fellatio facilitates a masculine dissociation of mind and body more readily than face-to-face coital positions. Whatever the reason, men cherish the illusion that their masculinity is not compromised by being fellated. Yet it's the other person, male or female, who's doing the work, really being active. So it is with action movies. In imagination, men can be Arnie or Keanu; in the seat, it's Arnie or Keanu pleasuring them. Now that's what I call speed.

MISSION: SUBLIME

José Arroyo

In the last scene of Brian De Palma's *Mission: Impossible*, Tom Cruise's love has been killed. The Bad Guy has escaped onto the roof of the train. Will Tom follow? 'Of course!' trumpets the updated theme music from the television series. Cruise takes off his tie and jacket; in his white shirt, he's ready for business. The wind lifts his body and throws it around. We know that won't deter him but we know the job won't be easy. The Bad Guy (in black) has an accomplice following him in a helicopter. They come to a bridge: camera follows as accomplice and chopper fly under it. They come to a tunnel: accomplice and chopper do the incredible and plunge into it. Bad Guy jumps onto one chopper leg, and Cruise onto the other: how will they get off? Cruise blasts the others with bubble gum (*special* bubble gum: it's explosive). Bad Guy and accomplice die; but our hero is thrown on top of the moving train. Will he hang on? Of course. But the chopper lands so close as to be practically on top of him. And its blades are whirring. Will it decapitate him? Of course not: he's Tom Cruise. The scene is impossibly silly, but also funny and exciting. *Mission: Impossible* forsakes the uncomfortable, 'Do you see what you believe?' to trick us into agreeing with a more delightful, 'Do you believe what you see?'

The word that recurs most often in the notes I took while watching *Mission: Impossible* is *Fab!* But I wouldn't suggest that it's a great film. I'd like to argue that it's rather good; even this is difficult. As yet we have no adequate vocabulary to describe or evaluate such films (which are now the dominant mode of Hollywood film-making) so we tend to dismiss them as popcorn. Your Mission, should you choose to accept it, is to take the Popcorn Movie seriously.

Part of the difficulty of appreciating such a film is that its story is so simple and so ludicrous. A mole is stealing a list of US secret operatives in Europe. Ethan Hunt (Cruise) and colleagues are sent on a mission to discover seller and buyer, apprehend them, and retrieve the diskette. During the mission, Hunt's colleagues are killed, he is taken to be the mole and spends the rest of the film trying to find the real guilty party, and to clear his own name while evading capture by his former employers. If one were to speak of this film in terms of character or issues (as in the nineteenth-century novel or even such contemporary films as *Leaving Las Vegas* or *Dead Man Walking*) one would come up pretty empty-handed.

Mission: Impossible is glamorous, exciting, sexy and sometimes witty. I love the way it looks, and the gadgets and the clothes. The film also contains inedible moments: Emilio Estevez impaled; Kristin Scott-Thomas' bright red lipstick against the *noir*ish blue background by the Charles Bridge in Prague; a hand in a black leather glove preventing a bead of sweat from hitting a pristine white floor in slow motion; the geometric design that the framing of rushing water forms as it chases after Cruise. But the film is gleefully superficial. It doesn't fit easily into any traditional discourse of aesthetics. It seems to lack coherence, balance, internal consistency and more importantly, depth.

Mission: Impossible belongs in a long history of the Cinema of Attractions. As with the early trick films of Georges Méliès, that made their audiences gaze with wonder at things and people seemingly disappearing before their eyes, *Mission: Impossible* assaults the senses by expressively conjuring a verisimilitude from the logically impossible. Like much current high concept cinema, the film strives to offer a theme park of attractions: music, colour, story, performance, design and the sense of improbably fast motion. The aim is to seduce the audience into surrendering to the ride. In an article run in *The Guardian* (2 March), Susan Sontag describes this as one of the strongest feelings movies can offer. Yet *Mission: Impossible* is a high concept film, the dominant mode of contemporary Hollywood cinema: in other words, the Popcorn Movie which Sontag and others see as the *death* of cinema.

As Justin Wyatt so well describes in his recent *High Concept: Movies and Marketing in Hollywood*, this type of film-making is partly defined by the reducibility of a story into a single sentence to facilitate marketing (along with a graphic or logo that can be associated with the film across various media). For example, when one reads 'Arnold Schwarzenegger and Danny De Vito in *Twins*', billing and title in themselves give away the film's plot, basic structure and most of the jokes. 'Tom Cruise in *Mission: Impossible*' operates in much the same way. It's the merging of two cultural corporations: Mr White-Middle-America-with-heart-and-guts meets the 60s pop spy series. The result is familiar. We know what to expect of a Tom Cruise film; we're familiar with the basic format of the television series, especially its unforgettable signature tune. But it's different, too, in the ways it combines and updates. And just because the plot is simple doesn't mean the movie is – or that it doesn't offer complex pleasures.

Applying the Frankfurt School's critique of mass culture to this type of film-making would not be hard: *Mission: Impossible* is not very original; the structure of the whole doesn't depend on details; it respects conventional norms of what constitutes intelligibility in contemporary film-making. It could be seen as an example of pseudo-individuation, that which seems different but is in fact the same, whose object is to affirm capitalist culture – Popcorn laced with discourses that propagate and sustain existing relations of power, lulling its audience into believing that they live in the best of all possible worlds. This type of criticism has often been levelled against Hollywood cinema. But though productive as *part* of a critique, it's a dead end when it results in mere dismissal.

Enemies of the West

The film also offers a pretty dystopic view of contemporary western culture. There is no longer any difference between the East and the West. What happens in Kiev and Prague or Washington and London is similar. All are corrupt places with citizens under continuous surveillance. Government, which is supposed to protect, throws out morality, ethics, justice and law to get what it wants, going as far as attempting to kill an honest Cruise, who is simply and desperately trying to do the right thing. Family is far away, ineffectual, vulnerable. Friends are unreliable: they may have killed your other friends and may yet kill you. Love, as personified by Emmanuelle Béart, is a source of longing, an object of desire (seemingly always deferred) and an instrument of betrayal (the *femmes* are pretty fatal here – and structurally subordinate in the narrative, as is Hunt's black sidekick, played by Ving Rhames; *plus ça change...*). The worst enemies of western culture are the 'Third World' and terrorists. The worst thing that can happen to an individual is to be 'disavowed', to be cut off from one's corporate community; to survive the hero must remain nomadic. It's a bleak view. The film's utopia is a masculinist fantasy: that if one is Tom Cruise, all such problems will eventually be resolved.

This is a reading of the film that appears to give it a degree of depth. But to look at *Mission: Impossible* only in this way is perhaps to miss what is most interesting about it. It's built around set pieces (the interrogation scene in Kiev; the Embassy scene; the aquarium scene and the Hotel Europa scene in Prague; the burglary at Langley, Virginia; and, finally, the train scene, which begins in London), each involving some element of action and ingenuity (from characters or film-makers). These scenes are woven through the film like songs and dances are in an old-fashioned musical: it isn't so much that they don't tell us anything about the characters, but that their function as spectacle exceeds their function as narrative. For example, though we may need to know that Cruise's colleagues are killed at the start, we don't need to see it in such detail or to such effect to follow the story. *Mission: Impossible* is a star vehicle structured around a protagonist: but it is not important to know much about Ethan Hunt, the character Cruise plays. What's important is how Cruise the star looks, smiles, jumps, leaps, outwits. In such movies, the star functions less as character than as an integral production value. Tom Cruise as 'Tom Cruise' in *Mission: Impossible* is its own kind of spectacle (as when he takes off his mask and is revealed to be 'Tom Cruise' during his star entrance at the film's beginning); what's more, it's an integral part of the spectacle presented during the more elaborate action scenes (as when the wind buffets his body on top of the train in the final scene).

Like the musical using the order of musical numbers to create change of pace and variation, *Mission: Impossible* tries to vary its own set pieces in terms of length, tone and desired effect: the scene at the hotel is medium-length and meant to be exciting; the scene in Langley where Cruise steals the diskette is long and meant to be funny and suspenseful; the scene where Cruise makes the diskette disappear in order to con Krieger (Jean Reno) is meant to be ingenious. The last action scene, the lollapalooza, is to function as the showstopper. It begins with a blast from Lalo Schifrin's energetic television theme-tune, and reprises all previous effects (it has excitement, speed, suspense, humour and ingenuity), but faster, with more intensity and at a higher pitch.

And like the musical, much of the beauty of and meaning in *Mission: Impossible* comes from the expressive use of non-representational signs: colour, music, movement.

The scene at Langley where Cruise and company download the names of undercover agents into a diskette is a good example of the pleasures on offer. While Rhames hacks away at the security with his computer, Béart, Cruise and Reno disguise themselves as firemen to get into the building. Béart injects the coffee of the computer worker with a serum to force him to go to the bathroom, and plants a bug on his jacket so that his movements can be traced. In the meantime, Cruise and Reno have managed to get to the room via an air vent. So far, so familiar: this is reminiscent of the pleasures of James Bond, with gadgets, wit and a few punches thrown. As the scene proceeds, maintaining the humorous tone, a shift registers. Will the computer operator return too soon, intercepting Cruise stealing the diskette? Cruise is hung from the ceiling with wires, handled by Reno. We see a rat waddling next to Reno. Will this cause him to lose control? Will the sneeze he's been controlling simply erupt, setting off the alarm? De Palma is a brilliant student of Hitchcock: these bits are funny and suspenseful.

And Reno does lose control. Cruise, previously floating downwards, now drops abruptly to only inches from the floor. He's hung from wires, waving his arms as balance, to avoid touching the floor: thus the film offers us the pleasure of Cruise's physique, his physical prowess. But his body is also reduced to a graphic element of the composition, albeit a gorgeous one: for example, in the high-angle shot which shows us Cruise (dressed in black) against a white floor crossed with thin black lines. His body seems two-dimensional; it seems to disappear into the pattern as if matter had dissolved into geometry.

Two separate moments make this scene thrilling: a drop of sweat about to hit the floor and Reno's knife falling to the floor. Both are exciting only because of their context (if either lands, this could ruin the mission). They involve quick cuts, to enhance the sense of danger and to give an impression of movement. But they also involve the use of slow motion, to arrest and break down movement.

Thrilling fascination

The combined effect is that of the sublime. The slow motion fixes our gaze with awe; the quick cuts rush us headlong into terror. It's thrilling to watch, but it's also fascinating because such a technique, so typical of the contemporary action/spectacle film, reduces difference into equivalence while divorcing an object from its properties. Here a drop of sweat and a knife are equally dangerous, one a natural process which does the body good, the other produced by human ingenuity and human labour to cut and harm: moreover, the knife is dangerous not because it can pierce but because it can fall.

We could interpret this by arguing that in the postmodern world, culture is more the source of terrorised amazement than nature; except its awesomeness derives not from God but from humans. But if we think of this at all, we think of it afterwards. *Mission: Impossible* is so thrilling that even hermeneutics are left behind for a while. On the ride, the viewer is too busy rushing through its aesthetics to think of anything but its erotics. *Mission: Impossible* is a delight because, in pleasing the eye and kicking the viscera, it continually asks the audience to wonder. How did they do that? And that the film does this, and *how* it does it, is at least as important as *why.*

Batman & Robin (Joel Schumacher, 1997)

Section 2: Arnold Schwarzenegger as Spectacle in Action (and some Moore)

Arnold Schwarzenegger is arguably action/spectacle's most representative star. The articles in this section are in chronological order so that the reader will be able to trace the development of the star's persona throughout the 90s. Of the articles and reviews in this section, only J. Hoberman's 'Nietzsche's Boy' takes Schwarzenegger as the central subject of analysis. Yet, though the rest focus on individual films, their observations on the way Schwarzenegger's star persona is used by particular directors within each film build into a cumulative argument that delineates Schwarzenegger's changing star persona, explores its connection to the action genre and, through the Schwarzenegger/Cameron films, investigates the relation between star vehicle and authorial signature.

In J. Hoberman's piece we are told that Schwarzenegger is 'the most potent symbol of worldwide dominance of the US entertainment industry'; that he is the current American ideal with a body that is 'its own stunning special effect'; and that he returns the movies to their fairground origin. Hoberman writes that the vehicles that made Schwarzenegger a star are distinguished by their can-do attitude; that the star has racked up the highest body count in movie history; and argues that Schwarzenegger's star persona reconciles 'father and destroyer, America and Germany (and Russia), man and machine, freedom and authority, terminator and redeemer, Rambo and Cary Grant, gym class and kindergarten, teacher and cop, the barbaric past and the awful future, the triumph of the will and the death of the subject, American hegemony and American vulnerability'. He is a muscleman pregnant with sociological and semiotic significance.

Jonathan Romney extends the analysis by exploring the connection of Schwarzenegger's persona to the action genre in relation to *The Last Action Hero*. Romney focuses on the film's self-reflexiveness, one that is associated with both high art and the music-hall/ burlesque tradition. But Romney argues as well that series such as *Die Hard, Lethal Weapon* and Schwarzenegger's own vehicles also exhibit a high degree of self-reflexivity. According to Romney, these films parody their own conventions in order to signal themselves as 'quality' genre product – as being more aware of their own constituent parts and, therefore, theoretically at least, superior to 'pure' genre fodder like, for example, the Chuck Norris oeuvre. Romney notes how in *Last Action Hero* the action genre is presented as worn out 'because it has run through all its possibilities' and that, in the process of showing the constructedness of Schwarzenegger's persona, the film exhausts it. Romney writes that the film is cinematic hara-kiri and that it is hard to imagine that any other Arnie will be possible after it.

José Arroyo's piece demonstrates that another Schwarzenegger was possible as Arnie returned in *True Lies* as an American James Bond – married, stronger than ever and, finally, with a soupçon of suavity. Arroyo's piece explores some of the characteristics and characteristic pleasures of action/spectacle as seen through the work of one of its leading directors, James Cameron. The piece also demonstrates how Cameron's work is indebted to the comic book and how it helped establish and develop Schwarzenegger's persona through the films they did together. Arroyo argues that, in its time, *True Lies* was the latest and most successful installment in humanising and Americanising Arnie and that, although it is not a good Cameron film, and in spite of its evident racism and sexism, it had all the necessessary elements to be a successful Schwarzenegger vehicle.

The feature articles are followed by reviews of Scharzenegger films subsequent to *True Lies*: *Junior*, *Eraser*, *Jingle All the Way* and *Batman and Robin*. The selection of films is interesting because they indicate that although Schwarzenegger always seems to appear in movies that are Big and Loud in both tone and mode, these films can also be characterised as belonging to different and distinct genres (comedy, action, comicbook spectacle). The reviews not only evaluate Schwarzenegger's films but also collectively comment on how the uses of Schwarzenegger's persona within each film are dependent on how it developed throughout his oeuvre and also on an audience's inter-textual and extra-textual knowledge of his life and career. Cumulatively, the reviews also raise the complex question of the relationship between acting ability, star persona and box office. An underlying narrative of a chronological reading of these reviews is that in the last half of the 90s Schwarzenegger exhibits increasing acting ability, maintains a potent star persona and demonstrates diminishing muscle at the box office.

This section ends with the perhaps surprising inclusion of Linda Ruth William's analysis of Demi Moore's star persona. It is not a tokenistic attempt at including a female star, and not because Moore is arguably one of the biggest female star of the 90s or even because she has done action films. Stars like Schwarzenegger and Stallone, via their dominance of the action genre created an archetypal body type for that genre. The juxtaposition of Schwarzenegger with Moore in *G.I. Jane* raises the implicit question of past influence and future possibility: is Schwarzenegger part of the reason why Demi Moore in *G.I. Jane* is showing us her 'musculinity' while fighting her way through the army and asking people to suck her dick? (Ripley never did.) And can a woman star in the genre, i.e. 'carry the vehicle', without aping a questionable masculinism both visually and behaviourally?

NIETZSCHE'S BOY

J. Hoberman

'The more contact I have with humans, the more I can learn,' ponderously enunciates killer cyborg Arnold Schwarzenegger in a rare lull during his multimegabuck super-spectacular *Terminator 2: Judgment Day*. The accent may defy transcription, but the humanising (or is it Americanising?) of our Arnold continues.

A film offering the most vivid thermo-nuclear firestorm in screen history, *Terminator 2* is more a remake than a sequel, less a homage than an obliteration. Among other things, it sets out to efface the implacable robot menace of *The Terminator* that elevated Arnold to super-stardom back in 1984. Opening unheralded on the eve of the US presidential election, *The Terminator* presented an alternative of sorts to the Reaganite 'new morning', unleashing der Arnold as the most compelling Frankenstein monster for half a century. *Terminator 2*, described by its director-writer-producer James Cameron as 'the first action movie advocating world peace', offers the monster's redemption.

T2 (as production company Carolco is hoping we'll call it) is more like *E.T. 2*, with a continual backbeat of *Die Hard* pyrotechnics – artfully pulverised walls and shattered glass, Evel Knievel cycle stunts, exploding skyscrapers and incinerated children. This time around, however, the bad old terminator (Arnold) protects the twelve-year-old future Messiah rather than trying to destroy his mother. Pitting the quaintly old-fashioned terminator against a new, liquid-metal prototype, *Terminator 2* makes the earlier model seem almost innocent. In a sense, it employs the same principle as US electoral politics: just when you think you've seen the worst...

The Terminator cost a mere $6 million; *Terminator 2*, whose budget is being estimated at fifteen times that, may be the most expensive movie ever made. And as we career into the 90s, it is the Arnold who seems the greatest of those extraterrestrial/immigrant/supernatural strangers in paradise who have wandered through the movies of the past decade, validating America's suburbs and shopping malls. It is Arnold who is the current American ideal, number eight (highest ranked actor) in *Entertainment Weekly*'s '101 Power People'. A self-made millionaire married to the glamorous newsreader and JFK niece Maria Shriver, our Arnold received $12 million to play the eponymous hero of *Kindergarten Cop* (1990), while, in an ancillary promotional move, his patron George Bush anointed him chairman of the President's Council on Physical Fitness and Sports. For *Terminator 2*, his estimated $15 million recompense included a Gulfstream G-III jet.

Yet, more than a public servant, Arnold is a strategic asset. During the 80s his films grossed $1 billion worldwide. He is the most bankable star in the US, Germany and Japan. (In the UK he should soon surpass Mel Gibson, although the French continue to prefer Depardieu, Gibson and even Dustin Hoffman.) In a story knocked off *Time*'s cover late last December by a piece wondering whether Kuwait was worth the price of war, Richard Corliss called him 'the most potent symbol of worldwide dominance of the US entertainment industry'.

While generations of would-be movie stars were compelled to Anglicise their names, this one sports the least pronounceable, most problematic moniker ever to emblazon an American movie marquee. Arnold is bad enough. As pronounced by an American, Schwarzenegger sounds practically obscene. Elevating those twenty letters is no small feat. But then, while other stars were born under the signs of Marx or Freud, this Austrian muscleman evokes that third prophet of modernity, Friedrich Nietzsche.

In *Conan the Barbarian* (1982), director John Milius introduced the five-times Mr Universe with a quote from *Thus Spake Zarathustra*: 'That which does not kill us makes us stronger.' Arnold's public statements reek of 'will to power', even as his image fulfils its manifestation, the *Übermensch*. (In the two *Conan* films, Schwarzenegger lords over the lower species – wrestling gorillas, punching out horses, cold-cocking camels – as if to illustrate Wilhelm Reich's observation that 'the theory of the German superman has its origin in man's effort to disassociate himself from the animal'.)

Even der Arnold's most famous line – the 'I'll be back' delivered with the full flourish of dull robotic menace in the original *Terminator* and echoed in *Kindergarten Cop* – has intimations of the Eternal Return. Yes, Arnold has willed the return of the American Dream. His parents, he says, wanted him to be a skier or play soccer, but he chose bodybuilding because 'it was a very American sport, and I thought, "If I do well, it could take me to America"'.

Culture of narcissism

But would the Arnold have achieved stardom during the breakdown years of the late 60s or early 70s? First had to come the decline of the western and the universality of hyperreal cartoon imagery, the canonisation of an antithesis (Dustin Hoffman or Woody Allen), the culture of narcissism, and the deployment of the artist's own person as sculptural material in Body Art. To become the Arnold, Schwarzenegger required the 80s fitness craze, the fifteen-year regime of 'body horror' movies, the proliferation of environmental cancers, the plague of Aids, the Reagan *Jawohl*. He had to transcend the suspect, sweaty fetishism of his chosen discipline and overcome suspicion about his sexual orientation. *Stay Hungry* (1976), the first movie in which Arnold had an important role, includes a scene in which a woman enquires whether his character is gay. Remarkably, this bit is reprised in *Kindergarten Cop*.

Still, for all the laboriously inscribed love interest in his recent movies, our Arnold is a man's man – or rather, a man's superman, or perhaps the simulation of a man's superman. 'Consider this a divorce,' he ripostes, shooting his treacherous pseudo-wife through the forehead in last year's *Total Recall*. Der Arnold perfected male character armour long before he became a movie star: 'I can hide my feelings under my muscles,' he told photographer George Butler, who with something of his subject's prescience has been documenting Arnold's thoughts and triceps since the mid-70s.

Not simply personifying the notion of the film star as an expensive expanse of well-lit torso, our Arnold returns the movies to their fairground origins. His seemingly indestructible body is, as *Time* observed, 'its own stunning special effect'. The sloping planes of his smooth, simian features are as chiselled as a comic book superhero. He is the blockbuster given human – or at least, humanoid – form. Mapped, quantified, evaluated, the Schwarzenegger torso is less a sex object than an object lesson, recapitulating the post-Renaissance transformation of the human body into something to be manipulated and rationalised, surveyed and regulated, subjected to the institutional discipline of prisons, schools, hospitals.

With his exaggerated 'perfect' form, the Arnold exemplifies those sci-fi cyborgs whose bionic technobodies render the human obsolete. ('When I'm training for a competition, I can be what some people call inhuman, but really I think it's more like being superhuman,' he told Butler.) 'John Matrix', the name by which he is called in the 1985 *Commando*, evokes both living cartilage and mass production. In *The Terminator*, the Arnold chose to play just such a matrix of metallic flesh and pseudo-human circuitry, as the movie invited us to share the joy of being a machine ('what some people call inhuman') by providing numerous point-of-view shots from the perspective of the Arnold's computerised videoterminal brain.

But even when Arnold does not play a machine, his behaviour is typically shown as an artificial construction. In *Twins* (1988), he has been genetically designed (by a German scientist, no less) to be a superman, then kept sequestered from the world. Arriving in America, an innocent in short pants, our Arnold must be taught by his dwarfish brother Danny DeVito to cope with the subterfuge of civilisation, even be tutored in his sexual instincts. In the far more radical *Total Recall*, the Arnold's memory is repeatedly wiped out and reconstructed, demonstrating that his personality, his personal history and his perspective are no less objectified than his body.

Given this materialism, it is hardly surprising that Arnold's movies are perceived as much as investments as they are entertainments. (*T2* was reviewed in the business section of the *New York Times* a week before it opened.) As a movie star and media personality, our Arnold is highly self-conscious. Albeit self-invented, the Arnold has a sense of himself as a historical being: 'With *Rocky*, I think Stallone did a big service to my career because he opened up a whole new type of movie, where the body is accepted and people go to see the body.' (Somewhat naively, our Arnold predicted that *Conan* would be his *Rocky*.)

Indeed, Arnold's relationship with Stallone seems to have been a virtual subtext in both the 1984 *Rocky IV* (the Soviet fighter Drago resembling nothing so much as Arnold gone blond) and the 1986 *Cobra* (Sly appropriating *Terminator* shades while his nemesis suggests Schwarzenegger gone to seed). And this despite (or perhaps because of) the fact that Arnold had helpfully supported Stallone consort Brigitte Nielsen in her ill-fated *Red Sonja* (1985).

Cary Grant with pecs

When in a 1988 *Playboy* interview, Schwarzenegger's interlocutor referred to Stallone as his 'friend', our Arnold strenuously begged to differ: 'He is not my friend... I make every effort that is humanly possible to be friendly to the guy, but he just gives off the wrong vibrations. Whatever he does, it always comes out wrong.' Unlike the tormented Stallone, the nonchalant Schwarzenegger is not haunted by the failure of Vietnam. Rather than dramatise old grievances or wallow in self-pity, *Predator* (1987) coolly reduces the war to the level of a video-game monster from outer space. Moreover, born and raised in neutral Austria, der Arnold is similarly unencumbered by the rigid categories of Cold War thinking. In *Commando*, he plays an East German immigrant; in *Red Heat*, his Russian cop is the ideal right-wing law enforcer – militaristic, hostile (when not oblivious) to civil liberties, economical in his instinctual application of justice.

The truth is, Sly has no *savoir faire*, while the Ivan Reitman comedies *Twins* and *Kindergarten Cop* allowed Arnold to become, as *People* had it, 'Cary Grant with pecs'. As early as *Commando*, our Arnold began to temper his aggression with corny puns and callous wisecracks in the manner of James Bond. His comedies deform the notion of amiability no less. We treasure the Arnold's tender concern for his stunted twin – whether it be Danny DeVito, George Bush or ourselves – because it is backed up by the threat of maximum force. We applaud Arnold's diligent public service in *Kindergarten Cop*, however threatening. 'Stop whining. You kids are soft – you lack discipline,' he tells his five-year-old charges, rationalising their chaotic play into regimented, meaningless activity.

Most American heroes are bugged by authority, but Schwarzenegger, the son of a cop, is not a cop-hater – despite *T2*'s clever opposition of Arnold's biker-clad terminator against the newer, police-disguised model. On the contrary: 'My relationship to power and authority is that I'm all for it. People need somebody to watch over them and tell them what to do. Ninety-five per cent of the people in the world need to be told what to do and how to behave.'

In *The Running Man* (1987), which unconvincingly attacked the cartoon world of the high 80s – the very robo-entertainment that provided the backdrop to Schwarzenegger's climb to fame – our Arnold mocks futile dreamers of social reform and demands immediate action. Order and discipline are the stuff of *his* fantasy life: 'I was always dreaming about very powerful people,' he confided to Butler. 'Dictators and things like that.'

Which 'things like that', you might well ask? Alternatively perceived as comic or sinister, the sound of a German accent serves self-consciously to unite Americans as Americans against an alien order. Camp fascist that he is, Milius attempted to shock the liberal media by opining that his *Conan* would have been popular in 30s Germany. The transplanted Dutch director, Paul Verhoeven, couldn't resist a similar gag, ending *Total Recall* with a mystical Alpine apotheosis worthy of Leni Riefenstahl. But our Arnold is not Conrad Veidt, a Nazi victim compelled to play Nazi villains. Unlike any previous star, he embraces and embodies the covertly admired Teutonic virtues.

The Arnold's autobiographical accounts are unselfconsciously filled with references to 'the Master Plan', 'iron discipline', and his own compulsive 'neatness'. An American citizen since 1983, he has scarcely shed his Austrian identity. Neither has his *Heimat* forgotten him. Kurt Waldheim's wedding present, delivered to the Kennedy family compound at Hyannisport, was a larger-than-life sculpture of a grinning, lederhosen-clad Arnold hoisting up his new bride, herself dressed in the laced-up blouse and dirndl of a Bavarian peasant.

America's reigning male star is *a priori* a political figure, as well as a didactic one. 'The most important American of our time is John Wayne,' wrote theatre critic Eric

Bentley in 1971. 'Granted that all good things come from California, Richard Nixon and Ronald Reagan are only camp followers of Wayne, supporting players in the biggest Western of them all.' From the Bicentennial through the Iran-Contra hearings, Stallone provided Americans with a decade's worth of political metaphor, while Clint Eastwood's old movies continued to supply tough-guy rhetoric through the 1988 presidential election – when, ever mindful of the wimp factor, George Bush campaigned alongside der Arnold and Chuck Norris. Thus, Arnold's innocent statements ('The joy in public office is a tremendous idea. I think it could be the greatest challenge yet,' he told *Entertainment Weekly*) are a factor of the seriousness with which he takes his exalted position.

It is time, as George Bush proposed (and *Premiere* seconded), for a 'kinder, gentler' Arnold. As *Kindergarten Cop* signalled, our Arnold is now a father. He has done penance for the sins of his fatherland, pledging $250,000 to the Simon Wiesenthal Center, which reciprocated with a dinner at the Century Plaza in LA honouring Arnold's work on behalf of physical fitness and handicapped children. This astonishing event featured a full-dress Marine colour guard, a US flag secretly stitched together by the inmates of the Mauthausen concentration camp carried into the ballroom by a group of Holocaust survivors, and a speech by George Bush. Not long afterwards, *Variety* reported Schwarzenegger's plans to run for senator from California, possibly as early as 1992.

Like Stallone, Schwarzenegger might be said to enact the masculine. The power of Stallone's alter egos, Rocky and Rambo, is, however, predicated on their ability to absorb physical punishment. (Rocky, in particular, embodies the pathos of the proletariat – the man who's only capital is his body.) But even as Rocky developed and the Gulf War relegated Rambo to a joke – a figure mocked by Saddam Hussein and debunked by US commanders – the Arnold, who once cheerfully asserted that 'for me, pain is pleasure', had already rendered Stallone's suffering obsolete.

While Stallone's movies were turgid exercises in regaining national self-respect, the vehicles that made Schwarzenegger a star are distinguished by their can-do attitude and insouciantly surplus carnage. On a per capita basis, the Arnold has surely racked up the highest body count in movie history. In *Commando*, he single-handedly kills dozens, if not hundreds, to save a single life. In *Raw Deal*, he decimates the Chicago mob, accomplishing 'a hundred years of police work in a single afternoon'. Unlike his macho predecessors, der Arnold has been an equal opportunity terminator, killing women on screen not only in *The Terminator* (where it is the subject of the movie), but, most famously, in *Total Recall*.

The perfect dad

In the new improved *Terminator 2*, Arnold kneecaps his opponents rather than blowing them away. The bloodlust in the world's greatest demolition derby is transferred to his former victim, Sarah (Linda Hamilton, her movie career seemingly on hold since she first played Arnold's snuff object). An even more crazed Rambette than Sigourney Weaver in *Aliens*, Hamilton is the mother not only of its Messiah but of all eco-terrorists – single-handedly pulverising a suburban ranch house and terrorising a family into submission. Although her character gets to trump Arnold's curtailed antisocial behaviour (reduced now to punching out pay phones to get a quarter), her nurturing side is not completely absent. Around the time that the terminator begins to wonder why it is that people cry, Sarah realises that this half-domesticated killer cyborg is the perfect dad.

Potent symbol of worldwide domination, our Arnold reconciles father and destroyer. America and Germany, and Russia, man and machine, freedom and authority, terminator and redeemer, Rambo and Cary Grant, gym class and kindergarten, teacher and cop, the barbaric past and the awful future, the triumph of the will and the death of the subject, American hegemony and American vulnerability. Proudly wasteful and bizarrely self-serving, *Terminator 2* suggests the merging of Schwarzenegger and Schwarzkopf. This is truly the Desert Storm of action flicks – a mindboggling display of state of the art FX angled at the international, as well as US, market.

Not only does *T2* advocate 'world peace', it illustrates the concept of 'collateral damage'. Too kind and gentle to massacre his opponents, too thorough and butch to let them live, too ambitious and socialised to divorce any more wives, our Arnold packs the cinema with invisible corpses. For an encore, he has enlisted Verhoeven to direct him in a twelfth-century version of Operation Desert Storm. They shall call it *The Crusades*.

ARNOLD THROUGH THE LOOKING GLASS

Jonathan Romney

Arnold Schwarzenegger seems to have been asking for trouble by parodying *Hamlet* in *Last Action Hero*: no one in Hollywood is immune to the slings and arrows of outrageous fortune, not even as apparently inviolable a sweet prince as him. *Variety* went so far as to suggest ways in which the titan – brought low by overweening hubris – could set about re-inventing his career. But *Last Action Hero* is already too thoroughgoing an exercise in self-reinvention, or at least self-deconstruction, to satisfy a market that prefers to take its stereotypes neat.

Among the charges brought against the film is that it is in bad faith. But bad faith is hardly a flaw of *Last Action Hero* – it's the film's *raison d'être*. The complex film-within-a-film framework means that it partakes at once of 'genuine' action-genre requirements and of the 'irresponsible' parody exemplified by *Airplane!*, *Naked Gun* and the Mel Brooks canon. *Last Action Hero* is neither fish nor fowl, but a strange self-regarding hybrid that owes its characteristics to a long line of nested narratives represented in film by *Hellzapoppin'* at one end of the scale, Godard at the other; and in literature by *Don Quixote* (whose hero, in Book Two, has the unusual experience of reading his own adventures in Book One). Another example, of course, is the play-within-a-play of *Hamlet* – suggesting that the trailer in *Last Action Hero* for an apocryphal Arnie movie is more totemic than arbitrary.

Last Action Hero has been criticised for the narcissistic pride it takes in refusing to provide the satisfactions expected from an Arnie movie proper. But the film constantly theorises its own relation to the Arnie canon. Much of *Last Action Hero* is taken up by a film-within-a-film, *Jack Slater IV*, supposedly starring Arnold Schwarzenegger. But the climactic twist comes at the New York premiere of *Jack Slater IV*, at which the real Arnold Schwarzenegger – or more accurately, Schwarzenegger playing a fictional representation of himself – tells the press that the body count in his new film is significantly lower than in its predecessors, in keeping with kinder, gentler public tastes.

Most reactions to this scene have been to accuse the film of mealy-mouthedness. For Arnie to pander to public tastes in this way, the argument goes, is both cynical and a denial of the reason people watch his movies anyway – precisely to see him waste bad guys. It seems like an excuse: a way of letting him off the hook for making an uncharacteristically tame kids' movie – *Last Action Hero*, that is. But this scene simply alludes to a debate already raised more covertly, but just as ironically, in *Terminator 2*, in which Arnie's android persona responded to the low-body-count imperative by maiming, rather than killing, his adversaries.

The argument against this interpretation is that *Last Action Hero*, by making its workings explicit, is trying to hoodwink us as to its true nature – giving us the impression that it is not an Arnold Schwarzenegger movie, when it knows damn well that it is. According to this line of reasoning, the film is trying to turn the patent flaws of *Jack Slater IV* into the manifest merits of *Last Action Hero*. Apparently selling itself under false colours, it is attempting to absolve itself from meeting the generic demands of the action movie.

Yet this same ploy is already at work within 'straight' examples of this sequel-ridden genre, which push their conventions to the limits of repetition and absurdity in order to revitalise them – the same old trick becomes a variation on the same old trick as long as a collusive understanding can be established with the audience as to how that trick might be perceived as being at once the same and different. At its simplest level, this strategy is exemplified by the hero's exclaiming 'Here we go again' when a situation repeats itself – as when Bruce Willis, in *Die Hard 2*, marvels that yet again he's required to save the day at Christmas (the opening of *Last Action Hero* immediately signals one referent when a harassed cop exclaims, 'This is one hell of a way to spend Christmas').

Series like *Die Hard*, *Lethal Weapon* and Schwarzenegger's own vehicles parody their own conventions, either within individual films or from film to film, in order to signal themselves as 'quality' genre product – as being more aware of their own constituent parts and therefore, theoretically at least, superior to 'pure' genre fodder, to the Chuck Norris canon, say. These films try to pass themselves off as being at least more honest about their own automatism. But *Last Action Hero* goes one step further. It is neither more dishonest nor more honest than those 'real' action thrillers; it simply takes self-awareness to an extreme.

Last Action Hero certainly makes its reception all the more difficult by espousing a form most commonly associated with off-mainstream areas – either modernist art cinema or the burlesque. As a film-within-a-film commenting on its own make up and reception, *Last Action Hero* is flanked on one side by the paradoxes associated with the literary tradition of self-referentiality, and on the other by self-deconstructing comedies like H.C. Potter's *Hellzapoppin'* (1942).

Last Action Hero's film-within-a-film is a classic example of *mise en abîme* – to use the heraldic term that André Gide brought into critical use to denote small-scale representations or analogues of a work within the work itself (for example, the play *The Mousetrap* in *Hamlet*, whose plot it mirrors). This is a tradition most famously represented in literature by the parables and paradoxes of Jorge Luis Borges, and by Gide's novel *Les Faux-monnayeurs* (*The Counterfeiters*), which concerns the writing of a novel entitled *The Counterfeiters*.

In film, Fellini's *8½* and Godard's *Passion* dramatise their own fabrication in similar ways to Gide's novel, addressing in particular authorship and its responsibilities, and the problem attendant on generating fictions. But outside such auteur-centric examples, filmic *mise en abîme* is likely to be concerned less with the author's travails than with the spectator's. Often, it is a case of undermining the assumptions of the viewing process by 'infecting' filmic illusion with the conditions peculiar to live performance. Starting from the bases of the non-illusionistic music-hall/burlesque tradition, such films have used *mise en abîme* to defuse cinema's claims to transparent representation of the world and to disarm the excessive readiness of viewers to project their desires into the celluloid image. It is a strategy that can be traced from Buster Keaton's *Sherlock Junior* (1924), in which a sleeping projectionist 'projects' himself into the screen; via more anarchic fantasies such as W.C. Fields' *Never Give a Sucker an Even Break* (Edward Cline, 1941), much of which consists of a producer's incredulous reading of an unfilmable Fields script; and up to Joe Dante's recent *Matinee*, which by way of tribute to B-film huckster William Castle, waxes nostalgic for an age in which cinema still partook of the unpredictable live dimension of music hall.

These all play on our desire to project ourselves into film space as if it were co-extensive with the space inhabited by the viewer. In *Sherlock Junior*, Keaton walks into the screen and gets booted out again; in *Hellzapoppin'*, the spectator is not only addressed directly, but also caught in the crossfire of banter between the on-screen characters, the projectionist and other figures who sporadically invade the stalls.

Such devices often lend themselves to tendentious agendas, notably the assignment of value to different types of cinema. 'High' cinema, supposedly, can be sorted from 'low' on the basis of the sort of illusionism entailed. Woody Allen's *The Purple Rose of Cairo* (1984) harks back to *Madame Bovary* in its evocation of the perils implicit in projecting one's desires on to the flickerings of celluloid. Its Depression-blighted heroine finds the hero of a romance stepping off the screen to woo her, sparking off much debate about the status of a character who becomes independent of his author. In one of those metaphysical disputes so beloved of Woody Allen, the existence of a controlling deity is argued for: 'There must be a reason for everything. Otherwise it would be like a movie with no point.'

Such dilemmas hark back to Borges' conundrums, in which *mise en abîme* as a literary device entails a wider uncertainty: 'if the characters in a fictional work can be readers or spectators, we, its readers or spectators can be fictitious.' In Maurizio

Nichetti's 1989 film *Ladri di saponette* (*The Icicle Thief*), the hero (also called Maurizio Nichetti) finds himself trapped in a television set, having entered it to correct the faulty showing of his own film (also called *Ladri di saponette*). Here, however, the metaphysical question – the status of the characters *vis-à-vis* their dethroned author-god – is put to the service of a specific comic agenda: at once to parody the neo-realist canon and to make a piqued comment on the way films shown on Italian television fall casualty to an enforced promiscuity with soap powder commercials (in this case, one bleeds into the other, and impoverished 40s housewives end up in a Shake 'n' Vac world).

However, *Hellzapoppin'*, the *locus classicus* of the burlesque *mise en abîme*, shows that such films can't be expected to adhere to their declared agenda. The film that most thoroughly establishes the possibilities of infinite regress, this comedy vehicle for the now largely forgotten Ole Olsen and Chic Johnson was inspired by – but in no way a direct transcription of – the Broadway show that made the duo's name. The film begins with the screening of a film called *Hellzapoppin'*, complete with credits, before we realise that we are actually watching the shooting of that film. The shooting is quickly aborted by an enraged director who goes on to show the comic duo his version of the film he wants them to star in. 'It's a picture about a picture about *Hellzapoppin'*', he explains, although the film we then see turns out to be nothing of the kind. One of the consistent pleasures of this form is the way films establish specific rules governing the boundaries between film and reality and then proceed to transgress them. Indeed, one of the most disappointing things about the Woody Allen and Maurizio Nichetti films is how rigidly they adhere to the schematic boundaries they set up for themselves: arguably, the pleasure of this form of narrative lies precisely in its willingness to lose track of itself.

What *Last Action Hero* has in common with *Hellzapoppin'* is an awareness of the exceptional density of possibilities that a film can accommodate, and that are precluded by simply demanding that it either concerns itself with a world of known rules or ignores the possible entirely by establishing its own hermetic schema of parallel reality. The pleasure of *Last Action Hero* lies in the way it exceeds the apparently stable distinctions it has established between the real and the non-real, between the picture and the frame. The seemingly coherent world of *Jack Slater IV*, a universe ruled by the laws of the action genre (people don't get hurt, good guys win), is riddled with flaws. In such a world, what would be the possible interest in watching *Terminator 2*? Yet the video is on sale at Slater's local video store – albeit starring Sylvester Stallone. And if *Terminator 2* exists in that world as a film, how can that film's evil android (Robert Patrick) turn up at the deluxe Los Angeles police headquarters where Slater takes Danny?

The sort of coherence that might prevail in a classic science-fiction, parallel-world story is clearly surplus to requirements here. It's the refusal to limit possibilities that's all-important. The police station is clearly not a real police station, even within the terms of Slater's world. It is simply Hollywood Central, the heart of movie dreams, where futuristic Amazons, robots and rabbis, and the real Sharon Stone, turn up between engagements alongside a 'sampled' image of Bogart and a cartoon cat out of *Roger Rabbit*. It's a Hollywood utopia in which all cinema's possibilities exist simultaneously.

This sense of impossible excess has its forebears in the tradition. In *Sherlock Junior*,

Keaton's dreaming self walks straight into the drawing room of the film he is watching. But no sooner is he within the screen than the scene changes in quick succession to a seaside, the African bush, a snowy waste – settings violently at odds with the syntax of a silent era detective drama. The point is, once again, that immersion in one film means immersion in cinema with *all* its possibilities. If a film flouts the divide between the real and the fictive, why not, then, flout the divide between one film and all possible films?

Likewise, Olsen and Johnson are seen striding across the sound stage for what is presumably the *Hellzapoppin'* they are about to make, and as they cross separate sets, their costumes change accordingly – tricorns for a Louis Quatorze antechamber, Eskimo suits for a snow scene with igloos (complete with a sledge marked *Rosebud*). None of these scenes could possibly figure within the film they are planning, yet they have a place in a virtual film that *doesn't* get made.

This sort of self-reflexivity refuses to limit a fictional world to the requirements of realism. The film within *Hellzapoppin'* may not require sledges and powdered wigs, and may not actually break all historical and geographical boundaries as well as all generic ones; the important thing is that we can imagine a film that would. All that is required is a skim through the repertoire of possibles, a visit to the prop room of movie dreams.

Implicit in this desire for totality, though, is a sense of exhaustion. *Last Action Hero*, like *Hellzapoppin'*, suffers from an omnivorous desire to exhaust every possibility, to sup, however briefly, from every generic plate. Both films also attempt to exhaust the totality of all commentaries that can be made about them by pre-empting them (in *Last Action Hero*, Danny comments on the impossibility of the films' stunts, while he performs them). But in *Last Action Hero*, which carries finality in its very title, there is the sense of a more drastic exhaustion. The action genre is itself worn out, because it has run through all its possibilities; and the genre fan, thoroughly schooled in its conventions by Danny's running exegesis, may never be able to watch another example of the genre again. The film does, indeed, represent a pre-emptive act of hubris on the part of its makers, who are effectively ensuring that we will never take seriously a *Die Hard III*, a *Lethal Weapon IV*, a *Terminator 3*. Sure enough, it's the end of the line for Slater, who lays down his badge and rails against his pre-scripted existence: 'Hollywood is writing our lives.' It's a neat touch – reality directly redeems the movies rather than it happening the other way round, as films have taught us to expect.

But what's also exhausted in the process is the Schwarzenegger persona, *Last Action Hero* is not simply a case of Arnie playing himself for laughs, as he did in *Kindergarten Cop* – it's a case of him playing against himself, devaluing his image as a 'real person'. The 'Arnold Schwarzenegger' we see at the *Jack Slater IV* screening – vain, garrulous, determined to plug his burger joint – seems a shadow of Jack Slater, the three-dimensional cop with a history, a lifestyle, a tragic side (even if it has been wittily demonstrated that the divorced-loner pathos that forms his character has been minutely constructed by screenwriters). When Slater and 'Schwarzenegger' meet, it's remarkable which seems the more real. The film demonstrates what, after all, we already know: Slater has been constructed, but so has Arnie, whose persona, no less than his body, is 'built'. Arnie as cop, as Hamlet, as 'Arnie', are all on the same level, sharing the same cartoon consistency.

Last Action Hero is cinematic hara-kiri. It's hard to imagine that after it, any other Arnies will be possible – at least, any Arnies that seem more real than a cartoon cat or a virtual Bogart. Not the least achievement of *Last Action Hero* is to make us ask whether or not we *want* to accept Arnie as anything more than the signature on the burger wrapper.

CAMERON AND THE COMIC

José Arroyo

Watching James Cameron's films, I sometimes experience what I imagine the Lumières' original audiences must have felt: a mixture of disbelief and delight, and a sense of wonderment at the magic of the movies. *True Lies* has several such moments, my favourite being the scene in which Arnie, on horseback, gallops after evil Aziz (Art Malik), who is on a motorcycle. The chase takes us through busy streets, a hotel lobby, up an elevator and across tall buildings. It is silly stuff – but silly stuff is rarely so thrilling.

Spectacle films don't rely on the same types of realism as genres such as domestic comedies, but verisimilitude nonetheless remains an important criterion. We know that Arnold Schwarzenegger isn't actually flying the jet in *True Lies*, yet if we could see how the effect was constructed (by detecting the matting, morphing or miniatures, for example), our pleasure would be lost. Part of the joy of Cameron's films (and this applies even to *Piranha II: The Spawning*) is that they trick us so well.

Critical response to *True Lies* has so far been mixed. My local newspaper in Montreal awarded the film only two stars, recommending that audiences wait until it is released on video – as ridiculous a piece of advice as one is likely to get. The film offers many pleasures (humour, romance), but perhaps the greatest, the one unavailable on video, is what the bulk of its reputed $120 million budget was spent on – the creation of particular kinds of spectacle (luxurious sets, exotic locations, huge boys' toys, high-speed chases, dramatic shoot-outs and extravagant explosions) whose enjoyment is predicated on widescreen viewing and increased by audience participation. Unlike *La Totale!* (the 1991 French film directed by Claude Zidi on which Cameron's work is based), whose effects are not diminished on a small screen, *True Lies* is a film to see at the movies.

A comparison of *La Totale!* and *True Lies* can probably tell us much about the specificity of French and American national cultures (and also their common features: both films are sexist and anti-Arab, albeit in different ways). But such a comparison also points up some of the characteristics of the contemporary big-budget American spectacle film. Cameron and Schwarzenegger's speciality both in their previous collaborations (*The Terminator* and *Terminator 2: Judgment Day*) and in the rest of their individual oeuvres. Watching *La Totale!* reminds us that *True Lies* is a type of cinema rarely feasible outside Hollywood. Smaller national cinemas cannot afford and do not have similar access to cutting-edge special effects technology (much less the opportunity to develop it with particular films in mind, as Cameron did for *The Abyss* and *Terminator 2*). Only Hollywood can maintain an infrastructure which keeps employed personnel skilled in a wide range of narrowly specialised areas of film-making.

In both *True Lies* and *La Totale!*, a couple, happily married for many years, find their marriage in trouble. The wife (Helen Tasker, played by Jamie Lee Curtis in Cameron's film) is approaching middle age and longs for excitement at least once in her life. She does not know that her husband Harry (Schwarzenegger) has lied to her throughout their marriage and is in fact a highly glamorous secret agent rather than the boring nine-to-fiver she believes him to be. Her would-be paramour Simon (Bill Paxton) is also lying to her: while trying to seduce her by posing as an agent and taking credit for her husband's exploits, he is in fact a used-car salesman. By the end of the film, the husband has neutralised the competition and recruited the wife into his organisation. Working together, they keep their marriage spicy and their country safe.

True Lies and *La Totale!* not only share this almost identical plot (and a subplot about Arab terrorists stealing weapons and wanting to blow things up), but the former also borrows situations, props and even lines of dialogue from the latter. Yet the two films belong to different genres (or perhaps more accurately deploy different combinations of elements from various genres), and indeed to different modes altogether. *La Totale!* mixes elements from the picaresque sex comedy, the domestic melodrama, the buddy-cop film and the spy film. But as one would expect from the director of *Les Ripoux*, the film's primary aim is to make the audience laugh. *True Lies* mixes elements from the screwball comedy, the domestic melodrama (both films are family romances), the buddy-cop film (the Tom Arnold-Arnold Schwarzenegger relationship can be read as a twist on that of Mel Gibson and Danny Glover in the *Lethal Weapon* films), and the spy film (though the spectacular elements and hero's panache are drawn more specifically from the big-budget Bond movies). But as one would expect from the director of *Aliens*, the film's primary aim is to provide spectacle that will thrill, chill and awe the audience.

The comic elements in *True Lies* are successfully realised, but though they are sometimes combined with spectacle, they most often alternate with it, just as the film switches between the domestic and public spheres, and push the narrative forward. The first scene in the film is an action scene; the last a comic one. Both feature a tango. At the beginning Schwarzenegger dances with the sexy Asian villainess (Tia Carrere); by the end he's dancing with his all-American wife. Their marriage is saved, the United States is free of Arab terrorists, the former suitor is made to pee in his pants at the feel of a lipstick and the hero and heroine tango into the night. *True Lies* may just be an embroidered *La Totale!*, but the embroidery is so extensive and skilful as to constitute a different object.

Gazing at Batman

All Cameron's films to date have been like comic books (he is presently in pre-production for *Spiderman*). This is meant as a compliment. Science-fiction literature has a long history of depicting fantastic imaginary worlds which are rendered legible (and 'realistic') to audiences through recognisable structural relationships (racial differences among species, for example) and analogy (space as the new frontier). Unlike literature, however, comics create concrete visual representations of these imaginings; they literally draw them out for us.

The best comic books endow their characters with an impression of movement. Action scenes are carefully constructed to make the most fantastic feats appear possible (as a child I used to gaze for hours at *Batman* comics thinking that if I bent my knees just so and twirled around a flagpole, I too could leap between skyscrapers). This care with movement is extended throughout the form: characters are given movement within and across panels and panels are juxtaposed so that the narrative moves throughout the page and from page to page. Comics have great flow – as do Cameron's films.

It is no secret that comic books are heavily indebted to cinema: they too rely on a type of *mise en scène* and montage to tell their stories and create their effects. But in the case of Cameron, the borrowing is reversed – the resemblance between the monsters in *Aliens* and the extraterrestrial brood who used the X-Men as human hosts is uncanny, while Charlton Heston in *True Lies* is a dead-ringer for Nick Fury. Like comics, Cameron's films give concrete visual expression to fantastic worlds or things through careful *mise en scène*: his action scenes are fluid and detailed and the use of inserts and close-ups gives impossible stunts a human logic. And the likeness goes further.

Marvel comics such as *X-Men*, *The Amazing Spiderman* and *Daredevil* depict a corrupt world characterised by conflict between species (as in *Aliens*); rampant and ruthless corporate interests which value profit over human life (the hotel owner in *Piranha II*, the corporate flunky in *Aliens*); stupid and careless government representatives (*The Abyss*, *Terminator 2*). As in Cameron's films, narration in Marvel comics alternates between spectacular action and a troubled domestic sphere in which surrogate families are created as alternatives to traditional ones and as a buffer to troubled love relationships – 'families' that are glimmers of utopia in otherwise dystopian worlds. Like Cameron's heroines, those in Marvel, by grace of their powers and intellect, tend to be equal to male heroes and generally superior to ordinary *homo sapiens*.

Cameron's films, like most comic books, construct imaginary worlds and render them believable, but with greater intensity, a greater impression of movement, and on a bigger canvas. This is usually accompanied by a critique of corporations (if not of capitalism *per se*), an interrogation of traditional gender roles and flashes of insight into what it might mean to be human in late capitalism. But if Cameron's previous movies are like comic books, *True Lies* is merely cartoonish.

True Lies is a disappointing Cameron film. It is too thin and long and too focused on its show-off, showcase scenes. Those sandwiched in between, skilfully directed as they are, are like stale filling. The jokes and explosions dazzle, but ultimately can't hide the film's shallowness. *True Lies* has little to say and most of that is unpleasant, to say the least.

The representation of Arabs reinforces many negative stereotypes: they are wealthy, devious, hyper-emotional and ultimately incompetent. Their function is to be held up for ridicule so the audience can laugh, and even applaud, as they are systematically eliminated. The film tries to buy a licence for this type of representation by having an Arab as one of the minor good guys – as if one computer nerd could compensate for reams of racism.

Cameron's previous movies have been critical of the established order, but *True Lies* simply affirms it. For instance, the family is usually an impossible ideal in Cameron's work – much longed for and highly valued, but out of reach. His characters end up making their own 'families' the best way they can. At the end of *The Terminator*, Linda Hamilton rides alone into the sunset, gun in her lap, ready to prepare her son for a post-nuclear future. In *Aliens* Sigourney Weaver becomes a surrogate single mother to Newt, partly to compensate for the death of her biological daughter (and I don't remember any mention of a father either). In *Terminator 2*, a cyborg is presented as the ideal parent. Even in *Piranha II* – which ends with a freeze-frame of the reunited family clinging to each other after the defeat of the mutant piranhas – Tricia O'Neil and Lance Henriksen (protagonists and parents) live independently, socially and sexually, for most of the film.

The family in *True Lies*, however, is an updated version of *Father Knows Best.* Mom may now work, but she still bakes birthday cakes and has supper ready on time. Dad's preoccupation with his job makes him a little absent-minded, but he always has the best interests of his wife and little girl at heart and always comes through for them, proving his love by saving their butts. *True Lies* perpetrates astonishing emotional violence in the name of the traditional nuclear family. As Harry Tasker, Schwarzenegger can eavesdrop on his wife, stalk her through the city, kidnap her and even lock her up for questioning. All this is excusable because it proves Mrs Tasker is faithful and thus helps keep the family together.

True Lies also affirms traditional gender roles. One of the most disturbing and telling scenes has Schwarzenegger interrogating Jamie Lee Curtis. He is with his colleague (Tom Arnold) behind a two-way mirror; she is a prisoner, target of masses of surveillance equipment that records and analyses her every gesture. The editing alternates between shots of Curtis and Schwarzenegger and of Schwarzenegger and Arnold, interrupted occasionally by close-ups of a featureless video image of Curtis, a visual lie-detector device. A woman is on trial for being a sexual person and her face, her greatest market of identity, is denied her. She will be freed only when she passes the boys' test.

Marital problems have been another favourite Cameron theme, a fertile context in which the domestic and the quotidian can intersect with the fantastic. In *The Abyss*, for instance, Ed Harris is saved from drowning because he keeps open his escape route by means of the wedding ring he had previously thrown down the toilet; the spectacular descent into the ocean depths is the setting for the couple to speak freely to each other again and to admit to their feelings. But *True Lies* presents an adolescent picture of marriage: a boring union can be saved if the pair are shot at and hang from helicopters. Schwarzenegger is contrasted with short, slobby Tom Arnold to lead us to conclude that to be a good husband is to be tall, macho and jealous (although Arnie also 'cares'). We are literally told that used-car salesman Simon is not competition for Arnie because he has a smaller penis. The Asian villainess (there was no such character in *La Totale!*) exists only as a counterpoint to Jamie Lee Curtis – the bad girl who makes Jamie Lee look good. The film kills her off so Curtis can appropriate some of her badness and become even better (a sophisticated sex-bomb and faithful wife) by the end of the movie.

Jamie Lee Curtis' role as Helen Tasker is written much as in the French film, but she does more with it than Miou-Miou. The latter is good as the mousey bourgeois house-wife, but her transformation into a sleek secret agent is less convincing. There is a scene in both films where the women have to pretend to be prostitutes. Miou-Miou simply turns around her dress and rearranges her belt, but Curtis' transformation is a star moment. She rips the ruffles off her black dress, pushes out her bust, sleeks her hair back with water from a vase and becomes Jamie Lee – The Body. She then turns around and, back in character, wobbles wonderfully on her high heels. Curtis can scream like a stereotypical bimbo, knock Arnie out, do pratfalls and still look elegant. And she is an excellent partner for Schwarzenegger.

Humanising Arnie

True Lies doesn't meddle with Schwarzenegger's star persona the way *Last Action Hero* did, but simply adds another facet. As another step in the carefully constructed career project of humanising Arnie, it presents him as emotionally and physically vulnerable (though only to his wife) as never before.

Thanks to his celebrity as a body-builder, Schwarzenegger had a persona before he was in movies; he starred in movies (*Hercules in New York*) before Bob Rafelson formally 'introduced' him in *Stay Hungry*; and the *Conan* movies had already made him a star before he hooked up with Cameron in *The Terminator*. But the Cameron film was the first Schwarzenegger movie to be awarded the kind of critical reception and academic interest that helps turn a commercial sci-fi spectacle into a contemporary classic. *The Terminator* continues to be a top video renter and aspects of the cyborg have remained central to Schwarzenegger's persona.

In his early films, because body-building has connotations of gayness, Schwarzenegger's heterosexuality had to be continually asserted, while his ethnicity also had to be explained. This was done in different ways: by making him a foreign body-builder (*Stay Hungry*, *The Jayne Mansfield Story*), by placing him in mythological settings (*Conan*, *Red Sonja*) or by giving him as little dialogue as possible (all of the above, plus the rest). In terms of coupling, he was sometimes estranged from his partner (*Raw Deal*) or paired with Amazons or women of colour (*The Running Man*).

Every film enlarged on his persona (particularly his comedies) and these impediments have now been overcome. His body, which often used to elicit laughter and derision, is now an ideal to many, while he is also widely perceived as American as apple pie. In *True Lies*, he is an American working for a secret government organisation and his body, until now his trademark, is kept pretty much under wraps. Yet the film knows when to leave the persona alone. For instance in *La Totale!* Arnie's character has two children, one of them a son engaged in an Oedipal conflict to assert his own identity. Against Schwarzenegger, who would dare?

Schwarzenegger's entrance in *True Lies* is revealing. We see someone in the water but we can't see the face. When it bobs to the surface we see a high-tech mask reminiscent of some alien or cyborg. Then the face is unmasked and it's Arnie. He plants his equipment and bombs, takes off his wetsuit and uncovers a tuxedo. For the next ten minutes, Arnie dances a tango, handles computers, speaks many languages – he's James Bond. But we also know the suaveness hides savagery – under the tuxedo there is also Conan and the Terminator. For the rest of the film, the Terminator is married, has a child, and is vulnerable, insecure and jealous. Harry Tasker is as much a cartoon as any character Schwarzenegger has played, but Cameron allows his actor's various cartoon images an airing at differing points in the film and offers him a few more single dimensions. It is a brilliant use of the persona – similar to the way new artists and writers bring new life to established comic-book characters.

In a recent television documentary, Dirk Bogarde said that stars could get by with one look. Schwarzenegger now has more than that but his jaw-clenched glare is still a trademark, and *True Lies* uses it cleverly. We know he can kill anyone with a blow and that the blow generally follows the glare. In *True Lies* sometimes it does and sometimes it doesn't; audiences at my screening enjoyed it either way. *True Lies* might not be good Cameron, but it is good Schwarzenegger. Racist, sexist and shallow, it is escapism into a white boy's fantasy land.

BODY TALK

Linda Ruth Williams

In the extended 'coming out' episode of the US television sit-com *Ellen*, blockbuster movie actress Demi Moore makes a brief cameo appearance, along with fellow lesbian icons Gina Gershon, k.d. lang and Laura Dern (who plays Ellen's love-interest). Moore is disguised as a shelf-stacking supermarket shlub, perkily boyish but undoubtedly Demi. This is the latest in a long line of self-masquerades, transformative acts by which Moore manages to bring off a curiously paradoxical coup: in the act of disguising, masking or completely making herself over, what emerges through the guise is an ever clearer image of Demi the star.

But what is a star in 90s Hollywood? Since the decline and fall in the 50s and early 60s of the studio system's controlling machines, how do we distinguish our icons? Female stardom may now be synonymous with $12 million pay cheques, final-cut control or the ability to open a movie. If the persona of the classical Hollywood star was once brought into being through the detailed manipulations of the studios, perhaps now it is that strength of control the star herself wields that guarantees stellar celebrity. In 1995, *Premiere* magazine voted Moore America's most powerful actress, placing her higher in their Power Top 25 (which judges 'actors with the most ability to exert their will on the making of movies in Hollywood') than Clint Eastwood, Robin Williams or her co-star in *Indecent Proposal*, Robert Redford. At number nine, she was also ten places ahead of her action-hero husband Bruce Willis. Lately Moore is as

famous for this power, for her talent at self-publicity and for her bodily transformations, as for her acting.

Moore has been around for 15 years now. As her career has progressed she has
honed an ability to appeal to men and women in equal measure: if male viewers want
to have her, female viewers want to be her – or vice versa. Either way, both want to
watch her. She is in many ways the perfect multiplex product, maximising audiences
across gender lines. One of the few survivors of that seminal 80s brat-pack vehicle *St
Elmo's Fire* (1985 – Ally Sheedy, where are you now?), she had even then long been a
regular on *General Hospital.* Catch the schlocky sub-*Shivers* 3-D creature feature *Para-
site*, her 1982 B-feature debut (just out on video), to see Moore in an early incarnation.
She soon progressed to tougher roles – models and hookers as in *No Small Affair*
(1986) and *We're No Angels* (1989) – or more vulnerable ones as Michael Caine's
daughter in *Blame It On Rio* (1983) and as the supernaturally haunted pregnant heroine of *The Seventh Sign* (1988). But it was her role as Patrick Swayze's bereaved sculptor
girlfriend in the massive 1990 hit *Ghost* which established the 90s Moore. She soon
gained major film work and talking-point parts: the rookie military lawyer supporting Tom Cruise in *A Few Good Men* (1992), the broke wife who sells herself to Robert
Redford in *Indecent Proposal* (1993), the sexual harasser in *Disclosure* (1994), the
improbably feisty Hester Prynne in *The Scarlet Letter* (1995), the 'sexy mother' of
Striptease (1996).

But it was perhaps only in the underrated *Mortal Thoughts* (1991) – which she co-
produced – that we began to see Moore open up a potential just glimpsed (albeit
insistently) in her other work: that she can be a subtle and surprising actress as well
as a compelling star. Sadly, intelligent parts in little-seen Alan Rudolph films do not
cement a star's position as an ongoing Hollywood power-broker. Since *Mortal
Thoughts*, Moore has traded the possibility of small, challenging and artistically risky
roles for huge salaries and tight career control. Her latest film, *G.I. Jane*, is the Cin-
derella story of a woman chosen to be the first female participant in the tough Navy
SEAL training programme, and it develops a number of issues which were bubbling
under in previous work. Directed by Ridley Scott, *G.I. Jane* is no *Thelma and Louise*,
though it touches on crucial debates about how women deal with male-minted power.
It also adds another texture to the fascinating story of Moore's stardom.

Image of a life

Threaded through this filmographic biography is another story – another fiction, perhaps – of how Moore's 'real' self is publicly displayed, of what we know and what we
are allowed to see. Her early marriage to English rock musician Freddy Moore, the
engagement to Emilio Estevez, the celebrated wedding of Bruce and Demi conducted
by Little Richard – these are the romantic coordinates. Add female support (neighbour
Natassja Kinski encouraging her teenage talent; her production company, Moving Pictures, being female-headed), scandal (battles with drink and drugs around the time of
St Elmo's Fire; rumours of cosmetic surgery; nude magazine covers) and some intriguing character details (Demi as devoted mother set against Demi as a tough cookie
on-set) – and you have a public/personal profile which builds brilliantly upon the star
commodity developed through the films. But her real-life image is partly the product

she herself constructs – pseudo-character-analysts could make much of her passion for collecting dolls. Even her name, she has said, came from a commodity: 'Demetria' was a cosmetic her mother saw in an advert. But Demi is quick to tell us how to pronounce its abbreviated form, with a stress on the last syllable (she is not half of anything).

Moore's consummate stardom is partly rooted in the way she has manipulated the boundary between screen and private selves. Her approach here is reminiscent of the old studio system's exploitation of the 'real' self as commodity, placed adjacent to the film persona, the two to be modelled, marketed and advertised as one. Moore is a quick-change artiste whose famously naked flesh is only one of her cloaks. But what is it about Moore's body that's so fascinating?

Moore's physical metamorphoses are a constant talking point in Demi-fan culture. An alternative biography could be described solely through the dramatic hair changes she has undergone. After the cute pixie crop of *Ghost*, her locks get progressively longer (and sometimes dramatically blonder) through *Mortal Thoughts*, *The Butcher's Wife*, *Indecent Proposal* and beyond. And now the no-nonsense power-bob of *A Few Good Men* and the shiny *femme fatale* mane of *Disclosure* have been dramatically topped by the most radical shave of all: in *G.I. Jane* she dispenses with her hair completely.

Yet, the most extraordinary thing about this new no-hair coiffure is not the style itself, but the fact that we see its creation. *Striptease*'s publicity machine rode on a 'Demi reveals all' promise (I still cherish the PR company's freebee gift which accompanied the video release, a 3-D postcard of Demi flashing open her shirt as you flick it from side to side). But one of the central scenes of the essentially chaste *G.I. Jane* is arguably far more pornographic – in the finest and most honourable sense of this term. Here, Ridley Scott shows us Demi *actually doing it* – not sex, but image control. Breaking into the military barbers after finally losing patience with her impractically flowing locks, she appropriates a razor and shaves off all those years of lustrous growth, right there, for real, in view. You can almost hear the crew holding their breath as she takes that first slice across the crown of her head and the hair tumbles. There could be no retakes, as Scott's multiple camera positions testify – you catch it from every possible angle, as once *has* to be enough. What we see isn't just Lt Jordan O'Neil taking control of her career by taking control of her body (a significant moment in her quest to become an equal-but-different Navy SEAL), but Demi Moore giving herself a Number One. The 'mondo' pleasure of the scene lies in this – the collision of star and role, with what the scene says about the star as important as how the character develops in the film.

Putting on the body

But Moore manipulates her flesh in other dramatic ways in *G.I. Jane*. Meredith, her *Disclosure* character, an executive involved in developing virtual-reality technology, promises a future in which humans can attain 'freedom from the physical body, freedom from race and gender... we can relate to each other as pure consciousness'. (Actually, even though she eventually appears in cyberspace as a virtual body resembling a suit of armour with her face pasted on it, the carnal Meredith wants none of this for herself.) But this speech resonates beyond the scope of this particular film, since it is the technology of cinema rather than virtual reality which has given Moore the opportunity to embrace bodily transformation and to put all physical femininity to the test.

'Disrobing' haircut notwithstanding, Moore 'puts on' far more in *G.I. Jane* than she takes off. Ridley Scott's trademark look, that lustrous widescreen low-angle precision which imparts a monumental slo-mo glamour to the most prosaic of objects, has had no more fitting a subject than the vest-clad Moore in the highly fetishistic working-out sequence, her astonishing one-handed press-ups no doubt destined to provoke rather less sublime one-handed responses in a future video audience. (And there are no body doubles here – she did the press-ups on Letterman to prove it.)

But once again Moore's body has become the site of a confusion about attitudes to feminism. *Striptease*'s genre confusions (soft porn masquerading as the tale of a feisty heroine challenging the misogyny of circumstance) made it a box-office disaster. Similarly, what *G.I. Jane* gives with one hand it takes away with the other, in the end preferring to assert that women in power are as bad as men and that a vague offend-no-one concept of 'personhood' is better than either. Countering her feminine disadvantages by re-creating herself in a man's image, Moore makes up for Jordan's lack of masculinity by her own (to use Yvonne Tasker's word) 'musculinity'. But her new-minted muscles can also give out ambiguous signals. Early in her SEAL initiation, Jordan overhears a conversation between the male trainees, in which they exclaim, with disgust, 'The average woman is 25 per cent body fat. That's a quarter fat!' Not so Demi, who hasn't been 'the average woman' since work-outs and alleged lipo-suction put paid to the objects of 'the average man'. Rather than challenge the disgust of this prevailing misogyny, she has rearranged the canvas of herself and dispensed with the fat. (That said, this is also the woman who displayed the full glory of her heavily pregnant body on the cover of *Vanity Fair*.)

All of which suggests a rather more nagging issue: since Demi is a woman, how do we read those muscles? And how do we read the controversial line of dialogue that ignited America's Southern Baptist moral majority into a frenzy of vitriol against Walt Disney Studios, *G.I. Jane*'s backers, when the film opened in the US? In single-handed combat with her own commanding officer, and all but beaten to a pulp, Jordan over-whelms her opponent, hoists herself up and cries 'suck my dick', achieving both combat ascendancy and the respect of her fellow trainees.

'Suck my dick' is *G.I. Jane*'s answer to *Jerry Maguire*'s 'Show me the money'. Liber-ated from an anatomical context, the utterance suggests that we may all have enough of a dick to make it available for the purposes of insult: you don't necessarily have to *have* one to be able to tell someone what they can do with it. In the light of the shav-ing and the working out which precede this line in the film – not to mention previous Moore incarnations, including having her naked body painted in male clothes for another *Vanity Fair* cover – it is particularly revealing. Yet oddly, the Baptists don't appear to be objecting to the discrepancy between Moore's gender and the line's mean-ing, only that its language is 'vulgar and profane'. As Dwayne Hastings, spokesperson for the Southern Baptists Ethics and Religious Liberty Commission argued, Moore's 'anatomical obscenity' is dangerous because it 'says to the kids who see the movie, "This is a cool thing to say."' The danger for Baptists is thus *not* that the line enables a woman to speak, in several senses, with the mouth of a man, but that it encourages a polite person to become an impolite one. Sweet.

A more challenging question would be: in what sense does Demi Moore have a 'dick' anyway? After the tit-fest of *Striptease* we might answer: in no sense at all. But you do not have to be well versed in psychoanalysis to know that dick means power, the power towards which everyone, more or less unsuccessfully, aspires. To grasp the position from which 'dick' can be spoken and then to yell the word back at your assailant makes the speaker – whatever anatomy has destined them for – the better endowed. We might also remember that Meredith, the boardroom bitch of *Disclosure*, is animated by so much sexual and corporate aggression that it's rumoured that 'she was once a man'. *G.I. Jane* builds on this, switching playfully between differently gendered ways of naming Demi-as-Jordan, whose calibre as top-notch SEAL material is underlined when Anne Bancroft proclaims that she 'really is top-drawer – with silk stockings inside'. Later she is called 'Joan of Arc meets Supergirl'.

The body beautiful as blur

Feminine musculinity is one manifestation of this gender meld. It also identifies star image indelibly with the demands of a role. The central spectacle of Moore's body beautiful increasingly blurs the line between the role and the star. More of Jordan there may be as the film proceeds, but her worked-on, worked-out, built-up body is still Moore's. It may seem an obvious point, but if Jordan shaves, Demi does too; if Jordan's pecs swell, so do Demi's. But is the Moore we see any more real than Jordan?

The body of Demi Moore is a costume, a mask, a masquerade conveying Jordan's development – but which Moore also carries through into all those photocalls with Bruce and the kids, those chat-show appearances, those shock-spreads in the *National Enquirer*. However much she takes off or builds up, the possibility that we are really seeing *her* is as big an illusion as those coy publicity shots of Judy Garland with her tennis racket, or Susan Hayward persuading us to use Lux soap. None of these faces, these voices, these actions is real – only the products these illusions of realness are marketing are different. Moore strips and shows a pregnant body, a painted body, a glamour body, and while all of these bodies are hers, they are also part of the skin-flick which is her ever-changing public self. Showing all, she actually shows very little, since all are part of the show.

Indeed, Moore has long recognised that what women do to their bodies they do, in the eyes of the world, to themselves. Female self- and body-image are inextricably intertwined, and Moore has chosen to celebrate or even exploit this, in a set of unshrinkingly headline- and cover-grasping moves. But how does this bodily transformation differ from a male actor's manipulation of a role (De Niro's weight gain for *Raging Bull*, for instance)? Why is one seen as the act of a literally selfless method actor, subsuming the personal into the professional, and the other as (at its worst) the move of a pushy self-publicist? Female stars have to fight to control the inevitable link made between the body of the role and their bodily public image. This Moore has done, risking the possibility of at least one of her parts sticking to her – *Disclosure*'s manipulative harpy, whose heart, someone says, is 'made of that plastic they use for football helmets'. That Meredith is eventually weakened and defeated by her male combatant, and that in general

Moore's roles are at least as characterised by the tragic manipulability of femininity as by its real power to control, are symptomatic of the risks she is taking as a star – even though on the surface her blockbuster 90s career does not look like that of a risk-taker.

Compare, then, that central image of Meredith scheming while on her stairmaster in *Disclosure*, with Jordan's one-armed press-ups sequence. Earlier in *Disclosure* the worried male victim played by Michael Douglas remarks to a colleague, 'That woman's probably on a stairmaster an hour a day – she can kick the shit out of both of us!' The tradition of Hollywood show-and-tell ensures that in due course we *do* see Meredith on her stairmaster, Douglas' words enforcing the view that this is no prudent act of physical fitness, but a *femme fatale* preparing her weapon. Jordan's press-ups also highlight the woman's body as weapon, except that here it's a weapon in service of the nation. Jordan is our heroine, acting on behalf of her sisterhood and the country at large, while Meredith only does things for herself. Furthermore, as Meredith works out she labours under the crucial misapprehension that controlling and honing the self into a singular trajectory of ambition will bring real public power. For this she must be punished. Still, Meredith's final words, the bitter bile of the defeated bitch, would in another world or another film (*G.I. Jane* perhaps) be the enlightened speech of a woman grasping the truth. Jordan could equally say, as Meredith does, 'I'm only playing the game the way you guys set it up – and I'm being punished for it. That's fine.' Bitch monster or action heroine, the force of Moore's roles lies in their exposure of the hypocrisies of power to which women are subject, combined with a refusal to let go of that power just because it is flawed.

War on weakness

If several films show Moore trying to reconcile female body image with this power, perhaps only *G.I. Jane* highlights what is at the heart of her stardom. Jordan's struggle is one of physical self-overcoming: the film lasciviously details the agonising tribulations of the SEAL training programme. Working on herself thus becomes key to attaining her goal. *G.I. Jane* is in the end *not* primarily a film about a solitary woman trying to forge a path for other women to follow in a sexist institution. It is about Jordan's (mythically American) war with her personal weakness. Her body, and her ability to control its limits, its involuntary failures and responses, becomes the film's prime battlefield.

The same might be said of Moore herself. The closer you look at her star biography, the more it seems to be modelled on the myths of fame woven around the icons of classical Hollywood. Moore might easily be read as the trailer-trash daughter of a Joan Crawford or a Lana Turner, rising from a tough childhood of extreme poverty and broken marriages to immense wealth and a conspicuously luxurious public life, via a struggle with dependence which mirrored her cocaine-addict role in *St Elmo's Fire*. 'Hard work' is the lauded quality which rings out through the biographies of each of these women, the drivenness of self-overcoming which makes individual glamour the all-American reward for a sufficiently motivated rise.

But Moore has gone one stage further, for in the age of the muscle-clad action heroine, hard work is no longer most visibly manifest in consumer rewards, in the designer wardrobe of a 40s icon, or the Malibu villa. If it is to be seen anywhere now, 'hard work' must be demonstrated, enshrined, lived out *first* in the body. Now that the showgirl must have more to show for her efforts than a gown by Adrian, Moore meets the challenge by revealing not just those famously augmented breasts but a whole worked-on physique. As in Crawford's day the star's rise from brutal poverty to an opulence 'earned' by personal graft was at the same time remote *and* attainable for viewers (a Butterick version of those Adrian frocks could be run up at home), so Moore's worked-on star body is something we could all achieve, if we only had that singular personal quality. She may have had $15,000 worth of gym equipment at her disposal when training for *Striptease*, but she also ran on the beach before dawn and did two hours of yoga a day, the publicity tells us – activities available to us all.

As ever, then, stars are like us and not like us, attainable role models and remote glamour icons, excessive versions of the fans who buy the tickets. Despite some inept career decisions in the last few years, Demi Moore treads this uneasy path with a gutsy skill. That she does so little to disguise her thirst for control makes her, like Meredith, a hard but compelling female icon.

REVIEWS

JUNIOR
USA 1994
Director: Ivan Reitman

San Francisco. Two men of science, cold researcher Dr Alexander Hesse and earthy Dr Larry Arbogast, lose university funding and facilities after the Federal Drug Administration refuses to approve Expectane, a fertility formula they have developed. Their boss and nemesis, Noah Banes, replaces them with clumsy female scientist Dr Diana Reddin, who is working on a different fertility project for which she has frozen some of her own eggs. Arbogast unknowingly steals them and combines them with Hesse's sperm. Desperate to validate the discovery and obtain funding from a pharmaceutical company, Arbogast injects Hesse with the mixture. The two men agree that they will terminate the pregnancy after the first trimester, but Hesse, who has begun to change both emotionally and physically, insists on carrying the baby to term. They continue to use the lab on a part-time basis, due to Reddin's generosity. Hesse and Reddin fall in love, and he decides to tell her of the condition that he has been successfully hiding. Initially angry, she becomes supportive, and they decide to raise the child together. When the opportunistic Banes discovers the scheme, Hesse, in full drag, checks into a home for unwed mothers, where he participates in all of the women's pre-delivery activities. Trying to appropriate the men's accomplishment, Banes calls the media to the delivery room, but the press find only Arbogast's pregnant (by Aerosmith's personal trainer) ex-wife Angela, with whom he is affecting a reconciliation. Arbogast delivers Hesse's baby by caesarean section, while Angela, with Reddin's assistance, gives birth in the next room. A year later, the two couples – Hesse with a pregnant Reddin, Arbogast with Angela – celebrate their offspring's first birthday on the beach. Hesse and the two women propose that Arbogast carry his and Angela's next child.

* * *

Junior is clearly keyed to the mood of America. A pro-life ode to the nuclear family, Ivan Reitman's film opened in the wake of the recent conservative Republican sweep of both Congress and the Senate – and yet another assassination attempt (in Canada) on a pro-choice doctor.

The fact that a man can carry a child might be a good subject for sophisticated parody or political theatre, but here it is only a joke stretched very thin. That the man – a bespectacled, brilliant scientist with tortoiseshell rims – is portrayed by Arnold Schwarzenegger, keeps the laughs coming far longer than the script deserves. Only a film archivist could withhold yucks when he explains his torrent of tears upon watching a schmaltzy TV commercial to surrogate father Danny DeVito: 'She was Daddy's little girl.' Or when, in dress and blonde wig, he clarifies the reason for his enormous size to the head of a fancy home for unwed mothers (played by 60s counter-culture folk-singing queen Judy Collins): 'The East Germans pumped up female athletes like me with anabolic steroids the way they dispense Gatorade here – but I'm all woman!'

What seems at first merely a weakly directed movie with more than enough juvenile humour to pull in the weekend dating crowd (close-ups of oversized urine cups, references to Schwarzenegger's large load, comments like 'My nipples are sensitive') soon becomes egregious. The scene in which Schwarzenegger and DeVito lovingly examine in detail a foetal sonogram smacks of the ubiquitous anti-abortion commercials ('Life: what a beautiful choice') running on American television. Conservative Republican Schwarzenegger takes on the most insulting external trappings of femininity and pseudo-wifeliness: nagging DeVito, berating his enlarged body, cooking obsessively – but the film refuses to push their relationship any further. Instead, Schwarzenegger's nascent sensitivity and his increased sexual drive lead him into an affair with fellow scientist Emma Thompson.

At first, Thompson chastises the two men for appropriating pregnancy from women, but this token feminism does not balance out the adorably bumbling traits given her (not to mention lines like 'a woman's life is a nightmare'): she falls regularly, she dances with toilet paper sticking to her shoe, she flips a lobster shell onto an adjacent table in a restaurant. She is a sort of British Mary Tyler Moore who metamorphoses from a no-nonsense, quasi-masculine, trouser-attired researcher into a softly coiffed caricature of conventional womanhood.

Junior reunites the team that made *Twins*, Reitman, Schwarzenegger and DeVito. Given his more typical screen personae, it's obvious why such a passive role might appeal to Schwarzenegger, and DeVito (recently charted in *The New York Times* as one of the best-connected people in Hollywood) has never been too choosy about his parts. What is unclear is why Thompson would play such a retrograde character.

Howard Feinstein

ERASER
USA 1996
Director: Charles Russell

Johnny C, a key witness against the Corelli family, is about to be slaughtered. John Kruger, an agent for the Federal Witness Protection Program, arrives to rescue them. He kills all the bad guys, burns the house down, and provides two fake bodies to take the place of Johnny and his wife.

Kruger's next assignment is to protect Lee Cullen, an employee of the Cyrez Corporation. Cyrez is supposed to be developing technology for US defence, but they are secretly selling it to the highest bidder. Having developed an assault rifle that uses electro-magnetic impulses rather than bullets and has an x-ray viewfinder which can locate a target through almost any barrier, Cyrez is planning a shipment to the Russian Mafia.

Cullen has acquired two computer disks as proof and is willing to testify. However, the disk she gives to the Feds disappears, and there's an attempt on her life, foiled by Kruger. He hides her in New York's Chinatown. Robert Deguerin, Kruger's mentor, turns out to be a Cyrez mole. He tries to con Kruger into taking them to Cullen. Kruger gets on a plane with Deguerin but gives him the wrong location. Deguerin drugs Kruger. When Kruger wakes up and realises what's happened, he starts a gun battle and parachutes out of the plane.

Having framed Kruger as the mole, Deguerin finds out that Cullen – warned by a call from Kruger – has fled to the New York Zoo. Cullen, Kruger, Deguerin and a small army of mercenaries fight it out in the House of Reptiles. Kruger saves Cullen and they both escape. Kruger finds Johnny C working in a gay drag bar and asks for his help. Kruger, Cullen and Johnny break into the Cyrez corporation to read the disk. Deguerin and the others are waiting, but are outsmarted. In a Baltimore shipyard, Deguerin and Kruger battle it out, delivery of the weapons is stopped and Kruger clears his name. Later, Deguerin reassures his ultimate boss, the Under-Secretary of the Defence Department, that the case can never go to court without Cullen's testimony. However, before they can eliminate Cullen, Kruger eliminates them.

*   *   *

The opening credits of *Eraser* hint at high-tech underhand high-jinks. Grainy steel-blue images of fingerprints, badges, plastic gloves, guns and bullet-proof vests glide through the screen at a precise clip in an elegant and evocative assemblage. The images and the accompanying names (Arnold Schwarzenegger, James Caan, Vanessa Williams and James Coburn) create expectations of a luxuriously crafted thriller with a whiff of mystery, a touch of safe social criticism and a great number of expensive quick-moving action scenes. Partly because a few scenes are almost good (Johnny C's 'erasure') and partly because the film closely traces what we normally want of a Schwarzenegger film, these expectations are maintained for roughly the first hour of the film. But *Eraser* never meets them.

No matter what it cost to make, *Eraser* is a cheap film. It seems to have been made with little effort or thought. The plot is full of holes (how do Kruger and Co. get out of the Cyrez corporation building?). A lot of the major scenes are derivative: the scene where Cullen copies the disk is done much better in *Mission: Impossible*; the scene where Kruger leaps off the plane was better done by Bond. In some scenes, it is clear that the film-makers were counting their pennies: the fight with the crocodiles, for example, is exciting but the blood splatters fade from the screen as if from a primitive computer game. In others it is unclear whether the problem was cash or craft: a few more shots and a sharper edit in the airplane sequence would have made it much more exciting.

Eraser is obviously an attempt to return Schwarzenegger to the less expensive successes he enjoyed in the mid-80s with films like *The Terminator* (1984), *Commando* (1985) and *Predator* (1987). Like the Terminator, Kruger is given few human characteristics (though why a person should be like a machine is never explained) and the colour scheme seems borrowed straight from James Cameron's movie (but if the latter's 'look' contributed to its *noir*ish expression, *Eraser* simply uses it as product differentiation). Vanessa Williams, like Rae Dawn Chong in *Commando* and Elpidia Carrillo in *Predator*, is simply the woman of colour presented for the male audience's sexual delectation (although, as in the previous films, not Schwarzenegger's). The body count in *Eraser* must be as high as in *Commando* and the star gets his usual share of one-liners. The irony is that whereas the earlier films were genre pieces that compensated for their modest budgets with wit and imagination, *Eraser* is a big-budget vehicle that can't even cobble together the basic conventions.

If *Eraser* truly represents what its makers think an audience wants of a Schwarzenegger film, their conception of that audience must be the contemptible one that they are a blood-thirsty mob of baying barbarians. Schwarzenegger's films were never popular just because a lot of people got killed in them (by that criteria a lot of straight-to-video action films would be equally successful) but because the action was exhilarating, sometimes even beautiful. Also they presented a new type of man in vividly depicted imaginary worlds (however true to life) that, in what they were showing and how it was shown, seemed to excitingly comment on our own.

In *Eraser*, Schwarzenegger is simply a killing machine without any motivation except a kind of professionalism. Characters are introduced to be killed off; Italians and queers are trotted out to be laughed at; shots seem designed to lead the viewer's eye to the obvious, as if director Charles Russell, who made *Nightmare on Elm Street 3: Dream Warriors*, *The Blob* and *The Mask*, filled the frame with anything else. The ending leaves the hero as amoral as the villain. As such the film is a cynical exercise, tawdrily executed. However, Schwarzenegger, looking leaner than usual, is fun to watch and so, despite their inferior quality, are the set pieces. Nevertheless, when the best things in an action film are Robert Pastorelli's performance as Johnny C, the ex-wiseguy, and the way James Coburn lends his authority to the role of the villain, Beller, the film is damned.

José Arroyo

JINGLE ALL THE WAY
USA 1996
Director: Brian Levant

Over-worked by the seasonal rush, furnishing salesman Howard Langston misses his young son Jamie's blue karate belt presentation. In compensation the boy demands a high specification Turbo Man action doll for Christmas. Realising that he ignored his wife Liz's reminder to buy the toy, Howard has to leave the house early on Christmas Eve morning, promising to return in time to take the family to Minnesota's annual Wintertainment Parade, where Turbo Man will be appearing 'in person'. The action figure in question, however, appears to have been sold-out for months, and as Howard's desperate search among local toy stores continues, he repeatedly locks horns with unstable postman Myron Larabee, who has left his run to hunt down Turbo Man, and strict veteran cop Officer Hummell, who has already given Howard a speeding ticket on the highway.

As the quest intensifies, Howard finds himself in a kiddies' playpen retrieving a bingo ball offering the chance to secure a Turbo Man. He also has to escape from the clutches of a corrupt mall Santa's illicit toy-fencing operation. When his car is vandalised, however, he returns home where oleaginous divorced neighbour Ted Maltin has been making moves on Liz while helping with the Christmas decorations. Remembering that Ted already has his son's Turbo Man safely stashed under the tree, Howard tries to steal it, but starts a fire when he's attacked by Ted's pet reindeer and is caught red-handed. In dismay, Liz and Jamie are driven off to the parade by Ted, and the pursuing Howard has to swerve into a warehouse to avoid aggrieved Officer Hummell. Before he can explain that he's not the stand-in, Howard is fitted inside the Turbo Man suit and is soon part of the parade, where he awards a 'Special Edition' Turbo Man doll to Jamie in the crowd, and uses his suit's jet-pack to fend off the advances of the crazed Myron, who has stolen the costume belonging to Dementor, Turbo Man's archenemy. As Myron is led away by police, Jamie gives him the doll, since he's got the 'real' Turbo Man at home. Father, son and wife patch up their differences with a smile.

* * *

It's easy to see how this vacuous addition to the recent ranks of Christmas movies was launched on an unsuspecting world, for the chief achievement of Randy Kornfield's screenplay is that it assembles a number of highly marketable ideas in a facile high-concept action-comedy. Like the earlier *Kindergarten Cop*, it offers Schwarzenegger a breather between action assignments, broadens the demographic across a younger audience with its pratfall gags instead of crunching violence, and allows the star to show a gentler on-screen side to his skills by relating to his character's small son. Add to that a storyline with a seasonal angle (it worked for *Home Alone*) and a thinly disguised plot-motor exploiting the popularity of Action Man and Power Rangers with younger viewers and you have a machine-tooled Yuletide Hollywood blockbuster.

Jingle's twin running gags involve a string of chance encounters with Sinbad's unstable toy-hunting postman and the repeated humiliation of Robert Conrad's silver-haired traffic cop. But director Levant's treatment of these displays the thudding comic timing and gift for wearisome slapstick overkill he already brought to the equally dire *Problem Child 2* and *The Flintstones*. Jim Belushi's corrupt mall Santa with his stolen-goods warehouse (peopled by sundry other nefarious Santas and elves making a swift seasonal illicit buck) provides the film's sole flash of dark humour. But this Christmas-as-exploitation angle sits uneasily with the consumerist aspirations – the must-have toy without which your child will be cast out by their peers – and the appropriation of the Power Rangers' brand of brightly costumed super-heroics (with a touch of jetpowered Buzz Lightyear thrown in) that drive the piece along.

Parents will surely boggle at the pat, cynical conclusion in which relations between father and son are repaired by the latter becoming the boy's super-hero idol and rescuing him from the very real dangers of a rooftop struggle with the evil Dementor (another of the unplayable scenes heaped on the hapless Sinbad). *Jingle All The Way* also seems to mark a point of decline in the Schwarzenegger career arc in that he's packaged in the relative anonymity of the Turbo Man outfit throughout the film's climactic flurry of fisticuffs and aerial derring-do.

Trevor Johnston

BATMAN & ROBIN
USA 1997
Director: Joel Schumacher

Crime-fighting duo Batman and Robin are notified that a new villain, Mr Freeze, is staging a robbery at the Gotham City Museum of Art. They arrive to find Freeze and his henchmen trying to steal a gigantic diamond. Batman is forced to stop pursuing Freeze in order to thaw out the newly frozen Robin. The Boy Wonder is irritated by Batman's paternalistic attitude towards him.

In a research laboratory, horticulturalist Pamela Isley is horrified to learn that her boss, Dr Jason Woodrue, has been secretly creating a destructive man-monster, Bane. Confronted by her, Dr Woodrue attacks Pamela and leaves her for dead, but she re-emerges as Poison Ivy, part-plant part-woman, with a mission to rid the world of polluting humans. In Gotham City, Batman and Robin learn that Freeze was once Dr Victor Fries, a scientist who cryogenically froze his wife after he was unable to save her from an incurable case of the disease McGregor Syndrome. He accidentally fell into her freezing solution and emerged deformed as Mr Freeze, who needs diamonds to maintain his freezing apparatus.

At Wayne Manor, the home of Batman's alter ego Bruce Wayne, Barbara Wilson comes to visit her uncle, Wayne's butler Alfred. To catch Freeze, Bruce holds a charity ball where diamonds will be auctioned, but Poison Ivy and Bane get there first. Ivy uses pheromone dust to hypnotise both Batman and Robin; they fall for her charms and squabble over her. Freeze attacks the ball and is caught and imprisoned, but not before Ivy is smitten by him. Alfred admits he is in fact seriously ill with McGregor Syndrome. Poison Ivy helps Freeze escape, but she switches off his wife's life support and blames Batman. Freeze vows vengeance, planning to freeze first Gotham and then the world. Discovering the secrets of the Batcave, Barbara reinvents herself as Batgirl and saves Batman and Robin from the clutches of Ivy and Bane. Batman, Robin and Batgirl find Freeze at Wayne Observatory and foil his plan. Batman tells Freeze about Ivy's treachery, and that his wife is still alive. Gratefully, Freeze tells Batman how to cure Alfred's McGregor Syndrome. Both Freeze and Ivy are incarcerated. Batman and Robin realise how much they still mean to each other and forge a new crime-fighting unit with Batgirl.

*   *   *

Potentially *Batman & Robin* is a film with something for almost everyone. Saturday night multiplex thrill-seekers can sit back and revel in the well-oiled spectacular destruction. Slumming psychoanalytic theorists can chuckle at Poison Ivy's enveloping fronds and the white stuff that shoots out of Mr Freeze's great big gun. Devotees of S&M can lap up the acres of moulded rubber. Gay men can muse on the fact that George Clooney and Chris O'Donnell are probably the most ravishing male couple ever to share a house in the history of Hollywood. And nerdy film buffs can tick off the inter-textual reference points that fly faster than the dynamic duo's fists. An initial survey might note *Nosferatu* (1922), *Metropolis* (1926), *Rebel Without a Cause* (1955), *Mad Max* (1979), *The Silence of the Lambs*, the Power Rangers and – a nice dig at this product's main marketplace rival this summer – *Jurassic Park*. Given such a semiotic cornucopia, the key question has to be: why does *Batman & Robin* nonetheless feel so hollow and hectoring?

The film's slick professionalism is undeniable – the opening battle in the Gotham City Museum of Art is a breathtaking beginning, dispensing with anything as sissy as narrative build-up in order to plunge the audience head-first into a gloriously excessive display of speed, sets, pyrotechnics and expenditure. It leaves you gawping and punch-drunk, but the very scale of its impact creates a structural problem for the film. The only way left to go is down – as if you'd blown your day at the theme park by going on the wildest, scariest ride first. The subsequent action sequences can only offer more of the same, and a law of diminishing returns inevitably takes hold.

Among the performances, the best news is Clooney, who displays exactly the right note of wry disbelief when in costume and manages not to giggle through the risible family melodrama sections back at Wayne Manor. The pointy ears and packed pouch are surely his for as long as he wants them. The wonderful and underrated Alicia Silverstone is largely wasted, but acquits herself well enough, while the witless and overrated Uma Thurman purrs and pouts in a way that might impress a few teenagers who've never seen Mae West or Jane Russell but is liable to leave the rest of us mightily unimpressed.

As for Arnie, his Mr Freeze can't help but be a step up from *Jingle All The Way*, but he still looks like a star in a tailspin. His classic *Terminator*-era roles were all premised on the fact that he was less (or more) than human, a machine or a monster splendidly isolated from mere mortals. Here, he is a cartoon surrounded by other cartoons; they're all as extreme as he is, and consequently he looks creaky, ponderous and foolish. He delivers the deliberately bad, cold-related puns ('Allow me to break the ice', 'Cool party' and so on) with all the panache of a discount warehouse on legs. Perhaps Poison Ivy's henchman, the man-machine character Bane, has been included primarily to mark out the distance Schwarzenegger's image has travelled – years ago *he* would have been playing Bane, but now he gets to banter with the classy actors. Unfortunately, he banters abominably, but in the realm of cinema that *Batman & Robin* exemplifies this doesn't seem to matter. It's Schwarzenegger's presence that counts – the fact that this is a *Batman* film (established franchise) with added Arnie (new ingredient! improved taste!) is supposed to leave us so stimulated by the very idea that we don't notice the unsatisfying execution.

More positively, *Batman & Robin* is by some distance the closest the film series has come to the once-reviled 60s television show. The perpetually tilted camera during fights and chases recalls the giddy disorientations and Dutch tilts of the small-screen version, to the extent that a psychedelic 'Thwok!' or 'Bammm!' would come as no surprise, and the brooding interiority of the *Dark Knight*/Tim Burton variants is kept to a bare minimum. Better still, two of the central, recurring male characters finally say 'I love you' before kissing. The fact that this exchange involves Bruce Wayne and a sickbed-confined Alfred rather than Bruce and the Boy Wonder, is, as any devotee of Bat-queer subtexts will attest, simply displacement. Bruce and Dick are far too busy gazing soulfully into each other's eyes or quarrelling like tetchy long-term lovers to have time to put their deeper feelings into words.

These, though, are slight and incidental pleasures amid the barnstorming callousness of the whole film. *Batman & Robin* feels hollow for the simple reason that all it can ever be is a prodigiously overblown joke, and it feels hectoring because of the deafening artillery of artifice it employs to try and shroud that fact. 'Look how expensive I am,' it shrieks, 'look at all the stars and the dazzle and the trickery, look how much effort I'm putting into entertaining you!' Indeed you are, this viewer answered while pining for the less bombastic diversions of *Speed* or *Twister* or *Anaconda*, but do you have to be such an attention-seeking little brat about it?

Andy Medhurst

Face/Off (John Woo, 1997)

Section 3: A John Woo Interlude

Hong Kong Action Cinema in general and that of John Woo in particular has been a tremendous influence on contemporary Hollywood film-making. As Manohla Dargis argues, 'when Western critics and audiences first made their acquaintance with Woo, the prevailing sentiment was that what they were witnessing was nothing less than the reinvention of the action film'. In this section, Berenice Reynaud takes us on location to the set of John Woo's first Hollywood film *Hard Target* where she meets the Hong Kong director. While describing the process of making *Hard Target*, Reynaud notes Woo's influence on *Reservoir Dogs*, remarks that the fashion for Hong Kong cinema in the West has largely been restricted to action and genre films and argues that 'the expressionist qualities the West so admires in Woo's films, far from being a given in his culture, are something he has had to fight to introduce'. In interview with Reynaud, John Woo describes his early Hong Kong career and his hopes for *Hard Target* and Hollywood. Writing four years after Reynaud, Manohla Dargis notes that the action movie is the most produced type of feature in mega-budget Hollywood but argues that it has 'solidified into a pattern so doggedly, persistently uniform that it has in the process become something like a genre unto itself' and that American film criticism is too debased to differentiate quality among action films as different as *Con Air* and *Face/Off*. In an appreciative article on *Face/Off*, Dargis affirms the influence of Woo in Hollywood but seems more pessimistic as to the influence of Hollywood on Woo: 'Woo has changed the terms of the modern action film with an influence that is ubiquitous and incessant. But even as Woo's influence grows, his own work seems to have become not only less vital but less personal: as the Hollywood action film has become more Woo-like, the director himself seems increasingly less so.' This section concludes with four reviews of Woo's recent oeuvre (*Hard Target*, *Broken Arrow* and *Face/Off* plus the made-in-Hong-Kong *Hard-Boiled*) which can be read in dialogue with the feature articles and with each other and which together, albeit through different critical perspectives, convey what makes Woo's work so special

JOHN WOO'S ART ACTION MOVIE

Berenice Reynaud

A foggy November morning in an unlikely seeming location in the marshland between Baton Rouge and New Orleans. The crew, carrying an assortment of portable telephones, cables and nasty-looking weapons, splashes through the rain-filled ruts dug by various vans and trailers. Stuntmen in helmets and black leathers ride motorcycles across the uneven ground. The plantation owners – frail and white-haired – seem oddly out of place, like will'-o-the-wisps from the swamp.

Neighbours have gathered too, remembering that in the distant past Charles Bronson shot a film here. The local police and volunteer firemen are on duty: a picturesque wooden shed, nested in the weeds of the Mississippi riverbank, is going to be blown to pieces, courtesy of Dale Martin, one of Hollywood's most highly regarded special effects professionals. John Woo, top-grossing Hong Kong action director and an international cult figure since his 1989 success *The Killer*, is shooting his first American movie, *Hard Target*. He is accompanied by the ever-modest Terence Chang: 'I'm just the seventh or eighth producer. To smooth out language difficulties, I'm doing part of the AD's job, I prepare shot lists.'

Soon after the release of *The Killer*, Woo and Chang founded their own company to produce *Bullet in the Head* (1990), a bloody tale of three young Chinese lost in 1967 Vietnam. This was followed by *Once a Thief* (1991), a charming comedy/thriller, and *Hard-Boiled* (1992), an intensely brutal police story in which the heroic protagonist hunts down an undercover cop passing for a killer. Woo was deluged with no less than 50 Hollywood scripts (Martin Scorsese, who adores *The Killer*, was even rumoured to want to produce Woo's next project; though Woo and Scorsese met, the latter is currently more interested in directing). Quentin Tarantino, whose *Reservoir Dogs* was visibly influenced by Woo's films, especially in the homoerotic choreography of gun-pointing that structures the ending, is writing a screenplay for his mentor. ('It's a very tightly structured kidnapping story, an almost perfect film for John,' comments Chang.) The film will give Chow Yun-Fat – Woo's favourite actor and alter ego – his first English-speaking starring role.

An action-packed remake of Ernest B. Schoedsack's *The Most Dangerous Game*, *Hard Target* was penned by a young screenwriter Chuck Pfarrer, who turned to Hollywood after seven years in the Navy ('Yes, I have killed men. I was in combat in Lebanon for nine months'). Two of his screenplays have been turned into films: the eminently forgettable *Navy Seals*, and more importantly Sam Raimi's cult horror film *Darkman*. Pfarrer has 'a deal' at Universal, and one day he received a phone call: 'They said they were running something for me in the screening room.... It was *The Killer*. When I came out I said I was convinced, and the next thing I knew I was on a plane to Hong Kong to meet John.'

James Jacks and Sean Daniel of Alphaville Productions are *Hard Target*'s producers,

along with Sam Raimi's and Robert Tapert's S & R Productions. Universal's participation is at the level of a negative pick-up, a relatively bold move on the part of a studio
which has never done action pictures before. Universal attracted Belgian martial artist
Jean-Claude Van Damme, an admirer of Woo. Van Damme hopes that working with
such a virtuoso will help him 'cross the line' into a more Schwarzenegger-type career.

Even before directing part of *Once a Thief* in France, Woo was no stranger to foreign-
location shooting. He made a number of low-budget films in Korea, then in Taiwan,
until New Wave film-maker Tsui Hark, repaying an old debt (Woo had given him the
opportunity to direct his first successful feature in the early 80s) produced *A Better
Tomorrow* (1986), which became the top-grossing film in Hong Kong history. But
despite his success, Woo has always felt a maverick, somehow 'not Chinese enough'.
His international success is a source of controversy at home: some critics dismiss his
cult status among English-speaking audiences as cultural misunderstanding.

The recent fashion for Hong Kong cinema in the West has centred on action and
genre films, largely ignoring other strands of the city's film production. Movies such
as Stanley Kwan's *Actress* and *Too Happy for Words*, Wong Kar-wai's *The Days of Being
Wild* and Lawrence Ah Mon's *Gangs* and *Queen of Temple Street* display modernist strategies for deconstructing history, sexuality, politics and the positioning of the subject
that make Woo's films appear frozen in time. Not only, as he acknowledges, are his
heroes paragons of a bygone code of honour, but there is no ambiguity, no shift of
meaning in his narratives. The homoerotic nuances of his stories never suggest a more
literal enactment of the fantasy, and in contrast with Tsui Hark's films, there are no
gay characters to function as comic relief, foil or return of the repressed – no delightful sexual ambiguity either, as in the love scene with the man-turned-woman in
Siu-Tung Ching's *Swordsman II*, produced by Tsui. In Woo's films, man is man, woman
is woman, friendship is what it seems (except in the case of betrayal, which is a quasi-
metaphysical abomination), and the narrative follows the laws of Aristotelian logic.

The Hong Kong Woo describes is conspicuously devoid of British characters. It is a
space that escapes colonial history, a place determined not by a difference of cultures
but by a plenitude of signs, a city to love with passion, to die for and to die within (significantly at the end of *A Better Tomorrow*, the Chow Yun-Fat character, instead of
fleeing with the money, turns back and gets killed in Hong Kong). Does Woo's oeuvre
seduce us by encoding such romantic nostalgia within the strategies of classical Western film-making? This is no idle question, for other games of Oriental/Occidental
seduction are now in progress: that of Woo by America, and of America by Woo. Will
success in Hollywood spoil him or will he impose his mark? Of course, the first non-
Chinese star of one of his films is not an American either.

Many directors want to work with Van Damme, whose presence in a movie is an
almost automatic guarantee of commercial success. Woo wasn't exactly first choice,
but the studio hired him in the belief that he could blow new life into an overused
genre. Without him, Pfarrer claims, *Hard Target* would be just another of those American action films that have run their course. For Woo, there is much more at stake: 'If
Hard Target is not a commercial success, it will be impossible to make another film in
Hollywood.' Studio executives have played touch and go: 'Even a month before shooting was supposed to start, they were trying to pull the plug,' recalls Chang. 'So we had

only three and a half weeks of pre-production. And the budget was nowhere near realistic – we would need another $2 million to be comfortable, which means we have to shoot six days a week. Now, after six weeks of shooting, we're four days behind and they're blaming John – he's too slow, his shots are too complicated. I don't think it's fair.'

Chang, a top producer in Hong Kong, has spent many years in the US, studying architecture in Oregon, then film at NYU. He is now a Canadian resident and has no desire to return to his native city: 'I don't like what is happening in Hong Kong. Crimes, robberies every day... China is already exerting a lot of control. We never had much freedom in the film industry: today we can't criticise the colonial government, and tomorrow all creative freedom may be lost.' Fearing the uncertainties of 1997, many middle-class Hong Kong residents are resettling in Canada, Australia, New Zealand and the US and more and more movies have this identity crisis as their theme. Shu Kei's *Sunless Days* (homage to Chris Marker's *Sans soleil*) documents the upset caused by the 4 June massacre. Evans Chan's experimental fiction *To Liv(e)* shows two couples caught between the misrepresentation of Hong Kong in the west and their desire to emigrate. Clara Law's *Autumn Moon* tells of the bittersweet friendship between a Japanese tourist and a little girl whose parents have gone to Canada.

Movie stars (Leslie Cheung, Tony Leung) are establishing residence in Canada too: 'There's enough talent in a city like Vancouver or Toronto to make a 100 per cent Hong Kong movie,' jokes Chang. He intends to start producing films – and not only Chinese ones – in the US and Canada, but for the moment he's riding in Hollywood on the John Woo ticket. 'If it weren't for John, I wouldn't be allowed to work here. But I like to think he's able to work here because I've come too.' Friendship is not an empty word in Woo's life. After his collaboration with Tsui Hark, he has found a true partner in Chang, whose professionalism, courtesy and reliability are a match to his own talent. It's a case of Chinese brotherhood: you help me, I help you, and together we'll make it.

Woo and Chang are the only Chinese on the set. Teamsters have been recruited locally, but most of the crew comes from Los Angeles. Some members worry that their last film, Sam Raimi's *Evil Dead III: Army of Darkness*, may have rating problems (in the US, *The Killer* got X-rated for violence). At first worried that he was not able to bring his action director to New Orleans, Woo is now getting along beautifully with stunt co-ordinator Billy Burton. In spite of the heavy shooting schedule – twelve, fourteen hours a day – the crew is taken by Woo's charm and brilliant professionalism. Even his hesitant English works in his favour. While absolutely precise in giving directions on the set, during breaks he smiles and takes his time, unless he explodes into passionate Cantonese, effortlessly translated by Chang. 'Look how hard the crew works,' says Pfarrer. 'They think they're making something special: an art action movie, probably the first one of its kind in America.'

The plot of *Hard Target* is simple, even cartoonish, with a hard-boiled romanticism that must have appealed to Woo. A young woman Natasha (Yancy Butler) comes to New Orleans to look for her long-lost father. She meets Chance Boudreaux (Van Damme), an unemployed seaman who, needing $217 to pay his union dues and board the next departing ship, agrees to help her. He uncovers the unpleasant activities of an elegant piece of Euro-trash (Lance Henriksen) and his sidekick, a white South African psycho (Arnold Vosloo), who, for a substantial fee, hire out homeless war veterans for rich men to hunt down in the swamps. Chance's snooping angers the

villains, who set him up as prey for their clients. The script has pages on nine different colours – one for every draft. Pfarrer is on the set, day in, day out, at hand for the
rewrites. 'John knows his stuff. For a writer, it's fantastic. What we're ending up with
is much better than what I wrote.'

For example, Woo has transformed a chase scene into a stunt never attempted on
film before, a head-on collision, almost lyrical in its choreographed violence, between
a motorcycle and a car. Yet he keeps on soliciting Pfarrer's advice, with his usual generosity and modesty. As Pfarrer explains, 'Hong Kong and US action films have
different rules: an American hero would never use a knife – unless he's taking it away
from the bad guy – and if the bad guy is hanging from a cliff, the good guy has to help
him.' But Pfarrer is there for another reason too: 'I'm learning at the feet of a master.
I'm in line to direct myself. Before I came here and saw John work, I thought I might
be ready, but now I just want to watch him.'

Other changes have been made to suit Van Damme's style. 'We've had to adjust the
dialogue for him,' says Pfarrer, 'and we've lost some bits of subtlety. However, he's a
very physical actor, who comes alive on the screen and can project emotions without
saying a word. Like a young Steve McQueen. And he's more charming than many
action stars. He's attractive: he could be a matinee idol.'

On set, Van Damme is charming but aloof. While the entire crew and cast eat
together, he lunches alone in his trailer, on a special body-builder's diet. For him, *Hard
Target* represents an opportunity to act the romantic hero, as when Natasha learns of
her father's death. Shot in a picturesque jazz club in New Orleans' *vieux carré*, the scene
begins as the camera moves from the face of the elderly bluesman who is performing
to the couple sitting at a table. As the young woman cries silently, Van Damme holds
her hand, comforting her in a low voice. The camera completes a long, sensual take.
'Cut!' (uttered by Woo, this command becomes a primal scream). 'This was beautiful,
but we'll do it again.' After four takes, the shot is in the can. Smoothly, with the
supreme ease Woo displays in every set.

The same evening the crew watches rushes. While a bit corny in the intimate
scenes, Van Damme's ponytail looks great when he's flying through the air in slow
motion. Hunted by an impressive array of cars and motorcycles, he seeks shelter inside
an abandoned sugar mill. A thug follows him. Suddenly, a motorcycle in flames
mounted by a leather-clad puppet representing the dead villain bursts through a large
window. 'We ran a cable and slid the motorcycle along it,' explains Dale Martin. The
spectacular stunt was performed only once, but for such scenes Woo runs six or seven
cameras simultaneously, offering long takes from different angles that will later be
spliced together in an orgy of fire, explosion and motion.

Back on the plantation while the experts are putting the final touches to their
pyrotechnics, the motorcycle stuntmen are at work. Henriksen and Vosloo are leading
the pack, encircling the shed in which Chance's uncle brews illegal whiskey. A motor-
cyclist takes off his helmet, revealing the long hair and fine features of a young woman.
She's Billy Burton's daughter, raised 'as a tomboy' to do stunts from an early age. 'I did
one dangerous thing on this film,' she recalls. 'I had to jump off a bridge with another
stuntman into the back of a moving train. To time the jump and make sure we were
both going at the same time, we dropped lemons, which fall at the speed of your body.'

The big moment arrives. The young PAs round up the onlookers, pushing them away from the action. The cameras are rolling. An explosion resounds and pieces of charred lumber fall from the air. The shed has vanished. The script describes the moonshiner's lair as bursting into flames, but Woo, fearing this might damage the vegetation, opted instead for a clean, combustionless explosion.

The same evening Woo, Chang and some journalists are feasting at a Japanese restaurant. While Woo seems to have adapted quite well to life in America, there is one point where he draws the line: food. So in the state of chicken gumbo and jambalaya, he stubbornly looks for Chinese restaurants (an almost impossible task) or Japanese *haute cuisine*. At The Shogun, after a few sakes, he becomes animated, his eyes smiling with kindness and cinematic passion. He talks about the first film he shot in Vietnam, *Heroes Shed No Tears* – once again the tale of his solitary fight against studio politics. The script was idiotic, crude, unnecessarily sexual and exploitative, so he changed it, turning it, in the process, into a much better film. But the studio hated it, changed it back and eventually shelved it until the success of *A Better Tomorrow*.

He also talks of martial arts director Zhang Cheh. This is not a subject on which Woo dwells easily, but in 1986 he had said in an interview for the Hong Kong Film Festival catalogue that the man had influenced him 'not so much in his way of portraying violence but his unrestrained way of writing emotions and chivalry. Chinese cinema has always been too low-key. We should be more expressive, put more of ourselves into our films.'

The quote is revealing. The expressionist qualities the West so admires in Woo's films, far from being a given in his culture, are something he has had to fight to introduce. Hence, perhaps, his solitude, his feelings of 'un-Chineseness'. Woo himself is reserved, gentle, almost shy, a man who likes to keep his mystery, his privacy. But shouldn't one expect such paradoxes from someone who may be the best action director in the world, yet confesses he's never fired a gun in his life, or even better, that he doesn't know how to drive?

WOO IN INTERVIEW

Translated by Terence Chang

'I started to make films – existential love stories – when I was in school. I was part of a small group of people who were stimulated by European art films, the French New Wave and contemporary Japanese cinema and were experimenting with film.

'I didn't go to film school because my family was too poor. The studios were very conservative and the industry was corrupt. Then in 1969 a company called Cathay welcomed a new generation of intellectuals and our whole group went in. I became a continuity person and was able to save enough money to keep on making experimental film. I was also writing film criticism.

'I later worked for the Shaw Brothers as an assistant director to martial arts director Zhang Cheh for *Boxer from Shantung* and *Blood Brothers*. In 1973 I was hired to co-direct an independent low-budget film called *Young Dragons*, which was eventually banned in Hong Kong because it was too violent. It lost money, and was sold to Golden Harvest, where they signed me up for three years. I directed kung-fu pictures – often shot in Korea for HK$200,000. This is not what I wanted to do, but I was under a lot of pressure. I was 27, and the youngest director working at Golden Harvest. Some people were assistant directors for more than ten years before they were allowed to direct.

'Jackie Chan and Samo Hung worked as stuntmen for me. I recognised their potential and gave Chan his first acting part in *Countdown in Kung Fu* (aka *The Hand of Death*, 1975). Then I made a Cantonese opera film, *Princess Chang Ping* (1975), which was very popular. Later I worked as a production consultant to help the great comedian Michael Hui on his first two films: *Games Gamblers Play* and *The Private Eyes*. And it was the comedy *Money Crazy* (aka *The Pilferer's Progress*), a smash hit in 1977, that really established me. In 1981, after my seventeenth movie, I left Golden Harvest to direct the first picture of a newly founded company, Cinema City.

'My film *Laughing Times* (1981) made money, and I was willing to accept a much lower director's fee for the opportunity to make the films I wanted. To my disappointment, the studio wanted me to do nothing but comedies. That was one of the worst times of my life. The three owners of Cinema City, finding me "too old-fashioned", sent me to Taiwan, where I was stuck for over two years. They let me direct two films there, but the less said about them the better. When I returned to Hong Kong, Tsui Hark, who was starting his own production company, the Film Workshop, offered me a job. This is how we came to collaborate on *A Better Tomorrow*. A lot of the emotion behind the film reflects my friendship with Hark.

'*A Better Tomorrow* develops an idea we both had, though basically it was I who wrote the script. Apart from the Cantonese opera film, I always wrote my own screenplays, even for the comedies – in this I'm an exception in Hong Kong, where directors mostly rely on others to write screenplays. For *A Better Tomorrow*, Tsui Hark first wanted to do a film about three women, and I changed it to three men. We both agreed that the film should stress human values, and Hark encouraged me to project my own feelings. The result was much better, much richer than he had expected.

'*The Killer* was my idea. Jean-Pierre Melville influenced me a lot, and I always wanted to make a film like *Le Samourai*. Professionally, I'm a loner, so I can identify with the solitary assassin. I also wanted to stress that justice is a universal value, shared by people who lead completely different lives. My killer is not very contemporary: he's a killer from several centuries ago, when they killed for a reason.

'As a Protestant, I am strongly influenced by Christian beliefs about love, sin, redemption. I designed the final scene of *The Killer* in a church because for the protagonist it is the only peaceful place in the world. I spent a lot of money to make the perfect Virgin Mary statue: when it is shot to pieces, truth is destroyed by evil, and with it the spirit of chivalry displayed by ancient warriors. In *A Better Tomorrow*, when Chow Yun-Fat is beaten up, the villain takes his scarf and wipes his hand: when Christ was crucified, Pilate washed his hands.

'I had a pietà image during the killing of the young bomb-thrower in *Bullet in the*

Head to stress the special impact the incident has on the three main characters, and because, regardless of politics, all killings are ugly. I only dramatised a scene that really happened: I saw, in a documentary, a kid taken away from the street and shot.

'*Bullet in the Head* takes place in 1967 because it was a dramatic year in Hong Kong: there were riots and people got killed. I chose the Vietnam War to demonstrate that war can turn good into evil and bring out the worst in human behaviour. I was an anti-war activist in 1969 and 1970 and went to a lot of demonstrations and rallies. I also wanted to use Vietnam as a mirror for what's going to happen in Hong Kong in 1997.

'I always supervise the editing of my films and edited some of the sequences of *The Killer*, like the dragon-boat chase, myself. I also edited the final duel in *Bullet in the Head* and inserted the flash-back shots alluding to the protagonists' teenage friendship. The duels in my films have a multiplicity of meanings. I believe that good will eventually triumph over evil, but it's going to be at a cost – of the good being misunderstood, or segregated. I am a pessimist, but I believe that the only possible redemption is from a religious point of view.

'I think I will stay in the United States. I know I can work here and make better movies than in Hong Kong. In some ways, I'm not very Chinese. My techniques, my themes, my film language are not traditionally Chinese.

'*Hard Target* is my first American film. It's my chance to gain experience in a totally foreign environment. I need the film to establish myself commercially in Hollywood. But in the future, I'll be writing my own scripts. And people like Quentin Tarantino, who knows my films very well, are writing scripts for me.

'The methods of the American crew are not so different from those in Hong Kong, but they are more professional. In Hong Kong the technicians work very hard, we've known each other for a very long time and they really understand what I want, but they were not trained by experience, by going to film school.

'I had shot in synch sound only once before, for the Cantonese opera film. It is not difficult at all, because I know this technique very well. In Hong Kong I routinely used several cameras. I shot in the American way. The most difficult thing for me here is to learn how to handle the studio politics. It can be very frustrating at times.'

DO YOU LIKE JOHN WOO?

Manohla Dargis

Some 45 minutes and numerous deaths into *Face/Off*, the new pulp extravaganza directed by John Woo, there's a scene in which John Travolta's face is peeled from his flesh like a new grape to be replaced by one removed from Nicolas Cage (later the face-less Cage forces the surgeon to graft Travolta's onto him). The nominal excuse for the first bit of radical surgery is that Travolta's character, Sean Archer, an embittered FBI agent, will be able to convince a villain named Pollux Troy that he is Pollux's older brother, Castor, Archer's long-time nemesis. For his part, Castor Troy has just fallen off the most-wanted list by landing in a coma, taking with him into the bargain the location of a bomb timed to bring cataclysmic ruin to Los Angeles. Armed with his enemy's face – along with other signature specifications, such as Travolta's womanly hips – Archer hopes to discover the bomb's location from Pollux, an inmate in a high-tech prison which looks halfway between a techno disco and some sort of Jeremy Bentham ideal.

There is an incontrovertible wit to a Hollywood action movie that hinges on a successful facelift, though it's an open question whether the writers of *Face/Off*, Mike Werb and Michael Colleary, were much concerned (when they turned their high concept into a bankable screenplay) with the politics and philosophy of plastic surgery – and both exist, especially in LA. Along with butchering scripts and terminating directors, plastic surgery is one of the most socially acceptable acts of violence you can commit in Hollywood. Indeed, this may help explain the linguistic kinship between film work and face work – cutting, suture – along with some of their shared imperatives: both are fuelled by illusion and both involve rearranging material into a harmonious ideal, which more often than not has nothing in common with the real world. Both, too, often require prodigious amounts of money.

The title *Face/Off* is of course a pun – both a description of the surgical procedure that creates the film's sparring doppelgängers and of the on-going confrontation between them. Although it's tempting to read the facelift metaphor as it relates specifically to Hong Kong denizen John Woo, something about the twinned countenances of China and the former British colony, it's more fruitful to think of the metaphor as it applies to the action film itself. The single most-produced type of feature in mega-budget Hollywood the action movie has solidified into a pattern so doggedly, persistently uniform that it has in the process become something like a genre unto itself. 'A genre film,' writes historian Thomas Schatz, 'involves familiar, essentially one-dimensional characters acting out a predictable story pattern in a familiar setting.' In Hollywood terms, this translates into an essentially good man (Travolta in *Face/Off*, Cage in *Con Air*, Harrison Ford in *Air Force One*) who employs first his wiles, then his brute strength, to triumph over the irredeemably wicked (Cage in *Face/Off*, John Malkovich in *Con Air*, Gary Oldman in *Air Force One*). In each of these cases, predictability isn't just inherent, it's welcome.

When Western critics and audiences first made their acquaintance with Woo, the prevailing sentiment was that what they were witnessing was nothing less than the reinvention of the action film. Although aficionados had long been journeying to the Chinatowns of their cities and cruising through film festivals to partake of Hong Kong's new wave, Woo's 1989 *policier The Killer* (*Diexue Shuang Xiong*) was the crossover hit which shifted the West's interest in modern Hong Kong cinema from the fringes to the happening mainstream. Following his 1992 film *Hard-boiled* (*Lashou Shentan*), Woo went Hollywood – first with the disappointing *Hard Target* in 1993, then with *Broken Arrow* three years later, his first feature with Travolta.

Released in the US in July, *Face/Off* is considered by industry watchers to be one of the few summer movies to have earned its keep. Upon its release, it was a designated box-office hit; by the time it reached its sixth play week, it had topped $100 million in receipts. In addition to being an audience favourite, this third of Woo's Hollywood films has been widely received by American critics as his flat-out best since leaving Hong Kong. Although a predictable number of reviews have made much of Travolta and Cage, who having swapped character identities spend a good part of the movie miming each other's vocal inflections and physical tics, critical attention has also focused on Woo himself, now a bona-fide Hollywood auteur.

It's to that end that critics of *Face/Off* have tended to employ the hyperventilated praise now the norm in American reviews ('thoroughly gripping,' pronounced *The New York Times*, 'Travolta is shockingly good'). A disquisition could be written about the debased condition of American film criticism, which over the last two decades has answered the problem of its own irrelevance with escalating levels of hyperbole towards Hollywood product. The reason for this has less to do with advertising revenue potentially risked by bad reviews (though that can't be ignored), than with the pressures brought to bear on any critic who fears writing herself into oblivion, and perhaps unemployment, by refusing to embrace – hugely, passionately, quotably – a certain number of Hollywood movies every year. No one, movie fans included, wants the bad news week in and week out. Those pressures to love movies help explain why even rotten films have their defenders (personal taste is, of course, always its own justification) and why the better movies, which include *Face/Off*, are habitually welcomed with more glee than thought. In this case, what made this glee seem odd was that the praise was lavished on a movie which however entertaining was also extraordinarily violent.

The highly stylised blood-letting of Woo's movies, and all the ways in which bullets and bodies move through his frame, have become such critical clichés that writer-director (and former film critic) Olivier Assayas even goes so far as to send up Woo's most feverish fans in *Irma Vep*, his movie-about-a-movie, in which Hong Kong action veteran Maggie Cheung, essaying a version of herself, plays a thoroughly modern variant on Feuillade's eponymous silent-age thief. During a break in the production, in a scene that pointedly recalls Jean Seberg's cat-and-mouse session with Jean-Pierre Melville in *A bout de souffle*, Cheung is interviewed on camera by a young French journalist who heaps scorn on his country's cinema even as he lavishly extols Hong Kong movies.

'Do you like John Woo?' the fired-up journalist demands of Cheung, who barely manages to explain that she's not worked with the famed director before getting blasted with more blandishments. At first glance, this casually funny encounter seems like one of those throwaway scenes directors keep in their movies more out of nostalgia than logic. In many ways, though, the scene cuts to the heart of Assayas' film, a film that is at once dazzled by and critical of the Hong Kong action movie, and that knows far too well that exploding squibs, heavy artillery and the detailed choreography of death are increasingly the prevailing currency of contemporary cinema.

Still, Assayas' target isn't Woo, but rather those critics whose love for Woo's work and for Hong Kong action movies in general is so totalising – and so unself-consciously culturally fetishistic – as to be ludicrous. To an extent, the most myopic of these enthusiasts have functioned as a kind of advance guard for a mainstream critical tendency that increasingly favours action over introspection, gimmicks over stories, heroes over human beings. That doesn't mean that Woo is to blame for such producers as Joel Silver and Jerry Bruckheimer, or such directors as Michael Bay. Nor does it mean that Woo's fans are to blame for those critics who either can't tell the difference between *Face/Off* and *Con Air*, or refuse to distinguish between them because it suits their careers. Certainly in the US, Steven Spielberg and George Lucas carry far more blame than Bruckheimer, say, when it comes to Hollywood's pervasive will to spectacle, or its blockbuster fixation. The irony is that these same impulses which have guided Spielberg, Lucas and the industry they've deeply influenced over the last two decades are exactly what transformed John Woo from an interesting unknown whose sensibility worked as a corrective to Hollywood bloat into the newest industry hire, with tens of millions of dollars and a couple of top-flight stars at his disposal. Woo has changed the terms of the modern Hollywood action film, with an influence that is ubiquitous, incessant – traceable from the lower-budgeted extremes of John McTiernan (*Die Hard With a Vengeance*), Bay (*The Rock*), and just about every other film released during the last few Hollywood summers. But even as Woo's influence grows, his own work seems to have become not only less vital but less personal: as the Hollywood action film has become more Woo-like, the director himself seems increasingly less so. Part of the problem is that without the distraction of the subtitles it's considerably easier to grasp just how foolish and lugubriously sentimental Woo's movies can be. It's a foolishness and a sentimentality that's simply exacerbated when the film is loaded not with low-key exotics like Chow Yun-Fat but with high-profile powerhouses like Travolta and Cage.

Not that *Face/Off* lacks in beauty or delirium: the film roils with gorgeous menace. There's the way Cage's black overcoat whips around his body like the devil's own cape, and later the way his eyes bulge wide as, now cloaked in his new identity of a bad guy, he samples his first taste of sin. There's the dementedly delicious moment when Travolta – who floats through his role as a bad guy as if unmoored by gravity – leers at the fourteen-year-old girl who's meant to be his daughter, then brushes past her to grab a pack of cigarettes. 'Papa's got,' he teases, 'a brand new bag.'

Still, if the movie shimmers with stylistic and performative flourishes, there is something altogether numbing about much else that transpires in between Cage's agony and Travolta's delight. Of all the violent films to come out of Hollywood this year, *Face/Off*, one of the most unrelenting, actually aims to be something more than just another exercise in cinematic blood-letting: it yearns for importance. But for all this, it opens with one of the single most brutal acts in recent screen memory – the murder of a child. Before any of the characters are introduced, we see a man fire a bullet into another man's back, wounding him and killing the young boy he'd just gathered up in his arms. The assassin is Castor Troy, the victims Archer and his only son. This sequence, shot in slow motion and drained of bright colour, precedes the first of the movie's many big set pieces: a fiery showdown at an airport that concludes with a plane crashing into a hangar and Castor Troy's coma-inducing mishap.

Curiously, the murder of Archer's son comes off as strangely nonchalant, almost unremarkable, despite the molasses-like slow motion, the celestial choir and the lacerating anguish which works across Travolta's trembling body. Woo has put children in the line of fire before, most famously in the hospital nursery scene in *Hard-Boiled*. There, though, the babies looked like the fakes they were, swaddled trophies tucked under Chow Yun-Fat's arm as he fought his way to the finish. There was something goofy and campy about all those babies, even the real ones strategically planted throughout the chaos, perhaps because – unlike Archer's murdered five-year-old – they come across, not as victims, but as almost willing co-conspirators in a spectacle that's every bit as unreal as it is daft. The murder of the child in *Face/Off* is, in contrast, calculated, not to amuse, but to appal; it's an unspeakable tragedy not only because it destroys an innocent, but because it comes close to destroying a family and unleashes waves of wholesale destruction. But while the extremity of the destruction at times suggests Ancient Greece – an intimation borne out by the mythological names Castor and Pollux – the ways in which the devastation swamps the narrative and the characters is overwhelmingly Hollywood. Throughout *Face/Off* the effect is the same: vaguely real characters – an unhappy wife, a rebellious teenage daughter – are introduced for emotional effect only to be summarily whisked off screen to make way for another burst of gunfire, another fallen soldier, another radiant catastrophe.

Last year, in *Mission: Impossible*, Tom Cruise clutched the back end of a train speeding through the Chunnel, his body framed by fire; this year Travolta and Cage fly through the air, bodies hurling through a fiery explosion, much as two years ago Robert De Niro's body soared through the air during the opening car-bomb fulmination in *Casino*: the image of characters framed against a wall of fire is perhaps the single most persistent visual cliché of 90s action movies. Generally, the characters run or leap from the fire, but sometimes they float in front of, or even sail through it, much as the Wicked Witch is tossed along in that Kansas tornado.

When it comes to torturing human flesh, modern Hollywood seems to have an insatiable appetite for pyrotechnics and a profoundly finite notion of how to deploy them. The familiar wall of fire is present in *Face/Off* – actually there are several fiery explosions – but there are other convulsions of violence in the film as well, the most memorable being a scene in which a child listens to 'Over the Rainbow' on a headset while stranded in the midst of an apocalyptic gun battle. The kid gets off easy: he lives. Most of the adults aren't so lucky, however. One man dribbles vomit down his uniform during an electric-shock treatment. A drug dealer holds his hand to his wounded neck, trying to stop his life from spurting out. Several characters are burned alive, another gets a harpoon through the middle.

Watching this parade of mutilated and violated flesh, it's difficult to believe there remains one single death which hasn't yet been imagined by either Hong Kong or Hollywood; watching *Face/Off* as it chugs from fight to fight, death to death, false ending to false ending, it's equally difficult to believe that at some time soon the movies won't have fully exhausted fictional screen violence. Jackie Chan, who in movie after movie cements the devotion of his fans by serving himself up as a potential sacrifice, would likely agree. The real violence of Chan's films, adventure yarns characterised by the star's buoyant charm, is generally evident only in the end credits of his features. These out-take glimpses of those stunts that went wrong have become a constituent element of his work, where you can see the world's most popular star grimace in pain, break bones and, in *Armour of God*, nearly die. They're a strange kind of pornography, like rehearsals for Chan's very own snuff movie. It's no wonder that midway through the end of the world John Woo slipped a pair of headphones on a kid in *Face/Off*. Like the kid, the Hong Kong director needs a way out of the wreckage, a way somewhere over the rainbow – and soon.

REVIEWS

LASHOU SHENTAN (HARD-BOILED)
Hong Kong 1992
Director: John Woo

Hong Kong. Police detectives Inspector Yuen (nicknamed Tequila) and A-Lung attack a gang of gunrunning gangsters in an extended shoot-out, during which A-Lung is killed. Yuen is reprimanded by his Chief Superintendent for his excessive use of force. Gangster hitman Tony – in reality an undercover detective – assassinates Little Mustache, a member of gunrunner Hoi's gang, who was supplying information to Hoi's rival Johnny Wong. Tony joins forces with Wong's gang, which includes Little Koi, also a police informer. This group is confronted by Yuen, who attempts to arrest Tony; Little Koi saves Yuen's life by knocking him to the ground. Later, Yuen meets Little Koi and is told that Wong is planning to attack Hoi's warehouse arsenal that night.

Wong and Tony oversee the assault, in which gun-wielding motorcyclists massacre Hoi's workers. Hoi and his minions arrive and are surrounded by Wong's men. Hoi attempts to do a deal with Tony, asking that his people be spared in exchange for his own life. Tony pretends to agree, shoots Hoi, then massacres his surviving underlings. Yuen, who has been hidden, now swings into action and another gun battle ensues. After Tony has declined to shoot Yuen, Yuen realises he must be an undercover cop, and surprises him at his boat, where they join forces repelling a further gun attack. Tony is wounded, and Yuen hides when Wong arrives; Wong promises medical aid for Tony in the hospital he owns – which also houses his main weapons store.

Ordered to kill Little Koi by Wong, Tony intervenes when he sees Koi set upon by Wong's gunman Mad Dog. Tony arranges for Koi to survive the shooting; Koi then tells Yuen about the hospital arsenal and is taken there for treatment. Tony goes to the hospital to save Koi with Yuen's help. Koi, attempting to escape, is killed by Mad Dog. Tony and Yuen sneak into the basement armoury, but attempting to break in, Tony is electrocuted. Yuen revives him but Mad Dog appears and another battle ensues.

Amid the mayhem, Mad Dog objects to Wong's attempt to demolish the building with explosives; he tries to kill him, but is shot by Wong. Yuen goes back to help his sweetheart Teresa rescue a baby left behind in the building; Wong takes him prisoner and drags him out of the hospital to confront Yuen and the police. Tony grabs Yuen's gun and shoots him by firing the gun through his own body. Yuen then shoots Wong. At police HQ, Tony's file is ritually burned.

*   *   *

Hard-Boiled's press kit carries quotes from the likes of James Cameron, Quentin Tarantino (who calls John Woo 'the most exciting director to emerge in action cinema since Sergio Leone') and *Variety* ('the Mozart of Mayhem'). This lavish quoted praise signals an intention on the part of the film's British distributor to market the film both as an 'action' spectacular and as the work of an auteur whose boldly kinetic style has already achieved much critical approval. This approach will probably reap dividends, despite the fact that, compared to Woo's 1989 *The Killer*, *Hard-Boiled* is a disappointment. The energy, wit and panache with which Woo stages his massively extended action scenes remain as potent as before, but what the film fatally lacks – as the absurdly contrived plot indicates – are characters and a story which would invest these scenes with a worthwhile moral impact. Instead, the emphasis is on action as an end in itself.

In *The Killer*, much is made of the friendship between Chow Yun-Fat's character Jeff and the cop on his trail; Jeff is granted a definite moral and emotional stature despite the patent absurdities of the storyline. *Hard-Boiled* trades in similar ideas, with nowhere near the same success. Tony makes a paper crane every time he kills; he also says he wishes to escape from his 'dark' life (to the North Pole) and there's some budding respect between him and Yuen. But here these laboured kinship notions seem second-hand and merely incidental to the main business of setting up the next spectacular action set piece. Whereas in *The Killer*, the shoot-outs served to define the characters and the relationship between them (and allowed Woo to have much fun at the expense of genre conventions), here such elements have a musty off-the-peg quality – they're simply a loose framework from which to hang the big production numbers.

The action numbers certainly are immense, with a prodigious body and bullet count and a dynamic fluency in their choreography, editing and sheer speed that is frequently stunning. Perhaps no other director can currently match Woo's heavy calibre finesse in combining gunplay and movement. Characters almost always run, leap and dive while firing. Bullets weave intricate patterns of blasted bodies, windows, furniture and fluttering masses of paper. Slow motion frequently extends pivotal moments and emphasises the grace of destruction, the beauty of disintegration and the raw power of pyrotechnics. The film's musical-like choreography and the overall rhythmic quality of the destruction suggest a directing style that has as much in common with Busby Berkeley as it does with Sam Peckinpah. It's an essentially decorative aesthetic of destruction in which pyrotechnics and firepower are celebrated for their own sake. In absurdly close proximity to each other, the leading characters shoot less to kill than to sustain their perverse dance-of-death courtship for as long as possible. In *Hard-Boiled* this is best illustrated in the scene in which two characters run alongside either side of a shattering glass partition while harmlessly blasting at each other. As in a dance routine, it's the performance rather than its goal that's important. The killing zone in front of camera is like the endlessly extended stage in a vintage musical, its many disposable villains arrayed much as the scores of anonymous showgirls in a Busby Berkeley revue. On the evidence of *Hard-Boiled*, John Woo fits snugly and unproblematically into the same straightforward 'action' category as workaday straight-to-video directors like Aaron Norris and Craig R. Baxley, rather than with such films as *Taxi Driver*, *The Wild Bunch* or John Milius' *Dillinger*. These films all have their pivotal action sequences, but they're also more than 'action' films, because their directors use the 'action' as a way to explore their characters and the social milieu in which they struggle – through violence – to define themselves. Such films creatively blur the distinction between safely synthetic screen action and the kind of gut-wrenchingly physical violence that we recognise as real. *The Killer* at times moves into this dangerous territory, but *Hard-Boiled* signally lacks such an exploratory urge. Though the stunts are magnificent, the casual plotting, low comic asides and thin characterisations most often recall the busy but emotionally sterile antics of James Bond or The Man from U.N.C.L.E.. The implausibly foolish villain Wong is especially mundane and derivative.

Perhaps the scene that best sums up *Hard-Boiled*'s moral timidity is the one in which Yuen blasts at least six anonymous gunmen while holding a baby, then exclaims, 'Hey, X-rated action!' before wiping a victim's blood off the child's face. That line is a wink to the audience that Woo is sending up the action genre, but it's also an admission that the movie won't stray out of that genre's bloody but bland parameters. The baby won't get its head blown off – if it did, we'd be in a much more dangerous, far more interesting film.

As it is, *Hard-Boiled* is a little like what *The Wild Bunch* might have been if William Holden's character hadn't been killed at the end; or *Taxi Driver* if Travis Bickle hadn't been mentally unstable; or *Dirty Harry* if the lead had been played by Elvis Presley or Glen Campbell. On this evidence, John Woo is indeed 'one of the best action movie directors working in the world today'. However, that's as much a criticism as a compliment, because *The Killer* had strongly suggested that he could also be much more than that. His forthcoming Hollywood debut, *Hard Target* with Jean-Claude Van Damme, will hopefully confirm he can be again.

Tom Tunney

HARD TARGET
USA 1993
Director: John Woo

New Orleans. The wealthy and refined Emil Fouchon runs an exclusive business organising the hunting and killing of men. Aided by South African ex-mercenary Pik van Cleaf, he gives his clients access to sophisticated weaponry and a lethal team of armed motorcyclists. The quarry is chosen from ex-Navy men, combatants out of work, down on their luck and without living relatives. These men are procured for them by Randal Poe who uses the cover of his flyposting business to make contact with likely victims. Their latest victim, Binder, is killed with a sophisticated crossbow as he flees. But Randal has slipped up, and shortly afterwards Binder's daughter Natasha arrives in New Orleans looking for her father. When she is attacked by a group of thugs, an out-of-work sailor, Chance Boudreaux, comes to her defence. She offers to pay him to help her find her father. With the help of Roper, another ex-serviceman and a habituee at the mission Natasha's father frequented, his possessions are located. Natasha lodges a missing person's form with Carmine, a woman police officer and soon after she is given the news of the discovery of her father's body, identified by dental records and service dog tag. Leaflets among Binder's possessions lead Chance and Natasha to Randal Poe, and a visit to the scene of the fire leads Chance to the discovery of a dog tag matching the one in the police's possession – this one bearing marks suggesting a shooting. Carmine orders an autopsy.

Pik meanwhile punishes Randal, slicing off one of his ears. Morton, a police doctor who has been helping Fouchon by faking autopsy results, is shot in the eye by Pik. Randal meanwhile makes contact with Roper, offering him work, but is subsequently killed by Pik. Roper is offered $100,000 by Fouchon and Pik if he can use his military training to escape an armed pursuer and make his way across the river. Fouchon's new client Zenan is terminally clumsy and is himself shot by Fouchon while Roper, wounded and bleeding, makes his way downtown. There his cries for help go ignored by passers-by and he is finally dispatched in an orgy of gunfire. Carmine herself is later shot, and Chance – with Natasha in tow – himself becomes Fouchon's next quarry.

Chance and Natasha make their way through the bayou to his Uncle Douvee's illicit whiskey still, which they wire with explosives against the imminent arrival of the gang. While Fouchon in a helicopter pursues Chance, who is now on horseback, Douvee and Natasha lie low. The final battle – with Natasha and Douvee taking part – is waged in a vast hangar used to store Mardi Gras costumes; Pik and Fouchon are killed in the onslaught of grenades, heavy weaponry and physical dexterity.

*　*　*

The dream of breaking into the international – meaning American – market has been a potent one for the Hong Kong film industry for the past thirty years. Director John Woo seems better placed than most to realise it. Woo has made the transition from the conventions of a resolutely low-tech martial arts genre – he trained with Shaw Brothers' most impressive martial arts director Chang Cheh, working on two of his best films, *Vengeance* and *Blood Brothers* – to a high-tech one of super stunts and sophisticated weaponry, without losing touch with the gut reality of the physical struggle the genre explores and embodies. But he has also garnered a swathe of plaudits from some of Hollywood's most bankable names, including Martin Scorsese and Quentin Tarantino, who admits Woo's influence on *Reservoir Dogs*, and who is writing a script for him. The current film, however, most noticeably does not have a Tarantino script, but the fact that it is a reworking of Ernest Schoedsack's 1932 film *The Most Dangerous Game* should be some compensation. Schoedsack's way with fairytale, nightmare and myth is not actively antagonistic to Woo's own mix of naive genre and nightmare. The theme of killing for sport and the struggle to resist the extinction of the self is close enough to Woo's previous film *Hard-Boiled* to bode well.

Beneath a thick wrapping of wordless and extended scenes of destructive mayhem, the earlier film contains a meditation on personal and national identity and its loss. It suggests itself as a kind of nightmare about Hong Kong's, and indeed China's, future. Menace is generated not merely from stunt pyrotechnics but also from Woo's Oshima-like awareness of the threat contained in sterile modernist spaces and the fragility of the human body. No favours have been done Woo's thesis by the relative bloodlessness of *Hard Target*. An awareness of physical frailty has been turned into a mere felling of trees. If vulnerability is of central importance, then the casting of Jean-Claude Van Damme poses problems. Here is an actor of small range, not given to suggesting self-doubt, and his presence in the lead ensures that the kind of drama that can be enacted is strictly in the Superman vein. When someone reassures Natasha that 'he'll be all right', we know he will – hence the array of daring stunts involving motorbikes, cars and trains, all travelling at full speed.

This leaves only the two villains Fouchon and Pik as bearers of self-doubt and vulnerability, marginalised by the script, but at once more interesting in themselves and in their relationship with each other than the protagonist. Arnold Vosloo gives a suggestive account of Pik, the killer proud of his professionalism, although he is not called upon to question his beliefs as the villain of *Hard-Boiled* is. It is only in the closing moments that Lance Henriksen, distraught as he closes the eyes of his dead friend amid the chaos, is able to suggest very much beyond an aesthete of violence given to pounding through Beethoven's Appassionata at his grand piano.

Hard-Boiled's seamless and impressive merging of the personal and the national finds no coherent development here. Instead the script takes pains to point out the un-Americanness of the two villains, rootless and cosmopolitan, who make plans to ship out of New Orleans for some of the world's more notorious trouble spots. What price then Henriksen's frequently uncanny resemblance to a recent American president and the fact that he is shown to live in a very white house indeed? But traces of a harsher moral critique do remain in places, in a sequence filmed amid the squalor of St Louis' homeless, and in the facile use by Fouchon of the language of democratic choice and market economics to mask his own and others' corruption. He is, he argues, only extending to civilians options open to the professional soldier.

There are clumsinesses in the dialogue, in the performances, in the scenes involving Uncle Douvee and in the throwaway comic ending. But Woo is a director with something to say and an eye for the poetic and resonant. One has to admire the daring stunt work and the intense bravura of the opening sequence, in which a New Orleans street in darkness and rain becomes as threatening and insubstantial as a nightmare. There's also considerable horror in the scene in which the wounded Poe is shunned as he lurches through the brightly lit downtown streets. At this particular point in history, however, we cannot but ask whether the use of ultra-violence in film can still be taken as mere hyperbole; and whether the use of weaponry – however excessive and fetishised – can still be seen as a simple 'empty sign' to be given meaning through the genre in which it occurs or by the auteur who uses it.

Verina Glaessner

BROKEN ARROW
USA 1996
Director: John Woo

Vic Deakins and Riley Hale, crack pilots in the US air force, square off in a boxing ring. Deakins, older and more experienced, wins the contest, but refuses his $100 prize from Hale: he claims the younger man didn't have his heart in the fight. Hale urges him to accept the money as Hale had picked Deakins' pocket while he was in the shower.

Deakins and Hale are sent on a mission to test a top secret B3 Stealth bomber carrying live nuclear warheads. During the flight Deakins tries to shoot Hale in order to take command of the plane, but ends up merely ejecting him from it. Hale is spotted by Terry Carmichael, a police officer. She tries to arrest him but, after a fight which Hale wins, he convinces her to help him retrieve the nuclear weapons from Deakins.

Deakins delivers the bombs to his associates and sends a helicopter to kill Hale but Hale and Carmichael destroy it. They then try to take over the bombs' motorboat transport, but fail. Carmichael hides in the boat while Hale travels to meet it at its next destination. The US government, realising that it has a 'broken arrow' (a code name for the loss of nuclear weapons), sends a squad to retrieve the bombs. However, some of the squad are in on Deakins' scam and the rest are easily eliminated.

Hale and Carmichael capture one of the jeeps carrying the bombs. They take it to an unused copper mine which turns out to be the destination Deakins was heading for. Deakins tricks Hale into activating one of the bombs and manages to steal the other inactive bomb. Hale and Carmichael are stuck in a pit with the active bomb. They escape via a river. The bomb explodes but it is so deep in the mine that most of the damage is contained. Deakins blackmails the government into paying for the other bomb. Hale and Carmichael discover that Deakins is taking it to Denver instead of Salt Lake City on a train. They destroy Deakins' escape helicopter. Deakins activates the remaining warhead. Carmichael fights with Deakins' associates while Deakins and Hale engage in a final boxing match which Hale wins. He deactivates the bomb.

*　*　*

Long before the opening credits tell us, we know that *Broken Arrow* is directed by John Woo. The film begins with an image of a little white square surrounded by black. As the square grows bigger we realise it is a boxing ring: Travolta and Slater are fighting. Close-ups alternate with two-shots; the film speeds up for a punch and slows down on impact. It's a knock-out beginning, gorgeous to the eye and a rush to the senses: very John Woo.

Great opening scenes set up expectations that are often difficult to meet. Those who go to *Broken Arrow* expecting 'realism' will be disappointed. For the rest of us, *Broken Arrow* mostly delivers on its promise. Its plot is somewhat rickety, dialogue too often laughable and characterisation clichéd. (Travolta falls back on the same charming mannerisms he coasted along on in his doldrum years.) But the film is really a string of excellent spectacular setpieces: the boxing match at the beginning, the fights between Deakins and Hale in the plane and Hale and Carmichael in the desert, the destruction of the helicopter, the car chase and the nuclear explosion.

Violence in *Broken Arrow* is part of the film's aesthetic. In the scene where Hale and Carmichael disable the helicopter, the propeller gets dislodged and hangs suspended in the frame. The slow motion invites us to appreciate the graphic qualities of this object. Divorced from its function, framed in a balanced composition, glistening in the sun, the propeller is a vibrant abstraction. Suddenly the film speeds up and the spectator is recoiling at the sight of a body suddenly sliced. No pity is spared for the body because, within the film's terms, it is not a person but an object to be sliced beautifully and thrillingly. This is how contemporary Hollywood evokes the sublime: awe comes from the beauty of images, terror from beauty metamorphosing into destruction.

The film's treatment of violence is not, however, amoral. In *Broken Arrow*, as in other contemporary action films, the protagonist is differentiated from the world he lives in by valuing right over might. In this genre, the traditional purveyors of morality (the government, the church, authority figures) are generally corrupt. Good and bad are thus relative values that vary in relation to power. The world is represented as rough, tough and eminently unfair. The military gets to play with its toys at unimaginable risk, but poor campers get blown up for being in the wrong place at the wrong time.

Broken Arrow rises above run-of-the-mill action films in that instability is rendered visually as well as narratively. The climax of each setpiece generally involves slow motion, balanced compositions and excellent choreography. These brief moments are from the world of classical aesthetics, representing proportion and harmony. As the film speeds up, equilibrium dissolves into chaos and destruction. To argue that these representations are beautiful is to say that chaos is counterbalanced by the order inherent in the elegance of the film's formal elements.

As an action film, *Broken Arrow* is pretty good. The sets, props and special effects are first class, the action scenes rather more than that. As a John Woo film, however, the best that one can say for *Broken Arrow* is that it is better than *Hard Target*. On the evidence of his American films, one would think that Woo didn't know about characterisation, comedy or acting. If *Broken Arrow* had been directed by anyone else, it wouldn't matter that the film has no depth beyond a visceral kick, but several of Woo's Hong Kong films (*Hard-Boiled, A Better Tomorrow, The Killer, Bullet in the Head*) easily combine superb action with funny and moving meditations on community, friendship, faith and even American cinema. If one didn't expect the very best that action cinema can offer from Woo, *Broken Arrow* would be worthy of praise. But that *Broken Arrow* can be considered very satisfying genre work is not a brilliant reflection on either contemporary American cinema or John Woo.

José Arroyo

FACE/OFF
USA 1997
Director: John Woo

FBI agent Sean Archer captures slick terrorist Castor Troy, who killed Archer's son six years earlier. Castor and his computer-nerd kid brother Pollux have just planted a bomb, scheduled to go off in six days somewhere in LA. Pollux is imprisoned, but Castor remains comatose. To find out where the bomb is, the FBI arrange for surgeons to cut Archer's face off his head and save it. They remove Castor Troy's face and attach it to Archer's head. Archer is to assume Castor's identity (Archer's voice and body shape will also be altered), go into the prison holding Pollux and get him to reveal the location of the bomb.

Inside the prison, Archer instigates a fight and meets up with Pollux. Meanwhile, Castor comes out of his coma and has his henchmen force the FBI surgeon to attach Archer's face to him. As Archer, he arranges Pollux's release and tells Castor that he's torched the FBI surgery and everyone who knew about the identity switch. He assumes Archer's identity at home. The real Archer escapes from prison with another felon.

After 'heroically' defusing the bomb, Castor convinces the government to put him in charge of anti-terrorism activities. He goes home and makes love to Archer's wife Eve and shows Archer's daughter Jamie how to defend herself with a switchblade.

Soon, he gets a call from Archer, who has returned to LA and put the FBI on alert. Archer goes to Castor's waterfront hangout, where he greets Castor's henchmen and, to prevent them from becoming suspicious, ingests some drugs. He passes out and when he comes to, Castor's girlfriend Sasha is seducing him. She tells him that her son Adam is his. He apologises for his hurtful behaviour in the past.

An FBI SWAT team storms the building and a huge gun battle ensues between the two factions. Castor shows up and, after most of the SWAT team and terrorists are killed, Archer and Castor confront each other in a hall-of-mirrors shoot-out. Both escape and Archer finds his wife. A doctor, she becomes convinced of his true identity when she types a sample of his blood. Archer's boss tells Castor to put a stop to his activities, but Castor kills the boss and makes it appear a heart attack. At the boss's funeral, the two men confront each other. Sasha shows up and gets killed in the gun-play. Archer's daughter also arrives and realising who her real father is, stabs Castor with her switchblade. Eve phones the FBI and explains what's transpired. At the docks, Archer and Castor engage in a speedboat chase until both boats crash into a pier. Finally, the real Archer harpoons his nemesis. The FBI arrive and tell Archer that they've got a surgeon on the way. Back in his original body, Archer returns home and reunites with his wife and daughter. He introduces them to Adam, who needs a place to live.

*   *   *

In John Woo's most fully realised English-language film to date, two characters liter-ally become their own worst enemies. The movie propels itself on this role-switching gimmick and on Woo's trademark excess. It's a star vehicle, a tenderly executed acting exercise, and a bone-crunching, hilarity-inducing example of what fans hoped would happen when the Hong Kong director's cartoon pyrotechnics collided with Holly-wood production values and matching budgets.

A sci-fi film wrapped around a Shakespearean romantic comedy of assumed iden-tities and exchanged lovers, *Face/Off* turns Woo into the ultimate crowd-pleaser, which, in this case, is not a bad thing. In sci-fi, medical experiments gone wrong lead to violence. In romantic comedy, mistaken identities resolve with domestic stasis. Here, we get both, and the result is as suspenseful as it is liberating. Can a person right his doppelgänger's wrongs? It appears so. The script requires that its stars John Tra-volta and Nicolas Cage take over each other's roles, which they do, gleefully sending up each other's mannerisms. More importantly, the ensuing confusion leads to trans-formation and redemption for each man: as Archer, Castor makes the FBI drone care about his life. As Castor, Archer makes amends for the terrorist's actions.

Like Woo's Hong Kong work – as well as his two earlier English-language films *Hard Target* and *Broken Arrow* – *Face/Off* is punctuated with gravity-teasing acrobatics, comic mayhem and mindboggling sentimentality, which somehow manage not to cancel each other out. Cheeky scenes occasionally mock the outré nonsensicalness of it all ('It's like looking in a mirror, only not,' says Travolta at one point). In one scene, a gun battle seethes around a little boy whose stereo headset is playing 'Over the Rain-bow' while the grown-ups around him shoot it out in slow motion. In another, an actor announces the movie's theme – 'good versus evil' – after parodying the posture of Christ on the Cross.

The secret of Woo's appeal is that he takes all the familiar clichés and throws them back at us. Not only does he use, without an ounce of compunction, the hackneyed plot device of a lawman out for revenge against a villain who killed his son, but he stages this murder, in a breathtaking sepia-and-slow-motion style, on a merry-go-round, complete with sad calliope music. Trite, yes, but so over-the-top trite it makes a statement.

Woo seems determined to prove that any plot event can be turned into a flaming inferno, as in the overextended finale in which every piece of wood in an LA harbour, drenched or not, seems transmuted into a stick of self-combusting dynamite. With his dark, Deco-futuristic sets and setpieces, Woo quotes from such sci-fi classics as *Metropolis* (1926) and lesser-known works like *Seconds* (a 1966 film in which men bored with their lives elect to have a face-swap), as well as, with its hall-of-mirrors shoot-out, such noir dramas as *Lady from Shanghai* (1948). Woo drops in these allusions not just to show off but because he knows we also love the spot-the-influence game. Indeed, *Face/Off* is, at heart, a high-budget B-movie with great B-movie moments. One of the finest is when Archer, residing in Troy's body and confined to an Orwellian hellhole of a prison, learns that Troy has escaped and is impersonating him. Our hope for his salvation sinks even lower than his below-floor-level prison cell.

Face/Off's screenplay, originally written for Sylvester Stallone and Arnold Schwarzenegger, leaves plenty of room for hamming it up. But it also contains the magic that works the spell that unravels a world in which one man inhabits another's body. It helps that Cage and Travolta seem like separate ends of a large blob of taffy – a tug on one end affects the other. What's amazing is that on such a big canvas, both Travolta and Cage set down their small moments with delicate strokes. 'I'm Castor Troy,' yelps Archer as he tentatively tries out his new identity. Then louder: 'I'm Castor Troy.' We watch him go through a baptism of fire and come out laughing all the way.

Robin Dougherty

Judge Dredd (Danny Cannon, 1995)

Section 4: Blockbusters and 'Trash': Comics, TV, SFX and 'the Ride' at the Movies

Contemporary Hollywood cinema evidences recent changes in its economic infrastructure, mode of production, mode of narration and in the context in which it is produced and consumed. The action/spectacle genre seems to embody the worst aspects of postmodern culture: the prevalence of images constructed from the trashy detritus of our cultural history in the service of the evocation of empty sensation to provide a linchpin to an intertext that has a semiotic function (the branding and marketing of a High Concept) and a commercial one (the product gets channelled through various modes of delivery – film, TV, Video, HBO, cable, video games, theme park rides, novelisations and comic book adaptations) that are intertwined (the former brings a coherence to the product's travel through the chain of modes of delivery). This section explores the cross-pollination (some would say cross-cannibalisation) of the cinema with cartoons, comic-books, television, special effects and theme parks, but also with its own history – a history of connections with all of these other forms that is much longer than is commonly acknowledged.

This section begins with Mike Atkinson discussing the connection between cartoons, comic books and film. Atkinson argues that cartoons have always battled to 'bridge an imaginative gap between what we feel and what ordinary live action movies can show us', a gap that the development of computer-generated special effects is attempting to bridge. Atkinson says that comic and cartoon imagery is today an established movie aesthetic but notes that there is a disjunctive ontology between the 'comic book's two dimensionality which implies an artist's whims and the intractability of photographed reality'. Atkinson's essay focuses on how films like *Batman* have provided a paradigm of how images and stories that are created for a 2-D medium can be re-imagined for movies which try to provide the illusion of three-dimensionality. With reference to *Batman Forever*, *The Mask* and *Casper*, Atkinson tells us that the capabilities of computer animation are snowballing and soon 'virtually anything will be possible, except perhaps the certainty of realism – or the present segregation of cartoon imagery from cinema as a whole'.

In a discussion of fans' expectations for the film adaptation of *Judge Dredd*, Martin Baker and Kate Brooks agree with Mike Atkinson about the difficult impact 'the 2-D gravity-busting possibilities have on screen aesthetics' but note with interest that the relevant history of both industries dates from the 1890s and argue that, by the 50s, a large two-way movement was underway, with comics offering their most mythic characters to radio, TV and film whilst at the same time, one or two comic book companies, primarily Dell and Gold Key, specialised in doing conversions of box-office successes, a tradition that can be seen today in Marvel's comic-book versions of *Indiana Jones*. Martin Baker brings a tighter focus to this discussion of influence by looking at Michael Mann's version of *The Last of the Mohicans* in relation to previous versions (screen, novels, TV series and comic books) of James Fenimore Cooper's 1826 novel.

In 'Sibling Rivalry', David Marc contributes an analysis of film versions of TV series. Marc delineates the changing relation between the two media over the past half-century and asks, 'How did the movies slide from guarding the public's interest against the brute of television to churning out homages to the likes of *The Beverly Hillbillies*?' Marc argues that films like *The Beverly Hillbillies*, *Maverick* and *The Flinstones* don't have a discernible story to tell. 'Indeed they are offered as pure settings inhabited by pure gestalts. The film-maker provides the viewer with a vehicle to the old show's cosmological space: once there, tourists may do as they please.' Marc notes that, in the age of Spielberg, shortcomings of story, character and dialogue are often compensated by special effects.

In the last piece in this section, Janet Abrams explores the work of Douglas Trumbull, a pioneer in special effects and talks about the connection between special-effects movies which people like Trumbull made possible and the theme park rides that Trumbull is now designing. Abrams discerns 'an augmented public appetite for the experience of speed itself, as visceral commodity, and for thrills without threat to personal danger. Arguably this appetite has been the common driving force behind a diversity of entertainments over the last century, including theme park rides and the movies.' We will return to these themes (and theme parks) in the final section.

DELIRIOUS INVENTIONS

Mike Atkinson

As children, when we first saw a lusty Tex Avery wolf's eye explode out of his skull to the blare of a car horn, it was as if a window had suddenly been thrown open on a world we'd sensed was there but could never see. Like drugs, only better, because we can still trust our senses, though human heads take the shapes of frying pans and Bugs Bunny need only reach beyond the edge of the frame to find an anvil, a sledgehammer, a banana cream pie. If comics and cartoons have a ruling principle, our most chaotic impulses have the mandate. From George Herriman's *Krazy Kat* in 1916 to John Kricfalusi's *The Ren & Stimpy Show* today, the landscapes are fashioned of raw will, unfettered by morality or physics. It may be tiresome to debate whether EC Comics, Wolverine or Beavis and Butthead really warp juvenile minds, but we can't deny that the relationship of both cartoons *and* comics to actuality has always been antagonistic. In comics, stylised forms and eye-stretching compositions have been devised to express motion where there isn't any; frame by frame, some strips become restless metamovies that endlessly strive to burst free into a third dimension. Likewise, cartoons have always battled, often deliriously, to bridge the imaginative gap between what we feel and what ordinary live-action movies can show us. Both are blindly determined, it seems, to hang in mid-air over a yawning chasm of visual possibility.

Trash culture

Perhaps this is why comics and cartoons have always been highly prized as a source from which to recycle trash culture, though never quite so much as now: with such major studio releases as *Dennis* (based on the American *Dennis the Menace*), *The Flintstones, The Mask, The Crow, The Shadow, Timecop, Richie Rich, Tank Girl*, the ongoing *Addams Family* and *Batman* sagas and now that F/X juggernaut *Casper*, live-action transcription of 2-D phenomena has become a Hollywood passion. Upcoming is *Judge Dredd*; in production or pre-production are films of *Catwoman, Black Panther*, James Cameron's *Spiderman* (in which Arnold Schwarzenegger almost played a villain: the Rhino), *Dr. Octopus, Prince Valiant, Speed Racer, George of the Jungle, Sgt. Rock* (Arnold again), *Daredevil, X-Men, Blade* and *Watchmen. Johnny Quest, Magilla Gorilla, Betty Boop* and *Green Lantern* cannot be far behind.

Simultaneously familiar and unexamined, this odd meeting of media goes back to the early days of cinema, with the likes of *Little Nemo* (1911) and *Ella Cinders* (1926) thereafter. The concept-hungry movie industry has been purloining the flotsam of daily comic strips, periodic comic books or intentionally ephemeral cartoon shorts ever since. Live-action comics were always considered adaptable fodder (*Joe Palooka, Gasoline Alley, Blondie, Barney Google, Ace Drummond, Little Iodine*) as were serials (*Dick Tracy, Red Ryder, Flash Gordon, Chandu, The Phantom, Terry and the Pirates, Superman, Captain Marvel*).

For the most part these were too constricted by budget and time even to attempt recreating the dense, propulsive *mise en scène* of the originals. Today, however, the impulse to resurrect and reinvent fond childhood hours wasted reading *Silver Surfer* or watching *Bullwinkle* can run to the looney tune of $30–50 million; whereas in the 40s Hollywood could previously afford to make 28 *Blondie* films (sometimes four in one year), today one *Flintstones*, with its tsunami of merchandising tie-ins, could make or break a studio all by itself.

Moreover, hyperbolic comic and cartoon imagery is today an established movie aesthetic – a berserk but ironic Pop Art expressionism. Back in the days of *Blackhawk* and *Congo Bill*, all a film-maker required was a nylon costume and a few undressed backlots. Today the manner in which 3-D cartoon movies appropriate the intensity of a comic's or a cartoon's visuals is all-important. When using actors and real settings, the armour-plated, turbo-charged panels of a Jack Kirby or Steve Ditko comic and the protean physical madness of a Tex Avery cartoon can only be approximated: and what results is perilously entangled in formal incongruities. Movies exist in that dimensional state that comics and cartoons have always – by their very nature – tried to invade; yet via extravagant lighting, clownshow-bright colour schemes, aggressively unreal decors, obvious models and make-up designs meant to look drawn, recent films have been struggling to break back across this same border.

The irony here is obvious; but the universe that live-action cartoon movies engender is rarely considered, nor how its laws might be rooted in the incongruity of rooting a style in hand-drawn art. It's this schizophrenic frisson that makes films from *Popeye* to *The Mask* and the current *Casper* fascinating in ways normal movies, or comics, can never be.

2-D culture is a world of both desolate and chaotic landscapes, where art styles (Arcimboldo, Rousseau, De Chirico, futurism, cubism, surrealism, Pop Art, Op Art and so on and on) are simultaneously amplified out of control and folded back into the mix, only to be rediscovered and reconstituted as art (witness Roy Lichtenstein's comic panel versions of classical paintings, complete with giant-size Ben Day dots). On one hand these cartoon stylistics are graphic compensation for a lost dimension; on the other, flatness is the form's trump card. The illusion of depth can be manipulated or discarded altogether; the suspension of movement can become a compositional *modus operandi*; raw shape and texture can take on a primal significance. Settings can vanish in the whirl of the moment, or warp to accord with the protagonist's worldview, all without camera tricks or in any way jarring us from our narrative trance. After all, drawn two-dimensionally implies an artist's whims just as cinema implies the intractability of photographed 'reality'.

This is the ripple in the continuum that distinguishes the 3-D foray into the 2-D lowlands. The rainbow colours, acute angles and Basil Wolverton freakishness of Warren Beatty's *Dick Tracy* bear no logical relation to the film's narrative or worldview, which is essentially kiddie noir. Rather, these changeling visuals are meant only to invoke, outside the context of the film's self-knowledge, the simple, pop-cult beauty of the original Chester Gould strip, and of 2-D-ness in general. Taken literally, the vivid, dreamlike designs and mutant villains (especially William Forsythe's Flattop) are free-floating concepts, disconnected from either the realism or the bare-bones resourcefulness of a tabloid comic. Where the stylisations of noir, say, or musicals, create an unreal universe reflective of its characters' inner life, the characters in a live-action cartoon are oblivious, and the inner life reflected really belongs to us, collectively, as we trip out of the maximised junk phantasia of two-way wrist radios, Batmobiles and Acme Atomic Bombs.

Though most pre-80s live-action cartoon movies ignored style altogether, there were some pioneering efforts, however campily dated they may now seem. The 1966 *Batman*, and its accompanying TV series, punched up its genre satire with lurid lighting, camera tilts and on-screen exclamations ('KA-POW!'). Roger Vadim's version of Jean-Claude Forest's sketchy *Barbarella* played like a Haight-Ashbury Halloween party, complete with play-acting, glitter drag and let's-put-on-a-show set-clutter. But it wasn't until Robert Altman's *Popeye* (1980) that there was genuine traffic between comics and flesh-and-bone. Its immediate predecessors, from the expensive *Superman* to the many cheap made-for-TV offerings (*Captain America, The Incredible Hulk, Wonder Woman* and *Spiderman*) had been merely prosaic. By comparison, so thoroughly incongruous is *Popeye*'s universe – as if caught in mid-metamorphosis between solidity and eccentric caricature – that anyone unfamiliar with the original cartoons would surely find it utterly incomprehensible, its founding texts turned to mysterious glyphs. Bringing a Max Fleischer scenario to life is unquestionably daring; not significantly retooling it to make sense in three dimensions and with living actors is, in its denial of aesthetic integrity, almost Dada. Robin Williams is Popeye, with one eye inexplicably squinted shut and with huge, foam-rubber forearms that look tumorous; the landscape around him is equal parts Boys' Own bric-a-brac and jolly-roger jungle gym. This idiosyncratic aura worked fine in the comic strip and cartoons; it hardly does so here, because its *raison d'être* is outside the film's experience. But this disjunctive ontology is the film's most beguiling feature. Somewhere in the co-opted chaos you can see the melancholy rituals of pop culture run like clockwork, and hear their songs of desire for a world better, and simpler, than the one we've got – one where Olive Oyl is the prettiest girl in town, and one where spinach will make us strong.

Cartoonish casting

Popeye, transmuted, is both surreal and poignant. Though similarly esoteric, the 3-D world of *The Flintstones* – with its relatively jejune source – is counterfeit, simply aping the original's most popular tropes ('Cha-a-a-arge it!'). Too nakedly engineered for maximum culture-sponging, *The Flintstones* displays nothing but a deep ignorance of cartoons, live-action movies and any ontological distance between them. In truth, what ultimately differentiates *The Flintstones* and *Popeye* is that *Popeye*'s failure is one of lack, rather than one of greed.

Unsurprisingly, given these intractable difficulties, most attempts to confront the vision of a film's graphic source material have been half-hearted. *Conan the Barbarian* and *Brenda Starr* achieve a degree of synthesis via fortuitous casting. Like *The Incredible Hulk*'s Lou Ferrigno, Arnold Schwarzenegger (Conan) and Brooke Shields (Brenda) are both just as two-dimensional and physically grandiloquent as comic characters come to life – the Kirby-like Schwarzenegger is actually rather more cartoonish than artist Barry Smith's gritty Conan. *Howard the Duck* and *Teenage Mutant Ninja Turtles*, both based on semi-subversive underground comics, featured too-obvious anima-tronic creatures in otherwise mundane milieus – in comics, *everything* is real and of a piece. *Sheena, The Rocketeer, Swamp Thing, The Punisher* and *The Fantastic Four* have only their ad art to recommend them; Stephen King's and George Romero's *Creepshow* so aped the formal outfittings of a comic that one wonders if it ought still to be called a movie at all.

Tim Burton's *Batman* and *Batman Returns* effectively established the 2-D-into-3-D paradigm for some time to come, and without dissolving the artifice in winking irony – even if Jack Nicholson's conspicuously Jack-like Joker does sometimes crash out of the movie's macrocosm into our laps. Burton's films erect a fully integrated urban nightmare that Dr Mabuse himself would be perfectly at home in: a world where it is always night and heroes and criminals, alike, are so tortured by bitterness and hate they've edged into nocturnal sociopathy and fetishism. Long stretches of both *Batman* movies take place on the roofs and in the sewers of Gotham City; even the ghoulishly mutant pathology of the Penguin is believable given his history and habitat. This Pen-guin, played sleazoid by Danny DeVito, is hardly the monocled, top-hatted gadfly the 2-D Batman originally battled, while Catwoman and Batman are both dark angels with far messier psyches than their drawn counterparts. Less effort is spent in trying to replicate the original iconography than in reconceiving it all within a context that's at once fantastic, crowded with childhood fears and scrupulously adult-directed.

Among their other triumphs, and despite their narrative cloddishness, the films proved, with the chill and dark bughouse qualm of their cityscapes, that it was for-mally and economically viable for a big-budget Hollywood movie to indulge in visual stylisation and create its own hermetic Caligarian cosmos. *Batman Forever*, though less inspired visually, and greatly dependent on the elastic presence of Jim Carrey (a man whose genre has truly arrived), proves that the strategy will outlive Burton's interest in it as long as scene-stealing villains are available. (*The Crow*, a close cousin, takes this Fritz Lang menace one step further, towards monochromatic, drizzly doom, approxi-mating the arcing perspectives of comic visuals by ceaselessly scanning the alleys and pinnacles of its city miniatures as no film has done since the 1930 mystery *The Bat Whispers*.)

Perhaps it's just that a measure of respect for the 2-D mediums is required (admit-tedly it's easier to find it for Bob Kane's Batman, and more recently Frank Miller's, than for later Hanna-Barbera).

This makes sense: after a century of cinema, cartoon environments have become a way of life. After all, the dominant cultural persona of twentieth-century America is a cartoon rodent's, Mickey Mouse. Disneyland and Disneyworld are autonomous, hyperreal city-states that native citizens Mickey, Goofy, Donald *et al* roam freely while we can only visit. The Disney nation even has its own flag, a silhouetted Mickey on a white field. What could be more of a live-action cartoon? The baroque, shadowless, faerie grotesquerie of Disneyworld's architecture is as close to an ideological 2-D secret garden as we may ever have in the 3-D world. As one strolls through its *faux* byways, it may lack the mysteries of 3-D reality – and yet this apparent lack of depth can come to seem its most mysterious feature. Hitchcock would have loved to set a thriller within this deranged perimeter; that the city elders would have forbidden such a tourist-trapping project further indicates a certain nationalistic sense of sanctity, as much motivated by idolatry of the cartoon ideal as of money. There may be fewer crackpot goings-on than in the Toontown of *Who Framed Roger Rabbit?*, but because Mickey's city's real, it's all the stranger.

The depthless and the deep

Roger Rabbit itself, though in fact based on a novel, owes more to the currents of cartoon life than any other film. Here the mixture of the depthless and the deep coexist without cross pollination, a touchy situation reflected in the ghettoised nature of Toontown. The film's proposition – a parallel world in which cartoon characters are a real race relegated to particular social roles and their own walled-off quarter, otherwise mixing uncomfortably with a noirishly stylised human society – becomes a hall of mirrors once we see Mickey, Bugs and Betty Boop among Toontown's denizens. The talent duel between Donald and Daffy Duck cordons off an imaginative territory for such figures more chaotically democratic than a state like Disneyworld. If they can't come to us (that is, become 3-D), we must go to Toontown, and meet them on their own terms.

Toontown is intended affectionately, but it's a concept that spills into possibly the most disquieting domain between the two realms – the potential tooning of the 3-D human body. Somewhere between the flat, exaggerated, endlessly malleable figure of a cartoon specimen and the breathing physique of an actor (even an Arnold) lies an undeniable anxiety the forearms of *Popeye* only barely suggested. The dynamic freedoms of 2-D systems represent a kind of wishful thinking; it would be a peril to our collective sanity if the fearless cruelty of a Daffy Duck cartoon entered our world, or ourselves. When Christopher Lloyd's black-robed ur-villain peels himself off the floor after being steamrollered, reinflates himself with helium and takes off his hand to reveal a looming, hand-drawn buzzsaw, it's a profoundly befuddling sight – though we're getting what we wanted, we realise at the same time that we were wrong to want it: please send him back to Toontown before it's too late! Throughout *Roger Rabbit*'s climactic scene Lloyd's blood-red eyes fibrillate and bulge in a lurid animated whorl: we have seen eyes like his a zillion times before in pure cartoons, and yet, especially for kids, the effect can be outright terrifying. The impulse to ghettoise is, under the circumstances, understandable. Call it depth supremacy if you will, but although Toontown as a notion means to poke sly fun at racial prejudice, we may find ourselves thinking this ghetto as necessary as a leper colony.

It's this that makes the *Roger Rabbit* finale the forerunner to *The Mask* and *Casper*, just as *Steamboat Willie* long ago pointed to *Pinocchio*. The bedlam suggested by Lloyd's seething cartoon body parts becomes wholesale in *The Mask*. Thanks to computer animation, Jim Carrey explodes like a big bad Avery wolf, but in three solid dimensions: his eyes fly out of their sockets like solid glass fastballs, while his horny heart bursts out of his chest and nearly tears his shirt open. And *Casper*, which is based on the utterly guileless Harvey comic and TV series *Casper the Friendly Ghost*, boasts 'more' visual effects than any movie ever made. Here nothing is safe from possible transmutation: in one (incidental) sequence Bill Pullman gazes into the bathroom mirror only to see himself morphed into Clint Eastwood, Rodney Dangerfield and Mel Gibson. The ghosts themselves are simultaneously 3-D and transparent, and capable of anything; computerised and bursting with cartoon hubris, they retain as much visual integrity as co-stars Cathy Moriarty or Eric Idle. One of the film's cleverest subtexts is the very characterisation of ghosts as cartoon-like beings – when Moriarty and Pullman pass beyond the veil their animated spirits are 'drawn' caricatures of their fleshy selves. We even get to see the live boy Casper once was, and he's decidedly uncartoonish. This is a more subtle MacGuffin than *The Mask*'s mask, a simple metaphysical observation that nonetheless rationalises *Casper*'s entire universe. There are no incongruities here: given a rationale and a raw moment of state-of-the-art F/X, we have no reason not to believe our eyes.

Opening the gates

At last the dementia of 2-D art has genuinely entered the third dimension. Consider the perpetually snowballing capabilities of computer animation and you realise soon virtually anything will be possible, except perhaps the certainty of realism – or the present segregation of cartoon imagery from cinema as a whole. If someone decides that Bruce Willis should run out of the film's frame and past the sprocket holes, or that Meg Ryan should get sucked into a vacuum cleaner, nothing holds them back. Little reason remains why Silver Surfer or the Road Runner or Pogo cannot be perfectly realised as live movie phenomena. The gates of Toontown are now open. Finally, and forever, the creatures are free.

WAITING FOR DREDD

Martin Barker and Kate Brooks

More than 100,000 people have waited for over fifteen years for *Judge Dredd*: there can't be many other films for which there has been that kind of anticipation. Fans of the comic book have been hearing rumours of a film since the late 70s. In the time since, they have played games with ideas for the film: who should, no, who *could* play Dredd? Which story would be best to adapt to film? What would Megacity One look like on celluloid? Above all, would the film dare to show Dredd's face? Every year at the UK Comic Art Convention the *2000AD* panel would face the inevitable questions.

Now it has come. The long wait is ended. And the most remarkable thing we've found, in talking already to a good many fans, is *how much they all want it to succeed*. Still, the overwhelming response has been strongly proprietorial: accept Sly Stallone, accept seeing Dredd's face, even accept the inevitable touch of romance – inconceivable in the original comic – between Judges Dredd and Hershey. But please drokk, let it be a success. Why are they so keen for this? Partly, of course, so that Dredd and his comic vehicles will survive and grow. But perhaps there are other more interesting and noble instincts at work: to spread the word, to share the pleasures and – perhaps most of all – to see the 'sheer epicness' of the story enacted in the medium for which it was surely intended.

It's too soon to say how present and former fans of *2000AD* will respond to the film, let alone whether *Dredd* will hold its own against the likes of *Batman Forever* (its most serious challenger), *Waterworld* (by all the signs destined for turkey roast) and *Mighty Morphin Power Rangers: The Movie*. It certainly won't be for want of trying. A megabudget for publicity has very much put the movie about: bus-shelter campaigns, press opportunities, even a travelling roadshow of Dredd vehicles. And it goes beyond the usual kitbag of merchandising: there are T-shirts ('Suck my glove, punk!'), chocolate bars, pencils, Dredd-shaped soap, a book of the film, a comic of the film, a giveaway mini-comic, a promised Judge Dredd cake ('trust there's nothing illegal in its ingredients, citizen') and an 'educational package' sent to every school for GCSE media studies teachers, to go with a much-repeated BBC schools programme, on the marketing of, yes, *Judge Dredd*: a pack produced with the 'full co-operation' of the film production company. Remarkable. It's lucky we don't hold to the pessimistic beliefs of the Frankfurt School about the circuit of produced and controlled pleasures of mass consumption.

Still, there *are* things to be asked and explored here. Just what is it that happens as *Judge Dredd* passes from its comic origins to the world of Showcase cinema? *Dredd*, as most people know by now, began its life in the second issue ('Prog Two') of the British comic *2000AD* in 1977. *2000AD* was a product of a crisis in the British comic industry. Since the 50s, that industry had produced and reproduced formulaic copies and spin-offs of a few originals, among them the Reverend Marcus Morris' *Eagle* and *Girl*. The rise of TV, pop music, the 60s earthquakes in youth cultures and the sheer exhaustion of the formulae meant that by the early 70s sales had slipped desperately near and even below break-even. Fleetway responded more bravely as a company than D.C. Thomson (who have today all but abandoned comics beyond the *Beano*). First they put out *Battle*, a hard-edged World War II comic; then the 'dangerous' *Action*, which pillaged from the period's most popular films (*Jaws* and *Rollerball*, for example), creating 'punk' versions of the stories, and then in a sideways move to deflect the wall of criticism that followed, the future-critical world of *2000AD*.

Within a very short time, *2000AD* made itself into an icon with which a number of pop groups associated themselves. *I AM THE LAW* T-shirts appeared on *Top of the Pops*, alongside songs on the same theme. This happened, not simply because of the brilliance of the conceptions of Pat Mills, John Wagner, Alan Grant and such early artists as Brian Bolland, but also because of a slippage inside Fleetway. For a time, editorial control operated virtually like a fan club. The result was an anarchic playing with story ideas, artwork and forms of presentation. *2000AD* at this time sang like a taut wire with the cynicism of young people's responses to the Thatcherite 'revolution'. And nowhere, perhaps, more effectively than *Judge Dredd*.

The more gargantuan Dredd became, the more the fans loved him. When artist Mike M. Mahon had trouble drawing ordinary-sized boots on him, so that he became vastly club-booted, it only added to the joy. 'A brick shithouse with a helmet on' was one fan's apt summary of the Judge.

The world of *Judge Dredd* is a deeply paradoxical one. Here is a consumerist nightmare, with gameshow hosts who will literally kill you if you get a question wrong, with beauty products and plastic surgery to make you ugly – and a global competition for one-ton heroic fatties, in a world where food is desperately short. Conceived by Carlos Ezquerra as Metropolis rendered by Gaudi, Megacity One is a claustrophobic, teeming, urban nightmare, where all citizens are potential perpetrators, where the line between guilt and innocence is determined only by the Judges, and where Dredd judges without mercy.

It was, of course, crucial to the success of Dredd that he is within the epic frame of 'America'. The dreamland of dreams has so long provided us with scenarios for futurity, land of freedom, home of the brave, refuge of crime, cityscapes of misery. *Dredd*'s version of this was extraordinary. For the comic readers, there are various pleasures to be found in Megacity One: the in-jokes (City Block names from politics and popular culture, Bet Lynch Block being a particular favourite); the risky storylines (one, on the Jolly Green Giant, got the comic into bad trouble); the general feeling that the comic was a secret satire.

And there was this sense that, like a vast off-frame space behind the comic panels, somewhere out there in strange corners of the Megacity, there was an infinity of stories waiting to burst through. Many of them hardly featured Dredd at all – he *might* arrive incidentally at the end to arrest or blow away the central figures, but mostly the strip was about their crumbling, bizarre lives in this most postmodern world. We just saw, week by week, fragments of this exploding city, policed to death by the machine that was Dredd.

And that was the point. Consumerist nightmare aside, Megacity One enacted the *Daily Mail*'s recurring nightmare of an urban future of multi-pop-cultural street anarchy. The slightest lifting of the oppressive lid and the whole lot would go up. Dredd the Lawman acts like a machine, his occasional doubts (when faced with, for instance, a 'democracy movement') were like small malfunctions before steady state was restored. Which side the readers were on was a matter of genuine doubt.

How on earth do you translate that to film? It's not easy, one reason why it took so long. When Charles Lippincott (who had made his name with his marketing of *Star Wars*) finally took the plunge in 1988, the problems were just beginning. Read the book *The Making of Judge Dredd*. A remarkable document, it reveals just how deep the fears ran that *Dredd* might end up a fascist film. Avoiding that cost its creators more than a year, and some ten script versions.

It certainly is a problem. In *2000AD*, there are layers of irony interposed just by virtue of its 'comic-bookness'. Drawing styles intervene between us and the characters: there is always 'on-screen' narration: the episodic nature of the stories means that each narrative is one in an open-ended line. Film just doesn't work like that. It takes real work to stop a narrative feeling closed and complete. Acting may not be simply naturalistic, but Hollywood facetiousness of the '*Hasta la vista*, baby' variety might not be enough to secure the film against criticism. Making *Dredd* was never going to be easy.

It's a problem accentuated by the virtual failure of the comics in America. There have been several attempts, from the mid-80s, to launch Dredd there, first through Quality Comics, most recently through DC Comics. DC seem most likely to succeed, not least because of the association with the film. But – perhaps wisely – they have written whole new stories rather than reprinting the British originals. And there is a crucial but hard-to-define difference which, if it can be placed at all, lies in *how we know whose side we are on.* In the British stories, there is a deep, ironic ambivalence about Dredd. In the American stories, there's no doubt he's a hero. The same, sadly, is true of the film. It is just too easy to be on Dredd's side.

If we are honest, we are uneasy about the film. Certainly the first forty-five minutes are just glorious. And it is to director Danny Cannon's credit that in the end it actually feels *right* that Dredd takes off his helmet. The setting is splendidly evoked. The city is the right kind of ferment. It doesn't matter that there are echoes of previous sci-fi films, from *Star Wars* to *Battlestar Galactica* to *Blade Runner*: it's even a good thing. Cannon sought and achieved a mock-Roman Senate look, with an admixture of *Ben-Hur* and other epics, and it works. Stallone is admirable as Dredd. His stiff visual presence, carapace musculature, deep grunting voice and almost unfocused eyes serve perfectly to evoke the machine. Watch the perfect moment of this, as he recounts his loss of his best friend (who returns as the ultimate villain, and is revealed to be his brother). Hershey to Dredd: 'Haven't you ever had a friend?' 'Yes. Once.' 'What happened...?' 'I *judged* him.' The last line is epitaphic in its quality. Brilliant.

Also brilliant in the first half are the little touches, such as the robotic go-kart that trundles, almost unseen, behind Dredd as he and Hershey attend a block riot. 'Eat recycled food,' it chunters, as it careers pointlessly down corridors – only to be 'arrested' by Dredd. Such mini-narratives make the comic what it is: they're central by virtue of their being incidental.

The difficulties arise when the film seeks to humanise Dredd. It is as if Cannon, a fan of *2000AD* since his childhood, is *too* in love with his subject. In the Press Preliminary Notes, he writes: 'I didn't want audiences merely to be dazzled by the special effects, I wanted them to connect with the characters, with their lives. With the storyline we developed, and the actors we cast in the roles, you truly feel the jeopardy with the characters; you really care what happens to them.' Which ain't the comic, of course. And in the film this caring is achieved at a cost. After those wonderful establishing scenes, the film departs to another sector. The street life – so central to everything in the comic – recedes. The seething citizens, the 'perps', become a backdrop, a manipulable but distant mass. The film enters a world of conspiracies. Rico, Dredd's genetic brother, becomes pure Evil Villain with appropriate Evil Chuckle, returning not just to destroy Dredd for 'judging' him, but to seek world domination – as if *anyone* would dominate the mess that is Megacity One!

The oppositions within the film now take on more overtly political meanings. Rico to Dredd: 'We're here to achieve the same thing: an ordered society... The only difference between us is that you destroyed life to embrace the law, whereas I destroyed the law to embrace life.' By the end of the film, Dredd has rediscovered the life within himself, has become more human and less of a law machine, no longer simply the embodiment of order. 'My whole life's a lie,' he grunts, as he uncovers the deep conspiracy to create a genetic super-race, a conspiracy of which he himself is a product and a victim. You just can't help but *care* for Dredd...

And you *have* to loathe Rico. He's not been degraded enough by his time in the penal colony to make you even half-pity him, while his philosophy is pure fascism: 'We are guilty of being human when we could have been gods!' he yells at Dredd, as he seeks to activate the genetic super-clones with which he will take over the Justice Department. Too much of the latter half of the film takes place within such 'corridors of power': above the heads of the Megacity masses both thematically and filmically. The camera roams down tunnels and enters womb-like chambers within the Hall of Justice; the chase sequence takes place in the air, at times resembling a computer game. The dangerous, crowded streets hardly appear; when they do, opportunities go begging. Dredd at one point almost crashes to the ground when his 'anti-gravity' Lawmaster IV motorbike malfunctions. In the comic, he'd have fixed a dozen citizens to holding posts for obstructing his passage. In the film he just missiles over their heads, making them duck and cover.

Is this just an issue about this particular adaptation, or does it have wider resonance? We think the latter. The history of comic/film relationships is more complex than Mike Atkinson's article (*Sight and Sound*, July 1995) allows. Though he is right about the difficult impact the 2-D gravity-busting possibilities of comics have on screen aesthetics, he reads history too much backwards from the present. We are in the middle of a wave of comic book adaptations, from *The Punisher* to *Tank Girl*. This is because of a desperate need in the current film industry for trailed concepts: that is, characters and scenarios whose capacity to speak to audiences is known in advance. The risks on big-budget movies are now so great that it is simply essential to test their likely success beforehand. Comic books allow that testing, and are being increasingly raided for their filmic potentials. But this is changing the comic industry more than the film business.

Ironically, the relevant history of both industries dates from the decade, the 1890s, when the first regular strip, *The Yellow Kid*, appeared in a New York newspaper and the first moving picture was shot. The industries met with the first cartoons. But it was actually comics which first displayed that a character-concept could be the basis of substantial licensing. By 1908, Buster Brown was endorsing a range of merchandise of which any modern film company would stand in awe. (In Britain, the process had started even earlier, via the figure of Ally Sloper.) However, it took a combination of factors to drive the two industries into parallel. First was the recognition of the market for films for young people; second, the rise of the adventure strip in the late 20s, arising from King Features' demand for syndicable storylines and Hollywood's move into the production of serials.

By the 50s, a large two-way movement was underway, with comics offering its most mythic characters (centrally, of course, Batman and Superman) to radio, TV and film. At the same time, one or two comic book companies specialised in doing 'cover versions' of predicted box-office successes. Dell and Gold Key alone covered more than 150 films in a ten-year period, adapting everything from *The Way the West Was Won* to *The Mummy*. There were also uncountable western adaptations, from film and TV. Looking back, it is fair to say that no one particularly worried about the *politics* of such characters or stories – they were so overwhelmingly 'American' no problem could possibly arise – and certainly no one bothered about the rival aesthetics of films and comics.

However, there were moments which brought the issue of visual potential to the fore. During the 30s, for instance, it was the fad for comic-strip advertisements. The newspaper strip revealed to commercial companies the power of narrative as a carrier for ideas, and how it could be linked up with endorsement. In the 50s, when comics for a brief time escaped censorious control, they held up to film-makers new modes of story-telling. Notoriously EC Comics experimented with the filmic possibilities of panels. Just one example: Bernie Krigstein, in his extraordinary *Master Race*, married a mini-study of the psychology of fascism with an array of experimental visual effects. In one panel, he evoked the visual confusion of watching a metro train accelerate past a puzzled man's eyes. These glorious results were learnt from not only by the underground artists of the 60s, but by such film-makers as Hitchcock.

There were subsidiary histories, too. Classics Illustrated developed their line of comic-book adaptations of great novels and plays after 1941. After their collapse in 1970, their inheritance passed into the hands of Marvel Comics, who in the 70s not only did a series of Classics adaptations but also took on the mantle of Dell and Gold Key. Marvel served up melodramatised renderings of such films as *Indiana Jones*, and kept the stories alive by telling new tales, which then returned to TV and film as *Young Indiana Jones*. The circle was completing and returning onto itself. This was the inevitable outcome of the emergence of the new corporate giants. Marvel changed hands several times among film-related companies. DC Comics was taken over by Warner.

The great hunt for concepts was on. Some were found by accident. *Teenage Mutant Ninja Turtles* was such a concept, launching from a spoof underground platform into the mainstream. (But with *Turtles*, faithfulness to the original was never an issue.) It was inevitable that Dredd would be discovered. In some ways he was filmed *before* he was discovered, *Robocop* owes so much to the concept of Dredd the machine-like lawman that it delayed the filming of *Dredd* himself by seven years.

Finally, a significant difficulty with *Judge Dredd* is just how much the stories owe to their original Thatcherite and Reaganite context of production. Dredd is only Dredd because he is the opposite of punks on the street – in whom we half-recognise ourselves. We are the powerless, resentful 'enemy within' whom Thatcher attacked. The comic transposes us to 'America' to play out the futuristic drama of the complete realisation of Thatcherite law-and-order politics, on a world scale. Dredd *must* be both hero and villain, and Hollywood just can't do that.

It would probably be better if they didn't try. When they intrude a conscious politic into their films, there is an overpowering smell of burnt good intentions. There is something horribly, terribly wrong in the Press Notes when they try hard to summarise the world of Joe Dredd: 'The Judge Dredd universe represents a totalitarian response to rising crime and a vision of the results of loss of nationalism.' Loss of *what*? *2000AD* and Dredd were global Reaganism, to the extent that both Thatcher and Reagan actually appeared in muffled, satirical form in the stories themselves. And the comic's fans knew it well.

Judge Dredd 2 is at the starting gate, awaiting box-office returns on number one. Even before seeing the first, the fans are talking about sequels, eagerly anticipating seeing, computer enhanced onto the screen, the hideous quartet of 'Dark Judges' (especially Judge Death: '*The crime iss life, the ssentence iss DEATH!*'), or the radioactive panorama of the Cursed Earth and its bizarre, dangerous 'mutant' inhabitants. Will *Judge Dredd 2* make it? Will the compromises enable Stallone to wrench the strings of 'poignancy' (his word) in enough American viewers? On that, *judgement deferred...*

FIRST AND LAST MOHICANS

Martin Barker

The video release of Michael Mann's *The Last of the Mohicans* gives a chance for a second, longer look. The film did moderately well at the box office, greatly enhancing Daniel Day-Lewis' reputation, but otherwise was granted a mixed reception. I suppose that most viewers appreciated it on the level of a simple action-adventure story with a historical setting, and it certainly mixed in just the right amount of violence and filmic mayhem to work in that way. (Several reviewers in fact welcomed what they saw as its unpretentiousness.) But outside that, it hit problems. *Sight and Sound*'s review half-panned it as 'Adirondack Vice' (a reference to Mann's other best-known work), suggesting he lacked the skills to handle such an expansive movie. Yet perhaps that too misses the point.

It seems a wise idea instead to relate Mann's film to the long tradition of versions of James Fenimore Cooper's 1826 novel – and there are certainly plenty of them. Counting English-language versions alone, I have so far hunted out ten films, three plays (the earliest from 1842), one opera, two television series, nine comic books, two animated cartoons and two British radio versions (I have no information available for the US). Alongside these are countless book abridgements and adaptations – countless, because publishers often did not bother to give copies to the collecting libraries, so to find them is a matter of serendipity. Then there are at least two versions of versions: one, a book of a television series of the book (1958); the other, a film of a comic of the book (1978).

The Last of the Mohicans seems, despite itself, to have had the narrative energy to become a certain kind of mythic classic. I say 'despite itself' because more literary critics are agreed that the book is intolerably badly written. This dismissal began almost as soon as Cooper died, when Mark Twain delivered a famous damnation of his writing skill. Indeed, of all Cooper's mythic novels, *The Last of the Mohicans* is probably the least critically regarded. Yet something about the story has continued to 'work'.

This is especially so in this century. In about 1910, in both Britain and the US, a process began of converting a number of 'classics' into 'children's stories'. In Britain this was coupled with the rise of 'English' as a school discipline. Brian Doyle has argued in his *English and Englishness* (1990) that this burgeoned as a practice following the 1921 Newbolt Report (Newbolt being otherwise famous for his imperialist panegyric 'Play up, play up, and play the game'), which praised literature as a conveyor of a national imagination, a common sensibility uniting people across class. A number of publishers subsequently pushed out abridged 'classics', and later illustrated comic books, to help make such good works readily available to young minds – only to be met with stern disapproval from many teachers.

The Last of the Mohicans seems to have been ideally suited to this purpose. But it also proved particularly amenable to adaptation as a movie. Indeed, *The Guardian* greeted Mann's film with the ironic comment: 'Once upon a time this was actually a novel, but it has been adapted so many times it's moved entirely into the visual domain.' Of all the adaptations, only the comic book versions (whose publishers were generally the most nervous about teachers' responses) stick reliably to the original narrative. Certainly the plot followed by Michael Mann's version is markedly changed.

How should we understand this narrative? An obvious starting point has to be the novel's deep concern with 'difference': the 'essential' differences between whites and Indians and the running concern about 'miscegenation' with its connected fears about interracial sexual attraction. In Cooper's novel, and in most subsequent versions, Hawkeye is the site of all virtues: simplicity, honesty, strength, manhood, essential 'Americanness'. Repeatedly Hawkeye comments that he has 'no taint' of Indian blood. Yet this is not a simple assertion of white superiority. In the Delaware council scene, the aged Chief Tamenund is given narrative authority to pronounce with scorn on white people's assumption that they own the world. And Hawkeye himself talks of the separate 'gifts' of the different races. Admittedly, the twin deaths of Uncas and Cora prevent the *reality* of interracial sex. With the 'disappearance' of the Mohicans, Hawkeye effectively inherits their qualities.

So there is a complexity in the novel's attitude to 'savages'. The Hurons, no doubt, are portrayed as irredeemably vicious and untrustworthy – at least when they are under the sway of Magua's rhetoric. In the book, his tremendous skill at persuasion acts like a 'wild card' – the Hurons have traditions, customs, beliefs and rules of justice, but Magua is able to pervert these into a force for his own ends. The Hurons' malleability is not simply the result of an inherent childishness, as a lot of Tarzan stories suggest about Africans.

If there is a weakness which the novel condemns, it is a strange one. In one scene the Hurons 'try' one of their own tribe, Reed-That-Bends, who ran away from Uncas. He is condemned for his 'cowardice' and is killed. His father is so shamed that he has to leave the tribe, even though he tries to deny his own son. 'The Indians, who believe in the hereditary transmission of virtues and defects in character, suffered him to depart in silence.' If the novel can mark this out as an odd belief, there is surely no simple racist doctrine in it.

The other famous aspect of the novel is its terror of cross-racial sex. Cora's horror at Magua's vengeful proposal that she become his squaw is clearly meant to engage with readers' anxieties. Yet the story assumes this reaction without approving of it. Cora, herself a 'half-caste', is in Cooper's words a 'lovely being', brave, self-contained and strong far beyond her 'pure' sister Alice. Colonel Munro is filled with anger when he thinks that Heyward is rejecting his daughter Cora on racial grounds and Heyward has to convince him of his genuine love for Alice before Munro will let it pass. Yet while Heyward is left at the end to marry Alice, Uncas and Cora die. It's as if Cooper is aware of his readers' horror of interracial sexual attraction and miscegenation, but is horrified by that horror. The clash is unresolved – except in as much as the virtual death of Indian culture makes its resolution unnecessary.

What to me makes the novel effective is the interplay between two systems of narrative organisation. In one, there is endless discussion of 'essential qualities'. This is carried in particular through the narrator's comments on the characters' motivations. Yet the resolutions in the book are founded on historically specific relationships and cultural traditions.

At the Fort, the French defy all Colonel Munro's expectations by allowing an honourable surrender. And at the end, the Delawares – 'savage' though they are – are not only seen to be scrupulously governed by laws and rules of justice, but clearly have a determining history. When Uncas is revealed to be the Chief of the Mohicans, the Delawares override Magua's claims because the Mohicans represent their ur-tribe, from which they are all descended. Without this second principle, the story could not be resolved in the way it is.

We might represent this clash of narrative principles as a conflict between racial theory and determinate (albeit mythologised) history. Because the two cannot be resolved, the novel is inevitably 'incomplete'. Think of it as a flexible template. This is worth noting because each adaptation has shifted this uneasy balance and resolution into a new orbit. And more significantly, each recasts the myth to the political temper of its own time.

Red hordes

Two things seem to be going on simultaneously. On the one hand, there are clear, self-conscious traditions within the adaptations. For example, just about every comic book references an N.C. Wyeth illustration to a 1919 edition of the book. Wyeth depicted Heyward wrestling, legs intertwined, with Magua. In all subsequent versions, the stance and setting are identical, but the opponents are two Indians.

Similar links can be found in the films. George Seitz's 1936 movie borrowed whole sequences from the Tourneur/Brown 1920 silent film, and was in turn looted for footage for the 1956 American television adaptation. Michael Mann acknowledged his debt to Philip Dunne's 1936 screenplay, from which many memorable lines are taken wholesale. (In both versions, Hawkeye is arrested at the Fort for helping the colonials to escape to their homes. In the ensuing confrontation, he addresses Major Heyward, who has demanded his hanging: 'Major, some day you and I are going to have a serious disagreement.') Yet whatever the continuities, the story remains a malleable source for the stating of different political positions. This flexibility is achieved through three processes: alterations to the sequence of events, shifts in motivation and the moments of philosophising.

There have been so many changes in plot that it's hard to know which to choose as illustrations. The 1920 version, for example, not only isolates Magua as a lone villain, but introduces an English equivalent: a Captain Randolph, 'more interested in women than in war', who betrays the Fort to the French and then dies in the ensuing massacre. It also introduces the most common change of all in having Magua die at the hands of Chingachgook rather than Hawkeye – having the father revenge his son's death seems to enshrine a more basic sense of justice. Both the 1936 and 1992 film versions deny Cora's mixed race, reverse the characters of Cora and Alice, and have Alice commit suicide at Uncas' death. But where the 1936 version has an English troop rescue both Hawkeye and Heyward at the end, Mann inserts a terrifying death-by-burning for Heyward, who thus saves Hawkeye's life and vindicates himself.

We can learn even more from the ways motivation is altered and from the moments when privileged characters are allowed to give their views – or are not. Sometimes such changes are crude statements of ideology. The 1942 Classics Illustrated version, for example, produced just as the US was about to enter World War II and in the midst of a fever of anti-Japanese prejudice, simply reduced all Indians (including the Mohicans) to subhuman chatter, while the French were carefully 'excused' any role in the massacre. White unity in the face of yellow or red hordes clearly had priority.

Other versions, particularly the films, are more sophisticated. The 1936 film, very much a 'New Deal' adaptation, focuses all philosophising in Hawkeye. Following the first escape from Magua, he talks to Cora (who had begun with a deep English mistrust of him, based on 'old principles'): 'A man could spend his life walking this country, and never walk the same trail twice. Every time I blaze a new trail I imagine new cities springing up at the end of them. I wonder if you can imagine what it feels like to be the first.' One can easily see audiences imagining their own history through this. And certainly by the end of the film Cora can, so a new alliance of old and new is achieved through their budding romance and through Hawkeye becoming a scout for the English (a noteworthy narrative change).

Hollow promises

The 1977 version is balder still in its rhetoric. After their first escape from Magua, Cora, gazing on the handsome, watchful Uncas, says to Hawkeye, 'I find it difficult to keep in mind that a man with such sensitive eyes can be a savage... the horrible stories I've heard about the Indians – the way they torture... scalp.' This hilarious remark is treated very solemnly by Hawkeye: 'You'd better bone up on your history, ma'am, scalping started in Europe long before the white man brought his poison here and taught it to the Indians, so that the Indian could be paid a bounty every time he brought in a scalp from an enemy – proof of the kill.' Can you imagine that from Cooper?

In Michael Mann's version, the English are unreliable, arrogant imperialists, whom ordinary Americans must defy in order to protect their homes. And, whereas in the book Magua is motivated by revenge for having been punished like an animal by Colonel Munro, for Mann his motivation is a desire to become a 'white capitalist', giving up the 'ways of the Hurons' for trade, wealth and luxury.

This shift in perspective is linked in Mann's version with an overall tendency to make Hawkeye the most Indian character of all. Whereas in the book Hawkeye often comments on Uncas' greater tracking skills, in Mann's films all the skills are Hawkeye's. And while in the novel great attention is paid to distinguishing the different 'virtues' of each people, in Mann's film you often can't tell them apart, as in a scene near the beginning, when Hawkeye and company return from a hunt to the inhabitants of their village – a mixture of whites and Native Americans filmed so they are indistinguishable. The screen presence of Daniel Day-Lewis participates in this myth: his stillness, wild hair, few words and physical poise resonate with classic 'good Indian Chief' depictions that I can still remember from childhood. Hawkeye/Day-Lewis *is* interracial, therefore all political issues about race are 'resolved' in and through him. Thus does multiculturalism find a myth to bear it.

Mann has made a clever, beautiful but, in the end, hollow film, celebrating cultural pluralism but depoliticising racial politics. The final shot, of Hawkeye with his new girl by his side and Chingachgook surveying the tree-clothed hills of America, seems to celebrate a merging of the races, a new hope and a cleansing reminiscent of the hollow promises of Bill Clinton's 1992 election campaign. It's an over-simplified and ultimately meaningless promise of simple renewal, in which all issues of power, oppression and injustice are smogged out by a rhetoric of vague hope and kindness.

It is curious to compare Mann's film with the Jack Jackson comic book version of the same year (from Dark Horse Comics). Jackson, one of the original Underground Comix artists, has built his subsequent reputation on a series of 70s comics depicting Native American tribal histories (most famously *Comanche Moon*, 1979). His new version of Cooper's novel is curiously the most reliable in terms of following the original plot, and is the only version I have come across which includes the disturbing incident where Hawkeye slits a horse's throat lest it reveal their hiding place.

But because of the manner of his retelling, Jackson turns Cooper's ambiguous racism into a strongly pro-Indian argument. Through simple comic-book devices, he causes us to question the reliability of English accounts of their own motives, while inviting us to see ourselves through the Indians' picture of the impact of whites on them. Alice is made to seem 'flighty' compared with Cora's *gravitas*; even though Magua does turn out to be bad, the prejudice against him is noted as a problem; Chingachgook is given space to comment on the destruction of his people. Without adjusting the story at all, Jackson comes close to making it a Native American myth.

The pity is that of the two, it is Mann's film that will be remembered. And the next version of *The Last of the Mohicans* will no doubt pillage bits of his movie, as it rewrites this malleable mythology of 'America' to whatever new circumstances call it forth again.

SIBLING RIVALRY

David Marc

The Clampetts serving dinner on their billiard table in 'the fancy eatin' room', Bret Maverick waxing philosophic from the wrong side of a gun with something his 'old Pappy used to say', Fred Flintstone getting knocked on his bottom by Dino, the hyperactive family dinosaur. What do these televisual snippets from the ancient burial grounds of the medium have in common? As well as being the postmodern remnants of life lived in front of a television set, they are bankably inexpensive, high-concept, self-promotional devices with which to market feature films.

In systems of mass entertainment, as in weapons of mass destruction, human beings have shown a greater capacity for producing delivery systems than for things needing delivery. Nowhere is this more apparent than in the US, where a 15-year-old in a rural county has more opportunities to view drama during the course of a day than the most avid theatregoer in Elizabethan London might have hoped for in a lifetime. Every new cable channel adds a couple of million empty seats. How to fill them? The relentless search for fuel to keep the culture factories humming constantly requires new sources of raw material. With demand outstripping supply, innovative recycling processes become increasingly attractive.

In its latest forage for salvageables, the entertainment industry has been testing the viability of old TV series as an alloy for new feature films. A trio of such experiments will be demonstrated to British moviegoers this month: *The Beverly Hillbillies*, *Maverick* and *The Flintstones*. These movies constitute the most recent wave of a trend that took off with *The Addams Family* in 1991 and has continued with *The Fugitive*, *Dennis the Menace* and *Car 54, Where Are You?*. *Gilligan's Island*, be assured, is in the works.

In fact, what Hollywood is doing here is reviving an old and generally forgotten approach. In the pioneer days of television, when fewer than half of American households had sets, it was common practice for movies to scout for likely properties among the TV dramas that were broadcast live from New York. The networks unwittingly obliged the studios by commissioning a steady supply of non-serial teleplays – fifty-two-minute, commercially segmented mini-dramas – from such writers as Paddy Chayefsky, Rod Serling and Gore Vidal, and the Hollywood studios' adaptations were generally impressive. In 1955 Chayefsky's *Marty* dominated the Academy Awards, winning Best Picture, Best Screenplay, Best Director (Delbert Mann) and Best Actor (Ernest Borgnine). Few cared to dwell on the concept's humble birth as *Marty*, a 1953 episode of *The Goodyear Tire Playhouse*. Other noteworthy transformations included Oscar winners *Judgment at Nuremberg* (1961) and *Requiem for a Heavyweight* (1962), as well as the Jerry Lewis vulgar modernist classic *Visit to a Small Planet* (1959), which was adapted from a 1955 Vidal teleplay.

By the mid-60s, the march of technical progress had completely reversed the flow of adaptation between the two media. As the NBC, CBS and ABC networks achieved coast-to-coast saturation, they blithely cancelled what is now remembered as the golden age of television drama and got down to the serious business of lowest-common-denominator programming. As the brainless shriek of sitcom laughter grew louder, the movies, just by staying where they were, forfeited their position at the base of the mass-culture pyramid. Compared to the despised idiot box, Hollywood cinema now found itself in the unfamiliar business of peddling 'quality' entertainment.

During this period sitcom adaptations of feature films became common practice, as if the lineage of the silver screen could confer prestige. In most cases the results came out looking like crass vulgarisations: *Gidget* (ABC, 1965), *Please Don't Eat The Daisies* (NBC, 1965) and *The Ghost and Mrs Muir* (ABC, 1968) are just a few examples. The two most successful in the ratings were both for CBS: *M*A*S*H*, which ran for nine seasons and was easily the pick of the litter, and the maudlin *Alice* (from *Alice Doesn't Live Here Anymore*) which ran for eight seasons.

This film is genteel/TV is vulgar structure gradually disintegrated in the home-video boom of the 80s. As the showing of reels of celluloid to popcorn-chewing audiences in public theatres became a quaint form of presentation in the mix of broadcast, cable, VCR, laser disc, in-flight projection and the like, so-called feature films gradually found themselves as a long form of their old nemesis, the TV show. Editing was speeded up to video-friendly rhythms. Successes were routinely extended into tube-like sequels and prequels. The thirty-year paradigm of film and television as aesthetically distinct media became obsolete: in practice, they were revealed as merely two forms for distribution of a single product. A preference for celluloid over videotape became something akin to a preference for reading the hardbound edition of a book rather than the paperback.

Cineastes, of course, find themselves alternately remonstrating against the barbarian tide or entering into trance-like states of denial. Television had always been the enemy – and a fine whipping boy at that. As long as the 'two separate media' illusion was maintained, the Edisonites did not have to kowtow to applause signs and severely depleted attention spans. Quite the contrary: in the old days, American commercial cinema shamelessly paraded its new-found pedigree by mocking the manners of the upstart.

In *A Face in the Crowd* (1957), Elia Kazan interrupts his plodding group theatre naturalism to offer a hysterical parody of commercial television camera styles. But the movie's message is not so light-hearted: television poses a serious threat to American democracy and all that thinking liberals hold dear. In his script for *Network* (1976), an embittered Paddy Chayefsky lambasts the greedy conniving bastards who had betrayed television's (and his own) artistic potential. In *The China Syndrome* (1978) we are warned that even the nightly local newscast is fraught with lies. So how did the movies slide from guarding the public's interest against the brute of television to churning out homages to the likes of *The Beverly Hillbillies*?

When practice affords such little comfort, it is perhaps better to seek refuge in theory. No genre is inherently worthless, no matter how poorly its possibilities have been realised. If movies based on old television shows should prove successful at the box office (and on cable, in broadcast and as cassette, laser disc, CD-ROM, videogame, and so on), this type of film is likely eventually to yield a genre's usual share of masterpieces and geniuses (check *Cahiers* 3001). Suffice it to say that with *The Beverly Hillbillies*, *The Flintstones* and *Maverick* we have not yet reached that stage. Instead, what you get is no more than the kind of thing that is often done – and done better – by a bunch of strangers reminiscing in a pub about their childhood viewing habits. Though all three relentlessly attempt to poke the viewer in the ribs over bits and pieces of trivia and nostalgia, not one of them is loving enough to qualify as an appreciation, witty enough to make for good satire or even smart enough to tell you something you didn't already know about the series or about television in general.

It is said that the hook to watching reruns of old television series is not the plotting of the individual episodes or the long-term character development made possible by scores of hours of air time. Instead, the attraction lies in the programme's quality as a place to enter another universe, a location once visited often and perhaps enjoyable to visit again. If this is true, then maybe it is not surprising that none of these films has a discernible story to tell. Indeed, they are offered as pure settings inhabited by pure gestalts. The film-maker provides the viewer with a vehicle to the old show's cosmological space: once there, tourists may do as they please. The superimposition of a feature-film plot structure seems like a clumsy afterthought: a half-hearted hedge against the chance that these movies might seem less like the originals if they had no plot at all. Perhaps Hollywood is developing its first non-narrative, or at least a-narrative, genre. What next: *Sgt. Bilko* directed by Stan Brakhage?

Boomtime hedonism

But though they have no on-screen tales to sell, these films do possess a commodity that is far more prized in the contemporary market: built-in public familiarity, or what television executives call the 'F-score'. The property comes fully equipped with a track record – translatable into charts, graphs and vinyl-bound reports that 'prove' a proposed movie's market value – which is an invaluable asset for producers seeking finance and much more convincing than the fact that you find a comedy funny or a mystery gripping. Available figures include the profitability of the series in the syndicated rerun market; the demographic character of its viewership; product licensing reports; public perception of the property's position in the family viewing/adult entertainment grid and plenty more.

The Beverly Hillbillies, the most popular sitcom on American television during the 60s, comes with reams of such information. Paul Henning, the series' creator-producer, dominated prime time for most of the decade with his hit show and its two popular spin-offs, *Petticoat Junction* and *Green Acres*. During the *Hillbillies*' production run on CBS (1962–71) it finished number one in the national Neilsens twice and was consistently top rated until the early 70s. According to a study published by *TV Guide* in 1982, nine weekly episodes of *The Beverly Hillbillies* ranked among the 50 most-watched programmes in the history of television, drawing ratings comparable to those of Super Bowls.

The premise of the series is succinctly stated in the song Henning wrote to accompany the opening credits: 'Come and listen to my story 'bout a man named Jed,/A poor mountaineer, barely kept his family fed./Then one day he was shootin' at some food,/When up through the ground came a'bubbling crude,/Oil that is: black gold, Texas tea.'

In this recapitulation of an epic American legend, Henning offers the story of a rugged individual who begins life behind a plough and ends up master of a great estate. But the Puritan basis of the myth has been updated for the boomtime hedonism of the 60s: hard work, once essential, has been deleted. No Horatio Alger, Jed Clampett simply pulls the trigger of his gun, his bullet lands on $25 million worth of buried fossil fuel. Henning further plays with tradition by opening each episode with a visual allusion to no less tragic a tale than John Steinbeck's *The Grapes of Wrath*, via the John Ford movie. As with the Joads, we see the Clampetts loading up their quaint belongings for the epic trek West. Just like Grandpa Joad, Granny must be forcibly removed from the house in her rocking chair and tied to the back of the flatbed truck. But the image that follows deviates sharply from the Depression-era parable: the next shot is the Clampett truck rolling down the tree-lined streets of Beverly Hills on its way to the family's thirty-two-room California mansion.

Over the course of the series' nine-year run, five plot lines developed that account for virtually all of the 216 half-hour episodes: 1. sophisticated city folks try to hustle the Clampetts out of their money, but fail because they outsmart themselves; 2. Elly May, Jed's daughter, has reached majority without a husband, and urban suitors – corrupt, effete and/or mercenary – come courting to no avail; 3. Jethro, Jed's nephew and an utter moron, tests the waters of various careers, including brain surgeon and 'double-nought' spy; 4. Jed, a widower, meets a woman; 5. Granny, the family matri-

arch, battles for the birthright of her folk heritage against the forces of post-industrial culture.

It is the last of these that provides many of the funniest moments of the 108-hour
text. Granny's proven folk talents as small-game chef, organic healer, moonshiner,
matchmaker, meteorologist and much more turn her into a lunatic in Beverly Hills,
where the status of an individual is measured by the quantity of their leisure time
rather than by the quality of their work. For example, Granny makes her own lye soap
in an open kettle down by the 'cee-ment pond'. Her neighbours do not envy or respect
her for this; they just call the police.

Manic feistiness

While director Penelope Spheeris attempts to cover the first four of these narrative
development lines in her ninety-three-minute film, Granny is almost completely
missing. Moreover Spheeris shows little of the genius for banal detail that made her
exploration of public-access cable in *Wayne's World* so rich. The little we do see of
Granny finds Cloris Leachman dull as paint. Completely lacking the manic feistiness
which Irene Ryan gave the television character, Leachman sleepwalks through, stealing not even a modicum of viewer attention, let alone a scene.

A stronger effort, but in some ways even more disappointing, is Lily Tomlin's rec-
reation of Jane Hathaway, the hyperliterate secretary of the Clampetts' greedy banker
Milburn Drysdale. Nancy Kulp, who played the role (and one rather like it in an earlier
Henning sitcom) made this merciless caricature of a polysyllabic-but-plain Vassar
graduate wandering through a world of Angelino airheads and country bumpkins
into an object of schoolyard hysteria for a generation of American children. Tomlin
becomes caught between a loyal imitation of the original and a script that utterly rein-
terprets the role. Most of Mrs Hathaway's humour in the sitcom is derived from her
frustration and female-eunuch impotence; in the movie, she turns out to be the hero
who saves the day.

The Flintstones isn't much kinder, either to its origins or its audience. John Goodman,
who is making a career from being the only good thing in a boring movie, tries very
hard to persevere with a miserable, disjointed script that can do little else but repeatedly remind its audience of how wonderful all those old *Flintstones* animated sight gags
were and how cool it is to see them unanimated – very unanimated. Every time someone starts a car, we get a close-up of revving feet. Every time Wilma and Betty laugh,
they do their famous duet laugh. Fred must say 'Yabba dabba doo' – well, a lot. Goodman does get some help from Kyle MacLachlan, who somehow manages to look as
though he's being directed by David Lynch in the midst of a kiddie movie. MacLachlan
plays a thoroughly evil character, the kind that would never appear in *The Flintstones*,
The Jetsons, *Yogi Bear* or any other Hanna-Barbera cartoon. But loyalty to the model is
hardly an issue as this still life plods on. Rick Moranis and Rosie O'Donnell seem only
slightly embarrassed as they drift through assignments as Barney and Betty. The fact
that Elizabeth Taylor appears at all completely overshadows any qualities that might
be discerned from her performance.

By some accounts as many as thirty two writers were used by director Brian Levant.
A patient viewer might just be able to pick out the work of each of them. In the age of

Spielberg, bad dialogue is often compensated for by special effects; ten-year-olds may well be floored by the technical dazzle of a pig puppet acting like a garbage disposal, a bird puppet mimicking an effeminate man and a Mastodon puppet giving Fred a shower with his trunk.

A shallow interpretation that has followed *The Flintstones* since its debut on ABC in 1960 compares it with *The Honeymooners*, probably because both Fred and Jackie Gleason's Ralph Kramden are explicitly blue-collar characters, even rarer then than now in American sitcoms. But a comparison of the Kramdens' bare-bones apartment – no radio, no television, not even a telephone – with the Flintstones' Levittown consumer utopia quickly gives lie to the idea. Unfortunately, Levant pushes the movie precisely in this fruitless direction. 'I am the KING of MY castle,' Fred tells Wilma in a line and style lifted directly from Gleason. Goodman's imitation is the film's best entertainment, but the *Honeymooners* parallel works against the most powerful metaphor to be found in a Hanna-Barbera cartoon: all human experience – from caveman past to space-age future – seen as life in an affluent American suburb.

Thickening plots

Maverick, directed by Richard Donner, is a different kind of project. First, the show belongs to a dormant genre, the TV western, which maintains only a limited following. Second, though the series was popular enough to crack the top ten one season, it was not a long-running mega-hit, nor did it ever achieve the status of an 'evergreen' – a series that always makes money by syndication of its reruns. It is this last feat, thoroughly accomplished by both *The Beverly Hillbillies* and *The Flintstones*, that turns a mere TV show into a cultural institution.

Premiering on ABC in 1957, *Maverick* had a refreshingly laid-back style in a TV action environment still dominated by bullet-headed McCarthy era law-and-order types. Roy Huggins, the show's creator-producer, introduced an echo of the Hammett-Chandler tradition by focusing the series on a poker-playing rogue rather than on the sheriffs, marshalls, gunfighters or vigilantes who otherwise dominated the format. Maverick's primary motivation, Huggins wrote in a memo to his writing staff, had to be 'easy money' rather than justice. Like Sam Spade, Bret Maverick is a hero by default, not intention.

Years later, Huggins revealed the autobiographical source of his career-long insistence on grey-hatted heroes to have been his own unheroic experience as a friendly witness for the House Un-American Activities Committee. Huggins told Victor Navasky that he had in fact 'named names', citing a failure of nerve which he would regret for the rest of his life. Accordingly, his protagonists, from Maverick to Dr Richard Kimble of *The Fugitive* to Jim Rockford of *Rockford Files*, do not seek the limelight, but typically find themselves pushed into dilemmas that force them to take action, even though they'd rather be at home watching television. But these characters succeed in doing the right thing anyway, something the man who imagined them had been unable to do.

In the movie, Mel Gibson plays the title character created by James Garner for television, and, in the kind of ineffectual self-reflexive flourish that characterises all three films, James Garner plays the father of the character he created some forty years earlier. In a reasonable updating, Jodie Foster is added as a professional and romantic foil to Gibson. Interestingly, Huggins had tried a similar female character during the 1958–59 season, but dropped her the following year. The Gibson-Foster-Garner combination makes for some snappy repartee and things might have worked out if only somebody on the set had been paying attention to continuity.

Maverick contains a plot that does nothing but thicken until it cannot function as a plot any more. The movie keeps promising some kind of spectacular dénouement, but delivers nothing but more promises. Whenever the disarray tests the limits of audience attention too severely, a scene with a shirtless Gibson or provocatively dressed Foster, or both, is added as a holding action before returning to the mystery of the sclerotic narrative. In the last scene, as it is becoming apparent that nothing is going to be resolved in any kind of satisfying way, Gibson is placed in a public bath, wet and wearing nothing but a towel. Weak dramaturgy? Flaccid softcore pornography? Demographic targeting? You've paid your money, take your pick.

The corporate restructuring of the culture industry over the last fifteen years means that today each giant communications holding company owns a diverse collection of broadcast transmitters, satellite transponders, movie studios, cable franchises, recording libraries and most even keep a publishing house or two. Such mergers have reduced the market to so few distributors as to make competition for an audience minimal. It would be hard for anyone to get through a day in America without consuming at least one cultural product each from Time-Warner, General Electric and Ted Turner. It is the search for raw materials that has become desperate. The cultural takeover of movies by television is but one result.

ESCAPE FROM GRAVITY

Janet Abrams

Best known for creating the special effects on such science fiction landmarks as *2001: A Space Odyssey*, *Close Encounters of the Third Kind* and *Blade Runner*, along with *Brainstorm*, which he directed, Douglas Trumbull has devoted his career to motion, as a route to utopia if not as utopia itself. He has consistently aimed to transport the cinema viewer into imaginary landscapes and infinite space, devising techniques and film formats that harness the sense of sight to the sensation of speed.

Ever since the hallucinogenic 'Stargate Sequence' in Stanley Kubrick's *2001*, Trumbull has been preoccupied with overcoming the limiting condition of the cinema screen, as if, with enough acceleration, the audience could actually be propelled across this spectatorial boundary, and the spatio-temporal distinction between 'what lies ahead' and 'the future' might finally be collapsed. Just how much speed does it take? This is the question underlying his film work and, more recently, the motion-simulation rides which employ electronic representation technology to convey the roller-coaster rush of early cinema, and which also recall its antecedents, such primitive 'virtual realities' as painted dioramas and turn-of-the-century mechanical rides to exotic destinations and faked natural disasters. Whether the vehicle in question is man-made and headed into outer space (*2001*, *Silent Running*), alien and headed down to earth (the mother ship in *Close Encounters of the Third Kind*), an LAPD vertical take-off prototype (Deckard's Spinner, a quasi-helicopter, in *Blade Runner*) or a real-life car-of-the-future that simply didn't fly (the DeLorean at the heart of *Back to the Future: The Ride*), the subtext of Trumbull's work is the desire to escape from gravity. The architecture of *Blade Runner*'s begrimed and retrofitted Los Angeles of the early twenty-first century may be curiously nostalgic, with references to visionary designs for the city of the future that date from early *twentieth* century. Yet the whole idea of this aerial motion above and through that encrusted urban domain – as traversed by Deckard's Spinner at corporate heights and polyglot depths – remains compellingly 'futuristic'. The Freudian dream of flight has been accomplished as a purely optical experience through motion-control cinematography; now, in the rides that Trumbull's IMAX Ridefilm Corporation has developed for the Universal Studios Theme Parks in Florida and California, and for Circus Circus' Luxor Casino, Las Vegas, that experience can be extended to the entire body.

Back to the Future: The Ride first opened in Orlando in May 1991 after three and a half years of development; since the opening of the second installation in Hollywood, in June 1993, the two riders have drawn an average of 25,000 people per day and the combined attendance now exceeds 30 million. The overwhelming popularity of this ride suggests an augmented public appetite for the experience of speed itself, as visceral commodity, and for thrill without threat of personal danger. Arguably this appetite has been the common driving force behind a diversity of entertainments over the last century, including theme park rides and movies; the railroad vista and chase sequence have long been staple elements in adventure movies. But such recent films as *Speed* and *Terminal Velocity* indicate that motion, if maintained at frenzied levels and channelled through sufficiently varied modes of transportation, can provide the narrative thread on which to hang a suspense story on its own. This points to a qualitative change in the social threshold of perception – as if we now require higher doses and a greater rate of acceleration to register speed at all, and feel innoculated against the risk of technological catastrophe which such speed implicitly portends.

As Wolfgang Schivelbusch has observed in his study of early rail travel, *The Railway Journey*, the cultural response, in the nineteenth century, to this new form of accelerated motion, was a kind of trauma analogous to industrial fatigue, likened by contemporary medical experts to the 'shock' of battle; the elaborate upholstery of railway carriages was a conspicuous attempt to alleviate both the physical *and* psychological symptoms of this trauma.

'One of the essential new stimuli of the train journey is its speed, which expresses itself as dispersed perception of foreground objects, as the feeling of the annihilation of space and time. This new stimulus at first merely irritates the traveller, who is still accustomed to the old velocity of the coach. Yet gradually everything connected with the new velocity becomes psychically assimilated.' Schivelbusch argues that the development of 'panoramic vision' was a significant part of this psychic adaptation;

by the late nineteenth century the train traveller had adopted forms of behaviour – such as reading on board – that would have been unmanageable for the early traveller because 'the journey still is, for him, a space-time adventure that engages his entire sensorium'.

In a curious reversal of the earlier situation, late twentieth-century travel has effectively been stripped of any such sense of adventure, and indeed is almost devoid of physical motion. We have become accustomed to the plane journey as a period of enforced stasis, strapped into regimented rows of seats, while the journey's primary 'view' is the in-flight movie. Inside this cylinder, the only real gauge of movement comes from the 'soundtrack' of the engines, and any untoward turbulence that may intervene to remind us of the oddity of floating – or hurtling – through air at high altitude.

This very denaturing of velocity has perhaps stimulated some of the craving for artificial re-enactments of the 'annihilation of space and time' that early rail passengers encountered. Motion-stimulation rides once again 'engage the entire sensorium', thoroughly disrupting the viewer's sense of space and time by synchronising the hydraulics of a seating platform with the kinetics of motion-control film. In these rides, the nineteenth-century railway traveller's 'panoramic vision' has its counterpart in Omnimax cinematography, projected with a fisheye lens onto a spherical screen – the surrogate carriage window.

Trumbull's Luxor ride entitled *In Search of the Obelisk* offers a fairly dazzling (and deafening) illustration of the late twentieth-century genre of 'immersive' entertainment. It is the first of a trio of attractions that opened at the casino/hotel in October 1993; they are conceived as a prototype that could fit in a shopping mall or other urban venue, rather than at the theme parks and World's Fairs which have, until now, been the primary locations of such non-conventional film presentation.

You enter the motion base, sit down in one of the sixteen high-backed seats moulded to resemble those in fancy racing cars, fasten your safety belt and pretend that you feel confident about what's going to happen next. The lights go down. Suddenly there's a jolt, you reach instinctively for the sides of your seat, and for the next four minutes you feel like a solitary sock in a demented spin dryer.

Centre-screen, a man on some kind of space-age moped is careering through a forest of crystalline obelisks; you follow, as if riding pillion, as he veers over precipices and around sharp corners, narrowly avoiding collision with looming obstacles and other flying contraptions. When he lurches, you lurch; when he jolts back, you hurtle sickeningly hard in the same direction. Looking over his shoulder, he purports to catch sight of his unexpected payload, then proceeds to yell out warnings to his passengers as the journey spirals through increasingly turbulent terrain, a giddy vortex of stalactites that's part pyramid, part Piranesi. The sound is enveloping, the visual landscape kaleidoscopic.

Trumbull disparages much other work in the simulation business for having 'headed down the path of cheap commercialisation. Mounting the camera on the front of a dune buggy or a jet ski, to get nothing but the rush of speed, may be OK for a carnival environment, but it's not cinema as far as I'm concerned.' What differentiates Ridefilm motion-simulation rides from mere carnival rides, he claims, is drama. 'There's dialogue, character development, suspense – all the normal cinematic elements. But it's not somebody else who's getting shot at or catapulted out of a rocket. It's you. This is what I'm most interested in: the direct first-person experience.'

Thus the Luxor ride places each spectator, as it were, *inside* Dave's cockpit in *2001*; the feeling of disorientation that the viewer registers, empathetically, on actor Keir Dullea's face in the Stargate Sequence counter-shots, now becomes their own. The role of the cockpit is significant, or rather, the absence of such a definitive enclosure is crucial to the commercial viability of the Ridefilm module. Whereas in *Back to the Future: The Ride* viewers are seated inside a DeLorean car, in the Luxor ride the vehicle is shorn of its roof, strangely denuded, or half-evolved like a funfair carousel minus its colourful turret. This partial characterisation avoids foreclosure on what can be told: the appropriate vehicle interior can be 'completed' via on-screen projection. Environment changes as a function of the film being screened; cockpit hardware rematerialises as computer software.

As an industrial object that occupies resolutely earthbound real space, the Ridefilm motion base is fascinating in its sheer hybrid awkwardness: part flying carpet, part fantasy conveyance and (mostly) cumbersome contraption. Styling is reserved for the seats and their immediate surround, but the anchoring undercroft – the criss-cross lacing of hydraulic rams, valves and metal beams that actually makes the whole platform move in x, y and z axes – can be clearly seen as the 'working parts' by departing punters. Like gigantic bedsprings under a vast mattress, this heavy structure is left unconcealed, perhaps with the intention of arousing the kind of awe that the dynamo inspired in Henry Adams at the 1900 Paris Exposition. But such admiration is pure nostalgic displacement, since the true 'mechanism' of the ride is now embodied in digital code on Silicon Graphics computers; the motion-base armature is merely its robotic extension. (The 'narrative' of the ride appears on the ride-operator's control screen as a graphical display like a musical score or electrocardiogram, a visual abstraction that condenses two kinds of movement, actual and recorded.)

One of the more obvious features of ride-simulators is their disruption of one's sense of time: a mere few minutes seems to expand to a different order of duration – compensation for the eternity spent queuing up for the eventual thrill. One 'pays' for the short burst of intense motion with a *longue durée* of stasis. Though physically often banal and about as architecturally distinguished as jetways to planes, with which they bear a functional kinship, these queuing spaces (as any visitor to Disneyland knows) are far from neutral. Calibrated into successive zones of different duration, they are characterised by contextual props and a profusion of overhead monitors on which video interviews with cast members and other phoney 'backstage' information is relayed. In *Back to the Future: The Ride*, these spaces are used to reintroduce the characters from this trilogy of films that most visitors have seen, and to establish the plot for the ride. Five stages precede the ride itself: the Main Queue Line (45 minutes), the Lobby queue (30 minutes), Pre-Show (six minutes), Holding Room (six minutes) and, finally, Vehicle Garage (the payoff, six minutes).

Carefully modulated storytelling is required in order to ensure that the narrative doesn't overwhelm the effects, and thus dampen the potential for repeat visits. 'You can kill the fun of the ride by telling too strong a story that you don't want to hear again,' Trumbull explains. 'A direct experience is similar to listening to music. You can have it multiple times without any degradation or loss of interest.' Whereas movies have a theatrical lifespan, on first release, of only a few weeks, rides are a more durable form of entertainment. 'A ride may have a market life of ten years. It takes on some of the qualities of *Cats* or *Phantom of the Opera*.'

Trumbull has long been interested in how cinema could change people's physical behaviour. In the early 70s, while developing the Showscan process (a method of photographing and projecting film at 60 frames per second), he found that a dramatic increase in frame-rate produced corresponding increases in a viewer's heart rate, galvanic skin response, respiration level and electro-encephalogram.

The physiological effects may be understood but the psychological ramifications are less certain. 'There's a tremendous appetite for altered states,' Trumbull asserts, quickly modifying the remark. 'For *socially acceptable* altered states.' When he talks of motion-simulation rides as 'having the potential to offer profound transformational experiences... to modify the way people feel and behave', he surely intends to imply the kind of spiritual transcendence that has always been an undercurrent of his work.

But the focus on the technology necessary to produce such brief interludes of otherness diverts us from a more elusive question: what *is* The Ride and where does it lead us? Is it a quest to be ejected from our normal, grounded bodily selves and then brought back? What does it mean to take a seat – whether in the plush of the cinema, or the seat-belt secured rows of the jetplane, or the vibrating platform of the motion-simulation ride – and submit to a journey whose destination is anticipated but ultimately indeterminate? Motion-simulation rides, for all their vaunted 'modernity', may be closer than we might think to the mechanical rides which emerged in parallel with the railway. Those rides sought to domesticate the 'shock' of emerging industrial culture by mimicking its routine, and re-enacting its physical and psychological disturbances under safely contained circumstances. Contemporary rides could be seen as the equivalent for an age in which information technologies are vaunted as conduits to another kind of sublime yet amorphous landscape: the abyss of infinite data. As the primacy of the physical body in real space yields to the miasma of free-floating minds in cyberspace, perhaps these cinematic diversions offer short, sharp shocks that shake us from our post-industrial fatigue.

*   *   *

Blade Runner: Tyrell Building – Approach

I proposed to Ridley Scott that the Tyrell Building be a sort of Mayan pyramid with Art Deco detail. We didn't have much money to build models, so we kept flipping them around. We only built one pyramid and it only had two sides; it was about six feet wide at the base and two at the top. We shot it two ways and then composited them together. This scene is actually comprised of six different optical elements; the building on the left, the building on the right, the lens flare, the vehicle itself, the sky and the distant horizon. Each element is shot individually on colour negative, then processed, screened and checked for focus and movement. Then we make an inter-positive as well as a matte of each element. For instance, a piece of white card would be placed behind the pyramid to create an edge, and we'd shoot the matte on a separate piece of film using exactly

the same motion – that's why motion control is so important. Deckard's Spinner is actually not moving at all: it's just a miniature mounted on a rod from behind. The camera is on a motion-control rig, so it can pan, tilt and track in and out relative to the Spinner. The Spinner alone requires several exposures; in addition to the lens flare, which happens in the camera, there are four separate exposures: the Spinner's surface, illuminated with off-camera lights; the inboard lights; the very bright lights coming off its top that expand beyond the vehicle; and the Spinner body, shot as a silhouette, to produce a matte. A combination of maybe thirty different lights, inside and out, are used to create the reflective sheen on the Tyrell pyramid.

Blade Runner: Tyrell Building – Inside

The upper part of the window and the column tops are a matte painting. The background was a retouched photomontage front-projected onto a large screen. The sun was added at the very end, as a separate exposure. When the actors walk in front of the sun we had to rotoscope them. We replaced the sun matte painting with a very bright light, behind a hole on the animation stand, and hand-painted a little black mask so that the actor would appear to be blocking the light for a moment, but you'd get a natural lens flare as though ten stops overexposed, creating a big halo.

Blade Runner: Memory Bubbles

While we were shooting the film I was anticipating all these memory bubble sequences. So we had a 35mm camera with a fisheye lens on it standing by, alongside the main unit, to grab shots simultaneously with the main unit, of images we knew would need to be in the memory bubbles. So there were thousands of feet of that. There were also a lot of still photographs in the memory bubbles – they weren't all moving, it was only the foreground ones that were moving. The memory bubble photography

was extremely complicated; it was shot on a motion-control rig called COMPSY, computerised multiplane camera system. This was about the most sophisticated motion-control camera my partner Dick Yuricich and I built. Some of those scenes had virtually hundreds of exposures on each frame of movie film; it was the same technique I used at the end of the film for the angelic, god, infinity sequences, and some of those were over 750 exposures on each frame of film. It was horrendous. That was the peak of that kind of photography. These days we would do it with computer graphics, much more quickly.

2001: Pod Sequence

In some of these, when Keir Dullea has his helmet on, you're seeing the reflections of off-screen 16mm films, as well as all the lights and instrumentation and the HAL readouts inside the Pod. In the sequence when he's being locked outside, and doesn't have his helmet on, some films are being projected on to his face. It makes no sense, but it looks great.

2001: Stargate Sequence

I'd met the experimental film-maker John Whitney, so I had some idea about his technique of making many exposures onto a single frame of film, automatically. John was working on a device for moving a slit across a film frame, and moving artwork behind the slit, to create patterns and textures and things. I never actually saw this thing; I just had a picture in my mind. But it occurred to me that if you could do that flat, you could do it three-dimensionally as well. After an experiment, I walked across the studio to Kubrick's office and said, 'I'm going to need to build a machine as big as a house, with tracks and motors, and big pieces of glass to scale this whole thing up.' He said, 'I think you're right. Do it, get it, whatever you need.' The pieces of artwork were on kodalith transparencies about four or five feet tall by ten or twelve feet long: hundreds of patterns from Op Art books; strange grids out of *Scientific American* magazine; electron microscope photographs blown up high contrast and reversed; lots of things I drew. Very strange patterns, plus coloured gels, mounted together on a huge light table. The camera was mounted on a track, moving in one direction, while the artwork was moving behind the slit in another. There's the sense of plunging into a space that has infinite depth. There was no name for this procedure, because it had never been done before. I called it Slitscan. I don't know what Whitney called it.

Back to the Future

This is a miniature DeLorean car flying into a miniature dinosaur. The car is actually about a foot high, hanging on wires. The dinosaur was a 29-channel digitally controlled robot, about nine feet high. Everything was scaled to facilitate the pivotal scene where the car goes into the dinosaur's mouth, using a specially made 5" by 15" camera.

Luxor: Pyramids

We created the Luxor ride in 18 months: a real crash program. Many of the scenes are mostly models with some computer graphics added, but this scene, where we're entering one of the underground pyramids, is entirely computer-generated. It would be virtually impossible to do as a miniature. Whatever the shortcomings in the images, in terms of colour and so on, the fluid could be moving, and there could be reflection, and self-matted things. Every pyramid is undulating while vehicles fly among them. We felt the potential of computer graphics was just passing some critical feasibility point at that moment.

Luxor: Crypto Egypt

This is a live action full-scale set piece, foreground, with two actors having a fight. The background is a miniature, and the whole thing is digitally composited. There's a moment in the simulation ride where we have several vehicles flying through a completely computer-generated environment, and there are rockets flying around leaving con trails. That's when the computer really got bogged down: dealing with reflection mapping, texture mapping, multiple vehicles and trying to compute how much opacity there is through the smoke of the con trails. We got to the point where this giant IBM Power Visualisation Computer could only manufacture twelve frames a day. That's two hours of computing-time per frame. We had to write a lot of special code to link up the Wavefront computer to the IBM PVC, and also to create the fisheye view, which is then projected onto a hemispherical screen. The computer actually has to warp the image.

The Luxor's orthogonal motion base allows you to keep the audience together, because if you rolled or pitched, you would disconnect from the screen: the person sitting in the left seat would be moving up while the person in the right seat is moving down. In the film you're seeing a certain kind of motion – diving over a cliff or turning right, or whatever – and everybody on the motion base must feel the same thing. One of the things about a simulation experience is that you not only have to feel the dynamic motion of flying or turning, but also very subtle motion: vibrations. If you were driving down Broadway, you would feel the texture of pitted asphalt plus potholes – a series of very subtle vibrations. We record that as a sound wave, and put it directly into the servo-electronic system that operates the valves controlling the flow of hydraulic fluid into the hydraulic rams. So we can create a physical sensation of sound. This is a process we've patented, called a 'high-frequency injection'.

L.A. Confidential (Curtis Hanson, 1997)

Section 5: Indie Pulp and Neo-noir

'The 90s are full of dumbness,' writes B. Ruby Rich. The pervasiveness of High Concept since the 80s, in which the marketability of a film was measured by whether the film could be summarised in a pitch of twenty-five words or less, meant that the Action/Spectacle film in the 90s was widely believed to have deteriorated into an assault on the senses whose hyperinflated production values underscored its basic infantilism. The opposite of this type of cinema – the subject of this section – was seen to be another type of action or crime film, an independent or lower budget alternative, which also offered violence as spectacle but with an even greater brutalism, and which combined pulp and noir references in a leaner production with heavy dosages of pop cultural pastiche. These films were seen to have the story, characterisation, subtle use of *mise en scène* and the stylish cine-literacy that cloddish big-budget efforts seemed to lack. This section examines some of their origins.

Manohla Dargis argues that this type of cinema, perhaps best exemplified by the work of Tarantino, is indebted to old pulp fictions that cut across genres but whose mainstay was the detective novel. Dargis notes that 'pulp is lurid, wild, sensational, cheap. Located in mean and naked streets, trailer parks, coughs of dust off lonely ribbons of asphalt, pulp movies are non-suburban and agressively anti-80s'. Dargis sees Tarantino as 'the new point man on pulp', but argues that directors as dissimilar as Carl Franklin, Tamra Davis and Peter Medak are also limning similar terrain. In the piece that follows, Amy Taubin delineates the controversy over *Reservoir Dogs* and analyses the film's representation of violence arguing that the film is 'desperate to preserve screen violence as a white male privilege'. B. Ruby Rich also looks at *Reservoir Dogs* and argues that art movies and independent films are now cornering their share of the market by trading in violence. She discusses a range of films including *Reservoir Dogs*, *Hard-Boiled* and *Bad Lieutenant* and bemoans them as examples of how 'the self-consciousness of neo-violence has become the ultimate hip'.

In Rich's second piece, she traces the genre of neo-noir. Just as Dargis found *Reservoir Dogs* to signal the return of pulp, Rich finds Tarantino to be the 'magician' of neo-noir. Neo-noir is seemingly the key exemplar of contemporary pulp. Rich describes the genre as one where 'the women are irresistibly sexy and inexplicably evil, the men as dumb as they come and heading for a fall. No one can be trusted and everything is *déjà vu*, and happy endings aren't even a dream in anyone's head. The style is over the top, the camerawork flashy and giddily self-conscious, and the script tends to a certain smugness toward its own characters.' Rich argues that 'the vacuum of authenticity is a key component for neo-noir, signifying as it does its membership in postmodernism. Thus the reliance on quotations, homage and appropriation, all elements that fuel the audience's pleasure and undermine the character's claim to meaning.' The last piece in this section is Amy Taubin's interview with director Curtis Hanson on *L.A. Confidential,* glossily noir and, according to Taubin, 'the kind of picture that supposedly couldn't be made in Hollywood any more'. Throughout this section we get an illustration of how indie films, suckled as they often are on old Hollywood pulp, in turn help nourish Hollywood's newest noir.

PULP INSTINCTS

Manohla Dargis

Bone-shattering, skin-splitting, blood-spurting, Quentin Tarantino's cinema of viscera is written on the flesh of outlaw men and women. In his latest movie *Pulp Fiction*, he returns to a world of casual violence and blunt sentiment, one fuelled by a hard-boiled past and fired by a pop-happy present. In this world, where the coffee's always black and the cigarettes are surely unfiltered, the divide between the normal and the pathological isn't just blurred, it's obsolete.

Tarantino is the new point man on pulp, but he isn't the only director twisting hard-boiled style into contemporary paradigms. Directors as dissimilar as Carl Franklin (*One False Move*), Tamra Davis (*Guncrazy*) and Peter Medak (*Romeo is Bleeding*) are limning similar terrain, seduced by an aesthetic whose allure is obvious, if not always simple. Pulp is lurid, wild, sensational, cheap. Located in mean and naked streets, trailer parks, coughs of dust off lonely ribbons of asphalt, pulp movies are non-suburban and aggressively anti-80s. Their meat is murder and all manner of mental, emotional and physical rot – a poverty-row vision at far remove from the steadicam, no-grain gloss of Spielberg, Lucas and their technologies of opulence.

The term 'pulp' comes from magazines that surfaced around the turn of the century, deposed the dime novel and endured through World War II. Although the name originates from the groundwood paper on which the magazines were printed, the christening was felicitous given the condition of the heroes and miscreants by the stories' end. Pulp cut across genres, embracing westerns ('oaters') and tales of horror, mystery and adventure, but its mainstay was the detective story. Dashiell Hammett and Raymond Chandler wrote for the pulps, as did Cornell Woolrich, John D. MacDonald, Mickey Spillane and a company of others. James M. Cain and Jim Thompson made their reputation through novels that were definitively pulp.

Every so often the pulps made it on to film, where the gore was staunched and the sex turned down to a careful simmer. The most celebrated of these movies were adapted from popular detective fiction – for instance *The Maltese Falcon* and *Double Indemnity* – studio pictures with stars and plenty of A-movie lustre. Far closer in spirit to the pulp writing, however, were the films critic Manny Farber described as 'roughneck'. Directed by the likes of Hawks, Wellman, Walsh and Mann, these were 'faceless movies, taken from a type of half-polished trash writing... Tight, cliché-ridden melodramas about stock musclemen.' It was these that the young men of *Cahiers du cinéma* claimed as their own, even if, as with the 'cinema of quality', they sometimes had to kill Daddy first.

In a 1955 *Cahiers*, Claude Chabrol wrote rather disingenuously: 'The [American] film thriller is no more: the novel likewise. The source has dried up; renewal is impossible.' In the March 1959 issue, Luc Moullet characterised Sam Fuller's work with bombast: '[W]e see everything other directors deliberately excise from their films: disorder, filth, the unexplainable, the stubbly chin, and a kind of fascinating ugliness in a man's face.' Moullet called Fuller a tellurian director, a primitive. That same year Godard began work on *Breathless*.

Chabrol and company championed Hollywood hires such as Nicholas Ray (especially), Hawks, Mann and Aldrich, drawn to the raw passion, poetic *mise en scène* and consummate professionalism of their movies. So it's no surprise that when these critics turned directors, they looked to the same pulp wellspring that had supplied their idols. Truffaut's second feature was a lyrical take on David Goodis' novel *Shoot the Piano Player*. Made in 1960, the result is at once *nouvelle vague* and Hollywood noir, the cigarette that droops from Charles Aznavour's mouth as authentic and heart-rending as any of Bogart's Lucky Strikes. Truffaut would later make *The Bride Wore Black*, based on a *roman* noir by Cornell Woolrich.

Meanwhile, in Hollywood, sociological changes and a slackening production code created an atmosphere in which an American New Wave could thrive. In the 60s and into the 70s directors as distinct as Penn, the later Siegel, Peckinpah, Friedkin, Coppola and Scorsese reinvigorated genre with graphic, highly personalised stories of outlaws, gangsters, mobsters and detectives. From *Bonnie and Clyde* to *Mean Streets* and beyond, pulp defined the subject matter, look and texture of the great US films – except that now the directors weren't hacks but auteurs, begging the question of how genuine this new instinct for pulp was, and the aesthetic limits of blood and guts.

Pure pulp went subterranean in the 80s, though A-list horror and action franchises such as *Alien*, *Die Hard*, *Lethal Weapon* and *Terminator* flourished. Then, in 1992, came Quentin Tarantino's *Reservoir Dogs*, and 'bang, bang' pulp was back. A narrative of torture and tortured narrative, *Reservoir Dogs* is the story of a well-planned heist that turns bloody. Although based loosely on Kubrick's 1956 feature *The Killing* (co-written by pulp icon Jim Thompson), Tarantino's film is in fact more Fulleresque, but refracted through *Black Mask* pulps, European art movies, Roger Corman's New World Pictures and Godard – the red that oozes out of Mr Orange's body as self-consciously gaudy as the tissue gnawed by the cannibal radicals in *Weekend*. A pasticheur and pop-cultural relativist, the Thirty-one-year-old Tarantino is as at home with Elvis as he is with Steve McQueen, Pam Grier and Shakespeare. And even more than with *Reservoir Dogs*, his screenplays for *True Romance* (directed by Tony Scott) and *Pulp Fiction* are scattershot with references to movies and TV ('Riddle me this, Batman').

Tarantino shares in his generation's cheerful bad taste and prodigious appetite for the good, the bad and the idiotic. Sonny Chiba, *The Partridge Family*, *The Brady Bunch*, 'Frankie Says Relax', *Superfly T.N.T.*, *The Guns of Navarone*, *Deliverance*, *La Femme Nikita*, *Kiss Me Deadly* and A Flock of Seagulls are just some of the most obvious allusions in *Pulp Fiction*. Like Godard, who once described the initial period of the *nouvelle vague* as '*films de cinephile* – the work of film enthusiasts', Tarantino enjoys raiding movie history, which is why in *Pulp Fiction* a steak isn't just a slab of beef but a joke-in-waiting.

VINCENT: 'I'll have the Douglas Sirk steak.'
WAITER: 'How d'ya want it, burnt to a crisp, or bloody as hell?'

An admitted Godard enthusiast, Tarantino writes scripts that recall the French auteur's work pre-1967 – in style, if not in politics (his are the children of Godard and

Coca-Cola). *Reservoir Dogs* not only riffs on Kubrick's curves in *The Killing*, but in its linear kinkiness, casual nihilism and playful self-consciousness echoes Godard films such as *Band of Outsiders* (the name of Tarantino's production company), *Alphaville* and *Pierrot le fou*. *Pulp Fiction* too has a playful structure, with three bridged stories framed by a prologue and epilogue. Although the title refers to the hard-boiled writing of the past, the story and characters are straight out of the pop culture storehouse. Very loosely, the triptych rotates around the violent misadventures of a collection of couples including a king pin and his wife, a team of gangsters, at least two pairs of love-birds and a set of lunatic hayseeds.

Tenderised bodies

At its most demented, *Pulp Fiction* reads like a hybrid of women's romance fiction and EC Comics, equal parts love and splattertoon. Its funniest and grisliest scene turns on the efforts of a male foursome to clean the carnage from a Chevy Nova before the wife of one of the men returns. ('If she comes home from a hard day's work and finds a bunch of gangsters doin' a bunch of gangsta' shit in her kitchen, ain't no tellin' what she's apt to do.') In its step-by-step precision, the scene evokes the elaborate heist in Jules Dassin's *Du Rififi chez les hommes*, in which the thieves' impossible skill works as an ironic counterpoint to their disdain for the bourgeois workaday grind. It's also cheerfully self-reflexive, since the orchestration of the purge could easily pass for a crash course in spectacle-making with the Wolf (Harvey Keitel reprising his *Nikita* role) acting as captain of the clean-up and the scene's producer, negotiating the actors and their actions amid the slaughter ('Give me the principals' names again').

Tarantino played up the stagecraft of his violence in *Reservoir Dogs* and *True Romance* (Tim Roth's undercover rehearsal, for one). But, in *Pulp Fiction*, his elaborations exist in double time, in that the scene is as much about the damage unleashed by boys-who-will-be-boys as a poke at male-female relations through the women who either enter stage right, or don't. Even if the film's central relationship is between two men, virtually all the tough guys in *Pulp Fiction* are already hooked to a woman, or on the verge.

But so far Tarantino has written only one female part as juicy as the roles he has scripted for men (Alabama in *True Romance*), and in this respect his odds are comparable to many of the pulp auteurs. Women in pulp are more likely to be dead by act three than their men. In Peter Medak's slick neo-noir *Romeo is Bleeding*, however, screenwriter Hilary Henkin revisits the story of a bad man and a worse woman for some gleeful feminist sport. The Romeo in question is Jack Grimaldi, a crooked cop who's keeping himself busy with a wife, a mistress, a Russian gangster named Mona and the mob. Hard-boiled and soft-spoken, Mona is a *femme fatale* for the 90s, a woman who squeezes the fight out of a man just by clamping together her steely thighs (she's an aerobicised nutcracker). A film about the lies women tell men and the lies men tell themselves, *Romeo is Bleeding* takes its self-conscious inspiration from Chandler and the old hard-boiled school. But while the execution is more cool than pulp, the payoff is a film in which the conventional, overdetermined fear of women is the point and not the price of the story. ('She's very modern,' a character says of Mona, 'she wants it all, you know the kind.')

Romeo is Bleeding is just one of a clutch of new pulps that are revisionist in spirit and, occasionally in execution. Another is Carl Franklin's expert suspense movie *One False*

Move, which plies questions of race, sex and class with such discreet fluency it's easy to miss them altogether. Tamra Davis' *Guncrazy*, initially shot for television broadcast, is pulp through and through, from bad-seed star Drew Barrymore to its tale of doomed love on the run. But its title and *l'amour fou* hook notwithstanding, Davis' film bears little relation to Joseph H. Lewis' noir. Instead, with its trailer-park Lolita and wicked step-daddy, it echoes James M. Cain's trashy (pseudo-)incest novel *The Butterfly*, except that this time the point of view belongs to the vixen cum victim. The kick of *One False Move* and *Guncrazy* is that they put characters – who in the past would have been supporting at best, background at worst – front and centre.

But despite these nods towards women and blacks, the new pulp remains largely white and male – if white and male with a difference. An entire history of American genre film could be traced on the bruised and besieged white male body. From westerns and gangster films to male-centred melodramas and war movies, America's great directors have displayed spectacular fascination with male bodies at risk. And whether it's Dustin Hoffman's myopia in *Straw Dogs*, the tired bones of the gunslingers in *The Wild Bunch* or De Niro's bloat in *Raging Bull*, it's risk that is answered and redeemed by pain.

The new pulp spins that familiar male pain into different contexts and conditions. Unlike the slow-motion waltzes into death in Peckinpah's *The Wild Bunch* or John Woo's *The Killer*, the torment in *Reservoir Dogs* is measured out drop by anguished, elemental drop. From first scene to last, Tarantino decelerates pain. No longer discreet in its blood-letting, the wounded body in today's pulp spurts the fountains of gore that were once the reserve of Mario Bava and Hammer Studio spectaculars. It's this graphic aspect of cinematic suffering that excites censors and moral watchdogs who credit social ills to film violence, as if a gurgling bullet hole were more culpable than the neat wounds of Hollywood past and present. But there is something agonisingly poignant about all the meat, bone and viscera. Woo employs a tender violence in his films (his victims are tenderised). Riddled with wounds that yawn open like so many stigmata, his bodies are a graphic testimony to the humanity and divinity of human flesh.

In Hollywood action pictures such as *Die Hard* and *Lethal Weapon*, the hero is bruised but never beaten: like an inflatable rubber clown he bounces back with an idiot grin for more ('do it again'). In movie after movie, he takes punches, kicks, even bullets to prove the inviolability of both his body and the franchise (see it again). In contrast, Woo provides his stars with exquisite deaths – the crawl into fate in *The Killer* being exemplary – only to resurrect them in the next film. (Is it any coincidence that so many pulp directors are Catholic?) But the need for redemption reaches fever pitch in Abel Ferrara's *Bad Lieutenant*, in which a nameless man suffers for the sins of masculinity, whiteness and the law. Here, the Reagan hardbody once idealised by Schwarzenegger and Stallone is transformed into something vulnerable, soft, as if masculinity itself were being battered into new shapes.

Ferrara makes a strong case for the fact that in pulp the word 'why' is a waste of breath. Neither the detective nor the outlaw are creatures of deep psychology; they are men of action, sensation, occasional humour ('build my gallows high, baby'), even men of God, if not necessarily reverent. When Warren Oates shoots at a conspicuously dead man in Peckinpah's *Bring Me the Head of Alfredo Garcia*, he says to no one in particular: 'Why? Because it feels so good.' Hammett's Continental Op pursues a similar tack: 'I began to throw my right fist into him. I liked that. His belly was flabby, and it got softer every time I hit it. I hit it often.'

Terror in the mirror

For all its often cheap flourishes of Freud, pulp is best characterised by unfathomables such as alienation, absolutes such as greed. (In Fuller's *The Naked Kiss*, a man's sick sex-talk is explained post haste by the fact that he's a child molester.) In its deployment of such old-fashioned truths as lust and jealousy, pulp honours a Manichean universe, going against the swells of politically, morally and ethically correct behaviour. Pulp heroes smoke, they drink, fuck and sometimes kill with abandon. They aren't in twelve-step programmes, would rather give a bullet than take one, and are always and forever alone.

While the new pulp trades on familiar style – unornamented, violent and quintessentially American – the fears it traffics in are fresh. There's a scene in *True Romance* where a white character insults the white mobster who has been torturing him with a virulently racist and funny story involving Africans, Italians and eggplants. At first the story seems unmotivated – until the torturer shoots the storyteller and ends the abuse. That racism can be answered by death is just one of the scene's brutal lessons. Another is that there is a complex snarl of masculinity, race and ethnicity that binds the male body, no matter its colour. For Tarantino, race and masculinity are conspicuous, determining and never beside the point.

The great pulp writer Charles Willeford (*Pick-Up, Cockfighter*) begins *Miami Blues* with the line: 'Frederick J. Frenger, Jr., a blithe psychopath from California, asked the flight attendant in first class for another glass of champagne and some writing materials.' The words don't burn as brightly as Cain's legendary opener to *The Postman Always Rings Twice* ('They threw me off the hay truck about noon'), but Willeford's meaning is clear. Like the ticking bomb that launches *Touch of Evil*, the words signal new dangers and violences, unexpected, casual, unbound, close ('In his new clothes Freddy looked like a native Miamian'). *Miami Blues* is the first in a quartet of novels about a weary homicide detective by the name of Hoke Moseley. By the end of the last one, *The Way We Die Now*, Moseley will have been irrevocably forced out of bachelor seclusion into something very much like a female commune. That the final book also chronicles a case of black bondage is an index of the terrain Willeford charts, a world not unlike that explored by Eastwood in *Unforgiven* and *A Perfect World*.

As with the very best pulp authors, Willeford explores a landscape in which an obsession with safety (border controls, vaccines, defence initiatives, the 'armed response' signs that litter neighbourhood lawns) produces nothing but terror. It's a terror that can surface in a radioactive suitcase, in life on the edge, or in the strangulated comfort of home. But more often than not it's the kind of terror that turns up in the bathroom mirror first thing in the morning, terror that puts guns in hands, bullets in bodies, blood on the streets. 'And he was there, of course,' wrote Thompson in *Savage Night*. 'Death was there. And he smelled good.' Forty years later in *Pulp Fiction* Tarantino pens a character who witnesses a miracle. 'I'm tryin' real hard to be a shepherd,' says Jules. The wonder of it is, he's trying at all.

THE MEN'S ROOM

Amy Taubin

Tim Roth came to the US to act in the kind of films that aren't happening in Britain, the kind of films, he says, that Allan Clarke would be making if he were still alive. Roth made his television film debut in 1983 as the ferocious skinhead in Clarke's *Made in Britain*, then followed with Mike Leigh's *Meantime*, as part of an ensemble that included Gary Oldman and Phil Daniels. 'That's what I thought film-making was,' he says ruefully.

Currently Roth can be seen on screen in New York and Paris in Quentin Tarantino's *Reservoir Dogs*, coming soon to wherever else the international language of male violence is spoken. The film's structure is pegged to the length of time it takes for a man – Roth's character, Mr Orange – to bleed to death in front of our eyes. How's that for preserving the dramatic unities?

The debut film of director/writer Tarantino, *Reservoir Dogs*, a bungled heist movie, was notorious even before it premiered at the 1992 Sundance Film Festival. It did not win a prize; reportedly, the jury felt that since Tarantino had already catapulted, at age twenty-nine, on to the Hollywood 'A' list, he didn't need its help, reducing the status of the competition to a charity agency. Especially as the film that did win was Alexandre Rockwell's *In the Soup*, a more innocuous male-bonding film, which, like *Reservoir Dogs*, soft-shoes around the connection between independent film-making and gangsterism.

Cover-story material for the *L.A. Weekly*, the *Village Voice*, *Positif* and a slue of dailies, Tarantino's bio is already common knowledge: how he obsessively watched movies from the age of five; how he never went to film school, but honed his skills by simultaneously working in a video store (where he had unlimited access to the oeuvres of his heroes, Peckinpah, Leone, Scorsese, Ferrara, Argento, De Palma, Schrader), writing scripts (almost all of which are now in production) and attending acting classes (he had some bit parts on television).

Tarantino originally intended to make *Reservoir Dogs* in 16mm for $30,000. Then a friend got the script to Harvey Keitel. Keitel's commitment attracted several million dollars and the stellar cast. To the *L.A. Weekly*, Tarantino confessed to being, as a child, 'amazed at the genius of the concept of a horror film and a comedy together' in Abbott and Costello monster movies. To anyone who suggests a moral queasiness about *Reservoir Dogs*' *pièce de résistance* – a ten-minute real-time torture scene in which a psychopath slices up a cop's face, hacks off his ear, and then asks him, 'Was that as good for you as it was for me?' – Tarantino responds: 'I love violence in the movies.' Such surly moments notwithstanding, Tarantino is universally described as charming, enthusiastic, inspirational – precisely the adjectives that were applied to Ross Perot, although not exactly by the same people.

Reservoir Dogs opens with its other *pièce de résistance* – a pre-credit sequence in which a bunch of small-time hoods, breakfasting in a southern California fast-food joint, engage in a close textual analysis of Madonna's 'Like a Virgin'. 'Let me tell you what "Like a Virgin" is about,' says Mr Brown (played by Tarantino). 'It's all about a girl who digs a guy with a big dick. The entire song, it's a metaphor for big dicks... it hurts, it hurts her... The pain is reminding a fuck machine what it once was like to be a virgin. Hence, "Like a Virgin".'

The conversation turns into a debate over the ethics of tipping waitresses. 'Jesus Christ, these ladies aren't starving, they make minimum wage,' objects Mr Pink (Steve Buscemi) when his buddies try to shame him into leaving his buck on the table just like everybody else. To the nostalgic bubblegum rhythms of K-Billy Radio's 'Super Sounds of the Seventies', the group swaggers into the street. Dressed in identical sleazy black suits, narrow black ties and white shirts, they look as if they had migrated down from a poster for, if not the actual celluloid of, Aki Kaurismäki's *Calamari Union*, an influence Tarantino has never to my knowledge cited. The credits roll.

Cut to the interior of a car, where Mr Orange is spurting blood from a bullet in the gut (only his red-soaked shirt, already stuck to his skin, keeps his intestines from protruding). Convulsing, he's begging Mr White, who's driving, to take him to a hospital. Mr White insists that they proceed to a pre-arranged rendezvous point, a cavernous, fluorescent-lit warehouse (the basic location of the film).

With Mr Orange lapsing in and out of consciousness, sprawled on the floor in an ever-deepening pool of his own blood, Mr White and the speedy Mr Pink try to piece together what went wrong. They and the other 'professionals' had been hired by boss-man Joe Cabot (Lawrence Tierney) and his hulking son Nice Guy Eddie (Chris Penn) to carry out a major diamond heist. The robbers have never met before; their colour-coded pseudonyms are intended to protect their identities. Unfortunately, the cops show up before the heist is completed. The hoods shoot their way out, blowing away cops and 'real people'. The survivors are left to ponder who among them is the stooly.

Information accumulates a-chronologically. The set up and aftermath of the heist (although never the heist itself) are revealed in a flashback through the points of view of the various participants. Relishing the dramatic irony, Tarantino reveals the identity of the undercover cop half way through the film, implicating the audience in his point of view and the helplessness of his position. In this world, knowledge gets you nowhere. When the icy psycho Mr Blonde (Michael Madsen, who played Susan Sarandon's concerned boyfriend in *Thelma & Louise*) arrives with a young cop he's kidnapped during the getaway, the violence escalates. By the final blackout, the warehouse is as littered with corpses as the halls of Elsinore.

Though the theatricality of the *mise en scène* and the emphasis on play-acting makes the Shakespearean association inevitable, *Reservoir Dogs* is hardly a tragedy. Hyperbolically visceral and self-conscious (it's the combo that gives the film its bigger bang per buck), it's a black comedy of manners that both brags on and derides its genre and its characters.

Tarantino tips his hand in his bravura set pieces. The undercover cop prepares for his 'interview' with the boss like a method actor rehearsing an audition piece. Identity is a fabrication: lies are as convincing as truth, provided they reference a collective cultural experience and are told with an improvisatory abandon. An event that never happened is given equal screen time. And why not? Isn't this a film about film, about fiction. 'I love violence *in the movies*,' says Tarantino. It's the porno escape value – for him and for us.

Reservoir Dogs conflates masculinity, violence and the underclass. Tarantino's version of masculinity is deeply regressive, specifically rooted in the 70s mass culture of his own childhood. When the undercover cop checks his costume in the mirror, he's Robert Blake in *Baretta*. Indeed, what makes *Reservoir Dogs* such a 90s film is that it's about the return of what was repressed in the television version of 70s masculinity – a paranoid, homophobic fear of the other that explodes in hate speech, in kicks and blows, in bullets and blades. *Reservoir Dogs* is an extremely insular film – women get no more than thirty seconds of screen time, people of colour get zero – yet not a minute goes by without a reference to coons and jungle bunnies, to jailhouse rape (black semen shooting up white asses), to the castration threat of 'phallic' women like Madonna or that 70s icon Pam Grier. (Its insularity also makes *Reservoir Dogs* less interesting, for all its film-making pyrotechnics, than two other recent 'violent arties': Carl Franklin's *One False Move* and Nick Gomez's *Laws of Gravity*.)

If the unconscious of the film is locked in competition with rap culture, it's also desperate to preserve screen violence as a white male privilege. It's the privilege of white male culture to destroy itself, rather than to be destroyed by the other. Violence is the only privilege these underclass men have. It's what allows them to believe that they're the oppressor and not the oppressed (not female, not black, not homosexual).

The problem in *Reservoir Dogs* is that its critique of masculinity is tied up in its money shots; they're one and the same. Mr Blonde carving up the cop and the final bad-joke shoot-out are guarantees of box-office success. This may have been true of previous films that raised the ante on male violence (*The Wild Bunch*, *Taxi Driver*), but now the field is so littered with corpses that it's hard to make a couple of extra pints of blood seem like a transgression.

What's transgressive in *Reservoir Dogs* is not the level of violence or the terrifying realism of bodies that bleed and bleed, but the way Tarantino lays bare the sado-masochistic dynamic between the film and the spectator. The masochistic (feminised) position of the audience is inscribed in Mr Orange's bleeding body. Mr Orange's pain and Mr White's guilt at not being able to save him bind them together in a sado-masochistic relationship that supersedes Mr White's code of professionalism and leads to his destruction and everyone else's as well. Moreover, the torture scene, far from being gratuitous, as many critics have asserted, is a distillation of the slap/kiss manipulation of the film as a whole. Mr Blonde, dancing around the frozen, fascinated cop (who is literally tied to his seat), changing rhythm mid-step, cracking a joke here, slicing off a bit of flesh there, is a stand-in for the director. And his mocking 'Was that as good for you as it was for me?' makes us one with his mutilated victim and leaves no doubt about who's on top.

Amy Taubin talks to Tim Roth about class, acting – and why Tarantino's *Reservoir Dogs* upsets people

No actor, not even Ben Gazzara in John Cassavetes' *The Killing of a Chinese Bookie*, has ever bled as long, agonisingly and profusely as Tim Roth in *Reservoir Dogs*. It's a performance of amazingly technical skill, emotional intensity and, odd as it may sound, comic nuance. Part of what drives Roth as an actor is fierce working-class loyalty that encompasses punks and bohemians, cops and criminals, the mad and the lumpen – all of them aligned against 'yuppies', 'suits' and 'tea-cup holders'.

Roth was brought up politically active. His father was a left-wing journalist; his mother is still an activist. 'When I was a kid, we'd go boycott the National Front. Then I got political myself.' His father had been a tail gunner in the World War II. After the war he changed his name from Smith to Roth. 'As a journalist he was travelling to places where the English weren't welcome, which meant just about anywhere. I like to think he took a German-Jewish name as a political statement.'

In his last year of secondary school, Roth auditioned for a play 'as a joke' and got the part. 'I was very embarrassed. The first night, I got on stage and I pissed in my pants. It sounds like one of those actor tales, but it's true. I got through the first five minutes, and then I thought, this is it, this is what I want to do now, this is the most fun I can possibly have.'

He went to art school, but dropped out when acting in pub theatres began to take up all his time. His first screen role was in Alan Clarke's *Made in Britain* and he hasn't stopped working since. 'Alan was the best. I saw *Scum* ten times. After he died, there were all these Alan Clarke actors walking around London moaning "what are we going to do now".'

About a year and a half ago Roth came to the US to do *Jumpin' at the Boneyard*, an $850,000 indie by first-time director/writer Jeff Stanzler, shot on location in the Bronx. Roth plays an unemployed, massively depressed Irish-American who's desperately trying to save his crack-addicted younger brother. *Boneyard* has some predictable first-film problems, but it deals with class and race in a way that's rare in American movies.

Roth went straight from *Boneyard* to *Reservoir Dogs* and then to *Bodies in Rest and Motion* (described in the advance publicity as 'a blue collar *sex, lies and videotape*'). '*Jumpin' at the Boneyard* could have been set in England. We have that kind of poverty and those kinds of problems. These are universal problems. So to come to America to play that kind of American was important to me – not to play the English bad guy in a 'Die Hard' movie.

'We sell this ridiculous version of England to America. It's not for lack of government financing that the film industry is fucked in England. It's to do with what we let them sell. In the States, you can make a feature film like Nick Gomez's *Laws of Gravity* for $38,000. We could do that in Britain, but no, it's Jeremy Irons and Kenneth Branagh.'

In Roth's terms, the issue isn't nationality, it's class. What Tarantino, Gomez and Abel Ferrara are doing in the US in the 90s is what Clarke and Stephen Frears and Mike Leigh were doing in Britain in the 80s. But by upping the ante on violence, haven't Ferrara and Gomez pushed the working-class art movie into the kind of exploitation Hollywood finds highly commercial? Roth doesn't see it that way.

'I like violent movies if they're true to the experience of violence. Alan Clarke was the king of that because he made films about real people who were in sad situations. Did you ever see *Elephant*? The violence is real, it's political. I love violence in movies because it affects me, it hurts me. I love sex in movies, romance. Violence is just part of that. Christopher Walken – the most unpredictable performance. You never knew if he was happy or sad. You can meet these people on the street; it directly relates to the experience of your life. You got inside those people and an accurate script. They probably wouldn't have given him the money to make it if there hadn't been a lot of guns in it, but they also didn't know what they were getting into when they put their money down.

'Why are they getting concerned all of a sudden about violence. The people in Washington, they're the real gang-bangers. People get upset about *Reservoir Dogs* because Quentin shows you that violence has consequences. People have been lulled into advertising violence instead – nicely shot, beautifully lit, thank you very much, this guy dies, and Mel Gibson's already halfway down the corridor and you've forgotten about the person who's been killed because he never was real.

'People go away from *Reservoir Dogs* thinking they've seen a really violent movie, but they haven't. You see maybe only three specific acts of violence, but it's always impending. It's in the air, in the way they speak and communicate. It's what makes Quentin a great director as opposed to someone who does a violent movie.

'But I'm glad people get upset; it's an upsetting subject. Get used to it. It's going to be around for a long time.'

ART HOUSE KILLERS

B. Ruby Rich

Once upon a time, art movies and independent films were able to corner their share of the market by trading in sex. They delivered on an implicit promise to offer the public more than could be found in mainstream, above-the-waist product. But times have changed. The torch has been passed from sex to violence.

End of an era? The sex tradition goes back to the 60s as the common denominator linking European art cinema with the US and British avant-garde. Think Genet, Jack Smith, Warhol. Look at the post-neo-realism Italians (Fellini, Visconti, Pasolini) or the 60s heyday of British film (*Darling, Blow-Up, Sunday Bloody Sunday*). Nor am I just talking about the past. In the US alone, if you have any doubts about how long a tradition can last, remember that it was *She's Gotta Have It* that made Spike Lee a player and *sex, lies and videotape* that turned Steven Soderbergh into a bankable commodity.

But wait: I note this heritage merely to mark its passing. The new order is obvious in this season's film-festival rosters: both the Toronto Festival of Festivals and the London Film Festival greeted autumn with a wave of neo-violence. Critics are now interested in shining their flashlights on the nouveau thugs of murder and fisticuffs, shock and recoil. Caryn James at the *New York Times* noticed the trend at the New York Film Festival: 'Wading Through Blood to the Festival's Heart'. The Sundance Film Festival is considering a special panel on the subject for January. September's issue of *Movieline* even did a photospread of guns as glamour, with a Smith & Wesson 9mm DA Luger on the coffee table, a Heckler & Koch 9mm submachine gun by the bath, and a tag line that insisted: 'The word this fall on everyone's lips is *firepower*, and the accessory on everyone's hips is a *piece*.'

To replace sex, of course, violence has to provide its audience with the same kind of cathartic release. And it seems to be doing just that. Ignore the rhetoric to the contrary: people are getting off. The fix is in, the rush delivered. Otherwise, the films wouldn't work the way they do and the hype wouldn't be as hot.

Thus trends are made, with films enough to justify all the pontification. The first out of the gate came from the US: Quentin Tarantino's *Reservoir Dogs*. The European community's entry is Rémy Belvaux, André Bonzel and Benoit Poelvoorde's *Man Bites Dog*, which made it even into the New York Film Festival. The king of Hong Kong art-shock, John Woo, continues to draw admirers with his newest feature, *Hard-Boiled*, even as he shifts gears to US production, directing his first Van Damme movie. Abel Ferrara's *Bad Lieutenant* augurs a US rating war for Aries with its sex-violence combo. In the queer contingent, too, sex and violence cohabit and copulate (Gregg Araki's *The Living End*, for instance, or Tom Kalin's *Swoon*). There's even a league of their own for the girls: the London Film Festival has shown both Tamra Davis' *Guncrazy* and Stacy Cochran's *My New Gun*.

The films are pretty different from one another. *Reservoir Dogs*, for instance, signs on to Scorsese territory, starring Harvey Keitel himself as the goodest fella in a gang of heisters who range from professional to undercover to psycho in their behaviour – but are all unmistakably cinematic, their characters drawn from B-movie history. They stage a robbery, they get betrayed, loyalty gets a workout, and a lot of people get killed. It's violence as a language of communication. Nobody is likely to confuse movies with real life after seeing it, despite a publicity campaign that seems to want to sell us on authenticity. Maybe that's what makes a film more moral, less attackable.

Giving the lie to the real-life argument, though, Tarantino's next of kin aesthetically is John Woo. While it's easy to imagine someone thinking they'd found an insight into Hong Kong after seeing *Hard-Boiled* (especially since the Triad shoot-out at the last Hong Kong festival), it's hard to imagine that anyone could argue that its violence is naturalistic, realistic or believable. More likely, the violence brings to mind Peckinpah crossed with Kurosawa, choreography drawn with blows rather than pliés, lines etched into celluloid with blood instead of ink. It's Hong Kong movie tradition, at its best. Again, the themes are loyalty and betrayal, cops and robbers, the humanist versus the psycho. Just to prove where its heart is, the climactic scene is staged in a hospital – but the babies are saved.

Film-school revenge

Bad Lieutenant and *Man Bites Dog* are something else. Nobody is likely to be saved, nobody takes prisoners. Real life enters the movie theatre the second such films come on screen, and audiences have been known to vote with their feet. *Bad Lieutenant* is Ferrara's characteristic sex, sleaze and violence cocktail; the pitch is Scorsese but the mood feels more Polanski. The rhetoric accompanying *Man Bites Dog* is more fashionable, claiming that the snuff-film violence with which it slams its viewers is really a critique of violence in the media, a send-up of *verité*, and a satirisation of television's true-crime genre. Yeah, right. The film-makers themselves play the key roles in a fake documentary of a film crew following a serial killer, filming everything and identifying with its subject even as his acts grow increasingly heinous. Rape and racism are just two of the cards played in the high-stakes game.

The film-makers pitch a catalytic moment, insisting their audience switches from laughter to horror. But it doesn't work. The audience divided instead: some of *us* never started to laugh; some of *them* never stopped. In one post-film ramble, the film-makers admitted they made the film on the verge of being kicked out of film school. Think of it as the ultimate film-school revenge film: you thought I was bad, well take *this*. Yet another fuck-you movie in which we all must pay for somebody else's sins. Ferrara pitches his vision as a quest for redemption, reasoning perhaps that if a nun can forgive the crackheads who rape her with a crucifix, then an audience should be able to forgive Ferrara, right?

Wrong. And the women, so badly served by this genre as characters, what do they do behind the camera? Surprise, surprise, something rather different is happening in this post-*Thelma & Louise* moment. Not the male bonding of *Reservoir Dogs*, not the emotionless violence of *Hard-Boiled*, not the sadism of *Bad Lieutenant*, nor the misanthropy of *Man Bites Dog*. No, even though the old genre movies allowed no place for women (pre-Kathryn Bigelow, anyway), the Ridley Scott caper changed the rules. As a result, guns represent something very specific in *Guncrazy* and *My New Gun*: empowerment.

The common denominator of the two movies is mistreated women, the arrival of a gun (welcome or not), and James LeGros as the unlikely object of desire in a stylish man-woman-gun triangle. In *Guncrazy*, Drew Barrymore (who's never been better) is stuck in a trailer in a small town performing as high-school slut by day, stepdaddy's plaything by night, trapped forever in hell until her pen-pal correspondence with a convict ends up changing her life. Terminally, but what the hell.

Director Davis explained, between screenings at Toronto, that she'd modelled the film less on its Joseph H. Lewis namesake than on *Badlands*, *Bonnie & Clyde* and Warhol features (the stepdaddy is none other than Joe Dallesandro). Davis manages to open up the violence/sex equation and redefine the terms. What's the real violence in backwater towns: rapes or the murder of rapists? What's the real crime: religion or running away? It's hard to see the other movies as anything but film-school tricks or little-boy antics after an evening with *Guncrazy*.

Cochran's *My New Gun*, on the other hand, is an evening off: this is the story of a woman who doesn't want a gun at all. Is she rejecting the object or its acts, her potential or her marriage (it's hubby who brings her the gun)? Heavily Seidelman-influenced, Cochran spins red herrings into cotton candy and ends up with an anti-yuppie comedy in which violence turns out to represent boredom, bad manners or lack of imagination. Davis sees the two films as a paradigm of West Coast versus East Coast: 'In her film, the woman never gets to use the gun; in mine, her using it is the whole point.'

But what's the point of any of the boy-boy movies, after all? It's tempting to see the neo-violence phenomenon as a purely cinematic episode. The *New Yorker*'s Terrence Rafferty describes Tarantino as tapping into a movie tradition of 'exploding-bullet power'. John Woo has been around for quite a while, as has the Hong Kong genre that birthed his reinterpretations. And besides, it was the new African-American guys who transformed South Central from a neighbourhood into a genre and made the studios a bundle doing it. Is this just a continuation, then, with independents and Europeans jumping on the bone?

Not quite. It's no coincidence that these films are appearing at the very moment in which the Cold War has been decentralised, split like atoms into dozens of hot wars around the globe. The newspapers are full of the violence in 'ex-Yugoslavia', as they like to call it. The end of Soviet has spelled the end of Union too, as Balkanisation, ethnic hostilities, tribal wars, anti-Semitism and gypsy-hatred all take centre stage. Massacres erupt again in South Africa. In the months between the Toronto and London festivals, the Nobel Peace Prize went to Rigoberta Menchu and, implicitly, spoke against Guatemala's contemporary manifestations of colonial violence. Meanwhile, IRA bombs are exploding once again in London. And the genre status of South Central didn't immunise it from the Rodney King verdict or the LA rebellions that followed.

The 90s, in short, is a time of intensely politicised violence. It should not be surprising, then, that the film genre that has emerged is one of equally intense violence, but depoliticised and individualised, in keeping with so much movie tradition. In the old days of communism, it used to be said that capitalism thrived by using 'crime' to direct public attention towards lone villains and away from the criminal functioning of the free market. Today, the genre of neo-violence seems tailor-made to fit that analysis. The world has changed too fast. The level of conflict and violence is beyond comprehension. Confused and angry and full of rage (to borrow my favourite Culture Club phrase)? Go back to genre, back to the movies.

Dubious pleasures

Movies may be expected to reflect their realities, but more often they function as opposites or surrogates. This year, movie-going publics may well feel powerless in the face of overwhelming global forces of poverty, ideological impoverishment and hatred of self and others. Too angry and uptight for the old sexual fix? How much better to sign on to violence and see that rage explode on screen – but comfortingly restrained within the cosy familiarity of genre. Like children entranced by the murders, explosions and reincarnations of the cartoon characters they love, audiences today are prepared to cede their agency to the larger-than-life characters of celluloid.

So I skipped the dinner, in Toronto, at which Quentin Tarantino and John Woo fell in love – with each other's movies. A few days later, a press release in my mailbox announced that Tarantino would write the screenplay for Woo's next opus (after his Van Damme production). By that time, I'd seen Tilda Swinton in Sally Potter's *Orlando*, one of the many films this year with a focus other than violence. Orlando's mythic transformation from man to woman occurs at the exact moment in which he is required to enter into battle and kill: he falls into a weeks-long slumber, from which Lady Orlando awakens. Alas, in the 90s, even gender is not necessarily a refuge. Tamra Davis turns out to have just finished shooting *Cell Block 4*, Hollywood's upcoming mega-violence boyz in the hood movie, written and produced by Nelson George, Chris Rock and Bob Locash. The neo-violence of the art houses, meanwhile, seems set to take charge of 1993.

I admit that I enjoy some of these movies for the euphoric rush of their dubious pleasures, while I confess to despising others for the misogyny, race-baiting and downright misanthropy that drive their characters and narratives. Which is the 'politically correct' response? Do I think that movies like these create violence? Probably not. On the other hand, in the current moment, is violence really what I want to experience – witness and participate in – when I enter the movie theatre? Probably not. I guess I just hope that the other films now being made and shown can get a fair viewing in a context that sees the self-consciousness of neo-violence as the ultimate hip. I hope genres can still be replaced rather than just replayed. If not, I may have to sink into a coma, like Orlando, and wait for the war to end.

DUMB LUGS AND FEMMES FATALES

B. Ruby Rich

The time is 1948, the place Los Angeles. Meet Easy Rawlins, a guy whose luck changed when World War II ended: back from the battles, dismissed from his job for the kind of insubordination necessary to retain some dignity, he's desperate for mortgage money to save the house that the GI Bill bought him. Enter a bartender who knows a guy who's got a friend who's in a jam and needs some help. Don't these films all start out this way? Just find this woman and you'll find yourself some 'easy' money. Never mind why.

Soon enough, people start turning up dead, the hero gets jumped, and people are no longer what they seem, if ever they were. The blue sky and the palm trees turn threatening, and life itself shifts from the sunny certainty of day into the shadowing dangers of night. Daphne Monet is the ticket, but where is she and who is she, and can he find her in time, and if so, then what? When a man gets in that deep, he needs a friend, even if it's a trigger-happy pal from back home down south, way out of control.

Welcome to the terrain of film noir with a difference. The film is *Devil in a Blue Dress*, the writer Walter Mosley, the director and screenwriter Carl Franklin. Denzel Washington as Easy subdues his elegance in the service of noirish criteria for down-at-the-heels angst. Jennifer Beals plays Daphne as a *femme fatale*, but with a twist. The early *femmes fatales* had no explanation for their relentless pain or greed; Daphne's got one all right, and it's convincing, if nearly fatal. The setting is Central Avenue, back when the hood was a neighbourhood, the heart of a thriving black metropolis that vanished everywhere but memory. Carl Franklin has definitively put the black back into noir. Reviewers have been citing *Chinatown* (1974), but that's all wrong: blood runs thicker than water in the Mosley/Franklin universe, black and white signifies more than film stock and, no, this time around, we can't all just get along.

The old paranoia of classic noir is intact in *Devil*, but race now colours the coordinates of the compass instead of gangsters or Cold War spooks. This is revisionist noir, backtracking to the 40s with one eye on the kind of scenario that the O.J. Simpson case must have been unreeling across town while *Devil* was in production. Corrupt politicians, racist cops, mayoral candidates with something to hide, all timeless elements that can fuel paranoia whatever the decade. Easy does track down Daphne, with the help of partner Mouse (the charismatic Don Cheadle), uncovering the underbelly of white Los Angeles in the process; doubly endangered whenever he leaves Central Avenue for white neighbourhoods or hotel rooms, he is our guide to a virtually apartheid Los Angeles and the rules it makes and breaks.

Franklin's earlier *One False Move* (1993) squarely belonged in the neo-noir revival that's been exploding on the screens in recent years. To the extent that *Devil* has a 'happy' ending, and to the extent that Tak Fujimoto's dreamily amber cinematography lets it go down as smooth as cognac with nary a trace of noirish rot-gut kick, it qualifies as a high-class Hollywood addition to 90s noir, an adjunct to rather than a member of neo-noir. The period setting is as much a giveaway as the label: Franklin is faithful to Mosley's postwar setting, whereas the neo-noir films are fixedly contemporary, borrowing mood and characters but never trappings or dates from their forefathers.

Neo-noir, *qu'est que c'est?* Well, consider that the *Devil* reprises the heady, atmospheric times of early classic noir; those lovely days of *The Maltese Falcon* (1941), *Double Indemnity* (1944), of Laura and Gilda and a Postman who always rings twice. The neo-noir of the 90s, on the other hand, looks to the psychotic years of late noir (already tinged with parody and subversion) for its inspiration. Its power stems from those end-of-the-line dramas in which nobody at all could be trusted and not even the final frame held any explanation: films like *Gun Crazy* (1949), *Kiss Me Deadly* (1955), *The Big Combo* (1955) and *Touch of Evil* (1959) – the film that everyone fingers as the last of the line. Neo-noir picks up on the irrational universe embedded in these demonic narratives as fertile ground for the postmodern cultivation of our own *fin-de-siècle* nightmares. John Dahl (director of *Kill Me Again*, 1989) is its master, the Quentin Tarantino of *Pulp Fiction* its magician. But neo-noir has an overarching reach; as a category, it can handily include Tamra Davis's *Guncrazy* (1992) alongside James Foley's *After Dark, My Sweet* (1990). Add *Black Widow* (1987), *The Grifters* (1990), *Basic Instinct* (1992), *Final Analysis* (1992), *Night and The City* (1992), *Ruby* (1992) and *Romeo is Bleeding* (1993), and the contours begin to come into focus.

In neo-noir, the women are irresistibly sexy and inexplicably evil, the men as dumb as they come and heading for a fall. No one can be trusted, everything is *déjà vu*, and happy endings aren't even a dream in anyone's head. The style is over the top, the camerawork flashy and giddily self-conscious, and the script tends to a certain smugness towards its own characters. Reviewing Elmore Leonard's new book earlier this year, Martin Amis wrote: 'He understands the postmodern world, the world of wised-up rabble and zero authenticity.' That, dear reader, is the universe of neo-noir.

The politics of noir

To be sure, noir itself never died out in the first place. It's been one of the most enduring genres in the history of American, if not world, movies. Revivals of noir favourites have been a mainstay of repertory houses throughout the US for years, while periodic rewritings of the genre (*Chinatown*, 1974, *Body Heat*, 1981) have kept the tradition alive since its origins in the 30s and 40s. In the book *City of Quartz*, that brilliant meditation on Los Angeles, Mike Davis tried to pinpoint the nature of those origins. With a nose for cause-and-effect (not unlike the sheriff's wife in *One False Move* who discloses that 'I read nonfiction'), Davis backtracks not merely to the traditional pulp touchstone, James M. Cain's novel *The Postman Always Rings Twice*, but to Lewis Corey's *Crisis of the Middle Class* (1935), which explored the bankruptcy of Los Angelenos during the Depression-fed crash of real estate scams, oil speculation and land grabs, and their consequent sense of disenfranchisement. Corey seems to have hypothesised that the masses would turn either to fascism or socialism as a route out of their confusion, desperation and resentment. (Flash forward to Oklahoma City in 1995 for a suggestion of what's up next.)

With the world turned upside down, though, the movies were ready to give this topsy-turvy universe its due – and give the masses somewhere else to turn. 'Noir,' writes Davis, 'was like a transformational grammar turning each charming ingredient of the boosters' arcadia into a sinister equivalent.' Noir etched a metaphor of light and shadow into the popular psyche; rain-slicked streets, feelings of loss, fear and betrayal; male bonding, *femmes fatales*, postwar malaise, atomic pressures, Communist threats, melodrama and gangsters all coalesced under its banner. Capone met Mabuse in the darkness. As the genre developed and became, well, kinkier – and as US politics did the same, devolving into McCarthyism and xenophobia – film noir became a pressure-cooker of overheated desires and overwhelming drives, instincts pushed way past reason into an intoxicating delirium of film style.

Today, neo-noir once again demonstrates the success with which cinema on occasion can marshal a handful of paradigmatic elements integral to its social moment and catalyse them into master narratives of crisis and resolution. No wonder it's so popular. Besides *Devil*, two television series are stimulating interest in the UK – Channel 4's *Dark and Deadly* series programmes a sampling of American neo-noir, while the first Showtime series *Fallen Angels* (for US cablecast) has just been shown by the BBC. Why now? Well, one popular explanation for the first flourishing of noir held it hostage to its time: the postwar landscape was a whole new ballgame for those Americans who naively thought they'd triumphed over evil, then immediately identified a new evil empire called Communism. The paranoia of noir was the result: a world suddenly rearranged, a sucker punch from left field, and boom, Paul Schrader's 'darkening stain' was spreading fast. Stunned by the end of the world as they knew it, Americans flocked to noir to pacify themselves with its equally tangled narratives and unreliable narrators.

Flash forward to the 90s, with a scenario not very different, apart from its reversals. In place of Corey's disenfranchised Los Angelenos, there are the angry militiamen of Waco and Oklahoma City. Instead of McCarthy, there's Newt. Instead of xenophobia – well, xenophobia. The end of the Cold War seems to have thrown the US into as much of a dither as its beginnings, old ideological formations are once again destined for the junk heap, and faith has gone missing. Whenever nobody can be trusted, society may disintegrate, but noir can flourish. Enter neo-noir to rewire the genre's circuitry to the currents of the present, flashing across its screen some fascinating messages about the fears and dilemmas of our age.

Take women, for example. The *femmes fatales* of original noir had some kind of relationship to the brassy dames that flourished when the men were off to war, only to face banishment back to the kitchen and bedroom when their Johnnies came marching home. It doesn't take much feminist analysis to trace the short line from postwar gender regulation to film noir's embodiments of male fear and female treachery.

In neo-noir, women are usually pure evil, with sexuality and greed the primary markers of character. There's some precedent, of course: the greedy scheming Laurie of *Gun Crazy*, who literally takes our hero for a ride, and the relentlessly curious Gabrielle of

Kiss Me Deadly, whose greed carries a sinister price tag, are the foremothers of the neo-noir broads. It's a small hop and a skip from Laurie/Gabrielle to the larger-than-life women embodied by Linda Fiorentino, Lena Olin, Lara Flynn Boyle, Theresa Russell, Kim Basinger, Annette Bening and Joanne Whalley-Kilmer. Their blood runs green, not red, as they sacrifice the men who cross their path to their insatiable and inscrutable quest for big money – and big-time betrayal. In *Kill Me Again*, John Dahl's early outing, Joanne Whalley-Kilmer sets up the role of duplicitous female that would be filled in future Dahl films by Fiorentino (*The Last Seduction*, 1993) and Boyle (*Red Rock West*, 1993); she plays a woman seemingly on the run from an abusive partner in crime, who enlists a small-town innocent to help her fake her own death in order to escape together and start over. Naturally, it's not that simple. Though *The Last Seduction* has caught big-time critical attention, it's pretty flat and formulaic by comparison to *Kill Me Again*. It's fun to see Dahl putting the pieces together for the first time (let's see, try a bit of *Vertigo* here) and equally fun to see who's already cribbed from him: fans of *Reservoir Dogs* need to check out the scene of a psychotic Michael Madsen laughing and dancing around the character whom he tortures with a cigarette, then slits his throat with brio.

The women of neo-noir may be inexplicably evil, but that's what audiences love about them. Their rapacious acts, their disregard for human life, their greed and lust and lack of restraint all elicit cheers and whistles of approval and enthusiasm. Their display of power, however depraved and unmotivated, is being accepted as a new version (albeit warped) of female empowerment, the dominatrix as a model of agency. So happy are audiences to find movies in which women chew up the scenery and trap the wimpy men that no one seems to have noticed that they're utterly lacking in subjectivity. After all, they usually get away with it in the end (the *Basic Instinct* model).

The dumb-is-good philosophy

The problem is that neo-noir is an exception to the prevailing style of gender-bending fictions. Wolves in sheep's clothing, the new noir films trot out smart, treacherous *femmes fatales*, but the male patsies who seem to be no match for them at all turn out to be the sole repositories of authenticity. In a world of 'wised-up rabble', smarts are inherently suspect. It's a postmodern universe in which people frequently know too much for their own good: if you're smart, you're liable to cause trouble. Dumbness, then, becomes the only marker of authenticity, the only guarantee of any integrity in a universe of shady deals and double-crossing comrades. Take *After Dark, My Sweet*, for example, which was actually based on a book by Jim Thompson. Jason Patric plays Collie, a guy who's escaped from a mental hospital only to find that the outside world is crazier and more dangerous yet. He falls in with a sexy widow (Rachel Ward) and her criminal ex-cop sidekick (Bruce Dern) who together manipulate him to kidnap a rich kid and get rich themselves off the ransom money. It all goes wrong, of course. But Collie, the dumb bastard so impaired that a random doctor can easily spot him, is the locus of integrity.

The dumb-is-good philosophy, of course, isn't unique to neo-noir. Way back in the original Joseph H. Lewis *Gun Crazy* (1949), one character said to another: 'You were born dumb.' It wasn't a compliment back then, but today it seems to be. The 90s are full of dumbness, from Beavis and Butthead to *Dumb & Dumber* to *Forrest Gump*. The protagonists of neo-noir are patsies just like they were in the old days of noir, but now they're ennobled by their idiocy, with the women in turn demonised (big surprise) by their intelligence. Collie is a washed-up boxer, after all (and boxing, in noir and neo-noir both, is a reliable index of masculinity). Theresa Russell's victims in *Black Widow* may be rich men, but they're never shown as conniving or ruthless, only as lovable and swindled by her marry-for-money murderess. Even the psychiatrist in *Final Analysis*, who's weakened by lust and then duped by a pair of sisters into providing a fake alibi, plays the part of an idiotic but innocent victim of sinister entrapment, rather than an irresponsible professional violating his profession's code of ethics.

These dumb lugs are all accorded a morality denied to the women. At the same time, in a moment of crisis for masculinity in the movies, these dumb guys are real men. The bid for authenticity in the 90s is stupidity, as though you can only guarantee realness if you don't know any better and so are too stupid for cynicism. Dumb equals good, smart equals bad. But why? It's tempting to reverse the old noir logic and see the qualities in a national, not individual, context. According to this model, the United States would be the dumb lug who, post-Communism, can't figure out who or what he is or what he's supposed to do; feeling spurned and duped, all he can do is stumble on, clueless, in a world dimly perceived as dangerous.

Yet if noir the first time around was bent on capturing the instability of masculinity, now it seems equally determined to reinstate masculinity. The valorisation of stupidity is just a small part of that agenda. Neo-noir is a genre where a man is always a man, even if a woman isn't always exactly a woman (Sharon Stone's bisexuality and basic instincts, Anjelica Huston's oedipal drama in *The Grifters*, *The Last Seduction*'s transvestite ex-wife). The destiny of these dumb men with sex-addled brains is to be set up by the greedy women whose paths they're fated to cross. Nor do they always triumph. Their assignment is different: to hold fast in a postmodern world of shifting significances, to reject dispersal and masquerade and therefore corruption, to be 'themselves' in the absence of any other comprehensible rules.

The vacuum of authority is a key component for neo-noir, signifying as it does its membership in postmodernism. Thus the reliance on quotation, homage, and appropriation, all elements that fuel the audience's pleasure, and undermine the characters' claims to meaning. In *Pulp Fiction*, Tarantino doesn't so much quote past films as cast his actors, literally, as embodiments of their own past characters, rescripted, this time around, to be rewarded or punished for past behaviour (rewarded for his *Saturday Night Fever*-era sexiness, Travolta gets to dance; punished for his years of on-screen machismo, Bruce Willis gets to talk babytalk and eat pussy; in the end, though, it's Willis who gets away). In *Guncrazy*, Tamra Davis cast Joe Dallesandro, the former stud of Andy Warhol's Factory movies, as a wasted jerk who rapes his old lady's daughter, played by Drew Barrymore, and therefore earns his death. As with Tarantino, it's the appropriation that grants the scenes' meaning and deepens their emotional value, even though such pastiche is usually thought to do the opposite.

The arch synthesis of postmodernism turns out to work to neo-noir's advantage, a point underlined by the *Fallen Angels* programmes. Most of the shows are based on earlier novels and set in the original noir era; they're interesting and smartly done, but they don't revise the genre like neo-noir. Except for two. Significantly, these both recast noir as 'outsider' dramas. In *Fearless*, Jim McBride directs a Walter Mosley script with an all-star triangle of Cynda Williams, Giancarlo Esposito and Bill Nunn, somehow infused with both sexiness and comedy; in *Professional Man*, Steven Soderbergh directs Brendan Fraser, Peter Coyote and Bruce Ramsey in a gay triangle of killer, boss and victim, all of it filmed with stylish precision and paced with exquisite tension. Both scramble the elements, but they have no easy relationship to emotion: neither sentimental nor cynical, these programmes play with audience expectation and turn the viewers, finally, into the patsies up for manipulation.

Neo-noir can offer up cartoons, but it can also surprise its audience with moral dilemmas and serious questions. *The Grifters*, for instance, goes down easy until things start to go wrong for its characters, at which point it becomes unexpectedly poignant, almost against its will. When serious subject matter fills its formulas, they become transformed – as, sometimes, do we.

Ruby is a good example: an oddball in the Channel 4 series, it wouldn't seem at first to be a candidate for neo-noir at all. A docudrama history of the JFK assassination, *Ruby* reverses what the old noirs did to politics: they embedded their political narratives in the fairly melodramatic structures of the noir formulas, but *Ruby* embeds the neo-noir elements in its real-life story of conspiracy, paranoia, betrayal and disaster. Jack Ruby (Danny Aïello) is the epitome of the neo-noir patsy-protagonist, dumb enough to get himself in way over his head and not smart enough to get out in time. With the CIA and the Mafia filling the bad-guy roles, *Ruby* enlists our noir-trained sympathies in a rereading of history; amazingly, it works.

A touch of race

Similarly, Carl Franklin's *One False Move* might seem to elude the new noir category. Not so. Race may have been virtually absent from the first round of noir (and hardly more present in the contemporary literary landscape of detective novels, which have had a renaissance paralleling the revival of noir), but it has a singular capacity to reinvigorate the noir form. *One False Move* opened with a gang of violent drug-dealers running for cover after a big hit with their woman companion (Cynda Williams), who convinced them to go south so she can see her child; waiting there to catch them are some big-city northern cops and a small-town sheriff, whose connection to the case turns out to be more complicated than ever expected. *One False Move* seemed to offer itself up as one thing (urban ultraviolence) only to throw its audience for a loop with bold evolutions into more complex terrain (race crossing, urban/rural dynamics, mother-love, tragedy). In fact it echoes *Touch of Evil*, in that both explicitly repudiate audience expectations based on racism (against Mexicans in one, African Americans in the other) – and refuse the figure of a white sheriff as any bearer of rectitude, assigning integrity instead to people of colour (Charlton Heston's 'Mexican' detective, Cynda Williams' gangster-moll). It's in this sense that *Devil in a Blue Dress* can be seen to have been directed by the same man who did *One False Move* after all. Both films focus on dramas of good and evil, both believe that something momentous hangs in the balance, and both reject the casual nihilism that otherwise tends to accompany the neo-noir project.

In the end, Franklin's films invert not merely expectation but the moral universe that they address. This arc of triumph (or defeat) may suggest an alternate moral development for neo-noir – a route out of the grifters and dead-end futures that litter the byways of the genre. It's only made possible, though, by the deployment of an 'outsider' identity – African Americans, non-fatal *femmes*, gays and lesbians – which neo-noir has thus far been uninterested in taking on.

L.A. LURID

Amy Taubin

At age fifty-two, Curtis Hanson has made his first serious film, a film which will probably rack up a bunch of Oscar nominations, but which cinephiles – like Hanson himself – will also appreciate. Hanson's *L.A. Confidential* is the kind of picture that supposedly couldn't be made in Hollywood any more – an impeccably crafted, densely plotted, fast-paced *policier* with a sense of place so lush that you want to sink into the image and stay there forever. Adapted from James Ellroy's pulp novel, it evokes not only the Los Angeles of the early 50s, but the films that have defined the glamorous and corrupt image of that city, from *The Big Sleep* (1946) to *Chinatown* (1974) to Ulu Grosbard's underrated *True Confessions* (1981).

Mixing fiction with a smattering of characters and events from LA's shady history, *L.A. Confidential* is the story of three cops caught over their heads in an investigation involving drugs, prostitution, a late-night coffeeshop massacre and an organised-crime syndicate up for grabs after top mobster Mickey Cohen is put behind bars.

Bud White (Russell Crowe) is a brute of a man who thinks nothing about beating a confession out of a suspect he believes is guilty, but a real Galahad with women: his rescue fantasy is focused on Lynn Bracken (Kim Basinger), a prostitute whose prime asset is her resemblance to Veronica Lake.

Bud's opposite number is Ed Exley (Guy Pearce). Exley has the brains to match White's guts (together they'd make a fabulous man) but his veneer of moral rectitude is a cover for a Machiavellian ambition. The most overtly sleazy of this trio of tarnished protagonists is Jack Vincennes (Kevin Spacey) who's teamed up with a tabloid writer (Danny DeVito) to maximise the publicity he gets from busting celebrities for various indiscretions.

As the bodies pile up – and the solution to the mystery dances tantalisingly out of reach – these three join forces, putting aside the animosity they bear towards one another and acting, for one fleeting moment, as if they believed again in the fantasy that made them want to become cops in the first place – that they are the defenders of society, fighting the good fight for justice and the American way.

A Los Angeles native who never went to film school, Hanson backed into the movie industry in the late 60s on *Cinema*, a film journal still remembered for Paul Schrader's influential essay on film noir. 'In those days,' says Hanson, 'you could call up John Ford or Vincente Minnelli and get an interview. Doing the magazine, and especially taking photographs for it, afforded me the opportunity to be around movies when they were being made. So when I started directing myself I was somewhat comfortable with how it was done.'

Hanson directed a couple of well-acted genre pictures (notably *Bad Influence*, 1990, with Rob Lowe and James Spader) and then had two box-office winners in a row, *The Hand that Rocks the Cradle* (1992) and *The River Wild* (1994, with Meryl Streep). Suddenly he found himself in the position of being a director that every studio wanted to work with, though the picture dearest to his heart – *L.A. Confidential* – was still no easy sell.

*   *   *

Amy Taubin: *L.A. Confidential* is not exactly the kind of picture one expects a studio like Warner Bros to make nowadays. And I heard they didn't want to send it to Cannes.

Curtis Hanson: As far as Cannes goes, Warner's position – not just about our film, but in general – is that there's an anti-studio bias there, so why go and come home a loser? Our attitude was that although we knew we weren't going to win the prize, we loved the movie and we wanted to unveil it on that international stage. And David Matalon of Regency Entertainment, which actually financed the movie, was relentless in pursuing this. He secretly conspired with my editing room for us to send a print to France for the selection committee to look at. And the selection committee flipped over it and invited it, and that was that.

But this movie is a hybrid. On the one hand, because it's logistically a big movie with eighty speaking parts and forty-five locations, it needs the budget of a studio movie. But on the other hand, it's multi-character, the characters are ambiguous at best, it's period and it's related to film noir, the very reasons why I wanted to make it. I didn't look on it as a homage to the world of Raymond Chandler, or to *The Big Sleep, Chinatown* – movies I love, but didn't want to do. I wanted this to be a movie set in the forward-looking, splashy 50s. That's why it's *L.A. Confidential* – *Confidential Magazine*, lurid and fun. Funny even, yet dark. It's noir in the broadest sense, meaning the darkness under the bright.

Amy Taubin: Would you consider everything you did before this as working as a director for hire?

Curtis Hanson: You know how it is. First, you're struggling to get anything to direct. I wrote *The Bedroom Window* and developed it in the late 80s, but I wasn't able to make it the way I wanted to. *Bad Influence* is the closest to *L.A. Confidential*: it explores the same theme, of the difference between the way things are and the way they appear to be. It's very much the story of a man being introduced to the darkness of his own personality which he's repressed until then – and introduced by the charming and attractive Rob Lowe. The shame of *Bad Influence*, which I'm very fond of, is that Rob's performance was overshadowed by that videotape scandal he got caught up in at the same time. But anyway, as a director for hire, I would choose the project that interested me the most of the ones I could land, and I'd do the best I could with it. I was fortunate enough to have the last two – *The Hand that Rocks the Cradle* and *The River Wild* – be commercial successes, and that gave me a certain clout.

For *L.A. Confidential* I wanted to find actors who could pull off the pivotal roles of Bud White and Ed Exley, but also actors with whom the public had no prior emotional history, so that the audience could discover the characters in much the same way as I discovered them in James Ellroy's novel. Which is the way we discover people in life. Movie stars are great, and sometimes help an audience invest in stories they wouldn't otherwise invest in. But I wanted something different with *L.A. Confidential*. What I considered part of Ellroy's triumph was that he created these three characters I loathed when I first met them, because they were doing reprehensible things. But as I kept reading, I got caught up and started having complicated reactions to them and to their personal struggles. I thought that if I could pull that off in a movie, I would have something special.

Amy Taubin: This 'three' includes the cop played by Kevin Spacey.

Curtis Hanson: Yes, although Kevin is a better-known actor – most people remember him from *Seven* and *The Usual Suspects*, where he plays these creepy, dark characters. But here he's a character who, on the surface, is very smooth, the way that Kevin hasn't yet had the opportunity to be on screen. When I gave him the script, I said think of two words: Dean Martin. And I knew he could also play the man behind that veneer, the man who also lost his soul.

Amy Taubin: How did you find Russell Crowe and Guy Pearce?

Curtis Hanson: I'd seen Russell in *Romper Stomper* and I knew from that performance that he could pull off the dark, physical side of Bud. I didn't know for sure that he could pull off the other side until I met him and worked with him. So I put him on tape doing a few scenes and showed it to David Matalan and his partner Arnon Milchan, and they said yes, he was Bud. Guy Pearce I met on a day when actors were coming in the door every fifteen minutes to read for these different parts. Mali Finn, my wonderfully gifted and tenacious casting director, brought Guy in and he did a wonderful reading. When I learned he played a drag queen in *The Adventures of Priscilla, Queen of the Desert,* I decided not to watch it. I didn't want to have my confidence that he could pull off this part rattled by seeing him run around in drag for two hours. So I put him on tape doing a few scenes and showed them to Arnon, and again Arnon said fine. And then he said, 'But are we going to have any names in this picture?' And I said yes, because I always felt the Jack Vincennes character was a movie star among cops and could be played by Kevin Spacey, who has movie star charisma. And Lynn Bracken, the prostitute who's selling movie-star glamour, needed an actress with movie-star glamour and that was Kim Basinger.

Amy Taubin: I think that the other great performance is James Cromwell as the police commander.

Curtis Hanson: I'm glad to hear you say that, because he's been getting somewhat overlooked by the critics. The thing he does that's so marvellous is that he brings the paternal, protective thing that we all want from cops, but at the same time he's pragmatic in that old-school way that we're very uncomfortable with. It's the same with all these characters: we can't pigeonhole them and write them off. I mean Danny DeVito is doing these reprehensible things as a tabloid journalist, and at the same time he also has the enthusiasm of a visionary who's inventing an industry. The fact that he's causing havoc on a human level is beside the point to him.

Amy Taubin: All the acting is fantastic.

Curtis Hanson: It's an actors' piece. If the acting didn't work, the movie wouldn't. It's as simple as that.

Amy Taubin: But it's also a gorgeous-looking movie.

Curtis Hanson: That only goes so far. In fact, my number one directive to myself and to Dante Spinotti, my cameraman, and to Jeannine Oppewall, my production designer, was 'Let's create this world of *L.A. Confidential*, and let's give great attention to the detail of the period, but then let's put it all in the background and let's shoot it as if it were a contemporary movie. So that the audience forgets that they're watching a period movie and what they're aware of are the characters and the emotions.' The one thing that I wanted to avoid was telling the story through the lens of nostalgia. Because one of the reasons for making a picture set in Los Angeles in 1953 is that so many of the things that were starting in that era of economic boom and postwar optimism are still very much with us today, for better or worse. The freeways, which might have seemed like a good idea at the time, but destroyed much of what was good in Los Angeles. Tabloid journalism. And the remaking of the Los Angeles police force so that the old-time corruption of cops on the take was replaced with a force based on a military model, namely the Marines in World War II, the image of which was sold to the public through *Dragnet* and other television shows. And you end up with a police force that was clean, relatively speaking, but that has a host of other problems, a police force that is empowered because, supposedly, it can do no wrong. And we're living with that now and we've seen what it's wrought in terms of police brutality. So all of that makes the picture contemporary and relevant.

Amy Taubin: Could we talk a little about how you worked with the actors?

Curtis Hanson: I had the luxury of six weeks of rehearsal with Guy and Russell, which is almost unheard of. And as I cast the other actors, I'd feather them into the rehearsal process. I also staged a mini-film festival where, once a week, I showed a movie from the 50s that I thought would be instructive, not only for the actors but for the production people. It was about showing what the faces and the bodies looked like in those days – hard-drinking, meat-eating guys who never thought to go to a gym. I showed Vincente Minnelli's *The Bad and the Beautiful* because it captures and perpetuates the romance of Hollywood. I wanted everyone to see it so I could say this is what we aren't doing – except in the world of Lynn Bracken, whose house is like a stage where she's selling the illusion of that romance. I showed Nicholas Ray's *In a Lonely Place* because it shows the emotional wasteland behind the glamour, Don Siegel's *Lineup* and *Private Hell 36* for their lean and efficient style. And of course Robert Aldrich's *Kiss Me Deadly* which is so rooted in the futuristic 50s: the atomic age and so forth. Stanley Kubrick's *The Killing* was another – for that beefy manliness that came out of World War II.

I didn't pick these films to illustrate the look of the movie we were going to make. To show the look – and the characters and the themes – I had put together fifteen photographs. I had showed them to Arnon when I first met with him and without having read the script, he said let's make the movie. I did the same thing with Dante and costume designer Ruth Myers. And then, while I was writing the script with Brian Helgeland, I saw this wonderful exhibit of Robert Frank photos from *The Americans*. And I was so struck by their power, by how the emotions were what came through first, before you noticed the period. I mentioned that to Dante and he understood it right away, and it became our touchstone. It suggested a whole lighting approach as well. It's all about keeping the period in the background and having a naturalistic feel. So when we were looking at locations, we'd always say, where does the light come from? That's in direct contrast with the classic film noir movies where the lighting is more stylised, where you have the fantastic lighting with the long shadows.

Amy Taubin: Let's talk a bit about how you went about adapting the novel.

Curtis Hanson: The novel is incredibly convoluted, with many subplots and back stories. James Ellroy doesn't write novels that are blueprints for movies. Which is part of the reason his books are so incredible to read, and why ours is one of the first movies made from one of his major books. Our approach was to let the character, not the plot, be our guide. The first three scenes in the movie are there to introduce the characters; they have nothing to do with advancing the plot. That's a luxury that you seldom have in a studio movie these days where everything is about advancing the plot. Frankly, we focused on the characters because if we had attempted to deal with the novel on a plot level we would have ended up with wall-to-wall exposition.

We wrote for about a year. It took us seven drafts to get a script I felt reasonably satisfied with and that I felt I could show to Ellroy. When I called him, he said, 'My book, your movie.' I feel that is the only attitude for a sane novelist to have. And that he is out there singing the praises of the movie means more to me than any other praise the movie might get, because when we were writing our main goal was to preserve his voice.

But, going back to the characters, what interested me originally was how they all turn out to be different from what they appear to be. And Lynn Bracken is the character who most neatly sums that up. She's a prostitute who looks like Veronica Lake and that illusion is what she's selling. But only she sees the truth about herself and sees the truth of the other characters. And it gave me the opportunity to show Veronica Lake in a clip from *This Gun For Hire* and then to have Kim step in front of the screen and show that, yes, she looks like Veronica Lake but she's someone different. The audience might also notice that there's a certain resemblance between this movie and *This Gun for Hire*, but this movie is something different.

The fact that these men are cops is incidental to what attracted me to the story. I prefer stories about people who stumble into these mysteries accidentally, not professionally. But once I was in this cop world, I was determined to do it right. For instance, that key scene at the beginning, where the cops beat up the Mexicans on Christmas Eve, was based on an actual incident that resulted in a grand jury investigation. We set that scene in the Hollywood station. And we shot it in the Venice police station built a year after the Hollywood police station, which was the same size. And it's tiny – and that was the police station for all of Hollywood. At any given time, there would only be five detectives sitting in the LA police bureau.

We were all struck by how small everything was. And how great it was before the freeways. The neighbourhoods had such a distinct feel before the freeways cut through and linked them into a giant megalopolis. That's what's so fascinating about this period when much of what was good in southern California – this utopia in the sun – was literally being bulldozed to make way for all the people coming there in pursuit of the very thing that was being destroyed. I'm not one to live in the past and to be nostalgic about what's gone – I like Los Angeles today and part of what I like about it is that it's a working, living, breathing city. The tremendous ethnic influx has totally transformed neighbourhoods I remember from childhood, and that's interesting to me. I'd rather live in a city that's changing than a city that's a museum to its past. And that gets back to the characters. LA is one of the main characters in this movie and, like the other characters, it requires work to get beneath the surface and understand it.

Natural Born Killers (Oliver Stone, 1994)

Section 6: Serial Killers in 90s Hollywood

As Richard Dyer writes in the introductory essay to this section, 'serial killing is often taken to be the crime of our age'. The serial killer has appeared in films throughout the history of cinema (*M* and *Psycho* are only two famous instances) but the preponderence of the figure of the serial killer across media, national cinemas and genres as we approach the new millennium indicates that the figure is somehow also emblematic of our age. This section explores the figure of the serial killer in Hollywood cinema of the 90s while also bringing together some of the strands already explored in the book and reconnecting them to the action/spectacle genre.

Richard Dyer begins with a discussion of the relation between serial killers and seriality arguing that 'humans have always loved seriality, but it is only under capitalism that seriality became a reigning principle of cultural production'. For Dyer, 'the apotheosis of seriality as a principle is television, constantly interweaving serial strands, the orchestration of which is known as scheduling'. Dyer focuses his discussion on two films *Seven* and *Copycat* which he sees as 'rather old-fashioned works, what novels and movies are supposed to be: finished self-contained, separate from everything else'.

In 'The Allure of Decay', Amy Taubin connects *Seven* to 40s noir, describing the look of the film as 'shadows and silhouettes hurtling through crumbling corridors, down the sides of a rain-drenched building, into an alley that's as ominous as one in a classic noir'. Although it is a psychologically violent film, Taubin notes that 'there's almost no violence enacted on the screen. All we see is the end products of violence' and argues that *Seven* is 'as lush and lyrical a film as ever came out of Hollywood'.

In 'Exploding Hollywood', Larry Gross talks about another movie with people who kill and kill again, one written by Tarantino, where the killers are related to the broader image culture we live in. Gross sees all of *Natural Born Killers* as 'freighted with and at war with Hollywood action cinema' and argues that *NBK's* secret utopian ambition is to put Hollywood action cinema out of business. In his introduction to the interview with Oliver Stone, Gavin Smith describes the film's violence as cartoonish and argues that '*NBK* is an investigation into the limits of filmic representation' and that the film 'ranks among mainstream cinema's greatest formal experiments'. Nick James, in his review, offers good reasons why he doesn't quite agree.

Together, the articles in this section not only offer insights into the figure of the serial killer, but also raise questions about genre, mode and narrative in contemporary American cinema. Larry Gross notes that *NBK* is both 'bad' and also 'important' and necessary. 'It's confounding,' he writes. 'It reveals contradictions within the very framework of how we try to talk about films.' These contradictions will be explored into the next section.

KILL AND KILL AGAIN

Richard Dyer

Serial killers kill serially: one murder after another, each a variation and continuation of those before, each an episode in a serial. Then the police and the media identify apparently disconnected murders as connected, and the logic of the serial unfolds: the discovery of further corpses, the next instalments in the killing, the investigation, the culprit's apprehension, trial and even their life in prison. In turn, each killer is fitted into the wider phenomenon of 'serial killing' itself, with its stars, fact, fiction or both (Jack the Ripper, the vampire of Dusseldorf, Ian Brady and Myra Hindley, Norman Bates, Jeffrey Dahmer, Hannibal the Cannibal, Fred and Rosemary West) and its featured players, the police, victims, witnesses and acquaintances. And we have recently had *Millennium*, a television serial about serial killers.

There have of course been serial killers on television before. Several of the real-life stars of serial killing have had mini-series devoted to them, provided their tendencies were not too gross to be accommodated to television's 'family audience' remit. Thus we had Ted Bundy, the All-American guy so clean-cut he could talk himself into any young woman's company (*The Deliberate Stranger*, 1986) and John Wayne Gacey, respectable citizen and murderer of boys galore (*To Catch a Killer*, 1992). But Ed Gein, whose human-skin draping of himself inspired *Psycho* (1960), *The Texas Chainsaw Massacre* (1974) and *The Silence of the Lambs* (1991), has achieved nothing made-for-television – nor yet Jeffrey Dahmer with his charnel house, nor the Wests with their prolonged molestation, torture and incest. Serial killers have featured in most police and detective series, including the most recent *Murder One*; the first episode of *Cagney and Lacey* (1982) and the first multi-episode story of *Prime Suspect* (UK, 1991), both sold on the novelty of their women detective heroes; and the first series of *Band of Gold* (UK, 1995) about a group of prostitutes uniting under the threat of a serial killer. Nonetheless, there has probably only once before been a television serial posited on serial killing, *Kolchak: the Night Stalker* (1974–75) – and its multiple killers were vampires, mad scientists, werewolves and witches, never natural human males.

With *Millennium*, series creator Chris Carter is probably doing no more than cashing in on two current media success stories, his own with *The X Files*, and that of the serial killer, grafting one on to the other (which *The X Files* had anyway already done). But its appearance in the schedules today is also the culmination of a deeper logic.

Selling the pattern

It's clear that humans have always loved seriality. Bards, jongleurs, griots and yarn-spinners (not to mention parents and nurses) have all long known the value of leaving their listeners wanting more, of playing on the mix of repetition and anticipation, and indeed of the anticipation of repetition that underpins serial pleasure. However, it is only under capitalism, that seriality became a reigning principle of cultural production, starting with the serialisation of novels and cartoons, then spreading to news and movie programming. Its value as a selling device for papers and broadcasts is obvious, and never more so than in the wake of Gianni Versace's murder. Each day sold news of fresh revelations and speculations – the killer wore dresses, maybe the Mafia was involved, had the suspect been seen at a party at Gianni's only a week before – to the point that the alleged killer's suicide seemed almost spoilsporting, bringing a good story to so swift a conclusion. And the apotheosis of seriality as a principle is television, constantly inter-weaving serial strands, the orchestration of which is known as scheduling.

Serial killing is often taken to be the crime of our age. It is held to be facilitated by the anonymity of mass societies, and the ease and rapidity of modern transport, to be bred from the dissolution of the affective bonds of community and lifelong families and fomented by the routinisation of the sexual objectification of women in the media. It is supposedly a symptom of a society in which worth is judged in terms of fame, to the point that spectacularly terrible killing is just a route to celebrity. To these features we may add the amplified desire for seriality.

Towards the beginning of Fritz Lang's all-time serial-killing classic *M* (1931) we see the murder of little Elsie, the film's first. Haunting images signifying her death – her ball rolling to a stop amid patches of grass, her balloon man caught up in telegraph wires – are followed by a black screen then out of the silence emerges the cry of a newspaper seller, calling out 'Extra! Extra! Another murder!' over and over again; the scene fades up and his slowish, regular repetition is augmented by the shriller, faster, more irregular voices of book sellers running along a street, which is swiftly thronged with people jostling to buy the papers. Even before this a cappella celebration of seriality, Elsie was bouncing her ball against a poster proclaiming that 'The murderer is amongst us,' until the shadow of the man who will befriend and kill her falls across it. Then her mother, anx-ious that Elsie is so late getting home, relievedly answers a ring at the door, only to find a man delivering 'a sensational new chapter' of a story to which she subscribes. No less than the global media village after Versace's murder, the 30s Germany of *M* seems awash with seriality, its pull intensified by the horror and prurience evinced by sexual killing.

Seriality emphasises anticipation, suspense, what will happen next? It also empha-sises repetition, pattern, structure. We may enjoy the excitement of the threat posed by a serial killer – when will he strike next and whom? when will they get him? – but we can also enjoy discerning the pattern in his acts. This may be the same basic pat-tern in each act – the same selection of victim, the same method of killing – or it may be the way that a pattern emerges out of all the killing seen as a sequence. The com-monest form of the first kind of pattern is explanation – each act becomes an expression of the same underlying pattern of motivation. A classic example of the sec-ond kind of pattern – that virtually only exists in fiction – would be a series of killings based upon some numerical or alphabetical sequence.

Elegant menace, hideous pleasure

Two recent films in particular develop and play on this sense of the pleasure of dis-cerning the pattern in seriality killing: *Seven* and *Copycat*. In the first we share the realisation by the police detective Somerset (Morgan Freeman) that apparently disconnected murders are connected and later that the connection enacts the seven deadly sins. This elegantly simple design is underscored by the use of titles for each successive day of the week, indicating that there will be seven sins in seven days, and then reinforced by having each sinner killed through his or her own sin (the glutton is forced to eat till his stomach bursts, the woman of lust is fucked to death by a dildo in the form of a serrated knife, and so on). Both the killer, John Doe (Kevin Spacey) and the other investigating officer, Mills (Brad Pitt), are themselves drawn into the chain of murders, until the whole structure folds back on itself. Doe is killed for his own envy, and Mills' career and mind are destroyed by his own wrath; what's more, each effects this destruction on the other, Doe goading Mills into killing him (Doe), knowing this will destroy Mills.

Copycat also develops an exquisitely simple pattern into which killer and investigators are woven. Like the serial-killer expert Helen (Sigourney Weaver) and cop M.J. (Holly Hunter), we come to recognise the broad principle of the killing repetitions, each being based on the *modus operandi* of a previous celebrated killer. But the order in which these imitative murders are undertaken is a problem. Only near the end of the film does Helen realise that it follows the order these star killers were listed in a lecture she gave – and we witnessed – at the film's start. As the investigator, she discerns a pattern she herself supplied in the first place. A frightening logic ensues. After her lecture, she had been menaced by a serial killer (Harry Connick Jr), only narrowly escaping death. The copycat killer wants now to round off this unfinished pattern, to make a perfect series of killings. The film, however, wants to repeat *itself,* so this killing too must only be an attempted one, bringing the film to a perfect formal closure.

Not all serial-killer films offer such dispassionate pleasures (and it should be added that *Seven* is rich in menace and *Copycat* in hideous suspense). *The Texas Chainsaw Massacre*, for instance, is so remorselessly visceral a slasher that one hardly has time to sit back and discern patterns. Other films seem deliberately to work against the desire to savour structures. Henry (Michael Rooker) of *Henry Portrait of a Serial Killer* (1989) is versed in serial-killer discourse and knows he will be caught if he repeats himself in his murders; this basic tenet is one he teaches Otis (Tom Towles) as he inducts him into killing. Yet, paradoxically, the denial of distinctive form to the killing simply emphasises its sheer repetitiveness – no clever patterns, just on and on and on. This is further underlined by the film's absolute refusal to give explanations for what Henry does, no behavioural deviance (as in *M*), no woman-blaming (*Psycho*), no media infection (*Natural Born Killers*, 1994), nothing that would make a kind of sense of the endless slaughter. *Kalifornia* (1993) likewise upsets the hope that serial killing has a pattern and serial killers an explanation. As writer and photographer respectively, Brian and Carrie (David Duchovny and Michelle Forbes) set off across America to visit the sites of famous murders, aiming to produce a glossy book of entertainment and explanation. Through an advertisement, they take on Early and Adele (Brad Pitt and Juliette Lewis) to share the costs of the journey. But Early is a killer, and since he kills repeatedly, could be termed a 'serial killer' – except he does it mainly out of convenience. He doesn't kill for the sake of it, let alone to enact the elegant patterns of *Seven* or *Copycat.* When he has no money for petrol at a garage, he simply kills a man in the toilet and steals from the corpse to pay the bill. Though the film is less interesting than it sounds, *Kalifornia*'s premise – that serial killing is just a lot of killing done for different practical reasons by the same person – nonetheless subverts that longing for form and sense that makes *Seven* and *Copycat* so satisfying.

Indeed, for all *Seven*'s stunning bleakness, its assertion of a pattern to its killings seems reassuring beside *Henry*'s vision of killing without shape or sense. Both *Seven* and *Copycat* are actually rather old-fashioned works, what novels and movies are supposed to be: finished, self-contained, separate from everything else. *Henry* is more truly modern, more like television. It realises, in macabre and terrible form, the quintessence of seriality, the soap opera, the story with no beginning and no end. *Seven* and *Copycat* give us the feeling that we can sit back in the dark, see the pattern and make sense of it, however appalling. With *Henry*, there is no sense – it opens up the spectre of endlessness, forever trapped by the compulsions of serial watching, engulfed in repetition without end or point.

Men who kill women

Not that the compulsive repetitions of serial killing are ever random. Though such classy works as *Manhunter* (1986), *Seven*, *Copycat* and *Millennium* avoid this issue, serial killers – in fact and fiction – are not just people who kill people; they are men who kill women or socially inferior men (boys, blacks, queers). The numbers of women or of non-white men who are serial killers are so tiny as to be statistically negligible, as are the number of grown, heterosexual, white men who are victims (leaving aside the few killed for getting in the way).

Serial-killer fictions condemn the slaughter of women, of course, yet also provide opportunities for misogyny. One commanding pattern of explanation for the killer's behaviour is to blame it on women: on dominating and teasing mothers, on provocative flirts, on prostitutes as the repository of male sexual disgust. Is it not Mrs Bates' fault that Norman is so screwed up about women? Don't those flighty girls in *Halloween* (1978) deserve what they get? No film is ever this straightforward, of course, but woman-blaming is seldom entirely absent as an explanatory framework: it is nearly always available to those for whom it is congenial.

Moreover, cowering women – often with the camera bearing down on them – may provide opportunities for sadistic visual pleasure. The horrible *Maniac* (1980) contains one of the most unspeakably protracted scenes of suspense in all movies, with a victim huddling terrified in a cubicle in a deserted women's toilet in the notoriously dangerous New York subway. Are we to identify with her and her terror, either to remember just how terrible serial killing is, or else to experience fear vicariously, as a masochistic thrill? Or are we simply to enjoy watching her suffer? And who does the film think 'we' are, men or women?

Serial killers may be horrific, but at the same time they may be figures to be identified with. They are often cult heroes, from Jack the Ripper to Freddy Krueger; real-life serial killers receive stacks of devoted fanmail. This is a point picked up by *Copycat*, which ends not with the death of the copycat killer, nor the satisfaction and relief of the women who have despatched him, but with the killer from the movie's opening writing to a 'disciple' from prison. The misogyny within such identification or admiration may be quite explicit woman-hating, a dwelling and a getting-off on the killer's dominance and destruction of women, or it may be a fascination more with his power, even his genius. Hannibal Lecter (Anthony Hopkins) never verbally expresses hatred of women, is courteous to Clarice Starling (Jodie Foster) and seems mainly to kill men – yet his whole persona, not least his ineffable sarcasm, is founded on the supremacy of the powerful and the expendability of the weak, a glorification that sits easily with notions of masculinity. Not the least of the genius of the killer in classy films is an ability to discipline a murderous tendency into witty serial patterns.

The superdetective

Though women are central to the serial-killer phenomenon, the *raison d'être* for killer and investigator alike, much of the actual action in a serial-killing movie is between men, on-screen between killer and pursuer, and also to a considerable extent between screen and audience. And along with the misogynist pleasures noted above, these films tend to posit men as the only possible saviours of women.

Police detection, as such, is often shown to be feeble. In *The Boston Strangler* (1968), only the chance sharing of a lift between the detectives and Albert DeSalvo, arrested for housebreaking, leads to his identification as the strangler; in *Seven*, Doe simply gives himself up. Elsewhere, investigation often requires input from rival criminals: the underworld gets to the child killer of *M* before the police, while the FBI needs Lecter to track down Buffalo Bill in *The Silence of the Lambs*.

There is one exception to all this shaky detection: the 'profiler', the genius-like investigator able, on the basis of clues at the scene of the crime, to narrow down the social and geographical location of the killer as well as his psychological make-up. This figure has echoes of Sherlock Holmes, who has indeed been pressed into service in the hunt for Jack the Ripper (*A Study in Terror*, 1965; *Murder by Decree*, 1979); but its real-life exemplar is John Douglas, head of the FBI's National Center for the Analysis of Violent Crime, whose watchword – to know the criminal, one must study his crime – is pure Holmes. Author of the book *Mindhunter*, Douglas is clearly the prototype for Will Graham (William Petersen) in *Manhunter*, a film based on Thomas Harris' novel *Red Dragon*, and acted as consultant on Harris' subsequent, much larger hit, *The Silence of the Lambs*. Stories about profilers suggest almost preternatural powers. Douglas recounts the example of a psychiatrist, James Brussel, used by the police in the investigation of the 'Mad Bomber' (active in and around New York between 1940 and his capture in 1957); Dr Brussel's profile was exact in the smallest detail (the bomber was in his early fifties, of Slavic origin, lived in Bridgeport, Connecticut and wore double-breasted suits always kept buttoned up). Such astonishing ratiocination becomes, in *Millennium*, an extrasensory gift, whereby Frank Black (Lance Henriksen) has flashing visions which lead him to the culprit.

Manhunter, Seven and *Millennium* all emphasise the home life of the detective. Just as in the westerns and gangster films of yore, home is the realm of normal reproductive sexuality at stake in the hero's engagement with the killer's abnormal, destructive world. He is protecting home from what the killer represents, doing his bit to make the world safe for women and children. The potential invasion of the homes is the deepest anxiety in *Manhunter* and *Millennium* (where it provides a running weekly cliffhanger), and it is, of course, brought to devastating fruition in *Seven*.

In this context – of men killing women, and of men pursuing men, all in the name of women – *Copycat* is a surprising film. Other films (*Basic Instinct*, 1992, *Butterfly Kiss*, 1995 and every second Italian horror thriller) aim to surprise by flying in the face of statistics and featuring female serial killers. But *Copycat*'s opening scene has Helen underline in her lecture the fact that serial killers are overwhelmingly male and white. This moment counters two of the mainstays of serial-killer movies. First, it insists that the killers are (in all other respects) typical white men, not exceptional monsters; second, it is a woman who demonstrates this, with all the authority of expertise.

Another woman, M.J., then joins forces with Helen, to track down and destroy the copycat killer. The obvious predecessor, Clarice Starling in *The Silence of the Lambs*, has to turn to a male expert, Lecter, to help her. M.J. not only turns to a female and non-criminal expert, Helen, but in her first scene in the film, she is also shown to be more able to handle herself physically than her hunky male sidekick. Moreover, he is eliminated towards the film's end, leaving Sigourney and Holly alone to face the killer. Nor is it masculine-style heroics that destroys this killer, but instead female derision. When it seems that there is no way out for her, Helen just starts to laugh at the absurdity of it all – and it is the killer's confusion and dismay at this that unmans him, leaving the way open for M.J. to shoot him.

Why does Helen laugh? Perhaps a kind of hysteria, or relief that now her life of anxiety will be ended. But also perhaps because she sees the profound absurdity of the seriousness with which men take serial-killing. The destruction of others, the lethal pursuit of women, is of course serious. But when it gets dressed up in all these clever patterns (*Seven*, *Copycat* itself), or gets passed off as genius (Lecter), then it is also appallingly silly. *Seven*'s bleakness is sublime, a symphony of despair, but the end of *Copycat* accords with *Henry*: killing is just killing is just killing.

THE ALLURE OF DECAY

Amy Taubin

Despite corpses so grisly they turn the autopsy scene in *The Silence of the Lambs* into a pleasant memory, *Seven* is an overwhelmingly seductive movie. It's not easy to make a great film out of a tacky serial-killer script, but director David Fincher comes close. And if *Seven* isn't a great film (as *Touch of Evil* is, through and through), it *is* great filmmaking, from the Nine Inch Nails opening credits to the Bowie/Eno cut at the close. Fincher honed his techno-romantic aesthetic on music videos, and fast cutting has nothing to do with it.

Seven opened mid-September in over 2,000 theatres in the US; despite wretched reviews from most of the daily critics, it shot immediately to first place at the box office where it remained for five weeks. At the end of nine weeks, it was still in the top ten and had grossed about $85 million. Since it had been produced by mini-major New

Line (now part of the Time Warner empire) for around $30 million, it's among the most profitable films of the year.

Gambling on sin's enduring appeal as a subject, and (given the rise of the religious right) its propitiousness, as well as on the star power of Brad Pitt, New Line mounted a lavish, last-minute marketing campaign with primetime television trailers and double-page newspaper ads. The print ads, more murky even than the movie, depicted Pitt and co-star Morgan Freeman in close-up, almost cheek-to-cheek, like a double-headed hydra. Oddly, they look more like twins than the polar opposites they are in the movie (a sixty-year-old world-weary black detective, and the thirty-year-old white pup who hopes to follow in his footsteps). Between them, in white lettering, a list of the seven deadly sins, each crossed off by a single stroke in red ink.

The ad was arresting. It promised a darker twist on the infallible Mel Gibson/Danny Glover *Lethal Weapon* coupling. But were these good guys, or villains, or one of each? Was this a horror film or a *policier* or a combination of the two? There was something unsettling about the way the fungal greenish-brown of the background was etched with opalescent white, like indecipherable grave rubbings. Not only did the ad spell out the hooks in the film – the stars, the theme – but it also suggested the other element that makes *Seven* so alluring.

Seven rubs your face in the necrophilia latent, if largely abstract, in the horror-film genre (not to mention in film itself). Like Jonathan Demme's *The Silence of the Lambs*, *Seven* is a police procedural/horror hybrid in which perversion (in Freud's terms, 'the death drive') outweighs the logic of detection. 'Necrophilia is in,' said my friend, film-maker Daniel Minahan, an astute reader of the *zeitgeist*. 'Damien Hirst and Nine Inch Nails, it's the last transgression.'

To get the plot out of the way (and give fair warning to squeamish viewers): Somerset (Freeman), a veteran homicide cop who's six days from retirement, and Mills (Pitt), his eager-as-a-chipmunk replacement, are assigned to a particularly lurid murder investigation. A 500-pound man has been found naked and dead, his face in a plate of spaghetti, his hands and feet bound, a pail of vomit between his knees. He was force-fed until he burst. Before long, Somerset, the intellectual of the duo, realises that they're up against a serial killer with a twisted biblical road-map for murder. Each of his victims personifies one of the seven deadly sins: the first victim is gluttonous, the second greedy, and so forth.

If the screenplay sounds pat, it is. It's also pretentious, slipshod (you literally can see the *dénouement* coming from miles away) and as rightwing as Newt Gingrich's natterings about New York. In *Seven*, man is corrupt, and cities are cesspools of contagion, spreading sin faster than TB. Forget the inequities of class and race, we're all sinners, and urban blight is the Lord's décor for the gates of hell. *Seven* may be the only movie of the year where all the cops are decent guys, trying to do the right thing in evil times. Somerset has never used his gun in thirty years, Mills has only fired his once, and both of them are completely colourblind. Mills has a wife (Gwyneth Paltrow) who's a saint of domesticity right out of John Ford. Though she hates and fears the city, she stands by her man.

There are, of course, many contradictions at work here. *Seven*'s psychopathic killer is himself a product of religious fundamentalism and his particular brand of psychosis is as likely to be found in the rural heartland as in the city. Like most successful mass-market movies, *Seven* allows for multiple readings, offering something to everyone.

The film pays only the most perfunctory attention to character. The madman who fancies himself an avenging angel is no Travis Bickle or Hannibal Lecter. The narrative structure, however, has similarities to *The Silence of the Lambs*, though it's missing the crucial figure of Lecter. The killer *du jour* doesn't appear on screen until halfway through the movie, and as in *Lambs*, he's more confused and pathetic than frightening, less a subjectivity than a cliché of psychopathology. Pitt's Mills is less dedicated and less intelligent than Jodie Foster's Clarice, and of course there's no gender disruption at work here. If there's anything approaching a fully drawn character, it's Freeman's Somerset, Mills' reluctant mentor, the world-weary detective with a humanist's understanding of history. Somerset knows he's no match for the evil that's taking over. All he can do is stand by, grave and powerless. A witness rather than an action hero, he's our point of identification.

In *Seven*, the detectives never get the better of the killer. They're two steps behind him to the very end. There's almost no violence enacted on the screen. All we see is the end products of violence – butchered bodies, rotting flesh. Its director is an aesthetician of rot and entropy. If *Seven* lacks the mythic underpinnings of his first feature *Alien³*, its ambience is even more overwhelming. Every frame seems saturated with despair. His concrete sense of place is the cornerstone of his directing talent. Working with production designer Arthur Max, who developed his apocalyptic style as a stage lighting designer for Pink Floyd and Genesis, and cinematographer Darius Khondji, who's currently shooting for Bertolucci, Fincher brings forth an acrid vision of post-industrial decay – all dank greens and browns, the light filtered through pelting rain and smog so yellow you can taste it. The walls are peeling, the dust is thick, the clutter is out of control. If not for a couple of already obsolete computer terminals in the police station, you might think you were in a 30s Depression picture or a 40s noir. In any event, it looks as if things have been spiralling downhill since the time motion pictures were invented.

Fincher favours set-ups so dark that Freeman would become the invisible man if not for the hits of light off his cheekbones; while Pitt's face is as chalky as a corpse's. *Seven* was processed through silver retention, a seldom-used method whereby the silver that's leeched out during conventional processing is rebonded. Silver retention produces more luminosity in the light tones and more density in the darks, but it is so time consuming, not to mention expensive, that neither film labs nor producers want to get involved. Only a few hundred of the more than 2,500 prints of *Seven* in distribution are silver retention, which means that you may never see the film I am writing about. Fincher says that he and Khondji built the film around blackness and that it's unbelievably depressing for him to look at the non-silver retention prints: 'They're so milked out, it's as if you have glaucoma.'

Seven literalises the struggle of bringing things to light. As in his video for Aerosmith's 'Janie's Got a Gun', Fincher loves the look of flashlights penetrating obscure and terrifying places. The film hits its stride halfway through, with a chase scene so dark that we can't tell one good guy from the other, let alone good from bad. It's nothing but shadows and silhouettes hurtling through crumbling corridors, down the sides of a rain-drenched building, into an alley that's as ominous as one in a classic noir. *Alien³* all but fell apart in the clumsy chase scenes through the bowels of the prison. Here, Fincher manages the near-impossible feat of sustaining tension and suggesting spatial continuity even when we can't tell where we are or who's who.

There's an across-the-board revulsion for the body in this movie, not just for the marbled, putrefying flesh of the dead. Even in close-ups, Fincher keeps an uneasy distance (he favours low-angled shots, rather than eye-of-God overheads). The camera (often handheld or on a steadicam) sometimes seems to float, sometimes seems dragged as if by an undertow. The extremely shallow focus is a way of controlling the viewer's eye, making you look at what you don't want to see and suggesting that there's something worse that you just can't get a grip on lurking on the periphery.

While *Seven* is most distinguished by its camerawork, Fincher also has stunning control over the rhythm and pace of individual scenes (his choice of angles is always surprising), and over the film's general shape, which is very erotic in its rises and falls. This shapeliness is much abetted by Howard Stone's score, even darker than the one he did for *The Silence of the Lambs*.

Fincher doesn't hide his sources. *Seven* is blatantly reminiscent, not only of *The Silence of the Lambs*, but of Ulu Grosbard's underrated *True Confessions* and of Robert Frank's photobook *The Americans*. (Frank has become as much a reference point for American film-makers as Edward Hopper once was.) In the game of aesthetic one-upmanship, Fincher's ploy is to maintain clinical detachment while heightening the visceral quality of his imagery. The dead in *Seven* have met with very bad ends. If we are fascinated by their remains, it's because Fincher is so good at suggesting that there is nothing to prevent us from winding up just like them.

Fincher is like a Baudelairean aesthete in reverse: a modernist with stunning control over the great modernist medium, finding beauty in rotting corpses and reeking cities. Forget the puerile genre script: *Seven* is, beginning to end, as lush and lyrical a film as ever came out of Hollywood. Watching Mills and Somerset chase the killer, leaping and staggering through shafts of light diffused through centuries of dust, one thinks of Jacques Tourneur and Louis Feuillade (the almost monochromatic colour cinematography has the density of black and white). But Fincher not only moulds space with light, he shapes time with it too. Every time a shot changes, the light streaming softly from a window or a lamp hits the eye like a muffled drumbeat. 'Edgar Poe loves to set his figures in action against greenish or purplish backgrounds, in which we can glimpse the phosphorescence of decay and sniff the coming storm,' wrote Baudelaire. If Fincher wants to get down to cases, he should make Poe's *The Mystery of Marie Roget*.

AMY TAUBIN TALKS WITH THE DIRECTOR

David Fincher says he'd rather do an interpretative dance than give interviews. He claims he's only done three – one for *Premiere* magazine after *Alien³*, 'because they told me that if I didn't, they would blame me alone for its failure', and two immediately after *Seven* opened. What follows are excerpts from a phone interview in September, on the day most of the reviews of *Seven* came out, when the fate of the film was still uncertain.

In his mid-thirties, Fincher was born in California, fell in love early with movies, never attended college, taking a job instead, in an animation house, when he was eighteen. He worked for George Lucas' special-effects company Industrial Light and Magic, and began his directing career with commercials and music videos. He is a co-founder of the ultra-hip production company Propaganda Films. His first feature *Alien³* (1992) was a commercial disaster – although a few people, including me, counted it among the best films of the year.

'There's no one who hated *Alien³* more than I did,' he says. 'The movie I set out to do, the one in my head, was so different from what got made. I got hired for a personal vision and was railroaded into something else. I had never been devalued or lied to or treated so badly. I wasn't used to adults lying to me. I didn't read a script for a year and a half after that, I thought I'd rather die of colon cancer than do another movie. Then I read *Seven* and I thought there's something so perverse about this.

'*Seven* is the first time I got to carry through certain things about the camera – and about what movies are or can be. It came out of left-field, with this little twist on genre. I never thought New Line would get behind it and promote it the way they are. I thought I was making a tiny genre movie, the kind of movie Friedkin might have made after *The Exorcist*, a little handheld hippie movie. I tried hard not to have a hundred fucking trucks, but every time you take the camera out of the box, it gets complicated.

'Just in terms of the decisions with Darius [Khondji], we wanted to do something immediate and simple. We started with *Cops*, the television show – how the camera is in the backseat peering over people's shoulder, like the runt following after the pack, a vulnerable position.

'Staging to me is everything. That's the whole game – where do you place the window? Darius and I talked about, psychologically, where we wanted to be in any given room. We decided we wouldn't build any flyaway walls. If the kitchen is only twelve feet, then hem him in. We live in an age when anything is possible, so it's always important to limit yourself. It's important the blinders you put on, what you won't say. I wanted to take an adult approach – not, "Oh, wow, a Luma crane."

'The movie cost $15 million below the line. We wanted to shoot in Oakland. Beautiful clapboard houses. But we didn't have enough time. So it's all downtown LA. The reason it rains all of the time is that we only had Brad Pitt for 55 days, with no contingency. So we did it to stay on schedule, because we knew that if it ever really rained we would have been fucked.

'I never thought it was a violent movie. I was afraid people wouldn't respond viscerally. It takes place after the scene when we see the killer stalking someone – she's in the shower, he's outside the window... But the thing I found gripping about the script is the connect-the-dots aspect. It's a connect-the-dots movie that delivers about inhumanity. It's psychologically violent. It implies so much, not about why you did, but how you did it. It has this element of evil that's realistic. But I didn't want people to say, "Isn't this the grisliest thing you ever saw?" What grosses me out is violence you're supposed to cheer for.

'At the premiere in New York, I could feel that people were stunned. I guess I'm just a warped fuck, but I never saw it that way. At the LAPD, they have files of photographs that they pull out and show you. A guy shot in the head and his brains unravelled like shoe strings. If you took the pictures and put them in a movie, no one would believe you.

'I didn't set out to piss off the people who are upset. I was told that Michael Medved [the ultra-right-wing critic at the *New York Post* – AT] wrote that the movie was evil, but I'm sure he slows down when he passes an accident just like everyone else. Death fascinates people, but they don't deal with it. In Joel Peter Witkin's photographs, it's demonic to see people without muscles to hold their face in place, but it's also peaceful: I wanted people to know there are stakes.'

EXPLODING HOLLYWOOD

Larry Gross

I don't know of a movie that has made me more ambivalent, more undecided and more uncertain in my reaction than *Natural Born Killers*. As an experience for the average viewer, the blood-stained road-movie story of Mickey and Mallory is numbingly familiar, the satirical attacks on media and prisons pedestrian and all too easy. As actual film-making, the visuals of the film are rushed, awkward. There is no 'viewpoint' towards the killer-protagonists consistently and intelligibly assembled, and so the usual defensive arguments – that the film exploits the issues about violence it purportedly deals with – have some measure of truth. By almost every regular criterion *Natural Born Killers* is a failure as a work of art. Yet it is the film released by Hollywood in 1994 that most deserves serious support, respect and admiration. Oliver Stone, without entirely knowing how or why, went for it. He dared to put his deepest rage on screen. All of us who live and work in Hollywood stand abashed, first at how he manoeuvred himself into a position to do it, and second at how far he was willing to go; what he was willing to risk, what he was willing to question.

How can a film be 'bad' in the ways listed above, and be 'important' and necessary in other ways? It's confounding. It reveals contradictions within the very framework of how we try to talk about films. But this is the film's 'importance'. *Natural Born Killers* is one of the few Hollywood films that forces us to come to it, after a while, on its terms.

Everyone knows the imitation *Badlands/Bonnie and Clyde/Gun Crazy* plot of *NBK* by now, that is unless they haven't cared about Hollywood action cinema of the last three decades. Everyone knows that Stone pasted onto the basic situation a kind of Zolaesque allegory in the third act, where the punk killers Mickey and Mallory inspire a bloody prison revolt thereby acting out what TV is Doing To American Society. What five minutes of *NBK* tells us is that accounts of the stories and the characters' psychologies, these conventional ways of describing a movie, are all beside the point. Every attempt to describe this film, or admire it, in naturalistic vocabulary, or to explore the sensations that the garish rapid montage sequences produce, also misses the mark. *NBK* is not a meaningful disquisition on the impulse to be violent, nor is it an analysis of the role that media plays in making us more violent. Rather *NBK* is a film about film. It is Oliver Stone duelling with the recent history of the movie image. It is an attempt to look at how an 'image culture' has taken over from immediate experience. Violence is a secondary symptom of a primary disease, the sheer pollution of representational imagery.

Stone's decisive energy and will to subvert are directed against the Hollywood deal itself, the unholy pact between commercial cinema's practices, and the audience's jaded appetites. The film demands that the audience question all regular modes of identification, and all reality of character and situation. This is done as resolutely as anything by Bresson or late Godard or experimentalists like Stan Brakhage and Michael Snow. A brief exposure to Stone's aggressive montage style tells us that we're not in Kansas any more. We're in a radically disjunctive universe where image, action, and sensation are divorced from the narrative armature of cause and effect.

The second time I watched *NBK* and came to the film's centrepiece which is Woody Harrelson's lengthy jail house interview with media huckster Robert Downey Jnr, I realised that every Harrelson speech was a question, culled from interviews with various of the legends of mass murder, Gary Gilmore, Charles Manson, Jack Henry Abbot. As I sat there watching Harrelson's perfect imitation of wild things like Brando in *The Wild One* and Martin Sheen in *Badlands*, a thought went through me. What if Stone wants me to recognise the sources? What if Stone means to distance me this way from thinking of Mickey as a literal figure in a drama? What if instead of being a character, Mickey is rather a textual effect? An abstraction of imagery in the form of a figure, rather than a person I'm trying to care about? Suddenly other things in the film start to kick in. Stone creates for us the wacky sitcom *I Love Mallory*, to show that Mallory was abused by her oaf father (played by Rodney Dangerfield) which 'caused' her to become the poisonous thing she is now. The literal interpretation of this show-within-a-film is that Mickey and Mallory are 'victims' of abuse. But the sitcom format undermines that reading. Frequently Dangerfield's puffy saliva-oozing face will flash before Juliette Lewis' eyes, a film noir nightmare. Doesn't Stone stylise the characters' back story to undermine the *very notion* of causal explanation? Abuse 'explains' Mickey and Mallory? The sitcom literally tells us this but if we accept it we're as moronic as the people giggling on the laugh track.

NBK begins with a detailed shot-by-shot reconstruction of the opening sequence from *Henry: Portrait of a Serial Killer*; it ends with the phrase 'Let's make some music, Colorado,' thereby invoking *Rio Bravo*, one of Tarantino's favourite action movies. All of *NBK* is freighted with and at war with Hollywood action cinema. (Stone's own films such as *Scarface* – which he scripted – and *Platoon* are even invoked as part of the sea of visual shit.) What Stone wants somehow to do is slough off his Hollywood identity with this movie. He wants, in some deeply tormented way, to annihilate the shell of Hollywood norms that have heretofore controlled his own and everyone else's careers. This is an aspiration that everyone who works in Hollywood understands: the desire to make a film about characters who are not palatable, to deal with emotions and situations that cannot be resolved positively, to leave the regular, three-act, psychologically motivated story structure behind and finally, if you follow the logic, to question the whole of conventional representation.

Now, you may ask yourself, do any of the concerns I've described here, which show the film as a kind of allegory of Stone's Hollywood career, that interpret the film's goals as chiefly aesthetic, and not really political, have that much to do with the film's concerns that *are* political? The answer is, not much. As sociology *NBK* stinks, nowhere more so than in the very disappointing riot sequence. There, by some conceptual sleight of hand, Stone makes analogy between maximum security prisoners and the entire mass audience watching TV. Mickey makes them mad, as TV is making us mad. Get it? Well, this is profoundly untrue and unjust and unfair, both to the prison population and to the mass TV audience. The part and the whole are not identical. I read the 'ending' of *NBK* another way, of course. All of the final developments in the narrative – Mickey inspiring the prison population to riot, Robert Downey Jr's journalist 'joining' the killers, un-named prisoners slaughtering everyone in sight – occur at a speed and mania level that obliterates the feeling of casualty. The chaos of shifting arrangements and alliance among the characters is mirrored in the surface action of the riot, and together these give us an image of the film itself self-destructing, as if narrative is cannibalising itself. Mickey and Mallory make their getaway into a dreamspace beyond all narrative coherence.

Now what makes evaluating this movie so tough is that all the ideas I've just described operate largely subconsciously. I don't know if Stone 'meant' any of the things I've just attributed to the film. He is a compulsive, speeding-like-a-freight-train film-maker. The term 'shoot from the hip' has Oliver Stone's face next to it in the slang dictionary. There are things in the movie that very much don't fit into my reading: when Mickey and Mallory visit an Indian Chief who 'understands' them, he lives in a social utopia of wisdom, father-with-son (no women – get it?) which Stone doesn't seem to have too much irony about. Juliette Lewis' performance as Mallory, while superb, is emotionally 'real' in a way that contradicts Harrelson's astonishing Brechtian cool. I for one thought that Tommy Lee Jones' manic, Road Runnerish, cartoon performance was exquisitely in key with the film's stylisation, but another fine actor, Tom Sizemore, seems marooned in another picture, a realistic one. Sometimes I feel like all the actors in a Stone movie are completely on their own, left to go on whatever psychodrama of discovery they're capable of, while he just picks up on the results.

These are deviations in the film's abstractness, or they may be systematic contradictions, the way Rauschenberg will throw authentic photographic images into a completely abstract swirl. I don't know if Stone gives a solitary damn about the kinds of theoretical issues I've alluded to so far. I don't know that *NBK* has got to be both a bonanza and conundrum for theorists. Rigorous in its denial of regular film structure, it is sloppy, even incoherent, in what it wants to replace it with. Unlike the montage experiments of the early Soviets or the New Wave, Stone does not undo conventional narrative sequence in the name of other discursive or intellectual systems. Is theory that defends this film using it like a Rorschach test to confirm itself? A theorist needs to answer that question. I'm just a screenwriter.

What is fascinating and mysterious beyond words is to consider how Oliver Stone got here. In *Platoon,* ten years ago, his aesthetics were 180 degrees different. There, he wanted to present action, rigorously and directly. There was something Rossellini-like in the plainness of his film-making and the simplicity of the emotional demand that the scenes made on us. Now, a decade of high-rolling Hollywood play has been undergone, and the sensibility that made *Platoon* is in some obvious way blasted. *NBK* is a drastic, peculiar effort at self-purification on Stone's part. He lives in a contemporary Hollywood that prizes sensation at the expense of meaning. He has tried to pry that sensation mechanism open and then leave it exploded into a thousand tiny fragments. The media satire of *NBK* is its most tepidly obvious element (Downey has, in my opinion, seldom been worse) but the satire of Hollywood is fundamental. (A similar overlooked element constituted *Full Metal Jacket*, which invoked and parodied one detail or another from nearly every American film about the military made in the two decades preceding it.)

Stone wants to make it impossible for us to get into another festival of mindless explosions in the same comfortable way we used to. He wants to disturb the conditions of positivity we're all now bred to, that almost every successful Hollywood screenwriter is lavishly overpaid to produce. In the name of what? He is desperately unsure. Kubrick has been able to analyse Hollywood convention while preserving a surface intensity of accuracy or beauty. Stone can't, and his effort here is almost perfectly, purely negative. The truth is that *NBK*'s secret utopian ambition is to put Hollywood Action Cinema out of business. It can't be purified. It can only be razed to the ground.

I live and work in this business. All of us who do can identify with some of the self-hatred at work in *NBK*. All of us admire the prodigal giving of the finger that this movie represents, taking $40 million of Warner Bros' money, and insulting everyone's basic assumptions about movies. At the same time, for all the guts it took, one wants something more. Not 'positive' in the *Reader's Digest*/Norman Rockwell sense, but something articulated in the aesthetic sense. *NBK* wipes the slate clean, or tries to, but it leaves us and Stone with no place to go. I know art doesn't have to provide 'solutions', but this kind of lack of generosity and lack of intellectual rigour leaves the status quo unscathed and with too many options, too many ways to elude Stone's scattershot critique.

OLIVER STONE: WHY DO I HAVE TO PROVOKE?

Gavin Smith

At the climax of *Natural Born Killers*, white trash thrill-kill couple Mickey and Mallory Knox (Woody Harrelson and Juliette Lewis) take advantage of a prison riot to stage a live-on-TV jailbreak, using prison guards and the TV crew as human shields. The riot has been triggered by the inflammatory Nietzschean/metaphysical rhetoric Mickey used to justify himself in a ratings-grabbing TV interview with his would-be moral nemesis, star journalist Wayne Gayle (Robert Downey Jr), the self-righteous host of

American Maniacs, the *ne plus ultra* of tabloid TV. Their escape route blocked by a squad of armed guards led by the psychotic Warden McClusky (Tommy Lee Jones), Mallory demonstrates they mean business by firing a warning shot point blank through one of Gayle's hands. Cut to an outrageously unlikely reverse angle of Mickey, Mallory *et al* seen through the bullet hole in Gayle's palm.

Blink and you'll miss this throwaway gag shot – a frame of flesh within a frame of film – trimmed but not quite cut from the R-rated version of *Natural Born Killers* released this summer in the US (among the cuts: shots of prison guards being crammed into ovens, mass throat slittings, Warden McClusky's severed head on a pole and, in the film's most disturbing sequence, Mickey's motel room rape and murder of a hostage, which made crucial connections between sex and violence that were too explicit for the MPAA). This bullet-hole-through-hand moment is most representative of *Natural Born Killers'* approach to violence: cruel, mean, gratuitous even – but above all, absurd, blatantly cartoonish.

This unmistakably parodic manner is established in what must be the opening scene of the year: Mickey and Mallory dispatching an assortment of dim-witted rednecks in a roadside diner in an extended set piece complete with the mid-air over-shoulder point-of-view shots of a bullet and a buck knife specified by Quentin Tarantino in his original draft of the screenplay. (Tarantino has opted for a minimal credit and disassociates himself from the film, though I'd say that roughly 80 per cent of his script survives intact – the main addition made by Stone and his writers is the overlaying of a moral and spiritual perspective that is the logical outgrowth of the preoccupations of *The Doors* and *Heaven & Earth*.)

The anticipated firestorm of moral outrage in the US media never quite materialised at the end of a summer made safe by *Forrest Gump*'s pacification. Though critics were divided between those who praised the film's audacity and those who dismissed it as irresponsible cynicism, *Natural Born Killers* seemed perfectly timed to tap into growing public consciousness of the media's exploitative processing of crime and violence into amoral spectacle. A busy collage of visual innovation driven by a compelling industrial/alternative rock soundtrack and laced with ambiguous cheap thrills, it is unquestionably Stone's *pièce de résistance* and ranks among mainstream cinema's greatest formal experiments. Yet Stone doesn't make things easy for himself or the audience: *Natural Born Killers* is a double-edged sword, unafraid to implicate itself in the sadism of spectacle, its punishing, unrelieved harshness and in-your-face excess the only way to make its point.

Stone's film is a savage, surreal satire about violence in modern America and its representation on television and in the movies. Like all satire, it employs outrage, extremism, cruelty and indecency as rhetorical devices. That censors credit its visual simulation as having a morally corrosive power is ironic indeed, since *Natural Born Killers* arguably satirises that very notion. The words 'TOO MUCH TV' are projected across Mallory's body; intermittent flashes of nightmare imagery (Mickey bathed in blood, lungeing demons) seem to mock those who would attribute sociopathology to the malign, subliminal influence of film.

Of course, Stone is almost having it both ways: he's attacking television and the media for its exploitation, sensationalism and hypocrisy in what is at its core an exploitation movie – or a parody of one. Then again, exploitation movies are inherently self-parodic. *Natural Born Killers* has a knack of raising these sorts of questions about cinema, setting up a dialogue between social commentary and film. This is most explicit in a motel room interlude where Mickey and Mallory are bombarded with cable TV images from *The Wild Bunch*, *Scarface* and *Midnight Express*, while the motel room window behind them becomes a screen on which documentary images of the historical traumas of the twentieth century are projected. The two separate visual realities create a dialectic in which Mickey and Mallory are both subject and end result, while Stone provocatively dangles before us the notion of film's desensitising effect, employing highlights from two of his own greatest screenwriting hits.

So *Natural Born Killers* is also an investigation into the limits of filmic representation. The viewer is plunged into a phantasmagoria of aesthetic anarchy: critical distance, identification and narrative continuity are eradicated in a gleeful frenzy of deranged visual overload. Shifting formats (from colour to black and white to video to 8mm to 16mm to animation) with a manic overturning of visual consistency, the film flips in and out of different planes of reality – as if criss-crossing a half-dozen parallel universes – producing extraordinary moments of suspension and dissociation.

Indeed, the film denies the possibility of an objective, normative 'reality' as a frame of reference, insisting instead on multiple, hallucinatory subjective versions of the same approximate series of events, all of them given equal weight. Call it Schizophrenic Realism. Reclaiming in one sweep all the postwar American avant-garde experimental film techniques appropriated by MTV over the past ten years, then feeding them back as a critique of representation, Stone has made a film of defiant anti-naturalism that offsets its kamikaze sensationalism with authentic moments of twisted poetry and lyrical sensuality. There's probably not a single conventional image in the movie, a two-hour barrage of sound and image jump-cuts, canted angles, berserk handheld camera, outrageous process shots, overexposed and grainy footage, projected images, stock documentary and found footage, tacky optical zooms, multiple camera speeds, video noise and distortion, luridly stylised lighting, computer image morphing and so on.

If the very fabric of reality seems to disintegrate before our eyes, it may be because Stone conceives the ten-decade atrocity that is his twentieth century as a Vietnam without end, outcome of the ultimate conspiracy: human existence and history possessed and manipulated by invisible Forces of Evil. As his autobiographical persona said too portentously at the end of *Platoon*, the enemy is us. In a sense, Stone, a filmmaker who violently divides audiences with his fanatical commitment to an anti-authoritarian, proto-anarchic vision, has finally lost his grip on reality – and it's the best thing that could have happened to him.

* * *

Gavin Smith: Let's say *Natural Born Killers* is a film about the triangular relationship between crime, media and society that adopts the form of contemporary social satire, then feeds all that through two movie genres, the road movie and the prison thriller. What relationship did you try to establish between these elements and the film's style?

Oliver Stone: I have to be upfront and say that the film changed a lot as went along, it assumed new shapes. There are things in the movie that are still beyond my fingertips, beyond comprehension – the butterfly moment, the walk into the prison with Scagnetti and the Warden, the rabbit with bloody fangs Mickey mentions in the interview, which is the last image of the movie. It's the nature of the film and the nature of the ending.

Gavin Smith: Those are all moments I wanted to address – moments where the film seems to shift into another, almost mysterious, realm.

Oliver Stone: The movie evolved through the photography and editing, all the way along the line. When I think back to its origins, in my head, I'd say they were pre-Tarantino, back to 1981, my writing *Scarface* and saying to myself, this is a movie about crime and I want to make one myself. I wrote *The Year of the Dragon* and *8 Million Ways to Die*, but I had never had the chance to direct a gangster movie. Then when I saw Quentin's script, I thought, this is the perfect chance for me.

So it's a road movie/prison movie crossed with 90s media; criminals are perceived in the movie via the media. In the old days they would have had an independent existence – in *Scarface* you don't see much media – but in the 90s version of the gangster movie (or at least in this one) they exist only through the media.

The next step is to say, let's deliver the spirit of the time – and it's a heated, hyperkinetic, absurd time. We have a woman cutting off a man's penis and she's celebrated for it – when I grew up she would have appeared in the pages of the *National Enquirer* but the story would not have made network TV. Two boys kill their mother and father and they're celebrated and acquitted. The most ridiculous story is two female ice-skaters having a fight – a piece of trivia that made such an impact internationally that the Winter Olympics were watched for the first time by an extraordinary amount of people, putting, I estimate, $500 million into the network's pocket. Money has created the heat – Chayefsky was very clear about that with *Network* – which is also one of our godfathers. The money has driven 90s society to boiling point.

The movie in a sense is constructed via television and as a homage to television – someone said this movie is like watching two weeks of television in two hours. There's the aggression of the imagery, the channel-surfing philosophy of moving on. Mallory sees her life via television. You don't want to remember pain, you don't want to remember your father raping and abusing you, so you filter it via a sitcom TV unreality and then you can escape from it. Early on in the movie, form-wise, you see a constant shifting of channels – like when you jump television channels, the style of the movie is constantly changing. You go from Mickey and Mallory's point of view to Wayne Gayle's point of view to that of the Indian [Russell Means]. First we start inside Mickey and Mallory's minds. They're desensitised to feelings, they're television creatures, the products of their parents. They kill without realising the consequences. (As an aside, there is a justification for this in Mickey's mind, he gets busted for car theft and sent to prison, Mallory visits him, he's in love with her and she tells him her father is continuing to abuse her and is pressing for more charges.)

Gavin Smith: So that's all happening in an objective reality outside the film's subjective viewpoints? It's not Mickey's fantasy?

Oliver Stone: That's happening in the real world. We're out of the sitcom at that point. Mickey breaks out of prison – it looks surreal, but it does happen. Then once they've killed the father and mother they're on the road to hell – in Buddhist thought that's the worst crime you could commit. In the scene on the bridge, Mickey says, 'As God of my universe,' which is a key thought in the sense that the whole first part of the movie is structured like a virtual reality trip. The audience is in the driver's seat, but Mickey and Mallory are in charge of the world, they're having fun killing and you confront yourself. The unpredictability, the hallucinatory, feverish aspect of changing from black to white to colour to video to 8mm to animation – which is included because they are superheroes in their own minds – all these changes empower you, you control your environment, you can be what you want to be. Going from black and white to colour gives you a visual pop – such moments are not logical, but the return to colour makes the film look more vivid, which is the way Mickey and Mallory think.

Gavin Smith: It's a heightening of reality.

Oliver Stone: Yes. Controlling your universe, killing, having that power – all serial killers have talked about that sense of empowerment, they all feel a heightening of reality. That style is countered in the first twenty minutes by the TV-magazine slick style that applies to Wayne Gayle. Then we return to Mickey and Mallory, and in the motel room scene the style shifts back and forth. The style for Scagnetti [Tom Sizemore], because he wants to imitate Mickey and fuck Mallory, goes towards a lurid, cheesy lookalike style, but with more tacky lighting than Mickey's. The Indian sequence has a heightened, mystic realism – the fire, the sense of cutting, of catching your own words. It's deliberately slowed down to create an inward-looking mood.

Gavin Smith: Did you see this sequence as pivotal in the narrative structure?

Oliver Stone: Yes – killing the Indian gets them off the trip. What the American Indian gives them is some kind of spiritual consciousness. He gives it to Mallory and she gives it to Mickey. She changes first, then he changes over the course of time because he's a little more stupid than her. She has remorse, her feelings change, it's not fun any more.

Then in the prison we have another style – we're coming into the world of Warden McClusky and his style is one of paranoia and punishment. He is a highly aggressive man, as aggressive as Mickey; he keeps everybody down until they explode. In a sense it's Frankenstein's castle – there's a shot of Frankenstein in the montage. Everything is distorted: the cuts, the timing, big black faces come up because the Warden is scared. There's a moment where a black prisoner comes and talks to him and he can't hear what he's saying – it's a very paranoid style.

For me, Mickey writing the letter to Mallory is very important. He has been in prison for a year and he says, I'm thinking about you every day – he is reintegrating his feelings, getting in touch with himself. By the time he talks to Wayne Gayle in the interview he is no longer the Mickey of the first half, he has become an articulate individual, as do many people who go to prison and have time to think. I find him articulate; some people find him totally cynical, using Gayle.

Gavin Smith: You could also argue that he has the calm and clarity of a psychotic.

Oliver Stone: Great. I like that. The interview is based on the Manson-Geraldo interview of 1981 or 1982, which was fascinating. Essentially Mr Manson dances intellectual circles around Geraldo, who maintains one posture, condescension towards Manson: 'You're the killer, I'm the good guy, don't kid me, you're behind bars, thank God.' That's basically Wayne Gayle's attitude, though he's totally hypocritical because as we see later, his own violence erupts.

Gavin Smith: Both Scagnetti and Gayle act out their fantasies about being killers.

Oliver Stone: I can't tell you how many people I've met who have similar fantasies. I've been in Vietnam and people often want to talk to me about that and fantasise trying it. Mickey says to Gayle that the demon is everywhere – in prison, in the world – he was born in it, his father was born in it, the century is soaked in it. Then he says, 'Look at your shadow, you can't repress your shadow.' He's saying you must acknowledge the demon, that's the first step.

I believe that all of us are born violent – we're natural-born aggressors. We have a million-year-old reptilian brain with a neo-cortex of civilisation on top, but it's doing a bad job of concealing the aggression. Killing is a combination of genetics and environment. When I go to my son's school, I notice a lot of aggression in kids, a natural cruelty. How are we to deal with it? My way would be to show kids images of aggression – Kubrick's *2001* apemen, for instance – and say, this is you too. You are an animal. Next time you feel aggression in your schoolyard and want to slug your friend, recognise it as such – that's the beginning of getting a handle on it. If you know what it is that's making you blind with rage, you have taken the first step towards controlling the mood as opposed to having the mood control you.

Mickey is very sane when he says, 'Deal with your aggression. Don't run from it,' and then we cut to Warden McClusky sitting on his anger, wanting to kill Mickey. He's not dealing with his aggression, he's not acknowledging it. That's why the riot submerges the entire world of the prison. When Mickey says, 'Murder is pure', that's not a skinhead statement, it's in the context of the media which makes it impure because it buys and sells fear. It's a Nietzschean statement, but pure Nietzsche, not the false Nietzsche used by the Nazis to pervert the message.

Gavin Smith: In the interview, whose world are we in, Mickey's or Gayle's?

Oliver Stone: It's half and half. A lot of the shots are slick and there's a lot of stock footage when we cut to Mickey.

Gavin Smith: What about the riot, in terms of style?

Oliver Stone: [Laughing] Let's call it Pontecorvo's *The Battle of Algiers*! Chaos is an energy that takes over the movie at that point, it becomes a revolution of society, so we threw in every style we'd used until then in combination with a documentary style. When it cuts to the black people from the TV, it felt to me as though we were trying to cut to outside from an inner story and become more objective – these are the masses, or this is a Soviet documentary. These people who don't know Mickey have another goal, which is to break out and destroy.

Gavin Smith: How does *Natural Born Killers* stand in relation to the contract that exists between most mainstream American films and the audience?

Oliver Stone: Tough question. I'm not sure that this film obeys the contract. The usual characters are not there – who is the good guy, what is the catharsis of the film? It robs the audience of that and makes them question their watching, which is sub-versive. But why must there be a contract, why must there be a definition of a film? I prefer to go to a movie not knowing too much about it and just let it happen to me. It's a wholly subjective experience, going to the movies. It is the subjective chasing the subjective.

Natural Born Killers is not an easy movie to settle into, you can't get a point of view, you have to surrender to the movie. If you resist the movie with conventional ethics, you'll have a problem. The movie asks to be looked at as, in the old sense of the word, a meditation on violence. It's like taking acid in the 60s, you have to put aside your judgment. The first part is very disturbing, a desensitising rush. The second part in prison is about reintegration and has a different rhythm. And since for me the only relationship in the movie that is pure is Mickey and Mallory's, the conventional catharsis for me would be the moment where they're reunited for the kiss in the cell and the music breaks into 'Sweet Jane'.

Gavin Smith: It's interesting that you cut away to the TV anchorwoman's reaction at that moment – and she seems moved.

Oliver Stone: Yes, she's smiling. She's totally bewildered at the shock, but she just feels good, she doesn't care about anybody being killed. She's the audience, looking at the riot as though she can't believe it, and then going into this decontextualised moment.

Gavin Smith: She represents every television viewer who reacts in a moment-to-moment way to whatever they're presented with, without any sense of context...

Oliver Stone: ...History or future. And human too – emotions and sentimentality reign. In a sense Mickey and Mallory are the only ones you can root for, they're anti-heroes but the movie questions the concept of moral relativity. Yes, they kill fifty-two people and it's unpardonable, but in a century that has killed 100 million in genocide, how big is their crime?

Gavin Smith: In the courtroom sequence cut from the film, Mickey defends himself by making reference to the state's legitimising of murder through war with the line, 'How many people do you have to kill before it becomes legal – or even subsidised?'

Oliver Stone: He was talking about corporate predation. The movie plays on that relativistic level throughout. What is violence, what is murder?

Gavin Smith: To me, the key element of the ending wasn't the compilation of real-life media crime cases with Waco, O.J. and the Menendez brothers, but the rapid montage of demons that follows it.

Oliver Stone: I call that the demon gallery.

Gavin Smith: It seems to suggest that there is no escape, no end.

Oliver Stone: The movie has an ambivalent ending. The song Leonard Cohen sings over the closing montage says 'The future is murder,' but also 'Love is the only engine of survival.' Leonard is as tough as they come and he's grim. But there's a genuine romantic underneath the hardness of his lyrics and I think the same is true of myself. People say 'Heart of Stone', but others have pointed out that I'm a sucker and sentimental.

The underlying philosophy of the film is not the media satire, but the concept of aggression in this century versus compassion and love. You might say that's ridiculous because they never do anything totally loving, and they don't. But there's another Cohen song, 'Anthem', at the very end, where he says, 'You need a crack of light to come through.' That's what's happening in this movie – you don't need a lot of compassionate love to make the point. The fact that the most violent man in the movie can talk about love, whether you believe him or not, indicates a crack of light.

The highest virtue of Buddhism is non-violence because Buddhists understand that violence is all around. The nature of violence is the nature of man. Mickey has understood that – he says a moment of realisation is worth a thousand prayers. Somebody said that's a cynical remark, but I believe he means it. That's what makes him, for me, the character who is most easy to identify with.

Gavin Smith: You seem to be trying to use contemporary music and culture as a medium for communicating with a younger generation some distance from your own. I can't think of another film-maker in your position who has attempted to speak to mass youth culture on its own terms.

Oliver Stone: The younger generation is very ironic about media, they doubt everything they see, they're not cynical, they're sceptical and rightly so. When I made *The Doors* younger people would come up to me in the street and tell me they loved it. I was interested by that because the film had been reviled by older people. It made me feel there was a left brain phenomenon in films that could connect with kids. We felt it when we were kids, with films like *El Topo* where we'd go into a dream state. I was exposed to lyrics and music I hadn't heard before through my producers and editors. I particularly liked Trent Reznor's 'Nine Inch Nails' because of the pain in the music – maybe it's a hurt that goes to the collective unconscious. It doesn't matter if you're from the 90s generation or the 60s or the 30s, when you were young you were young, and if you're in touch with those feelings you remember them.

Eddie Vedder of Pearl Jam gave me a song, 'Footsteps', in which there is a line, 'In the old days you committed suicide, in the new days you lash out,' something like that. Hurt is in the collective unconscious, I was hurt as a kid. The reason I went to Vietnam was because I wanted to commit suicide, but I didn't want to pull the trigger so I went there instead. Younger generations have an essential agony that they go through – though not all: some just go right to the golf course. But this film feels right to me, for my age. The idea of killing fifty-two people would never have occurred to me in 1969, even after *Bonnie and Clyde*. The idea when they killed was that they were victims of the Depression. But in *Natural Born Killers* they kill because they kill, there's no moral sense or excuse for it.

Gavin Smith: Doesn't your Lee Harvey Oswald have a lot in common with Mickey and Mallory – generational social alienation, a kind of Cold War outlaw?

Oliver Stone: Yes, absolutely. Gary Oldman picked up on that right away. Oswald was not a bogeyman, there's an in-depth, anguished man in there who's very bright. There's a Charles Manson quality to Oswald that I can identify with. Manson is a brilliant man and his trial is still suspect. He never killed anybody, we all know that, he is convicted of inciting others to kill.

Gavin Smith: Don't you think he was dangerous?

Oliver Stone: Charles Manson is us. He is a product of our society. He had a horrible childhood and he was in prison at the earliest age. He's us because we created the system that's done this to him. It's come back to haunt us. *Natural Born Killers* is also about this us-them duality. You can't separate yourself from the aggression. It's universal.

Gavin Smith: In the prison sequence you used real convicts as extras. In the scene in the dining room where Warden McClusky breaks up a fight, were all those prisoners real?

Oliver Stone: Most of them. The two men who were fighting are both killers, both in for life. The white guy with the bald head is a real psycho who bashed in his wife's face and killed his kids. In the riot, the people the prisoners killed were our stuntmen.

Gavin Smith: The sequence where the Warden and Scagnetti walk through the prison is remarkable.

Oliver Stone: It was the hardest scene to cut. I think we cut it thirty times, and it's set to how many different songs? 'Checkpoint Charlie' and 'The Violation of Expectation', 'The Day the Niggaz Took Over', 'Ghost Town' – that was a long, loopy, hallucinogenic thing to create the impression that the warden had no concept of what was going on in that prison.

Gavin Smith: There are certain strange moments of suspension in the film that arrest the action for a few seconds – when Warden McClusky laughs, you go to a different angle, a different format and it's in slow motion, I think, and there's different music over it and the sound fades out.

Oliver Stone: You're looking for the fact that something is different in the Warden than has been pictured in the previous frame of him. The effect of the shot is, he seems nuts.

Gavin Smith: Many of those inserts suggest a bestial conception of human nature.

Oliver Stone: Yes. Impending violence. The best moment is when Scagnetti breaks into his own philosophical *raison d'être*, with his mother being shot by Charles Whitman, the Texas sniper.

Gavin Smith: Is that actual documentary footage of the shooting that we see?

Oliver Stone: Some of it is. So Charles Whitman killed Scagnetti's mom and we cut ironically to a boy who is supposed to be the young Scagnetti, but, in fact, is the young Mickey – it's done to suggest the concept of a collective unconscious of agony. His childhood is Mickey's childhood – what difference does it make? Then it cuts to a butterfly and a beautiful romantic moment. There is beauty in life, there is a moment in the midst of this hell where the butterfly can come in.

Gavin Smith: Was there any underlying logic to the intercutting of different formats?

Oliver Stone: No. It was based on editing gut-instinct. You could post-rationalise it, but you'd be hard pressed to write a thesis on it.

Gavin Smith: Not even the high-contrast black and white 35mm, which seemed to be used for all the flashbacks of true, formative memories?

Oliver Stone: Certainly that works, most startlingly with the close-ups of Mallory's father's eyes. But later we see his eyes in colour, through the fire, which defeats your analysis. If that was a true moment for her, it should have been in black and white throughout.

Gavin Smith: So it was shot in colour and processed to black and white?

Oliver Stone: No, the black and white was shot as black and white. We also filmed his eyes in colour. But certainly that flashback of her father's sexual abuse stands out because it alternates with the colour. We couldn't have done this movie without doing *JFK*, which also had a lot of fractured reality moments.

Gavin Smith: Most critical reception of the film has made reference to MTV, but, in fact, most of the film's techniques originate in the experimental avant-garde of the 60s and 70s, which MTV has plundered. Which reminds me – someone told me that Stan Brakhage is a fan of *JFK*.

Oliver Stone: I saw his films back in 1968 at a film cooperative in New York. They made a very strong impression on me. No storylines.

Gavin Smith: In terms of its form, doesn't the film raise a lot of questions about the medium of cinema? For instance, the idea of a unified, coherent text is all but swept away – or is the film only superficially incoherent?

Oliver Stone: [Laughs] Well, it's coherent to me. It's very clear to me that definite misunderstandings arise. Is it my fault for not having clarified? Possibly, but haven't I been criticised eternally for being heavy handed? This is a hall of many mirrors. I think it's coherent, but it's evolving too, with open-ended imagery at points which throw you off kilter.

Gavin Smith: For me, a good example is the recurring shot of the headless corpse in the armchair. I didn't think that was Mickey's memory of an actual event so much as of something he saw on TV.

Oliver Stone: Or his father with his head blown off.

Gavin Smith: But he committed suicide in a field. So was it transferred to a different setting?

Oliver Stone: It could have been. It's just a horror image. And it's an image of the demon inside. But an old horror movie could be just as true.

Gavin Smith: What about the rabbit?

Oliver Stone: At the end of the film montage there's the image of the rabbit. Mickey and Mallory may have got away, but our culture has left us with a residue of fear. Either in Hindu or American Indian culture the rabbit is a symbol not just of fertility but of fear. Let's say that fear is one of the legacies of our generation. We've bombarded the world population with bad news. Crime has remained flat as a statistic since Vietnam, but Vietnam, the television war, brought the virus into the living room. Nixon – law and order; Reagan – let's build up our muscles; Bush – Willie Horton, the black parolee. Crime has been politicised, crime is perceived as the number one issue in America. What's the American vision now? Orwell's *1984* come true: don't go out because there's a black mugger outside, don't have sex because you'll get Aids, dial Barry Diller's QVC Home Shopping Network. A joyless, non-thinking life – the ultimate passive consumer.

Gavin Smith: So the rabbit is an image of a fearful position – an image Orwell himself used in *1984*, I think.

Oliver Stone: That's what I'm trying to say.

Gavin Smith: This film suggests doubt about film's suitability as a medium of truth or to represent reality.

Oliver Stone: How often have we heard, 'The book had more density'? Reading allows you to experience multifaceted points of view and depth that you don't get in a movie. I feel the limitations of movies because I'm interested in writing. In a sense this movie for me has pushed to the limits of 2D.

Gavin Smith: Did you feel things went too far in any area?

Oliver Stone: The earlier cuts were more chaotic and I did screenings on an extensive basis before the ratings board because I was scared our grammar was too fast and over everyone's heads.

Gavin Smith: So do you have doubts about cinema?

Oliver Stone: I think I'm expressing doubt about life. This picture was made in a darker spot in my life. We were so far out there that it was scary. Our nature is a struggle between aggression and love. Obviously Vietnam clarified that for me, but I wasn't totally aware of it when I got back. I killed over there. I have still to deal with that. I have tried. It's become apparent to me that my films are violent. People would say that for years and I would deny it, I wouldn't face up to the violence in myself. I'm beginning to now. This film came from that spot. It was an explosion of violence right after the most non-violent film I've made, *Heaven & Earth.* Why would I do that? It was a totally contradictory move. What happened? I don't know. Part of me is scared, and wants to say, let's pull back, let's make a film that is understandable to everyone, that's sweeter, that the whole country can believe in, like *Forrest Gump.*

Gavin Smith: So does *Forrest Gump* prove that love beats the demon?

Oliver Stone: No. Because the demon is never allowed to manifest itself in its full force and clarity. Gump goes through a hard time but there's a denial going on about the Vietnam war, about protestors, his relationship to women... it's an ostrich type of solution to history – stick your head in the sand. I like the film, it works on many levels, but anyone who went out and experimented dies of Aids or gets their legs blown off. It's the opposite of what I'm saying. But I would like to make an escapist film. Why do I have to provoke each time?

REVIEW

Natural Born Killers
USA 1994
Director: Oliver Stone

In a diner somewhere in the mid-west, a young girl begins dancing while her boyfriend orders food. Three roughnecks assume she's easy bait and begin to taunt her. Immediately she and her boyfriend produce firearms and begin slaughtering every-one, leaving only one witness to tell the tale. The pair are Mickey and Mallory and they're on a killing spree. A back story in the form of a spoof television sitcom entitled

I Love Mallory sketches out how Mallory was prey to an abusive and violent father and how she and Mickey killed her entire family.

On a high bridge over a deep gorge, the two clasp hands in a blood bond. Their instant media history is then encapsulated by the television show *American Maniacs*, hosted by Australian Wayne Gayle. They are celebrity killers. As they drive along, Mickey suggests several passing candidates to take as hostage. Mallory leaves Mickey stranded, driving to a garage where she seduces a mechanic on the bonnet of her car before shooting him for giving 'the worst head I ever had'.

Together again, Mickey and Mallory run out of gas in the middle of the desert. An old Indian mystic gives them shelter in his hut. He seems to have some understanding and sympathy for them, but that night Mickey has a nightmare and shoots the Indian dead by mistake. Surrounded by deadly conjured snakes, the two both get bitten before making their getaway. They go to collect an antidote from a store, but the alarm is raised and the building surrounded. Hard-nosed detective Jack Scagnetti is soon on the scene to arrest them, hoping to consummate a perverse passion for Mallory.

A year later, Scagnetti is called in by the warden to deliberately assassinate Mickey and Mallory in prison. On Superbowl Sunday, Mickey gives an in-depth interview to Gayle and his *American Maniacs* crew. His unapologetic admission that he's a 'natural born killer' sparks an instant riot among the watching inmates. While his guards are distracted by the noise, Mickey grabs a shotgun and kills several of them before leading a procession of hostages through the prison to Mallory's cell. There he finds Scagnetti trying to assault her. Mickey shoots him dead and fights his way out, via the front gate, encouraging a frenzied Gayle to join in the killing. In a clearing in the woods, the couple explain to Gayle that he must die and together they execute him before his own camera. A flash-forward shows Mickey and Mallory living in a mobile home as a nuclear family.

* * *

After the much-discussed delay to its classification by the BBFC, what's most surprising about *Natural Born Killers* is not the visceral depiction of violent acts, but that anyone could have accepted Oliver Stone's putative satire as a serious work. Not only is the film played for grim laughs throughout (albeit by a director who is clearly not laughing), with Mickey and Mallory as overblown cartoon killers, but its black humour is so strained and hysterical that all satirical intent is dissipated. There's barely a trace left of Tarantino's usual cool wit (assuming it was there in the original script), no nice domestic touches to offset the mayhem; it's a straightforward rush of inexplicably raw visual data.

Stone's proclaimed target is the pernicious levelling effect of media saturation on moral questions, but if this full-on assault of MTV blip-editing and simulated channel-surfing hits any target at all, it would be the barn door marked 'overused imagery'. For all the hallucinogenic frenzy with which this film shuffles the full range of image-gathering options, it is a curiously second-hand experience. Its pictorial exuberance feels forced, a slap-dash imitation of music video and infotainment style. In attempting a self-lacerating version of Terrence Malick's *Badlands* and the tinpot imitations that have followed that film in mythologising 'misunderstood' hoodlum youth, Stone is clearly so afraid that his audience won't get the fact that he's engaged in parody, that he restates everything over and over, repeatedly cutting from wielded gun, to reacting victim, to entry wound, to gun again. But he also sends himself up, having Mallory rant at Mickey for killing the Indian – 'Bad, bad, bad, bad, bad' – as if she were giving notes on his performance.

Woody Harrelson and Juliette Lewis are nevertheless superb at exaggerating the archetypes of cool psychopathology forged around the mean and moody stars of the 50s and 60s. Harrelson's cocky smirk makes a particularly apt counterpart to Lewis' method pout (she could have parodied her own performance in *Kalifornia*: instead she plays a more decisive and self-possessed version of white trash womanhood). There are blink-and-miss-'em knowing allusions to films as diverse as *Detour* and *Scorpio Rising*, which can be seen as progenitors of the standard weirdness-is-all music video approach. But while it's undoubtedly true that the image bank of rebel youth mythology – of Dean, Presley, Brando *et al* – has been plundered to bankruptcy by the endless recycling of the music promo business, it didn't need a scion of the 60s such as Stone – whose own movie, *The Doors*, is similarly meretricious – to spend millions of dollars bemoaning it. To call it overkill would be an understatement.

What is unique and remarkable, however, is for a big-budget Hollywood movie deliberately to trash its narrative in favour of a nightmare logic. Perhaps Stone has no interest in telling more than a vestigial story because it's harder with narrative to predict an audience's reaction. He wants us to feel nothing but his own palpable disgust at the kind of true-crime cultural production spoofed as *American Maniacs*. But what he is holding up is a fairground's distorting mirror, to which we can only respond with a laugh or a shrug.

Of course, it will be argued that one-note-harping on one-note-harping is the whole point, that, whether or not you get the insider references, you will get the message. But Stone fails to follow his own logic. If an audience is sophisticated enough to read the stream of images then surely they deserve a coherent argument. Here the audience gets a deafening imprecation to think about every little thing from a director who seems to feel that they've already lost the ability to do so.

There might be another reason for Stone's abandoning the coherent narrative. Perhaps the least-discussed of recent new technologies is the computer-based editing systems, such as Avid and Lightworks, which enable a film to be edited digitally at speed in many different versions. Without this facility, *Natural Born Killers* would be almost unthinkable, not simply because otherwise the process of assembling such a random mass of footage would take too long, but also because linear hands-on editing arguably forces the film-maker to think the whole thing through, to keep the entire film in his or her head. No-one could possibly retain a complete and detailed picture of this film because it is so non-committal and open-ended.

As for the film's much-trumpeted ability to shock, it is set at the level of a prank, reminiscent of nothing so much as a heavy metal band adding a backwards voice track to an album simply to wind up Christian fundamentalists.

Nick James

Jurassic Park (Steven Spielberg, 1993)

Section 7: Critical Perspective on a Mode

In this section there is an implicit argument that the characteristics previously associated with high concept action movies have now become characteristics of big-budget Hollywood in general and should properly be looked at in terms of a dominant mode of film-making rather than as belonging to any particular genre. The films discussed in this section belong to many genres (sci-fi, horror, monster movies, disaster movies, the woman's film and even a Shakespeare adaptation), but their shared traits are made obvious upon reading the articles.

Martin Scorsese's place in this section might be open to question. However, it is instructive to begin with the articles by J. Hoberman and Jenny Diski because a comparison between the two versions of *Cape Fear* reveals the extent to which Hollywood cinema has changed in a period of thirty years, even in the hands of the revered Scorsese, who is seen, if not quite an outsider to Hollywood, certainly above it. In discussing the film, Hoberman refers to Scorsese succumbing to 'remakitis' and uses the notion of the set piece, while Diski notes that 'Scorsese doesn't hide his intertextuality under a bushel' and that Scorsese's *Cape Fear* resembles '*Poltergeist* or all those *Damiens*'.

If Scorsese is generally seen as an outsider to this cinema, Spielberg is often credited (or damned) as one of its founding fathers. Within a larger argument on fetishised attractions in the society of the spectacle, one which focuses on *Jurassic Park* whilst ranging from the nineteenth-century Dinosaur Cult to Hitchcock's *The Birds*, Peter Wollen notes that although Spielberg is an undoubted auteur, *Jurassic Park* is a 'film about a theme park (that) will itself end up as a theme park attraction. It's all as if *Jurassic Park*, the film, was really designed to end up as *Jurassic Park*, the ride.' In an accompanying piece, Henry Sheehan notes *Jurassic Park*'s pulp plot and lack of characterisation. He concludes that the film is both a 'technical masterpiece and an indifferent piece of drama', an evaluation that has often been extended to many Hollywood films.

The relevance of Hoberman's piece on *Mars Attacks!* to this section is made clear from its opening sentence: 'If the mission of the movies is, as Siegfried Kracauer wrote in his *Nature of Film: The Redemption of Physical Reality*, to preserve that which is transitory, to monumentalise the ephemeral and to celebrate the poetry of trash, then *Mars Attacks!* is pure cinema.' Kracauer's phrase offers an interesting criterion of value which, deployed dialectically, can be a fruitful way to begin a discussion of contemporary Hollywood cinema and, aligned with other methodologies, and in the hands of as skilful a critic as Hoberman, can contribute to our knowledge of it.

In 'Bigger than Life', Yvonne Tasker evaluates the career of one of the greatest directors of Action/Spectacle cinema, Kathryn Bigelow. Tasker notes the awkwardness of

Bigelow's position both in Hollywood and in film studies. Her films are not successful enough at the box office to place her on the A-list, yet her work is seen as too Hollywood to be classed as 'independent'. Perhaps because so much of her work is concerned with genres that are considered 'masculine' (bikers, vampire, police thriller, surfers, sci-fi) she has also not received as much attention from feminist film studies as one might expect. Yet, as Tasker persuasively argues, Bigelow's work deploys a distinctive combination of action and noir modes, which along with its conceptual complexity and graphic qualities, 'has redefined the visual possibilities of action as a cinematic mode'.

Michael Mann's cult status as an action director rivals that of Bigelow's but his commercial success affords him greater industrial clout. In 'No Smoking Gun', Nick James uses *The Insider*, atypical Mann in that it is not an action movie per se, as a springboard to a description and evaluation of Mann as an auteur of action as well as a commentary on contemporary Hollywood in general. James notes that the key Mann films are types of action movies that are aggressively hypnotic, characterised by muscular visual hyperbole and that grab you by the lapels and keep you there. James demonstrates the influence of TV in that *Miami Vice*, Mann's most famous creation for that medium, is seen as a structural paradigm for his subsequent film work. James also situates Mann's oeuvre in the context of contemporary big-budget action spectacle by arguing, intriguingly, that Mann's films 'can be characterised as artistically perfected structures crafted on similar genre real estate to that on which Simpson-Bruckheimer were happy to jerrybuild'. Yet James also demonstrates how Mann's visual sense, his mastery of widescreen, and the way in which his 'perfect' genre movies break out of their seeming perfection when the world being depicted becomes overwhelming for characters and viewers, are qualities that transform typical raw materials of genre into great movies.

In the last two pieces in this section, José Arroyo argues that the aesthetics of action/spectacle, the dominant mode of contemporary Hollywood film-making, are evident in films as diverse as *William Shakespeare's Romeo and Juliet* and *Titanic*. Arroyo argues that it is through the exhilarating movement of striking images, and it is in and through motion that both films move their audience emotionally and communicate meaning. Of *Romeo and Juliet*, Arroyo remarks on how, as well as being 'Shakespeare', it is also a 'kiss kiss bang bang' movie with a narrative framed by television, a story set in a 'constructed' world and a hybrid style that relies on an array of kinetic imagery to elicit visceral affect. In a similar discussion of *Titanic*, the most expensive and successful film to date, Arroyo relates the film to the Irwin Allen disaster cycle that Gross at the beginning of this book found a key influence on contemporary action/ spectacle cinema and concludes that for all the pleasures on offer the film is unsatisfying in a way that is emblematic of contemporary Hollywood filmmaking. Arroyo argues that 'in the twentieth century, speed, movement and action are synonymous with America itself: certainly they were what people all over the world loved US movies for. But US cinema was never just about action: it also had people whose freedom and energy were internationally emulated and stories that enchanted the world. Contemporary US film-making no longer runs to this type of characterisation and stories are now most often the domain of lower-budget films, whatever their quality. Generally (and *only* generally), the only thing big-budget Hollywood currently does well is action and effects – that is, only through action and effects does big-budget Hollywood have anything to say.'

SACRED AND PROFANE

J. Hoberman

The young Jean-Luc Godard wrote of Nicholas Ray that if the cinema no longer existed, Ray alone would be capable of inventing it – and, what's more, of wanting to. Looking at the roster of current American directors, the same might be said (and often is) of Martin Scorsese. Steven Spielberg has made more money, Woody Allen has received more accolades, Oliver Stone (a former student) has reaped bigger headlines – but nobody has made better movies. Scorsese is Hollywood's designated maestro: the most celluloid-obsessed and single-minded film-maker in Hollywood, the one American director that Spike Lee would deign to admire.

Although *Taxi Driver* and the title song from *New York, New York* are the only Scorsese artefacts to embed themselves in American mainstream consciousness (a television series based on *Alice Doesn't Live Here Anymore* barely lasted one season), Scorsese has never lacked for critical support. *Mean Streets* was the most highly praised debut of the 70s; *Raging Bull* topped several polls as the best American movie of the 80s; *GoodFellas* received virtually every critics' award in 1990. Even his so-called flops – the brilliant *King of Comedy*, engaging *After Hours* and heartfelt *Last Temptation of Christ* – have had their defenders.

Perhaps hoping to repay Universal for bankrolling his magnificent obsession, *The Last Temptation of Christ*, Scorsese has entered into an exclusive six-year directing and producing deal with the studio and succumbed, at last, to remakitis. With his edgily overwrought *Cape Fear* remake, he has concocted an admittedly commercial thriller more skilful than inspired and at least as cerebral as it is gut-twisting.

The first *Cape Fear* (1962, released by Universal-International) was knocked off by British director J. Lee Thompson between the martial epics *Guns of Navarone* and *Taras Bulba*. The hero, Sam Bowden (Gregory Peck), was an upstanding Georgia prosecutor who, some years before, had testified against one Max Cady (Robert Mitchum) in a particularly vicious rape case. The plot thickens when Cady, having served his time, comes looking for revenge, presumably to be inflicted on Bowden's wife and daughter.

Undeniably disturbing (the original trailers promised movie-goers that they were going to 'Feel Fear!'), Thompson's movie derived much of its frisson from Cady's anti-social assault on the good-good culture of the 50s. With the judicious Peck seemingly preparing for his Oscar-laureate role as the saintly Southern lawyer in Universal's *To Kill a Mockingbird*, which opened six months later, and his wife and daughter (TV personalities Polly Bergen and Lori Martin) so sitcom wholesome, one might well sympathise with the villain – at least at first.

The heavy, deceptively somnolent Mitchum – an action star with a hipster edge, having been busted for pot in the late 40s – brought a brute physicality and unprecedented sexual sadism to his characterisation. Barry Gifford, who would later pay homage to *Cape Fear* by incorporating its eponymous location in his meta-noir novel *Wild at Heart*, calls Mitchum 'the angel of death-with-pain, put on earth to give men pause'. But although *Cape Fear* is as much horror film as thriller – with Mitchum's virtually unkillable monster anticipating the slashers of the late 70s – there is another, equally disturbing subtext lurking in the film.

Cady wants to spook Bowden before he destroys him, and for much of the movie he is protected by the very law he places himself beyond. Set in the South and released at the height of the struggle for desegregation, *Cape Fear* conjures up the bogie of a terrifying rapist – albeit white – who proved inconveniently conversant with his 'civil rights'. In its nightmarish way, *Cape Fear* managed to suggest both what terrified the white South and the terror the white South itself inspired. 'You won't forget this movie,' Gifford ends his critique, 'especially if you're a Yankee Jew.'

In general, *Cape Fear* was received with trepidation. The film's British opening was delayed until early 1963, while Thompson and Lord Morrison, president of the British Board of Censors, argued over cuts. (The movie was eventually released with six minutes trimmed.) Calling it 'a nasty film', Lord Morrison objected to the sexual threat Mitchum posed to Lori Martin. Nor was the British censor alone. Pit in *Variety*, Dwight Macdonald in *Esquire* and Bosley Crowther in the *New York Times* all warned readers against bringing their children, Crowther adding that *Cape Fear* was 'one of those shockers that provoke disgust and regret'.

Of course, disgust and regret are scarcely emotions to make Martin Scorsese flinch, and he would doubtless endorse the sense the 1962 movie left that civilisation's veneer is somewhat less sturdy than the shell of an egg.

Scorsese's *Cape Fear* opens with the camera rising from the depths of the primordial swamp where all the protagonists will ultimately swim. Although the ensuing sense of beleaguered middle-class territoriality is as strong as ever, the new *Cape Fear* complicates the moral equation by shifting focus from Max Cady, flamboyantly played by Robert De Niro, to the Bowden family. In this *Cape Fear*, the Bowdens' lives are built on quicksand. Scorsese undermines their solidarity, wipes his hands on their reputations, sullies their laundry with a miasma of guilt.

Not simply a concerned citizen, the new Sam Bowden turns out to have been Cady's public defender against a particularly brutal charge of rape, who buried evidence of the victim's promiscuity so as not to jeopardise his client's conviction. The self-righteousness inherent in sensitive Peck has here coalesced into uptight Nick Nolte – a man built to absorb punishment, even as his menacing bulk suggests Mitchum's. As his wife Leigh (renamed for Janet?), Jessica Lange looks just as classy as precursor Polly Bergen, but she's considerably more bitter and a lot less supportive. Their teenage daughter Danielle, played by Juliette Lewis, is ripe and dishevelled, braces gleaming out of her unformed face. (Does Marty know how to pick them? Not long after *Cape Fear*'s US release Lewis replaced Emily Lloyd as the nymphet in Woody Allen's current project.)

Whereas in 1962 evil stalked the Bowden family from without, the threat is now to be found within. They are, as current parlance would have it, *dysfunctional*. Leigh, not irrationally suspects Sam of having an affair; to block out their screaming, Danielle – who is recovering, it is suggested, from a precocious drug problem – locks herself in her bedroom, flicks on both MTV and the radio and begins compulsively dialling her Swatch phone, as instinctive an ostrich as the rest of her clan. Meanwhile, his release from prison heralded by a drumroll of thunder, Cady is the return of Bowden's repressed – telling him later that while the judge and DA 'were just doing their jobs', Bowden betrayed his trust.

Even more than in the original, it's difficult not to feel a sneaking sympathy for Cady, particularly when the more physically imposing Bowden is trying to buy him off or, later, hiring goons to run him out of town. This Cady is less the snake in the Bowden family Eden and more the projection of their unconscious fears. Indeed, he first appears to them in precisely that fashion. Shuffling into a movie house (showing the horror comedy *Problem Child*), Cady positions himself directly in front of the family, blocks the screen and, brandishing his cigar while laughing like a hyena, subjects them to what must be the film buff's ultimate violation: 'Dad, you should have just punched him out,' Lewis admonishes Nolte, unaware that they've just encountered implacable evil.

Cross played across his back, religious mantras inscribed on his arms, De Niro's Cady is a self-taught psychopath and a refugee from Kafka's penal colony, as much a mythological beast as any unicorn or yeti. Although it's tempting to read his character as Scorsese's revenge on the Christian fundamentalists who attacked *The Last Temptation of Christ*, it's difficult to conceptualise the sort of born-again Baptist who would pray to Jesus beneath a Stalin pin-up and augment the scriptures with a combination of *Thus Spake Zarathustra* and Henry Miller. A two-bit De Sade with delusions of grandeur, Cady sees himself as avenging angel. By opening the family up to his blandishments, *Cape Fear* has perverse intimations of *Teorema* as well as *Straw Dogs*.

Johnny Boy and Travis Bickle, Jake La Motta and Rupert Pupkin have nothing on this nut. With his long black hair slicked back under a white yachting cap, mouth wrapped around the world's biggest cigar butt, and torso draped in a flaming Aloha shirt, De Niro is a cracker from hell. The conception is wildly baroque, and most of the time De Niro's Cady is more crazy than menacing. Although his tattooed slogans and religious rants evoke Mitchum's career performance as the psychotic preacher in *Night of the Hunter*, De Niro lacks Mitchum's insolent ease as a performer. His Max Cady is a riff and, half camping on his Southern drawl, he never lets you forget it.

The movie, too, is knowing without seeming felt. The rough sex here looks a lot rougher than it did in the original, but is actually less visceral. Where Mitchum cracks an egg on one of his victims, De Niro (like Dracula) takes a bite out of a woman's face. More overt, too, is the suggestion, repeated in various contexts throughout the film, that when a rape is reported, it is actually the victim who goes on trial. (Note: even though *Cape Fear* opened the very day the American public was transfixed by allegations of sexual harassment and achieved box-office saturation during the William Kennedy Smith rape trial, the operative movie metaphor for such cases remained *Fatal Attraction. Cape Fear*'s critique is softened by the use of the daughter's voiceover to frame the movie – the entire nightmare can thus be read as the hysterical fantasy of a teenage girl.)

In the movie's most daring set piece, De Niro makes a call to Lewis in the guise of her new drama coach (one more instance of subtext overwhelming narrative). The stunt nature of this self-reflexive turn is literalised by having the actor chat on the phone and even cue records while dangling upside down on his chinning bar (eventually the camera flips over as well). It's followed by another hot-dog scene in which, having lured Lewis down into her high school's basement and on to the stage where a play is to be rehearsed, De Niro seems determined to out-creep Willem Dafoe's 'seduction' of Laura Dern in *Wild at Heart*. This fairytale sequence in the make-believe gingerbread house ('I'm the Big Bad Wolf,' De Niro begins) has received near-universal acclaim. What's far more effective, however, is Nolte's subsequent rage at the nubile daughter with whom he can never quite make eye contact. 'Did he touch you? Wipe that smile off your face!' he screams when he discovers what happened. It's an indignity Gregory Peck never had to suffer – the autumn of the patriarch.

Does it sound as if *Cape Fear* is overdirected? The movie is undeniably gripping and it certainly looks great. Shot by Freddie Francis, director of the Hammer horror flicks beloved by Scorsese in his youth, it's a heady succession of extreme close-ups and artful reflections, luridly shimmering sunsets lit by flickers of heat lightning. If an unknown had signed *Cape Fear* it would have been heralded as an impressive debut. (Consider the delirious overpraise that greeted *Dead Again*.) But Scorsese is no twenty-five-year-old retooling antique genres, and more than one observer has attributed *Cape Fear*'s manic formalism to the director's alienation from the material (a similar hyperkinetic frenzy is evident in his last commercial assignment, the 1986 *The Color of Money*).

Scorsese's relationship to *Cape Fear* is, however, more self-conscious and complex. No less than Godard, Scorsese is prodigiously movie-literate. His VCRs work overtime, he employs a full-time film archivist, spends thousands on prints, and has supervised the restoration and re-release of movies as varied as *Peeping Tom*, *Once Upon a Time in the West* and *Le Carrosse d'or*. His grasp of film history far exceeds that of most American critics and is far too sophisticated for him to attempt anything so crude as an unself-conscious remake – let alone a heedless obliteration of the original version. If anything, the new *Cape Fear* assumes that the viewer has seen the earlier one, perhaps even as recently as Scorsese himself.

In effect, Scorsese has taken a piece of hack work and, like the archetypal auteur, filled it with his own directorial touches and perhaps subversive notions of guilt and redemption. Douglas Sirk is quoted in the film. As the *Nation*'s Stuart Klawans observed in his suitably ambivalent review, 'History robbed Scorsese of the chance to be an *auteur* in the full, oppositional sense of the term. So now, as compensation, he's gone back thirty years and inserted himself into a studio product, *Cape Fear*, giving it the one thing it lacked in 1962 – a star performance by the director.'

The new *Cape Fear* oscillates between a critique of the original and a variation on a common text: it's a choreographed hall-of-mirrors, an orchestrated echo chamber. The first version resonates throughout the second – often literally. Elmer Bernstein stridently reworks the original Bernard Herrmann score. An aged Robert Mitchum appears as the local chief of police, and his deep drawl, first heard over the telephone, haunts the movie. Martin Balsam, who played the police chief in the 1962 version, has here been promoted to judge.

Scorsese's witty casting includes using the archetypal Southern vigilante, star of

Walking Tall, Joe Don Baker, as a sleazy private eye whose idea of a mixed drink is Pepto-Bismol laced with Jim Beam. But the film's vertiginous sense of inversion is completed by the appearance of Gregory Peck as the enthusiastically slippery criminal lawyer who represents De Niro's smirking Cady. (It's as if Peck has become what he beheld.) Scorsese's remake thus contains its own negative image – a trope that's more than once utilised in the cinematography. *Cape Fear*'s tumultuous climax – a *tour de force* for De Niro, Scorsese and mainly editor Thelma Schoonmaker – completes the role reversals by putting the lawyer Nolte on trial, even while the boat of civilisation spins out of control and cracks up on the rocks.

Although De Niro's final scene is as powerfully crafted an exit as that actor has ever made, the movie – like his performance – is a good deal more spectacular than terrifying, and somewhat less than the sum of its parts. Blood is not an abstraction; De Niro is. (I never thought I'd say this, but what *Cape Fear* needs is a shot of Paul Schrader – Cady's particular nexus of evangelical fervour, sexual guilt and class resentment is more alluded to than fleshed out.) Like the villain, the location lacks specificity: it's a curiously all-white South.

Budgeted at $34 million, *Cape Fear* is Scorsese's most expensive movie, and his first commissioned project since *The Color of Money*. The project originated with Steven Spielberg, who interested De Niro in playing Cady, who then persuaded Scorsese to undertake a commercial thriller. And indeed, *Cape Fear* is structurally quite similar to Spielberg's *Hook*. A careerist father's failure to spend quality time with his children brings down a baroque threat to the family that can only be defeated by the father's capacity for regression. The difference is that *Hook* is filmically more impoverished, but psychologically far richer.

That absence of pathology seems to have left Scorsese with a guilty conscience. 'I think a lot of the pictures I've made are good,' he recently told *Premiere*. 'But they're not *The Searchers*. They're not *8½*. *The Red Shoes*. *The Leopard*.'

Although it's a disservice to consider *Cape Fear* more than middling Scorsese, the film has received near-universal raves. The major exception is *New Yorker* critic Terence Rafferty, who, no less hysterical than those who hailed *Cape Fear* a masterpiece, termed the film 'a disgrace... ugly, incoherent, dishonest'. Rafferty echoes the original's reviews – including the brief mention that appeared in the *New Yorker* back in 1962: 'Everyone concerned with this repellent attempt to make a great deal of money out of a clumsy plunge into sexual pathology should be thoroughly ashamed of himself.' And money has been made. *Cape Fear*, which seems headed for a $70 million domestic gross, needed barely six weeks to surpass *The Color of Money* as Scorsese's most financially successful film. (His reassuringly outré follow-up project is an adaptation of Edith Wharton's novel, *The Age of Innocence*.)

Directors are manipulative by definition, but I've never met a film-maker more adept at enlisting critical sympathy than Scorsese. 'For Scorsese, there's no such thing as a throwaway,' Peter Biskind wrote in *Premiere*. 'He couldn't sell out if he wanted to,' enthused Richard Corliss in *Time*. Their characterisations are not exaggerated; neither is their support unwarranted. Other directors wax self-servingly sentimental about the art of the movies; Scorsese repeatedly pledges allegiance, spending time and money on the job of preservation.

In extolling Nicholas Ray, Godard was reviewing his less than epochal *Hot Blood* – 'a semi-successful film to the extent that Ray was semi-uninterested in it'. *Cape Fear* is a similar sort of semiotext. More than a critic's darling, Scorsese is a national treasure – the only director in Hollywood whose devotion to cinema justifies everyone's notions of popular art. We need him. He needs a hit. *Cape Fear* is a semi-sacrifice to that faith.

THE SHADOW WITHIN

Jenny Diski

What will the kids say of our time, when in thirty years from now they see Scorsese's new version of *Cape Fear*? Perhaps, that although we understood the complexity of things, and the relativity of good and evil, we had no knowledge of the satisfactions to be had from the battle between light and dark on a human scale.

The original version of *Cape Fear* is pure film noir, one of those stories we tell ourselves on dark winter nights. It shows decent values under threat. The Bowden family is untouched by suffering and as nice as the apple pie Peg Bowden undoubtedly makes for Sam and their cutely precocious daughter, Nancy. They're wealthy, though not outrageously so, and they're happy together in a simple, enviable way that's as remote from passion as it is from divorce. There are no doubts and no clouds in the lives of the Bowdens until Robert Mitchum, barrel-chested, heavy-lidded and *bad*, takes the keys out of amiable, dull, puppet-wooden Gregory Peck's ignition and reminds him who he is. It's simple. You know where you are; the bad guy's come along, and the family – *The Family* – is under threat.

Cady's threat is sexual. He's after Bowden through his wife and daughter, and the film makes it clear he's a sadistic psychopath. He attacks a woman he's picked up, and we hear from his own lips that he abducted and assaulted the wife who divorced him while he was in prison. What he does to them is literally *unspeakable*. No detail is shown or said, it is all shadow and implication, but we are allowed to suspect the worst our imaginations can come up with. What *is* stated, however, is that Cady is an 'animal' with a grudge. We have to fear the worst for the Bowdens, but the fear is not about death, it's about defilement.

The problem, watching the movie thirty years on, is: what side are you on? There's good and bad lined up against each other for a classic confrontation, and shouldn't I be rooting for the insufferably smug Bowdens? Is it the effect of the passing years that makes me cheer on chaos, or is there fault in the balance of the original film that allowed only *models* of good and evil on to the public screen? Think of the hallucinatory *Night of the Hunter*, made not long before, when Mitchum's evil met with a more interesting mix of flawed, weird, but determined humanity. See that film even now, and you don't feel you're in a moral time warp; there's no doubt whose side you're on.

So, roll on thirty or so years, and what does Martin Scorsese make of *Cape Fear*? Scorsese doesn't hide his intertextuality under a bushel. Mitchum is there, and so is Peck, in cameo parts that reverse their moral positions in the first movie, and neither of them resists a hammy wink at the way things have turned out this time. Scorsese has some fun (his Cady drinks nothing but Evian water throughout the film), but he's a moral investigator, and three decades later things have changed on a grand scale.

Robert De Niro takes the part of Cady and turns Mitchum's single-mindedness into a diabolical obsession. He is covered in biblical tattoos that warn of time and vengeance. The sexual danger is accompanied now by religious vehemence. He has become a man of learning as well as a man of iron. Body and mind are dedicated to revenge for the loss of his freedom. Scorsese and De Niro have cranked Cady up to the final notch of power and threat.

But for all De Niro's sinister presence, it is the nature of his victims that has altered most interestingly. Bowden is no longer the man who put Cady behind bars. This time, Sam was Cady's *defence* attorney. His crime, in Cady's eyes, was that he buried evidence proving Cady's sixteen-year-old victim was promiscuous. Cady might have got off or got half the sentence. Bowden deliberately betrayed the oath as a lawyer in order to get a man he knew to be an 'animal' off the streets.

Here, we're in a debate about natural justice versus constitutional rights, and the simple good against bad tale of the earlier film has almost disappeared. We know that the right to an adequate defence is a fundamental of civilisation; we also know that Cady is too violent and vicious a creature to be allowed to roam free. We are implicated in a moral confusion at the heart of the movie, and Bowden is no longer simply a good man upon whom evil is unjustly unleashed. He is a much more modern hero, with a burden of ethical guilt. He faces not only violent retribution, but disbarment by his peers.

Cady's sexual threat has been brought up to date, too. De Niro's Cady is a man of our times, a post-Freudian laden with psycho-sexual knowledge. In the original film, Mitchum terrifies Bowden's daughter in her empty school; we see her running away in panic while a male torso stalks her. The child is almost run over in her desperate attempt to escape. But De Niro doesn't trap Bowden's daughter (who is now fifteen), he entices her. In the deserted school theatre, set for a production of *Little Red Riding Hood*, he offers her sympathy for the troubles and unfairness of a teenager's life – and a joint. He knows how misunderstood she is, how unhappy she feels at home; he's the 'Do Right Man', he tells her, moving closer, and he's on her side. In a scene that's more disturbing than all the violence to come, he plays delicately with the girl's confused, emergent sexuality. He holds her gently (while we hold our breath) and penetrates only her lips with his thumb, getting a tremendous mix of childlike trust and sexual excitement that makes the adolescent much more than physically vulnerable. Cady's sexual threat is all the more *unspeakable* thirty years on because its range is so much greater, encompassing the mind and heart as well as the body.

The underlying theme of both versions of *Cape Fear* is the brittleness of civilised values. We come to see that Bowden's rock-solid sense of lawful, civilised behaviour is no more than a veneer. Just a little chipping away, and the niceness and righteousness break apart, and then it's down to a Hobbesian reality of kill or be killed. Civilisation is tested and must fail, that is the tragic centre of both movies, but while in the first film we observe the process of breakdown, in Scorsese's version it's clear that the cracks had appeared long before Cady arrived.

In the 1991 version, Bowden's wife, a fidgety, sexually and emotionally unhappy woman, sees the inevitability of the test ahead of them. Before the final chaos comes down she tells Bowden, with curious acceptance, that she'd often wondered how strong or weak they really were, and that they have to go through the hell that Cady will make in order to find out. Thirty years earlier, there *were* no questions to be answered, no uncertainties, only inexplicable forces that attacked from outside. Since then, it seems we've learned that bad things are often shadows of ourselves.

But when judgment day comes in the remake, it's wildly over the top. The swamp and storm of the earlier film become the watery ninth circle of hell, swirling and engulfing all the human participants. If Mitchum was hard to kill, De Niro is immortal. He becomes the avenging Angel, the Devil, the speaker in tongues, the undead, that we all fear. Or, perhaps, so alienating and hysterical is the end, he just becomes Freddy, late of Elm Street. Disfigured, manacled, drowned, crushed, Cady keeps on popping up to remind us he'll see us in our dreams.

Scorsese's *Cape Fear* comes, finally, more to resemble *Poltergeist* or all those *Damiens*. The battle of the old black and white movies between good and bad on the small, but essentially human scale is lost. When De Niro becomes impossibly inhuman we lose the benefits of both the old simplicity and the new complexity. The family fights back against the chaos, but the force that threatens them is so monstrous that there is no moral satisfaction when they overcome it. Their triumph is arbitrary, not a result of having learned something.

It seems that as we have come to understand the flaws that run through all of us, so that good and bad are forever more or less relative terms, we have lost our belief in judgment. We know we have our faults, but the monsters out there waiting to get us belong on the big screen, shadow creatures of tricky camerawork. The more impossible they become, the less they have to do with us. De Niro might quote Dante to invoke the Inferno as his rightful home, but in the end it's clear he really resides on Elm Street – and none of us lives there. *Cape Fear* is still one of those stories we tell ourselves on dark winter nights, but these days we come out laughing.

THEME PARK AND VARIATIONS

Peter Wollen

To the cine-palaeontologist tracing the evolutionary history of film, Steven Spielberg's *Jurassic Park* appears at first to be a rather obvious hybrid of *Jaws* and writer Michael Crichton's earlier theme-park fantasy *Westworld* (1973). The hybrid is made possible at story level by the concept of genetic engineering. The idea of chromosome recombination has superseded that of robotics, which drove *Westworld,* a distant descendant of Fritz Lang's *Metropolis.* In *Jurassic Park,* the concept of genetic cloning allows the robot film to be interbred with the successful line of monster movies that runs from *The Lost World,* on through *King Kong,* and down to *Jaws.*

Jurassic Park also combines the *Westworld* concept of the theme park with the monster movie idea of *The Lost World,* derived from Arthur Conan Doyle. In *King Kong* the monster is captured and brought by a show-biz tycoon from its remote Pacific island home to the mass audience of New York, where it is exhibited in chains at what appears to be a version of Radio City Music Hall. In *Jurassic Park* it is the other way round: the audience is to be transported to a remote Pacific island, where the monsters are exhibited and restrained behind massive electric fences. Isla Nublar is an island resort like Cançun or Djerba, what economists call an ITZ (integrated tourist zone), self-contained and cut off from the depressing and dangerous rest of the world in the pleasure periphery. It is also a safari park, planned and built around the dinosaur theme by another visionary show-biz entrepreneur, complete with tie-in merchandising of dinosaur souvenirs and memorabilia. On the Isla Nublar, the safari park is further combined with the Natural History Museum, displaying fabulous creatures from the past whose gigantic skeletons we are familiar with from so many museum halls. Finally, there is an uncanny echo, not only of *King Kong,* but of the Galapagos Islands, which Charles Darwin visited on his fateful voyage aboard the *Beagle* and whose wildlife formed the centrepieces of his theory of natural selection.

On Isla Nublar, the technology of the future is used to re-create the extinct species of the distant past. Biotechnology, like cinema, makes it possible for us to engage in a kind of time travel. Again, instead of the tourist climbing into a time machine in order to travel back through deep time to the Age of Reptiles, the reptiles themselves are brought forward to the Age of Humans. Manipulation of DNA acts as a reverse time machine, harnessed now to the interests of the entertainment industry. Dinosaurs, in fact, have become commodities, fetishised attractions in the Society of the Spectacle. At the same time, they are like the prisoners in Jeremy Bentham's Panopticon, a prison in which every prisoner could be ceaselessly observed from a single vantage point. Michael Foucault, in his classic book *Discipline and Punish,* points out that the prototype for the Panopticon was the menagerie built for Louis XIV at Versailles, where all the animals could be watched by a single guard. In *Jurassic Park,* the captive monsters are observed electronically rather than optically, from a computer-driven control centre reminiscent of that for the space ship in *Star Trek,* another form of high-tech island resort. Isla Nublar hurtles through time as the *Enterprise* hurtles through space.

This island is also the isolated castle or fortified island where so many other mad scientists and mad doctors and mad sadists have held sway. Hammond, the Scottish entrepreneur played by Richard Attenborough, is another Dr Frankenstein, another Dr X, another Dr Moreau, another Dr No. Hammond has a Chinese American geneticist at his side, Dr Wu (shades of Dr Fu Manchu), who does the (ultra-hygienic) dirty work while he concentrates on the grand sweep of his vision and the construction of his crazed dream. Hammond's dream does not have to be concealed from prying eyes: he is not afraid of being exposed and lynched. On the contrary, his whole purpose is to display his monsters to an adoring public. We might expect that, in the end, he would be torn to pieces by his own vengeful monsters, like Dr Moreau. Hammond, however, escapes unscathed, presumably because he is too close, in some respects, to Spielberg himself.

At a critical point in the film, Hammond muses on his early days running a flea circus in Petticoat Lane, a realm of illusion, in contrast to Jurassic Park, where everything is real and tangible (and can eat you). Cinema, in these terms, is only a flea circus – the humbler, safer, insubstantial first beginning of the great Jurassic Park dream. But the comparison between cinema and theme park is still too close for comfort, especially when we think of Jurassic Park's museum shop, lovingly, and perhaps ironically, tracked around. Along with the box office, all those T-shirts and mugs and key-tags and toys are, after all, the fuel that drives both enterprises, real film and imaginary theme park. More than a hundred licensees are producing *Jurassic Park* merchandise: video games, action figures and play sets, breakfast cereal and hamburger promotions, plush toys, magnets, story books, lunch boxes, pencils and of course, a forthcoming *Jurassic Park* ride at Universal Studio's very own theme parks in California and Florida. A film about a theme park will itself end up as a theme park attraction.

It's all as if *Jurassic Park*, the film, was really designed to end up as *Jurassic Park*, the ride. The strip of film unspooling through the projector is like the single-rail automated people-mover designed to shuttle tourists safely around the park. In both cases the ride turns into a nightmare from which we will emerge safely in the end. The nightmare is caused, first, by technical breakdown, and then by breakdown of the barriers which separate the safe, 'civilised' world from the dangerous 'wild' world. Things no longer stay in their proper place. Like the Indians who have broken out of the western reservation or the rioting prisoners escaped from Cell Block 11, the dinosaurs tear down the fences and set out to hunt down their human prey. More uncannily, the monsters have not just run out of control, they have come back from the dead as real, living, calculating presences, confronting their human captors face to face. *Jurassic Park* is like a palaeo-zoological version of *Night of the Living Dead*, in which fearsome creatures exhumed from their fossil graves converge on the terrified humans in the resort's welcome centre. Dinosaurs, like phantoms or vampires, have come back to haunt the living – and not only to haunt them, but, of course, to hunt, trap and kill them.

Sweet and savage

All horror is based on the return of the repressed, on some metaphoric digging up of what should have stayed buried. In *Jurassic Park*, the metaphor is extended into deep time to bring back what has been buried for 65 million years, all the more potent for its long entombment. The fascination we feel for dinosaurs must be related in some way to their extinction, which troubles us. First, it makes us wonder whether we are not somehow usurpers who have taken the place which was rightfully theirs. Not that we actually did the deed, but we benefited from it and perhaps will be punished in turn for our arrogance. On another level, there are the infant's fantasies of the primal scene, of terrifying parents, now long dead but all the more able to torment us. In *Jurassic Park*, the children divide up the monsters into 'meat-osauruses' and 'veg-osauruses', carnivores and herbivores, in a way which is surely gender-related: the savage predators are demented father figures while the sweet-tempered grazers, their prey, are beneficent mothers. One leaf-munching monster is compared to a cow; the others are obviously raging bulls. Psychiatrists tell us that another common childhood fantasy is that of saving one's parents from monstrous attackers. This, too, is faithfully enacted in that it is the young boy who gets the central computer system working again and thus saves all the surviving adults.

The dinosaur cult began in the nineteenth century with the identification of dinosaurs as a specific order of reptiles by the great palaeontologist Richard Owen. Owen coined the word 'dinosaur' and used it for the first time at the annual meeting of the British Association for the Advancement of Science, held at Plymouth in the summer of 1841. As he explained, dinosaurs had common characteristics which he deemed 'sufficient grounds for establishing a distinct tribe or sub-order of Saurian Reptiles, for which I propose the name Dinosauria'. Owen, however, was troubled by dinosaurs for theological rather than psychological reasons. If they were part of God's creation, what was their place in the order of things? And in what sense did they point forward to the creation of man, God's masterpiece? Above all, Owen wanted to disprove the theory of progressive evolution, put forward by Lamarck, a process which culminated in the transition from ape to man. If man was to be clearly separated from the apes, then reptiles could not be the immediate precursors of mammals but must be separate creations who reached their peak early with the majestic dinosaurs and then declined into the pathetic swarms of lizards we see today. Dinosaurs, Owen argued, were not cringing creatures creeping about on their bellies, but upstanding beasts with advanced cardiovascular systems, almost like the mammals who eventually superseded them, just as man superseded the mammals. Life progressed in uneven steps rather than in a continuous upward curve.

We know exactly how Owen envisaged dinosaurs because he had life-size models built. When the Crystal Palace was moved from Hyde Park to Sydenham, after the closing of the Great Exhibition of 1851, Owen was given the opportunity to design a series of dinosaurs to be erected on an artificial island in the Exhibition Park, each consisting of up to 30 tons of cement and iron, and still standing today. The Great Exhibition, as Michael Sorkin points out in his intriguing book *Variations on a Theme Park*, was the Ur-form of the theme park, bringing together the wealth of nations into an enclosed palace for tourists, which 'depicted paradise. Not only was it laid out like a great cathedral, with nave and transept, but it was also the largest greenhouse ever built, its interior filled with greenery as well as goods, a climate-controlled reconciliation of Arcadia and industry, a garden for machines.' At Sydenham, now under commercial management, the exhibition became an expanded leisure centre and the dinosaur replicas were one of its main attractions. The artist given the task of 'revivifying the ancient world', as he put it, was Benjamin Waterhouse Hawkins, who had earlier done the illustrations for Darwin's report on the reptiles he discovered on the voyage of the *Beagle*. Hawkins is thus the direct ancestor of Stan Winston, whose studio built the models for *Jurassic Park*. Just as Winston was advised by a team of palaeontologists, so Hawkins was advised by Owen.

Spielberg and Disney

The iguanadon, then the largest known such monster, was designed as a four-legged mammal-like creature, 100 feet long and thirty feet high, reminiscent of a huge rhinoceros rather than some lowly reptile like the crocodile. To publicise the new attraction, a dinner was held on a platform inside the iguanadon, its back still open, with Owen seated at the head of the table in the dinosaur's head. The palaeontologists and geologists who gathered in the monster's 'socially loaded stomach', as the *Illustrated London News* reported, were there to form 'the best guarantee for the severe truthfulness' of Hawkins' work. The visitor to the dinosaurs' island was rewarded not only by the giant iguanadon, but by a monster sloth in the act of climbing an antediluvian tree, a fearsome-looking megalosaurus, a plesiosaurus wallowing in the mud of a pool whose waters were artificially raised and lowered from three to eight feet to simulate the tide and many other such wonders. There were tie-ins too: wall charts and small-scale models. Plainly the newly minted dinosaur was in at the very birth of the theme park, mixing science with spectacle as ever, each Brobdignagian creature frightening the Victorian tourist 'with ideas of retribution in its monstrous jaws', as the *Illustrated London News* gloatingly observed.

Richard Owen's main public antagonist in the battle over evolution was Thomas Huxley, who countered Owen's near-mammal theory of the dinosaur with his own innovatory claim that the dinosaurs were birds. After he left England for America, Hawkins set about building a new series of models, this time of bird-like dinosaurs, to be exhibited in New York's Central Park. Unfortunately this scheme never came to fruition and the bird-dinosaurs were vandalised and destroyed. In *Jurassic Park*, however, they are back with a vengeance, running around like bloodthirsty ostriches, as Huxley had imagined.

It is appropriate that *Jurassic Park* should popularise Huxley's belief that the dinosaurs were birds, recently revived by palaeontologists, since the film that is its own closest ancestor, I believe, is Alfred Hitchcock's *The Birds*. In *The Birds*, as in *Jurassic Park*, a couple is formed and a bachelor learns to care for 'wife' and 'family', as a prelude, we suppose, to marriage. He learns to care by protecting them from the threat of predatory creatures which at the beginning of the story seem perfectly harmless. As Carol Clover has pointed out, *The Birds*, like *Jaws*, is a 'marginal example' of the slasher film. With *The Birds* and *Jaws*, the slasher genre merges with the fantastic monster film, beaks and teeth substituting for knives or saws as instruments of savage yet intimate penetration of the flesh. With the dinosaurs, teeth are supplemented by claws, and instead of the woman victim as the focus, as in *The Birds*, it is men who are attacked and killed. In a notorious comment a propos of *The Birds*, Hitchcock gave as his guiding principle the maxim: 'Punish the women!' In *Jurassic Park*, Spielberg's motto could have been 'Terrify the children!' While *The Birds*, like the classic slasher film, represents displaced, stylised rapes, *Jurassic Park* seems to represent displaced, stylised child molesting. The dinosaurs do not simply threaten, attack and kill people, they threaten to kill the most vulnerable victims – children who loved and trusted them. Thus the slasher-monster sub-genre mutates again in Spielberg's hands.

Spielberg is an undoubted auteur and his fascination and identification with children and the child's point of view is a key characteristic of his work. Like Disney, another child-oriented auteur, Spielberg both seeks to nurture children and at the same time often threatens to terrify them. Disney's own dinosaurs, weirdly gambolling to Stravinsky's *Rite of Spring*, are innocuous enough, but other Disney characters are truly terrifying. Like Spielberg, one of my earliest memories is of being taken to see *Bambi*, a film which traumatised me. Looking back, I believe I can relate my fright to other fears, engendered by the Blitz and associated with the forest fire, the armed aggressors, separation from the mother, the absent father. In *Jurassic Park*, too, the children's fear is aggravated by being separated from their parents and then left alone to their fate. Painstakingly, in the face of repeated dinosaur attacks, a kind of safe family haven has to be created. As in other Spielberg films, there is a scientist, Dr Alan Grant, this time a palaeontologist – like the ichthyologist in *Jaws* or the archaeologist in *Indiana Jones*, but in striking contrast to the unworldly, accident-prone palaeontologist who stars in Hawks' *Bringing up Baby*. In *Jurassic Park*, Grant becomes the heroic father figure, able to draw on his dinosaur knowledge to protect and reassure the children.

Sadistic sublime

The dinosaurs themselves also have no parents, no family life, since they have been prevented genetically from breeding. Even more significant, they are sexually ambiguous. Although they left the laboratory female, they are able to change sex and become male. Thus like Norman Bates in *Psycho*, they are of uncertain sex and also seem to displace their sexual impotence into violence, itself another major trope of the slasher genre.

We know from *Metropolis* that technology out of control is closely associated with sexuality out of control, two particularly terrifying forms of disorder. They are combined in the robot Maria, the creation of another mad scientist, the magician Rotwang. Rotwang too is determined to recreate the dead, in the form of the woman he lost to his rival, Fredersen. He loves his monster as, I believe, Hammond loves his, endlessly denying and disavowing everything in the face of ever-growing evidence of viciousness and depravity. If Dr Wu is the blandly sadistic father who fertilises the eggs and then castrates the offspring, Hammond is the enthusiastically protective mother who ignores every sign of his offspring's monstrosity. He builds a paradise garden for his saurian children, a walled garden full of plants and trees and flowers. Paradise has become a theme park and the theme park replicates Shangri-La. But Paradise Regained quickly turns into Paradise Lost. *Jurassic Park* becomes the site of what we might call the 'sadistic sublime'. Nursery terrors of being torn to pieces and devoured alive are magnified to saurian scale.

Perhaps Spielberg should stop and ponder the fate of his monsters. Palaeontology shows us that the spectacular blockbuster was eventually doomed, to be replaced by a swarm of tiny, marginal, low-budget creatures.

THE FEARS OF CHILDREN

Henry Sheehan

At the start of Steven Spielberg's *Jurassic Park*, its hero, palaeontologist Dr Alan Grant (Sam Neill), indulges in a fantasy about killing a child. Having been pestered by a twelve-year-old boy asking antagonistic questions about dinosaurs, Grant tells him what would happen if he were stalked by velociraptors, viciously clever carnivores who, according to the scientist, hunted in teams and struck by surprise. The result of an encounter with these hunters, Grant explains, would be sure death. And to make his point he pulls a wicked-looking talon from his shirt and draws it over the child's stomach, describing the fatal wounds that would be inflicted. As a final flourish the scientist informs the kid that he would still be alive as the velociraptor began to feast on him.

From the point of view of the plot, this scene is a crucial step-up for what comes later in the film, which climaxes with a pair of velociraptors, who turn out to be just as clever and vicious as advertised, hot on the trail of a couple of children. It follows a sequence set on *Jurassic Park*'s island in which a worker at the dinosaur amusement park is torn apart by a mysterious something barely contained inside a crate. But in a film in which familiar Spielberg types make only the wannest of impressions, the association of children with death stands out as an unusually stark preoccupation.

This preoccupation goes beyond the mechanics of suspense, although it certainly lends an extra edge to the threat posed by rampaging dinosaurs who suddenly find themselves free to roam and hunt on their island domain. The two most terrifying scenes in the film revolve specifically around the children's near death at the hands first of a tyrannosaurus rex and then of the velociraptors.

But these encounters also serve to play out the child-murder fantasies of Dr Grant. Grant's girlfriend, palaeobotanist Dr Ellie Sattler (Laura Dern), claims laughingly that the scientist has a phobia about kids, as if it were a bachelor's tic. But the way Neill plays Grant, dark and morose, there doesn't seem anything lighthearted about his disdain for them. When he's sent on a tour of the Jurassic Park facilities with a small group that includes a couple of kids, he glowers and sulks.

Those kids are thirteen-year-old Lex (Ariana Richards) and nine-year-old Tim Murphy (Joseph Mazzello), the grandchildren of the park's owner, billionaire John Hammond. The wealthy businessman has hired Grant and Sattler to write a report that will assure his board of directors that the island is safe for paying customers (a lawyer for the board is also there with another scientist, Jeff Goldblum's Ian Malcolm, to prove the opposite). As a sign of his faith in his own creation, Hammond is willing to risk the lives of his grandchildren, vouchsafing them to the care of parental stand-ins, willing Sattler and unwilling Grant.

This set-up mirrors the structure of Spielberg's first big hit, *Jaws*. There another powerful paterfamilias, the mayor of the vacation town of Amityville, had badgered his employee, the local chief of police, into opening the town's beaches to prove they are safe from shark attack. As a result, the policeman's own kids find themselves in the water when a huge, voracious great white shark goes hunting among the bathers. The subsequent voyage out to kill the beast is not just a matter of public safety but an act of expiation.

Murder fantasies

Enacted murder fantasies have occurred in previous Spielberg efforts. In *Indiana Jones and the Temple of Doom*, the heroic Jones is drugged by members of an Indian death cult. He is in the process of sacrificing a female companion to the cult's deity when his side-kick, a little Chinese boy, manages to awaken him from his trance.

The dissatisfactions with family life that are implicit in *Jaws* are played out in *Doom's* symbolic fantasy. The peripatetic Jones, the personification of male independence, has been uncomfortably saddled with an instant family in the guise of a buxom nightclub singer and an orphaned kid and has frequently voiced his wish to be rid of them. The drugging doesn't impose the all-male cult's control so much as release Jones from his self-imposed social restraints. When the drug wears off, he not only rescues his own family group, but restores several dozen others by freeing captive children from the cult's enslavement. Even *Hook's* Peter Banning enjoys a resurgent pre-adolescence when the evil Captain Hook cooperatively kidnaps his children. The businessman is free to regress to childhood unencumbered by paternal responsibilities.

Jurassic Park doesn't probe into the source of Grant's child-hatred. He's a single man, after all, and his liaison with fellow scientist Sattler doesn't imperil his professional status in any way. The children he meets aren't particularly obnoxious; at worst they can be accused of being chatterboxes, a condition Grant appears to accept in adults. The association of children and death is just there in *Jurassic Park*, a stubborn fact to add to the genetically manufactured dinosaurs. The film, which otherwise carefully follows the rules of dramatic logic within its fantastic plot, even violates these rules in order to pursue the theme.

For example, the presence of that first boy, the one who hears Grant's story about the velociraptors, is inexplicable. Grant is out in the middle of a desert conducting a dig with a team of scientists and university students. Why should there be a single, pestering boy along? And why in the world should Hammond, a reclusive, security-conscious billionaire, entrust his grandchildren to strangers?

They are there because Spielberg is building up to the scene where the T-Rex attacks. The build-up is frighteningly tense, anchored by the film-maker's intimate familiarity with childhood fear. The party has been sent out in two landrovers guided by an electrically charged rail which runs down the park's main roads. When the power fails, the cars come to a halt.

The security fences lose their charge at the same instant, and it's not long before the rumble of huge footsteps ominously shakes the stalled vehicles. The sole adult with Lex and Tim – the lawyer – bolts almost immediately, sending the abandoned kids into hysteria. This notion of being left alone, that adults are untrustworthy protectors, pumps up the action that follows.

For when the T-Rex attacks – which it does with brutal ferocity – back in the other car Grant and Malcolm can only watch. Or so they tell each other. For it is motion that attracts the dinosaur's eye; he can't see a still object. Grant has all the knowledge of adulthood to justify his immobility.

The attack goes on for a long time, the better for Spielberg to lay out its details. He cuts into the scene, juxtaposing the dinosaur's teeth and the terror-stricken faces of the children again and again. The creature is relentless, systematically tearing apart the protective layers of the car to get at the squirming meat inside. The only time Spielberg cuts away is to show Grant sitting in his car watching, or to emphasise the space between the two vehicles, close but irretrievably distant.

Grant is eventually moved to action and with the help of Malcolm manages to escape with the kids. It's an impulsive act, as obscure as the source of Grant's dislike of children, although Neill's squirming, coupled with his impassive features, does imply a deeper struggle. You could say that the rest of the film is a ritualistic enactment of Grant's penance, like the police chief's voyage in *Jaws*. Grant and the children make their way through the manufactured prehistoric wilderness and have a final climactic bout with killer dinosaurs, this time with Ellie at their side.

Schindler's List

But you could also say that it is the automatic playing out of a pulp plot. All the digging in the movie is for fossils, not character. With its echoes of other characters from other movies, this is the remotest crew to people a Spielberg effort.

The power of the film's coupling of children and death arises almost solely from Spielberg's obsessive invocation of it. He hasn't often pursued it from the child's perspective: the exceptions being *Empire of the Sun* and *The Color Purple*, in which inconvenient children overcome death largely by their own initiative. In a comic variation, *Indiana Jones and the Last Crusade* features an adult child entangled in a near-fatal intrigue sparked in part by an ageing father's competition with him. But more often it's a case of the father or father figure trying to rescue a child just before it undergoes the death the father has unwittingly devised for it.

Certainly this makes Spielberg's pursual of his *Schindler's List* project more understandable. For years the director has been trying to film Thomas Kenneally's account of a German industrialist who rescued over a thousand Jews from the Nazis, and for years people have wondered why the entertainment king wanted to tackle such a sombre subject. As depicted by Kenneally, Oskar Schindler was a paternalistic figure whose tactic was to build factory camps which provided risky havens for Jews while seeming to cooperate with the Nazis. But there were moments when Schindler couldn't protect his charges from being rounded up for the death camps.

So less a sudden interest in history than a continuing obsession with fathers treading the line between life-giver and life-destroyer may motivate Spielberg's project, which he has now finished shooting. There's always been a dark, almost morbid streak in Spielberg's work that most people have overlooked in favour of its easier emotions. But here in *Jurassic Park*, a technical masterpiece and indifferent piece of drama, it's that darkness, not the light, that remains.

PAX AMERICANA

J. Hoberman

If the mission of the movies is, as Siegfried Kracauer wrote in his *Nature of Film: The Redemption of Physical Reality*, to preserve that which is transitory, to monumentalise the ephemeral and to celebrate the poetry of trash, then *Mars Attacks!* is pure cinema. Tim Burton's latest opus may not be the first mega-million dollar Hollywood block-buster based on a bunch of 35-year-old bubblegum cards, but it's surely the standard against which all such subsequent efforts will be judged. Certainly, no one will ever accuse Burton – among the few Hollywood film-makers with a modicum of aesthetic integrity – of betraying his supremely cheesy source. (Having previously worked from the compost heap of comic books, Grade Z sci-fi cheapsters and television kiddie shows, the director is practically the Merchant-Ivory of American idiot culture.) Like Burton's *Ed Wood* (1994), *Mars Attacks!* is rooted in what the horror-film historian David J. Skal calls 'Monster Culture'. A form of (mainly) male adolescent humour inspired by the campy telecasts of old horror movies that began in the late 50s, Mon-ster Culture was big in the Universal stable of Mittel-European bogeymen. In addition to reading the pun-ridden fan magazine *Famous Monsters of Filmdom* (an utterly dis-reputable publication whose adolescent devotees included Joey Dante and Stevie Spielberg), monster cultists might construct moulded-plastic models of the Wolf Man, the Frankenstein Monster and Dracula, some of which glowed in the dark. 'Perfectly Detailed Down to the Smallest Fang,' the comic book ads promised: 'Decorate Your Room! Surprise Your Mother!'

Monster Culture coincided roughly with the Khrushchev era (sputnik, missile gap, ban-the-bomb), reaching its mainstream apotheosis with such sitcoms as *The Munsters* and *The Addams Family*, both of which had their premieres during the pre-Vietnam 1964–65 television season. As obviously counterphobic as grown-up 'sick' humour, the craze peaked in the autumn of 1962 to merge with the imagined apocalypse of the Cuban Missile Crisis – the period during which the sepulchral tones of Bobby 'Boris' Pickett's novelty hit 'The Monster Mash' actually reigned as the number one single on the Bill-board Chart. Joe Dante's amiable and underrated *Matinee* (1963) provided a reasonably valid high-school view of the Missile Crisis by entwining the most angst-ridden week of the Cold War with a satire of the schlock apocalyptic radioactive mutation movies that everyone, even then, recognised as a primitive manifestation of nuclear terror.

It was during that same season that the original 'Mars Attacks!' made its sensational debut, as a series of fifty-five trading cards, conceived by the Topps bubblegum company in the wake of a successfully scurrilous series of centennial American Civil War cards depicting all manner of gross, bloody, *imaginary* battles. Despite their fictional details, the 'Civil War' cards were praised by the nation's educators. Not so the 'Mars Attacks!' series which, in showing scenes like a pet dog being vaporised, were deemed too lurid for kids. It was attacked in the press, as well as by a Connecticut district attorney, and effectively driven from the nation's candystores and hence into the realm of mass-cultural legend.

Like any self-respecting monster culture product, the movie *Mars Attacks!* has provoked grown-up disapproval. The sternly celebrity-driven *New Yorker* scolded
irresponsible Burton for squandering the capital of his success ('There's a strong whiff
of self-destructiveness in this picture... *Mars Attacks!* is *meant* to be a kind of anti-enter-
tainment'), while validating Burton in another way, *The New York Times* advised
anxious parents that, like *The Cable Guy* (the year's prize *film maudit*), *Mars Attacks!*
might be too dark for their children.

'More weird than funny' according to the *Times*, *Mars Attacks!* is also less camp than
hyper-real in adapting the Topps series – to which it is surprisingly faithful in representing the green-faced, bug-eyed, ecto-skulled martians and their flesh-burning
raygun violence. Given the potential to make *any* sort of alien creature, there is something irresistibly perverse in Burton's using state-of-the-art computer animation to
produce this simulation of supreme tackiness.

The theremins wail overtime as a flotilla of rotating saucers clutters up space, like
so many hubcaps on the cosmic junk heap. *Mars Attacks!* offers a sentimental taxon-
omy of Cold War extraterrestrial-invasion clichés, from the official all-purpose
scientific expert and the bellicose military commander to an anachronistic reel-to-reel
'translation machine' used to convert alien babble into English. That the movie is set
in a nominal future, resembling a more fabulous version of the High 50s, further suggests a particular form of cultural nostalgia (Washington DC never more resembled
Imperial Rome than during the prolonged saucer attack at the climax of the didactic
1956 'semi-documentary' *Earth vs. the Flying Saucers*). Infused with the Populux Jet-
sonism of the early 60s, *Mars Attacks!* draws on the entire 1948 to 1973 'Golden Age' of
Eric Hobsbawm's Short Twentieth Century, including the cycle of disaster films that
marks the Golden Age's end.

No less than the lugubrious *Independence Day*, but to far more desecratory effect,
Mars Attacks! celebrates the Pax Americana. Although *Mars Attacks!* often seems to parody *Independence Day*, it was actually longer in the production pipeline. The *War of the
Worlds* paradigm notwithstanding, the films' similarities are very probably a function
of market-testing. Both use the crowd-pleasing convention of a righteous black man
(essential America) punching out an alien's lights. And both propel their narratives by
channel-surfing the Land of the Free – but where *Independence Day* concentrates on the
power citadels of LA, New York and Washington DC, *Mars Attacks!* replaces the coastal
Sodom and Gomorrah with the fantasy heartland realms of rural Kansas and downtown Las Vegas. Where *Independence Day* revels in the survivalist scenario of public
order breaking down, the more honestly 'what-me-worry?' *Mars Attacks!* shows that
hope springs eternal for the television-blitzed populace.

While *Independence Day* pits a gaggle of hyped-up flyboys against a horde of inter-
planetary locusts (the movie's rhetorical highpoint being the hitherto wimpy
President's 'Let's nuke the bastards!'), *Mars Attacks!* allows Earth's marginal losers to
best the juvenile pranksters from outer space. And as *Mars Attacks!* ridicules Las Vegas,
America's fastest-growing metropolis (as well as the national Democra-city where the
architecture synthesises all human history and the casino dress code encompasses
everything from star-spangled tuxedos to damp swimming trunks), *Independence Day*
celebrates American military and cultural hegemony.

A pure cultural expression of what *The Nation* magazine has dubbed the National Entertainment State, *Independence Day* is the spectacle for which the Republican attack on the Clinton White House and the revelation that life may have once existed on Mars were but part of a three-month publicity build-up. Among other things, *Independence Day* afforded the key negative moment in America's interminable presidential campaign. Having played to the Religious Right by attacking America's foremost industry, the mired-in-the-polls Republican challenger Bob Dole created a midsummer media event out of his wife's sixtieth birthday by treating her to a box of Goobers, a basket of popcorn and a matinee showing of America's most popular movie in a nearly empty Century City cinema.

What did the candidate see? Accurate as far as it went, Dole's thumbs-up review ('Leadership/America/Good over Evil') only underscored his cultural cluelessness. Not only had he endorsed the movie's projection of an improved Clinton, but by failing to comment on the money shot – of the White House blown to smithereens – Dole served notice that he had never even caught the most successful trailer in recent memory.

War of the global moguls

As *Independence Day* united America before one movie, so the movie showed America organising the world to establish 4 July as a global celebration of independence – from what? Surely not Rupert Murdoch, the immigrant lad whose Twentieth Century-Fox studio bankrolled the flick. Among other things, *Independence Day* was an example of shameless synergy, plugging not only Murdoch's *Sky News* but *The X Files* – a Fox television show that refers regularly to the so-called Roswell Incident (in which an alien-piloted flying saucer crash-landed in the New Mexico desert in 1947, a world-historic event allegedly covered up by the US Air Force ever since).

In terrestrial terms, the confluence of these two special-effects invasion thrillers is an episode in the ongoing struggle between Murdoch and Burton's patron, the world's largest multi-media conglomerate, Time-Warner. In New York City, where Murdoch received a special waiver of the US anti-trust laws to allow him to be the only media mogul in America to own both a daily newspaper and a television station in the same marketplace, Time-Warner refused to allow Murdoch's new twenty-four-hour news station on its cable system. As Murdoch's *New York Post* lambasted Time-Warner's latest acquisition, Ted 'CNN' Turner, the city's mayor Rudolph Giuliani attempted first to pressure Time-Warner and then to put Murdoch's news station on a city-owned cable channel as a public service. (To add to the mix, Giuliani's wife Donna Hanover – seen to splendid effect in the role of former President Jimmy Carter's evangelist sister in *The People vs. Larry Flynt* – is a newsreader on a Fox station.)

Personal and anarchic where *Independence Day* is corporate and patriarchal, *Mars Attacks!* has an even purer hatred of politicians – and of adult authority in general. 'Extraterrestrial life – the people are going to love it,' President Jack Nicholson calculatingly smirks on seeing the first images of the approaching saucer armada and, as Manohla Dargis put it in her review, 'smelling [the] supreme Photo Op'.

Playing the nation's senior star as the Hollywood king he actually is, Nicholson's performance is so layered with insincerity that he's all but lost beneath the waxy build-up (a pompously rancid blend of Reagan and Clinton, he is truly the leader we deserve).

He even contributes a superfluous bonus stint as a leathery wheeler-dealer in a red-on-red cowboy suit and Stetson with attached orange wig; Burton's fondness for strapping performers into bondage drag notwithstanding, actors must enjoy working with him.

Mars Attacks! is overstuffed with cameos by Burton alumni, including Sarah Jessica Parker as a Barbara Walters-type television personality in go-go boots, Danny DeVito as a Las Vegas low-roller, octogenarian Sylvia Sidney as a nursing home diva and, topping her *Ed Wood* Vampira turn in the movie's one universally appreciated sequence, Lisa Marie as a seven-foot-tall, blankly gum-chewing bubble-coiffed, hip-swivelling, torpedo-breasted, alien-designed sex doll.

The most sensitive director of live cartoons since Frank Tashlin put Jerry Lewis and Jayne Mansfield through their paces, Burton here achieves a near Preston Sturges-like density (or at least a *Hollywood Squares* form of celebrity familiarity). He casts blaxploitation superstars Pam Grier and Jim Brown as an estranged couple; gets Annette Bening to play a New Age Spielbergette; recruits Glenn Close as the fatuous First Lady and Pierce Brosnan as a suavely inane scientist with a pipe attached to his jaw; has Paul Winfield impersonate a Colin Powell-style political general; and rehabilitates Martin Short to bob and grin as the President's mutant Stephanopolous. (That some of Short's antics anticipate the over-publicised peccadilloes of another Clinton adviser, the disgraced Dick Morris, just shows that American politics and American showbiz are two hemispheres of the same galactic brain.)

More stars than in outer space

All the more remarkable is that the human stars have to compete for attention with a screen full of computer-generated martians. (In this sense at least, *Mars Attacks!* is a glimpse into the Hollywood future. Though the synthesised creatures of the twenty-first century are more likely to be long-dead movie stars, Burton has allowed that the chief martian, distinguished by his plush crimson cape, is modelled on Gloria Swanson in *Sunset Boulevard*.) With oversized iridescent heads, half skull, half lushly exposed brain, these quacking, eye-rolling little cuties are as ferociously scene-stealing as they are lethal. Indeed, half the human cast is wiped out in the first spectacular attack of these killer toys, who (as gleeful in their destruction as Joe Dante's gremlins) pack heated-zapping rayguns that char their victims down to their green – or orange – glowing skeletons.

The *Mars Attacks!* narrative is so inconsistent that screenwriter Jonathan Gems, who brought the project to Burton, might have generated his script William Burroughs style, by tossing the Topps cards in the air and then tracking their random pattern. Who cares? No effect is too tacky – a herd of flaming cows (lifted from the original cards), a couple of transposed heads, flying saucers over Vegas, the notion of alien bachelor pads. *Mars Attacks!* is a form of pop surrealism. (Call it the chance meeting of Tom Jones and Godzilla in the Luxor parking lot.)

Burton is no more afraid to trash the bogus counter-culture piety of Spielberg's grotesquely revered *Close Encounters of the Third Kind* than he is to dress a set with violently polka-dot spherical chairs, to locate his trailerpark in the shadow of a massive Donut World, or to set an AA meeting in a Pepto Bismol-pink prefab church. As shot by David Cronenberg's favourite cinematographer Peter Suschitzky, the radioactive palette seems based on mood rings, lava lamps and tropi-holic slurpies. Fittingly, the martians are defeated not by Earth's indigenous microbes but by the endless permutations of America's naïve vulgarity.

Triumphantly solipistic, *Mars Attacks!* is the sort of movie in which the resident nerd triumphant (Lukas Haas) is serenaded by a mariachi band's 'Star Spangled Banner'. So, God bless America. When our maximum leader Jack Nicholson takes to the tube to tell his fellow citizens that 'a powerful memory is in the making... This is the perfect summation to the Twentieth Century,' he's actually providing *Mars Attacks!* with its perfect pull-quote.

BIGGER THAN LIFE

Yvonne Tasker

Why write about Kathryn Bigelow when there's no new film to discuss, nothing on the horizon since the commercial failure of *Strange Days* (1995), her vision of millennial LA apocalypse? The reason is because Bigelow represents an important contradiction. Self-consciously flashing her art credentials while working more or less in the Hollywood mainstream, she established herself as an auteur on the basis of just five features made over nearly twenty years. But she has become an exemplary auteur of big-budget action/spectacle at the very moment when Hollywood seems to have lost confidence in the idea that such films can be more than formulaic. Bigelow the genre-bender, purveyor of visceral cinema and fetishistic camerawork, may no longer fit in.

In fact, her position in Hollywood and critical hierarchies was always awkward: too perverse for the mainstream, despite the stars and budgets attached to *Blue Steel* (1990), *Point Break* (1991) and *Strange Days*; not quite maverick enough to warrant more than a brief mention in Geoff Andrew's recent study of US independents, *Stranger than Paradise*. Apparently not feminist enough either, since several anthologies on women film-makers exclude her altogether. In the context of the proliferating biographies of the movie-brat generation, Bigelow remains relatively obscure, though her status as *the* female action director in Hollywood brings her a strange visibility. In some ways her contradictory position reflects what is so distinctive about her movies: an artful immersion in generic popular cinema that is simultaneously stylish, seemingly ironic, but also so deeply romantic we're left unsure how to take it.

Bigelow has managed at least partially to dodge her framing as a 'woman in a man's world' via an opposition that casts her as an art-world formalist crossing over into popular cinema. Her background in painting is as recurrent a feature in profiles as her perceived transgression of an imaginary gender divide in film-making. Bigelow studied painting at the San Francisco Art Institute before gaining a scholarship to New York's Whitney Museum in 1972. Her experiments with film began before her move to Columbia's graduate film school, while she was still heavily involved in the art world as part of the Art and Language group and as assistant to video and performance artists including Vito Acconci. Laid-back publicity shots enhance her image: Bigelow in shades, tailored suede, jeans, leather, with a moody expression, looking like an extra from one of her own movies. She may distance herself from performance art in interviews, but the crafting of her persona is a performance in itself: a New York/LA composite, intellectual yet sensual, citing Barthes and Peckinpah.

Strange Days represents the most heightened example to date of Bigelow's characteristic mix of elaborately crafted images and sweeping camerawork with the conventions of commercial action cinema. Along with film-makers James Cameron (who wrote the treatment/script) and John Woo, she has redefined the visual possibilities of action as a cinematic mode. In Bigelow's movies, action sequences – shoot-out, chase, heist, fight, explosion – form only one element in a carefully stylised cinematic spectacle that includes such images as the atmospheric shots of graduating officer Megan Turner (Jamie Lee Curtis) and her colleagues in *Blue Steel.* Often quizzed about why she makes action movies, Bigelow has spoken of their filmic quality. Her rhetoric – 'action movies have a capacity to be pure cinema' – is part polemic, an assertion of the value of a form long held in low critical esteem, while the reference to 'pure cinema' harks back to the attempts of early film theorists to capture the specificity of the medium.

Bigelow's movies are marked by a strong sense of visual style – careful composition and lighting and an eye for iconography. No surprise, then, that she has been accused more than once of style without substance by critics who thus call into play what the films themselves so insistently question: the implicit distinction between narrative (finding out, cause and effect, moving forward) and visual pleasures (contemplation, beauty, display). Both *Blue Steel* and *Strange Days* develop their central narrative conundrums via fetishised images. In the former, the identity of serial killer Eugene (Ron Silver) is bound up with his/our eroticised perception of Jamie Lee Curtis' vigilante cop Megan, while the latter invites participation in point-of-view 'clips' – recordings made directly from the brain via SQUID technology which when replayed provide total involvement in the recorded experience – that serve both as visual spectacle (scenes of erotic and criminal 'action') and exposition.

As critics cast about for precedents to account for the Bigelow phenomenon, it is Hawks and Hitchcock who are repeatedly invoked, in particular the romantic articulation of the male group and gendered role reversals of Hawks and the dynamics of voyeurism and spectatorship associated with Hitchcock. Yet Hawks had no interest in the fluid camerawork, night shooting and sculpted lighting that have become Bigelow trademarks, and while *Strange Days'* explicit concern with voyeurism and point of view, sexual violence and spectatorship was bound to conjure up visions of Hitchcock, the comparison is more suggestive than sustainable.

Bigelow herself has talked about *Strange Days* in this frame – or more precisely about the film's controversial point-of-view rape/murder sequence, which draws explicitly on both *Psycho* and *Peeping Tom.* The scene revolves around Iris (Brigitte Bako), a prostitute who (like Jodie Foster's character of the same name in Scorsese's *Taxi Driver*) has seen more than she should. Forced via SQUID technology to act as an audience to her own murder, Iris 'sees' her own pain, participating in and heightening her attackers' pleasure. The sequence ends with an explicit evocation of the voyeurism of the killer/film-maker/audience as the camera closes in on the image reflected back to us from Iris' iris. Heavily criticised as this sequence was, Bigelow's allusions to *Psycho* in interviews are partly defensive. But the scene is more than a superficial reference – here too a transgressive woman is being killed/sexually assaulted in a bathroom. Bigelow speaks of her desire to match the shock effect of Hitchcock's original shower scene, of the need 'to create something as intense' in order to draw us in, to make us aware of our complicity as an audience via the SQUID technology, which serves as 'an extrapolation of the cinematic experience'.

The sequence also exemplifies a key contradiction of Bigelow's movies: a characteristic attention to formal style, which suggests emotional distance, coupled with an intense (and often intensely romantic) involvement in the scene. Iris' death – viewed and reviewed as it is – is simultaneously a scene of chilling violence, an experimental piece of camerawork and a moment of intense narrative involvement. This is the point, after all, at which purveyor of illegal SQUID images Lenny Nero (Ralph Fiennes) gets an inkling that the sleaze in which he trades might impact on his life in a very personal way. In short order the killer will leave another 'clip' for Lenny, revealing him stalked in his own apartment as he sleeps. While we shift in our seats, Lenny slips from the role of B film-maker, directing the participants in his 'clips', to find himself the key player in someone else's drama.

If Bigelow's films contain few of the allusive in-jokes so characteristic of contemporary indie movies, it's not that the films – or the film-maker – aren't intimately aware of movie history, rather that the relationship of cinematic past and present is not defined as ironic. Most evidently referential is her first feature – the 'biker-noir' *The Loveless* (1981) – which visually reworks Laszlo Benedek's *The Wild One* (1953) via Kenneth Anger, highlighting the eroticism of bodies and machinery. But *The Loveless* is well removed from the sort of redemptive romance that offers closure to *The Wild One*, carefully juxtaposing its knowing biker chic with a portrayal of the racial and sexual divisions of small-town life. Co-written and directed with Monty Montgomery, it was characterised by Bigelow in terms of her transition from the non-narrative art world to cinema: 'a visual tapestry with enough narrative to give you the illusion of a story'.

The Loveless' painful 80s evocation of repression is staged by means of highly coded moments reminiscent of 50s melodrama: Sportster Debbie (Tina L'Hotsky) in her red sports car, using a guilty father's gift to seduce biker Vance (Willem Dafoe); her suicide evoked by the soundtrack and Vance's expressionless face as he looks on; the envious gazes of the townsmen at the bikes and bikers. Heavily stylised, fragmented by editing and restrained by long shots, and with music foregrounded over dialogue, *The Loveless*' arch film-school allusions prefigure Bigelow's more substantial engagement with popular genres in the movies that followed.

The use of actors in Bigelow's movies similarly builds on type. The casting of Jamie Lee Curtis as a cop who becomes the eroticised object on which serial killer Eugene fixates in *Blue Steel* cleverly elaborates on the star's associations with stalk 'n' slash. *Point Break* – in which Keanu Reeves plays an over-achieving FBI agent Johnny Utah, who is assigned to work his way into LA's outlaw surfer community – brought a more sinister edge to the actor's anti-adult teenage roles, bridging his transition from airhead youth to action star in the process. Patrick Swayze's role as surfing-community guru Bodhi in the same movie built on his action/romance image as composite dancer/bruiser, while Angela Bassett's personal security expert

Mace in *Strange Days* reprises her strong survivor roles within an action narrative.

Bigelow has talked of her work – in particular of the vampire-noir-western *Near Dark* (1987) – as subverting genre: 'We were very conscious of taking a genre and turning it upside down, subverting it in some way.' And *Strange Days* co-writer Jay Cocks side-stepped a question about the movie's feelgood ending with an aside that emphasises its departure from formula, suggesting that Bigelow 'is the only director in the world that would let her leading man faint at the end'. Bigelow too has spoken of the contrast between Lenny's strong female cohort Mace and Lenny's own vulnerability in terms of subverting a formula, claiming that this 'would not be something I would pursue if the situation were reversed... it'd be generic'.

Bigelow never presents herself as making 'art' despite Hollywood's limitations – her subversion of genre is derived not from dissatisfaction or contempt, but rather demonstrates a genuine involvement with popular cinema. And this subversion is as often the result of stretching or combining genres as of up-ending them: *Blue Steel*'s compelling mix of the *policier* with the women's picture and stalk 'n' slash; the film's presentation of the police station through the eerie light of horror rather than the more usual camaraderie of the squad; Eugene as a gun-fixated, serial-killer werewolf, howling naked, bathed in blood, atop a building. By way of contrast with such striking visuals, Bigelow isn't particularly adept at either plot or naturalistic dialogue; as with Cameron, concept and image come first. This is yet another reason why she doesn't fit neatly within the alternative pantheon – it's quirky dialogue, black comedy and the spectacle of violence as much as visual innovation that give the spark to the mainstream edges of US independent cinema (though *Near Dark*, co-written with Eric Red who scripted the previous year's *The Hitcher*, has the sort of tongue-in-cheek quality that might qualify).

While Bigelow is usually classed as an action film-maker, the generic combinations with which she has worked suggest the need for an expanded understanding of that term. Action, like noir, functions as a mode that suffuses Bigelow's movies, and it's the combination of these two modes that gives her films their visual power, their simultaneous sense of artful distance and romanticism. Noir has increasingly come to signal 'quality' in an art-house context, but what classical noir offers, alongside its familiar thematic preoccupations, is the potential of visual style in popular cinema. Bigelow's films have mobilised with increasing confidence the central qualities of action cinema – camera movement, carefully choreographed action, bursts of explosive spectacle, rapid editing – in combination with stylised lighting, careful composition and an urgent, sometimes erotic investment in objects and images: costume and uniform, blood and night skies, the 'clips' in *Strange Days*, the gun in *Blue Steel*. She has spoken of becoming more familiar with the action medium, learning to use unbroken shots (or shots that look unbroken) and moving away from the restraint of *Blue Steel* to the adrenaline of *Point Break* and *Strange Days*. But it's noir that frames the pervasive mobilisation of generic iconography in fetishistic fashion across her work.

Termed by Bigelow a 'wet western', *Point Break* looks to noir the least obviously. Though the film centres on an ambiguous cop/criminal doubling so characteristic of noir, the doppelgänger narrative is located not in noir's rain-soaked streets and oppressive urban spaces but in self-consciously 'natural', sun-drenched settings. Yet even here Bigelow manages to weave in night shooting, with a scene of midnight surfing that represents a key moment of self-discovery (and romance) for Utah.

Point Break was met with critical bemusement – not noirish, ironic or feminist enough, not a worthy successor to the cult status of *Near Dark* or what was widely felt to be the latent feminism of *Blue Steel*, the film was judged to enact rather than subvert genre. Less attention was paid to what *Point Break* achieved: a vivid portrayal of the interplay of law-bound and lawless communities centred on the relationship between undercover cop Utah and bank-robbing surfer Bodhi and the genuine intensity of the buddy relationship expressed in the exhilarating surfing and skydiving sequences. In *Point Break* Bigelow took what was to become the quintessential 90s action format, the roller-coaster, and invested its carefully choreographed action sequences with emotional intensity – as in the breathtaking steadicam chase (shot by James Muro, who worked on the point-of-view sequences in *Strange Days*) in which Utah frantically follows Bodhi through alleys and houses but finally can't kill him.

Bigelow's films involve neither emotional nor political distance. In interviews she is at pains to stress the importance of emotional intensity: 'Without that stuff, it's an exercise in futility. You just go from one explosion to another.' The final scene of *Point Break* has Utah catch up with Bodhi on a storm-swept Australian beach. Though Utah manages to handcuff Bodhi, he almost immediately relents, setting his buddy/adversary free to surf out to his death before throwing his own badge of authority away. If this moment suggests (Dirty) Harry Callahan's bitter gesture of casting aside his badge, Utah's alienation from authority is bound into the romantic suicide of Bodhi. *Near Dark* ends with a blood transfusion by which vampire Mae (Jenny Wright) is reclaimed to embrace hero Caleb (Adrian Pasdar), foreshadowing the much-derided and debated ending of *Strange Days*. Here, as the year 2000 arrives, the bad cops are destroyed, riot becomes celebration and Lenny and Mace kiss, reconnecting him with the real world in shamelessly romantic fashion. But only up to a point, since slow motion acts as a visual cue for the unreality of both fantasy and romance.

Though Cameron left his treatment/script of *Strange Days* to direct family fun *True Lies* (he initially brought the script to Bigelow in 1991), the movie echoes the techno-noir, sci-fi paranoia of his critically acclaimed *The Terminator* (1984). As a spectacular film involved in a more or less explicit critique of spectatorship, *Strange Days* is for Bigelow aficionados the culmination of her previous movies, bringing together the darkly romantic outsider communities of men from *The Loveless* and *Point Break*, the noirish horror of *Near Dark* and the uncomfortable voyeurism and tough women of *Blue Steel* (though despite all her musculature and fighting, Angela Bassett is one of the least androgynous of Bigelow's female leads and the first mother, excepting Jenette Goldstein's vampire matriarch Diamondback in *Near Dark*). The film rehearses anxieties across the personal, technological and social – all related in some way to the visual. Lenny wires himself up to relive moments from his time with his ex-lover Faith (Juliette Lewis), at the same time marketing dark fantasies to his punters while Los Angeles falls apart. His preoccupation with memories and fantasies blinds him to what is going on around him; Mace's strength, by contrast, lies in her refusal of the sensual pleasures of playback ('porno for wireheads').

The movie draws us in via action and spectacle, posing the question of complicity in extreme terms. Pushing the serial-killer chic of *The Silence of the Lambs, Copycat,*

Seven, et al, it plays noir to the hilt, with Faith as the *femme fatale* to Lenny's ineffectual hero. And like other 90s noirs it makes explicit, or at least visible, the racial subtext of classical urban noir through the murder of black activist and pop star Jeriko One (Glenn Plummer) and the ensuing riot scenes.

Having always taken the time to develop her own projects – interspersed by occasional work for television – it's uncertain where Bigelow will go next. There's no doubt that *Strange Days'* poor performance at the US box office hurt her. And her thwarted and long-cherished *Company of Angels* project, a movie about Joan of Arc, received yet another setback when litigation failed to block Luc Besson's competing film set for 1999 release. But then, there's nothing like misunderstood movies and bad box office to aid the romantic image of the auteur.

NO SMOKING GUN

Nick James

'Al should really be in the fucking intense groove here.' This is a note scrawled vigorously in blue ink next to a scene plan for the coffee-shop meeting between Al Pacino and Robert De Niro in Michael Mann's *Heat* (1995). It's part of a cache of documents Mann sent to *Sight and Sound* at the time of *Heat's* UK release and it seems revealing. Of course, the idea is unintentionally comic – when is Al Pacino not in the 'fucking intense groove'? But, by implication, even though Mann must have known he was always going to get the trumpet without recourse to the mute, he's going to write the note anyway, because Mann the director is a perfectionist and he has to check: Al, make sure you're in the fucking intense groove, OK? Sure thing, Michael.

Pacino is back centre frame in Mann's new film *The Insider*, but he's not in the lead role. That's taken by a podged-out, grey-wigged Russell Crowe playing Jeffrey Wigand, an everyday tobacco-industry boffin so outraged at being made redundant and then threatened about the confidentiality clause in his contract he turns whistle-blower at grave risk to his life. Pacino gets the romantic end of the deal-playing Lowell Bergman, the investigative journalist behind CBS's famous *60 Minutes* programme, the man for whom Wigand will spill all, a tenacious figure who lives and breathes that near-mythical force for good: journalistic integrity.

Professionalism and ruthlessness
It's hard now to dissociate Pacino from the world of Michael Mann. Something about the actor's combination of swaggering, eyeballing and buttonholing, the aggressive intimacy he brought to the cop Vincent Hanna in *Heat*, makes him the quintessence of the Mann universe. Think of his arrival at the crime scene after the robbery near the beginning of that film, the way he struts his ground, processing the scene theatrically, barking commands to his officers – it's not unlike descriptions of Mann on set. Consider Pacino's perfect delivery of a line pointing out the professional ruthlessness

of his quarry: 'Drop of a hat and these people will rock and roll.' Or the way he mimics deafness when he's wanting to intimidate a vacillating stoolie who's trying to eat his breakfast. Why is Pacino so right? Because Mann's cinema is about professionalism and ruthlessness and it's always in the fucking intense groove.

That's what so simultaneously likeable and dislikeable about Mann's films: they are aggressively hypnotic, they grab you by the lapels and keep you there. Just as Pacino's slightly dead eyes can fix you with challenge or menace, so Mann's films require your complete emotional commitment, in worlds that are sometimes overwhelming, more often downright claustrophobic, to people who are demanding or needy. In Mann's films the *mise en scène* is so controlled, so entrancingly framed and lit, it constantly threatens to subsume or belittle the human action. His protagonists are people whose sharpness keeps them one step ahead of an encroaching environment, be it urban, suburban or rural. The key Mann films are types of action movie – *Thief* (1981), *Manhunter* (1986), *The Last of the Mohicans* (1992) and *Heat*. I don't know yet whether for me *The Insider* is good enough to keep these others company. I've seen it only once, and the thing about Mann's films – if you like them as much as I do – is that you tend to want to watch them over and over again. Moreover, while *The Insider* has many of the Mann hallmarks, it is not an action movie per se. It's a conspiracy thriller – imagine *All the President's Men* with the volume cranked up. Its plot is all talk and procedure, yet Mann can't help but intrude his favourite things.

Take the opening sequence. It begins with a shot through a lattice of cloth. It's the point of view of a hooded man being driven by armed guards in a four-wheel drive past posters of the Imam, barbed wire and other symbols of militarist Islam. The sequence has all the clip and rush of a superior action thriller, yet it has nothing to do with the main plot. Its sole purpose is to establish Pacino's character – the man under the hood – as a 60s idealist grown up, a man of so much apparent integrity he can negotiate aggressively for fair play even under such intimidating circumstances. So *60 Minutes* gets its Mullah interview, on its own terms.

Mann then has to rein his film back in and back home, because the main drama of *The Insider*, a true-story tale of American heroism, is an internal thing. It takes place mostly inside Wigand's head. He's fuming because his loyalty to the tobacco industry has been rewarded with contempt and suspicion. Wigand's heroism is all about bloody-mindedness. It's clear right from the start that he could have an easy life of well-heeled retirement and quality parenthood. His only motive, it seems, for blowing the whistle is a refusal to be pushed around. This formerly quiet man's unspectacular life then moves into meltdown and he can't understand why his need to reveal the truth puts what he cares about most at risk – the esteem of his wife and two daughters. Mann expertly draws us into this dilemma, mostly through quiet tension-building, though the action-movie reflex still kicks out.

Real people get scared

Just as the suspense of the mysterious meet at the film's outset reminds us of the fear of ambush lurking behind all Mann's high-flown action movies, so the situation Wigand finds himself in – as a 'suit' whose suburban domestic idyll is under siege from unseen corporate security stalkers – recalls the 'perfect' victim families in *Manhunter*. 'Look at the bloom on her,' says *Manhunter*'s empathetic detective Will Graham (William Petersen) as he watches the super-8 footage of Mrs Jacobi and her family that eventually leads him to the 'tooth fairy' killer. He's fascinated by this vision of an ideal family now slaughtered (an image echoed by the frontier family butchered by raiders in *The Last of the Mohicans*), which reminds him he has put his own wife and son under threat by agreeing to come out of retirement. Wigand is equally guilty of putting his wife Liane (Diane Venora) and kids on the spot through his stubborn belief, but *The Insider* is a true story, so his reward is not the loyalty shown by Graham's wife Molly, but desertion.

Even so, Mann, it seems, can't help but approach the Wigand family's suburban siege in reflex ways. That hard-edged, blue-washed night-time look cinematographer Dante Spinotti perfected in *Heat* injects menace into one typical action-like scene here. As I recall it, Wigand's pre-teen daughter tiptoes down the stairs in her nightdress. We see the dark basement den where her father keeps his gun and computer. Wigand hears her calling out that there's someone outside. He runs for his gun, finds the girl in the front doorway and clutches her to him. All he discovers in the garden is a shoeprint. And that's it. Nothing worse actually happens to his family apart from the inconvenience of sharing the house with security guards. Nevertheless, Mrs Wigand leaves with the kids. There's no 'stand by your man'. Real people get scared.

Mann dramatises this internal dread in terms of the genres he's worked in, which makes *The Insider* feel more of a patchwork than his other movies. And Wigand is the exception to the rule of his protagonists. His instincts are lousy. He doesn't foresee the desertion. He has no natural feel for surviving the media smear campaign raked up by the tobacco-company lawyers. That's where Pacino comes in. Lowell Bergman is that connected antennae man. He's the one who promises to protect Wigand from the shit that's bound to come down once he has recorded his testimony to the fact that the tobacco companies knowingly design cigarettes to enhance the addictive properties of nicotine.

As if to underline Bergman's affinity with such other Mann heroes as Graham, the *Manhunter* empath, and Neil McCauley (Robert De Niro), the consummate professional thief in *Heat*, we find him living, as they do, in a beach house overlooking the sea. But, yet again, Mann lets the real-life basis of his story win, undercutting his penchant for framing his heroes against raw nature – here Bergman has to wade out into the water to get his mobile phone to work. It's almost a comedy moment, but Mann's films are not exactly known for their humour. Rather it's a way of telegraphing Bergman as vulnerable, that he himself will be the victim of CBS's unwillingness to broadcast Wigand's revelations.

What we see here is Mann trying to move on from familiar genre-writ-large material without giving up the things he loves to do – the set pieces, the grandiloquent images that nearly but don't quite spill over with meaning. There are two *Insider* scenes in particular that strike me as demonstrating the parameters of classic Mann. In the first, Wigand, feeling he has been betrayed by Bergman, is cracking up. His family have left him and he's holed up in a hotel room, refusing all calls and visitors. The hotel wallpaper is a hideous pattern of tropical islands in blues, yellows and greens. We see Wigand in profile against it then suddenly the wall becomes a huge screen showing his kids playing in their garden. In the second, Wigand stands on the shore of a lake where a long convoy of official vehicles is waiting to take him to testify on behalf of the State of Mississippi against the tobacco companies. He has just learned that if he testifies he may be jailed on return to his own state for breach of confidentiality. He must make up his mind there and then whether or not to risk imprisonment. So internalised is the crisis Crowe's extraordinary performance has built to at this point that all Mann has to do is watch him waddle, dwarfing him with a crane shot. Both scenes are powerful emotional climaxes, the first is Mann at his most imaginative and risky, the second similar to big-scene moments from his other films. And it is the latter scene, which Mann says was shot exactly how and where it happened in real life, that feels the more contrived.

What is it, though, that Mann is trying to move on from? If asked to describe a typical Michael Mann film, most people would be likely to conjure up a cop movie set in the present day full of sports cars and guns, fast paced and slickly shot and edited, using a pounding metal-disco score. Some rugged, sharp-suited urban individualist would be out there with his colleagues riding shotgun for the good people, but unsure of his own moral centre. And what they would be describing, of course, is *Miami Vice.*

Mann was the executive producer of the 80s television series, and you can see some elements of the flashy *Vice* aesthetic at work in *Manhunter.* Yet that film was also was clearly the work of a totally distinctive director, one who had put the 70s grunge realism of his first heist movie, *Thief,* behind him and opted for a shiny modernist palette to emphasise the clinical pathology of his serial killers. Indeed, *Manhunter* is a rare example of a post-70s movie in which the montage design seems to have been developed in tandem with the script. Much as, say, Hitchcock's *North by Northwest* (1959) uses the lines of renaissance perspective as a consistent visual motif, so Hannibal Lecter's prison bars are echoed throughout the design scheme, usually through adroit use of modernist architecture.

Yet the streak of bombast and vulgarity that makes *Vice* such a compelling slice of 80s excess remains part of the Mann aesthetic. That Mann is mentioned a couple of times in Don Simpson's biography seems no accident – his films can be characterised as artistically perfected structures crafted on similar genre real estate to that on which Simpson-Bruckheimer were happy to jerry-build. After all, Mann revisited *Vice's* empathetic-cop theme in *Manhunter,* just as later he would take the plot of a short shlocky television drama and rework it into *Heat.* All these cop-swagger sagas have their cheesy moments, when you feel hemmed in by medallion men – but that's perhaps evidence more of this viewer's snobbery than of Mann's vulgarity.

Still, it might have been unease about such cultural stereotyping that led him to make an eighteenth-century costume drama, *The Last of the Mohicans*, after *Vice* had given him the financial muscle to be a totally independent auteur. The exactitude of *Mohican's* re-creation of the past cemented Mann's reputation as a perfectionist martinet, along with tales of an extremely punishing shoot. *Mohicans* represents the moment when Mann's auteur claims become unassailable. It also showed him making a commercial leap from the $3 million grossed by *Manhunter* after seven weeks in the top fifty to the $70 million *Mohicans* accrued after twelve weeks. So perfectly conceived and executed is *Mohicans* that, for all its careful costuming, it feels utterly stripped of excess meaning. To say that there's not a hair out of place is almost an ironic joke.

Mohicans shows Mann's mastery of widescreen at its most overpowering. Take the scene where Alice Munro (Jodhi May) is on a high rock. She's just witnessed the death of the young Mohican brave who loves her and she is now being beckoned by his blood-soaked killer Magua. A slo-mo close-up of her young face jolts us into recognition of her beauty; indeed it draws our attention indecently to her indisputably modern coiffure and unblemished complexion – it's almost a fashion shoot. The contrast with the truly savage Magua is all the more piquant. Irish folk music is keening away as blue mists of mountains behind her remind us of her vertiginous position. Then she jumps after the brave to her death. This is breathtaking modern cinema and nothing to do with heritage re-creation.

But this crafting of 'perfect' genre movies brings its own problems. In an incisive 'interim report' on Mann in *Film Comment*, Richard Combs persuasively argues that his films are hard to read as auteur works because as a supreme writer-producer-director he makes movies that are somehow sealed up. 'The film-maker who becomes an organisation,' says Combs, '…may lose his personality… a world so convincingly controlled may not be an easy one to enter.' This self-cancelling instinct in Mann is perhaps best epitomised by the coffee-shop scene in *Heat* mentioned above. For Combs, *Heat* is 'an 80-minute cops and robbers drama whose parts are subjected to such minute inspection that it lasts nearly three hours.' That cop Hanna and thief McCauley are mirror images of each other, workaholics chained to their perfectionism, means their so-called climactic meeting is really 'the sealing up for which every Mann film is headed'.

If we take Combs' assessment as accurate, then *The Insider* is the Mann film that opens up a fissure of incompleteness. Though it revisits many of Mann's themes, it's not afraid to trouble its surface with the irresolved. There are plenty of climactic head-to-heads – between Wigand and Bergman, between Bergman and his former mentor, *60 Minutes* presenter Mike Wallace (Christopher Plummer) – but they are not self-cancelling because the true story imposes its own loose ends. All the protagonists are real people, so the lifelong friendship between Bergman and Wallace is ruined over principle, while Wigand's life remains wrecked though his pride is somewhat restored when his daughters get to watch his testimony after Bergman has blackmailed the network into showing it.

Inability to correct

What, then, has this attention to reality opened up that could be said to be pure Michael Mann? For me the idea of the sealed-up film is partly an intellectual suspicion of mega-productions, of movies that marshal all the power of cinema and focus it like a laser. Muscular visual hyperbole is a given with Mann; it's in the moments when the world being depicted becomes overwhelming for both the characters and the viewer that his films break out from their seeming perfection. After many scenes of intense claustrophobic confrontation there is suddenly a release into action, into excitement. The way, for instance, the spectacular bank-raid gunfight breaks out in *Heat* seems an experience beyond any director's calculation. Mann's loners are ready to act at the 'drop of a hat', yet what his films are trying to articulate is their inability to connect. Haunted as the Mann hero of heightened senses is by images of domestic perfection laid waste, such perfection is held at a distance, unattainable. Genre expectations are often used against themselves. For instance, the damaged Graham seems unable to believe in his own beach-bum idyll, for paradise must not be allowed to corrode his vigilance. You feel he can't wait to get back into action.

Mann tends to portray work as a respite from what we do on vacation. Time and again he'll pose his figures against an awe-inspiring landscape in a way that suggests they are not just dwarfed by it, but framed alone together. In *Heat* McCauley stands on a balcony high over LA at night trying to open up to Eady (Amy Brenneman), the woman he's dating. Below them the city lights are flickering. 'In Fiji,' McCauley says, 'they have these iridescent algae that come out once a year in the water.' 'Have you been there?' asks Eady. 'No.' McCauley's professional dictum is that a thief should never be involved in anything he couldn't walk away from in fifteen seconds if the heat comes down. Eady is, of course, his tragic flaw, the woman he doesn't desert and who therefore is his doom. The heat in this context is not the cops but the warmth of human contact.

It's a truism to say that men in Mann's present-day films are nearly always hopelessly at odds with women. Marriage, for instance, is put under pressure in such a way that scepticism seems endemic. If the few articulations of women's views seem strained, they are at least leavened with acute male self-knowledge. When Justine (Diane Venora) tells Vincent Hanna, 'This is not sharing, this is leftovers. Because you prefer the normal routine – we fuck, then you lose the power of speech,' all Pacino's cop can come back with is: 'I've got to hold on to my angst, it keeps me sharp.'

That's what it takes to stay in the fucking intense groove. Mann's high-principled protagonists suffer from the feeling that others are not as there as they are. In *The Insider* the heroic qualities are divided up between Bergman and Wigand. Bergman is the one with the street smarts, but it's Wigand who becomes the true loner, the man who must confront death and violence and pay the price of solitude. Violence is often portrayed by Mann with an unlikely tenderness – a brave about to slit a woman's throat will hold her gently, a bank robber who snatches a little girl will address her as a parent would. Death is as intimate and sensual as smoking.

KISS KISS BANG BANG

José Arroyo

William Shakespeare's Romeo & Juliet is a kiss-kiss bang-bang movie. It's got action, spectacle and romance and it aims to entertain. Unlike other movies of Shakespeare's plays – the ones we all get bored by on school trips to the cinema – *Romeo & Juliet* doesn't salaam to Shakespeare's language. The words are all there, as glorious as always, but they are not the *raison d'être* of the film. If most other Shakespeare films nullify the expressive power of *mise en scène* by subordinating it, in the service of the language, the Australian director Baz Luhrmann (who made the high-camp dance film *Strictly Ballroom*) elevates Shakespeare cinematically. He makes Shakespeare's work relevant the way it rarely has been in films, by treating his words merely as great dialogue. *Romeo & Juliet* is a moving picture. The dialogue is performed and heard as much in and through the exhilarating movement of striking images, and it is in and through motion that the film moves its audience emotionally.

Romeo & Juliet is set in a 'constructed' world, one that is different enough from a 'real' one to allow for different ways of being and knowing, but with enough similarities to permit understanding. It is a device presently popular across a variety of cultural forms. In comic books, whenever writers want to experiment with risky storylines, they place their characters in a 'parallel universe'. (DC Comic Books has a whole Earth II where characters introduced in the 40s are older and have led different lives than the Superman or Wonder Woman of 'our' world.) Science fiction often constructs new worlds in which to set contemporary dilemmas, and fantasy novels brew epic potions of topical villainy by combining modern characterisation with medieval monsters and, sometimes, futuristic technology. In a broader sense, *every* movie could be said to construct its own world (that we accept the city in which *Casablanca* is set as standing in for the real place doesn't mean it's anything remotely like Casablanca). In the narrower sense I am using here, the convention of a constructed world has traditionally been associated only with particular genres; sci-fi, fantasy, horror and – to a different degree – the musical. But it is arguably now a dominant device, not only in a great deal of action/spectacle cinema, but also in such art fare as *Orlando* or *Swoon*.

Much of *Romeo & Juliet* was filmed in Mexico City, and the topography of that millennial urban nightmare is a key component of the film's look. Verona is depicted as a massive industrial sprawl. At the centre of the city, a gigantic icon of Christ, arms outstretched, ineffectually looms over its inhabitants. Skyscrapers indicate that the Montagues and the Capulets are rich and warring corporate owners. But the skyscrapers are so rickety, dusty and old that they indicate a crumbling social structure. The city is close to sunny beaches and open skies. Its citizens sport rich clothes, fast cars and flash guns. But the city these citizens move in, its streets, buildings and institutions, are all in decay. The clothes mark caste, while cars and guns may be mobilised to sudden and deadly consequence. The colour schemes change through the movie, but such bright pinks, blues and oranges are rarely to be found in nature. Verona's Prince, although powerful, is ineffectual against the anarchic gang violence that is the city's *modus operandi*. The way Verona is visualised evokes violent delights as well as violent ends. Pictorially it emphasises the ritual performance of ancient hates that is one of the film's themes.

The film's creation of this imaginary world, one like ours but different, allows us to recognise the actions depicted. We've seen that type of gang violence in news reports from Los Angeles, and the film borrows its iconography from LA gang culture (one gang member has the word 'Montague' tattooed on his scalp). Yet this imaginary construction also renders understandable a world where filial duty, religious devotion, family honour and the institution of marriage have an importance that they do not in ours. In other words, such a construction contributes not only a visual setting for the film's action, but also sets the dramatic terms for that action and therefore the conceptual schema for the audience's understanding. Constructing a world which combines the real with the imagined, the past with the present, results in a depiction of a sense of time and space which is quasi-mythic.

Fredric Jameson has argued that this is typical of the dehistoricising effects of post-modern culture. But one could counter-argue that what he calls dehistoricising can be a means of making past conventions of storytelling understandable in the present context. The construction of mythic time and place in *Romeo & Juliet*, a no-time that is all time, and a no-place that stands for anyplace, is built bit by bit out of previous, inherited modes of telling, showing and understanding. These operate allegorically, and involve the viewer in sophisticated strategies of interpretation. So we are required to decipher what this constructed world stands for and how it comments on our own.

Romeo & Juliet is complex but also direct, pleasurable and easily accessible. The story is framed by a television news report. The television slowly materialises from a dark screen until it takes over the frame. A black newsreader with the *faux*-friendly attitude, regulation hairdo and style of announcing so typical of American television, begins to tell us about 'the two households, both alike in dignity'. The camera then cuts away from the newsreader, as we get to the report itself. As the voice-over continues to tell us how 'civil war makes civil hands unclean', we get a tabloid television montage of quickly edited images of chaos: some from a helicopter, some out of focus, some zooms and quick wipes. The end of the film will reverse this process and the television newsreader will fade to black as we are told that there 'never was a story of more woe/Than this of Juliet and her Romeo'.

The brawl at the beginning of the play, which ends with the threat of a duel between Benvolio and Tybalt is filmed at a hysterical pitch. The audience seems to be assaulted by every cinematic trick in the book: impossible point-of-view shots (a huge close-up of Tybalt's silver-heeled boots); quick cutting of pans, zooms, wipes. The scene culminates in the most characteristic device in the contemporary action/spectacle genre: the moment when something potentially destructive, moving at great speed, is shown in slow motion, to evoke the beauty of anticipating the horror to come. Here, that moment is when Tybalt draws his weapon on Benvolio.

The frenzy of this first scene is so viscerally exciting that the language gets lost in the action. The intent is probably strategic: to announce that *Romeo & Juliet* will be a Shakespeare film like no other. However, one is grateful that this kind of loss is not compounded. How the language gets performed – by the director, cinematographer and other film-makers as well as the actors – is still the major attraction in seeing a Shakespeare film. Fortunately, from then on, no matter how action-packed or how excitingly filmed the scene is, the speeches will be heard.

We are introduced to Romeo via a helicopter shot in a setting that conveys his state of mind. Initially we just see something that looks like a Victorian monument with a hole apparently blasted through it. The sun is coming up over a new day, over the near-apocalypse of the past. When we get to Romeo, the camera comes to rest, as he sighingly foreshadows what will happen – the brawling love, the loving hate. When Romeo tells us that 'Love is a smoke made with the fume of sighs' and a 'madness most discreet', the camera is in close-up. This alternation – between filming public scenes as action-packed and quick-moving, and slowing down the pace and moving the camera closer when the protagonists are expressing emotion in private – is characteristic of the film; plot is filmed intensely with a complex array of film devices; the intense emotions of Shakespeare's characters are filmed quietly and more simply.

In this version of *Romeo & Juliet*, the Prince is something akin to a Chief of Police, Mercutio is a black drag queen, the Montagues are white while the Capulets are Hispanic. This amounts to more than just the attribution of ethnic or racial characteristics to characters: it helps to restore to Shakespeare's filmed work a polyphony that has been eroded through years of respect. Having Harold Perrineau depict Mercutio as a drag queen is a delight, if not too much of a surprise: a certain bawdiness is one of the pleasures of Shakespeare, and previous film interpretations (including John Barrymore in George Cukor's 1936 version) have tended towards camp. Even a black Mercutio will not seem strange: we've become used to blind casting in Shakespeare (good though Denzel Washington was in Kenneth Branagh's version, he was still Much Ado About Nothing). But what will (I think) surprise is Perrineau's recognisably black-American inflection; and that Vondie Curtis-Hall speaks the Prince role in the usual received pronunciation and declamatory style expected of Shakespearean princes, while Paul Sorvino as Fulgencio Capulet and John Leguizamo as Tybalt speak with a Hispanic accent. The language is just as poetic; and in the sense that it adds a racial and ethnic dimension to the characterisation, arguably richer, more relevant to contemporary culture. And it is undoubtedly more 'realistic' and (perhaps because of that) more accessible. The vocal performances here aren't as attention grabbing or as theatrical as the vocally complex and rich declamatory style usually associated with Olivier (though they derive from a great British theatrical tradition): yet I find that it's a style that works beautifully in this film.

The film's attribution of ethnicity puts an interesting slant on how the film depicts gender. As in *West Side Story*, Romeo's side is white, while Juliet's is Hispanic. This device attaches to Shakespeare's characters certain modern stereotypes, which make them more understandable. Tybalt, for example, is as sleek and agile as a puma. He wears Cuban heels, tight pants, a matador jacket and a pencil-thin moustache. Every movement he makes has the elegance and force of a flamenco gesture. His pride, temper and the importance he attaches to family honour are far more understandable to present-day viewers as Hispanic stereotypes than as the values of a Renaissance nobleman. Likewise, Juliet's refusal of her father's wishes becomes more transgressive when read through her ethnicity.

The way the film racialises the family is intriguing. It is the *woman*'s family which tends to be depicted as of a 'minority', thus doubly disempowering her. Within her family context here, Juliet has very limited power over her actions and her future – not only because she's a young girl, but because she's a Hispanic young girl. Romeo's love is thus also a promise of integration, one which gets fulfilled after their death when the two families reconcile at the end. Moreover, as in *West Side Story*, which has Natalie Wood as Maria, whose family is clearly marked as ethnically Other, the heroine is played by a 'white' actress. Thus, while Paul Sorvino can personify ethnicity as Capulet, Claire Danes as Juliet doesn't even use the accent. *Her* ethnicity is a kind of drag impersonation imposed on her character by genealogy. This adds a certain erotic *frisson* to the relationship while not burdening the love story with any extra social repercussions inherent in an inter-racial romance.

Perhaps *Romeo & Juliet*'s greatest success is in its depiction of the love story. The film really captures the romance of adolescent love: sometimes flighty but also exaggerat-edly obsessive, intense and secret, frightfully dangerous and touchingly pure. When Romeo goes to the party where he will meet Juliet, he takes some drugs and all of a sudden the black sky is full of red fireworks. Something explosive is about to happen. When he does meet Juliet, everything quietens down. He sees her eye through white coral in a fish tank. We see both of them in close-up staring at each other as tropical fish in brightly beautiful colours glide over their faces. Even as they are separated by the tank, their reflections are already side by side. The private moments of Romeo and Juliet are always shown as enclosed or submerged. In the balcony scene, they kiss under water. After they are married and he sneaks into her bedroom, we see them under a sheet. The morning after, we see them through an overhead shot that finds them grounded on the bed, their adolescent bodies unprotected even by a sheet, much less from the dangers that lie ahead.

Romeo & Juliet works on many levels, but it could all have fallen apart with the wrong casting. Leonardo DiCaprio and Claire Danes not only act the parts well but, more importantly (an importance we can glean from the success of the rather badly acted Zeffirelli version in 1968), they *look* like adolescents. Danes brings a quiet resol-ution to her part, a maturity and pragmatism evoked by her face and figure as much as by her acting, while still looking like an adolescent. DiCaprio is skinny and gangly, seemingly all arms and legs. His walk, somewhat pigeon-toed, makes him seem very vulnerable. This version of the film places rather more onus on Romeo than on Juliet. He is the one who bears the brunt of feeling: it's his face in close-up most of the time indicating how he wants, longs, feels and sometimes, eyes hidden by tears, suffers. His performance is all raw emotion. When he's in exile in Mantua, it's not just the flat bar-ren desert of red earth and regulation trailers that speak his desolation, but the way he moves. When he hears of Juliet's death it's not just that the camera lifts up suddenly to crush him that expresses his grief, but the way he falls on his pigeon-toed heels. It's a superb performance.

Romeo & Juliet draws on many genres. We can detect elements from *Rebel Without a Cause*. The *Dirty Harry* films are evoked, as are Fellini and Busby Berkeley. But they are all brought together through a camp aesthetic pitched at a melodramatic level. In tra-ditional melodrama, effect tends to be in excess of cause. A one-night stand, a missed encounter or a simple misunderstanding could lead to a lifetime of tragedy. Romeo and Juliet fall in love instantly; they promise to marry one another and because of this (and several misunderstandings) they both kill themselves. Geoffrey Nowell-Smith has written of the notion of conversion hysteria in melodrama: that which the text represses on the level of plot and dialogue returns in the *mise en scène* as 'hysterical' moments. Though Shakespeare's text doesn't leave much unsaid, the *mise en scène* excessively intensifies that which the characters are saying. Every emotion is overde-termined. When the two fall in love we're told so by the film on the level of the music, the colour and the camera movement, as well as the dialogue. The function of camp in the film is to add a layer of signification to the narrative while distancing the viewer from it. When the pair meet she's wearing wings and he's wearing shining armour. She's his angel; he's her knight. When Romeo goes to the party, the acid tab he takes is imprinted with a broken heart. On one level, this campy *mise en scène* contributes to what we are shown about the characters' state of mind; on another, it is so knowingly excessive that it has the paradoxical effect of making the dialogue and situation seem *more* naturalistic.

I am not sure that the film's campness is necessarily a gay camp. True, the story of a forbidden love whose discovery brings catastrophic consequences has traditionally appealed to gay men (it's no accident that Cukor and Zeffirelli directed previous Hollywood versions). This *Romeo & Juliet* could certainly and easily lend itself to a queer reading on many levels: the focus on Romeo, the display of the male body through the film, the types of sets, props and clothes the film utilises. But I don't think it specifically addresses a gay subculture through its campness in the way, say, that Derek Jarman's *The Tempest* does. Camp is just another element that – as in so many other postmodern films – helps *Romeo & Juliet* to construct its frame of reference and particular tone.

It's a very hybrid film, one that quotes and borrows from everywhere and yet garners the requisite effects. At Romeo's death scene, Romeo and Juliet lie on top of an altar. They are surrounded by crosses of red flowers in which blue neon lights are embedded. It could have become kitsch, but it isn't. Though the film is quite knowingly referential (we see the Globe Theatre Pool Hall at the beginning of the film), there is no irony in the emotional scenes. The crosses are theatrical, but they suit the film's world, complementing the tone of the scene and Romeo's state of mind. They are part of the film's construction of a vernacular that can convey Shakespeare's story to a contemporary audience in a filmic way, eliciting a variety of feelings which, in the appropriate places, include laughter. But not boredom.

MASSIVE ATTACK

José Arroyo

The sinking of the S.S. *Titanic* on the night of 14 April 1912 is one of the best-known disasters of the twentieth century; even people who don't know much history have heard of it. Movies have been made of it ever since 1912's remarkably instant German reconstruction *In Nacht und Eis* (Mime Misu): the all-star (Barbara Stanwyck, Clifton Webb, Brian Aherne) 1953 *Titanic* directed by Jean Negulesco still crops up on television occasionally, as does the British *A Night To Remember* (Roy Ward Baker, 1958), highly regarded for the way it builds a quiet power through a collage of vignettes. The sinking has also been a minor plot point in countless other films, including musicals: in *The Unsinkable Molly Brown* (Charles Walters, 1964), Debbie Reynolds plays the same Molly that Kathy Bates plays in James Cameron's new *Titanic*. The event has been interpreted as an allegory for capitalism, as divine punishment of human arrogance, as a symbol of the destruction of a privileged way of life and as a portent of the changes World War I was to bring.

It is understandable why Cameron would be attracted to the subject: a historical event loaded with significance, it offers a huge canvas, with potential for great action. And his film does try to bring in these traditional interpretations of the event: we do see class warfare erupting when the icebergs hit, with the lower classes getting locked up in the lower decks. We see the cosmopolitanism of the times, the radical break-through in the arts and the incipient feminism that were to transform the twentieth century; the bloody dialectic of enlightenment in which science and progress lead to destruction is illustrated for the umpteenth time. One can hardly blame Cameron for wanting to tackle so weighty a subject – but one can't help noting that he wrung more meaning, significance, seriousness *and* fun from his science-fiction work than he does here, from history.

And it would be surprising if audiences cared much about the meaning of *Titanic*. This is a film that would probably be just as popular (if twice as bad) at half the length, provided the last of its three-and-a-quarter hours, the one with all the action and the special effects, remained as it is here. For what we all want to see is how the ship sinks – and what we get to see here is not simply visually awesome but also great film-making. Indeed, there are amazing shots throughout the film. For example, one shot near the start moves from Leonardo DiCaprio as hero Jack Dawson standing on the banister of the ship's prow, arms outstretched – revelling in the air, the speed of the boat and the freedom of the ocean – through the whole length of the ship and beyond as we see people walking on deck and every detail. The shot is show-offy in its expensiveness and skill, and a sheer pleasure.

Wisely, most of the best is left for the latter part of the film, which thus seems to build and build. It gains speed from the moment Billy Zane as Cal Hockley hears Rose (Kate Winslet) and Jack declaring their love for one another, and it doesn't stop moving, until Jack dies. We see the massive ship break, thousands of extras sliding to their death, and gushing water destroying everything in its path. The way this is filmed turns these scenes into something more than merely spectacle: they are rendered so immediate that the destruction takes on a life of its own. Only with death imminent does everything come to life. Characters shake loose, scenes finally begin to play and drama to happen as the chaos commences. It's as if the icebergs that sink the boat had unshackled Kate and Leo from their keylight and Cameron from his yen for portentous significance. It is in movement that the actors become moving and funny. And it is in and through action that Cameron finally communicates anything worth saying. Cal frantically grabbing a loose baby in order to qualify for a lifeboat says more about his character, his class and the contrasted cultures of that time and ours than does the entire necklace subplot.

In the tradition of high concept cinema, the plot is easily reducible to stars, title and ad-line: 'Leonardo DiCaprio – Kate Winslet – *Titanic* – Nothing on Earth Could Come between Them' pretty much tells us the story. Jack Dawson, an artist, talented but poor, who won his fare at cards, meets upperclass Rose DeWitt Bukater when he charms her away from jumping overboard (reasons: boyfriend trouble plus general sexual-cultural oppression), saving her life. By the end, when both are in the icy waters, he's still trying to charm her into living even as he's dying. It's true love, you see. Befitting her more practical nature, she pushes his frozen corpse into the Atlantic at the very moment she promises never to let him go, remaining true to her word because (don't gag), she 'will always carry him deep in [her] heart'. For this is, after all, one of those romances where a lady with three names falls in love with an artist used to sketching one-legged prostitutes in Paris. And true to type, Everything on Earth *tries* to come between them: her selfish mother (Frances Fisher) is eager to imprison Rose in a loveless marriage, to maintain social status and increase her own standard of living (the father is dead; the family in debt); the intended husband is the sadistic Cal, who beats Rose for being belligerent – even in more tender moments he treats her merely as an expensive object and is willing to kill her rather than allow her into the arms of another man. The icebergs don't help. Nature fosters Rose and Jack's union only to demand an earthly separation which simultaneously guarantees the transcendental status of their love. Yes, *Titanic* is as trashy as it sounds, and so sometimes it's impossible to keep a straight face, but it is also a lot of fun.

'*Romeo and Juliet* aboard the *Titanic*' is not the most promising pitch for a film – nor is it improved by the decision to let Rose live to be a hundred years old, in order to tell us the story. For the story actually begins in the present, with Brock Lovett (a ruddy Bill Paxton) leading an expedition down to the wreck to find a necklace with a rare blue diamond, 'The Heart of the Ocean'. The safe where the necklace supposedly resides is located and opened – but all Lovett finds is a drawing of a young and topless Rose wearing it. The elderly Rose (Gloria Stuart) sees this picture on television, recognises herself, contacts Lovett and gets helicoptered onto his ship in order to tell him her story. The exploration of the wreck of the *Titanic* and the interaction between Lovett and old Rose takes up a fair amount of running time at the beginning and end of the film, and as a narrative device is not without its uses: the audience can be given contextual information on the history of the ship and its passengers, moving between past and present, while several questions can be set in motion. What happened to the necklace? What happened to Rose? But such benefits do not make up for the device's shortcomings. The good things one remembers in the framing-device sections are few: an abstract shot of submarines resembling spaceships descending towards the final frontier; a cute robot manoeuvring its way through the silt-covered remains of the wreck; computer graphics vividly illustrating what happened to the ship when it hit the iceberg. This section is still not worth the screen time that it occupies. More storytelling imagination could have structured the central narrative so as to accommodate exposition *and* set the central quests in motion.

Moreover, the director would have trusted the audience to make the link between the past and the present. That he doesn't is clearly exemplified in the two instances when the film cuts to the present. Each present-day section is introduced by Rose's voice-over. Each time there's a cut to the faces of Lovett and his crew listening to her. In other words they are the narrative's stand-ins for the audience. The crew is as visibly moved as the audience of the film is expected to be. But in effect what Cameron has done – probably the worst directing in his career – is to pre-empt and dictate audience response. So hackneyed is this shameless bit of manipulation that it's all too easy to resist.

Clearly the *Titanic* is ideal subject matter for a disaster movie, for an intimate epic and for a commentary on a mythic historical event and long-gone way of life. And

Cameron essays all three, with varying degrees of success. The film doesn't quite fit into the disaster genre as we recall it from its 70s peak. Such films as *The Poseidon Adventure* (1972), *Earthquake* (1974) and *The Towering Inferno* (1974) began (like *Titanic*) by telling us of a situation that couldn't possibly happen, and introducing us to those it couldn't happen to. Then – on as wide a screen as possible and preferably in sensurround – they showed it happening: the eruption of a disaster and how different people coped. Unlike *Titanic*, however, the classic disaster movie introduced a wide array of characters, requiring star casting in order to facilitate characterisation. And always part of the fun was anticipating which stars would live and how the others met their grisly fates (doing Shelley Winters in *The Poseidon Adventure* is still a popular party piece). We need to care – or rather, to judge how well or badly these stars behaved in the crisis – in order that affect be generated.

Titanic doesn't quite work this way. First, DiCaprio and Bates are the closest the movie gets to stars. Second, we simply never know enough about the many characters to mind about their fate. The unsinkable Bates, Fisher and David Warner are all memorable, but their roles have no character arc – while the evil Zane is all but pure cartoon. Fabrizio (Danny Nucci) is Jack's closest friend in the story, but when the ship's funnel falls on him, we're much more taken up in the aesthetics of the shot than the fate of the man.

By focusing on a single relationship, in the context of some earth-shattering event, it's clear that Cameron and crew strove to make this movie an intimate epic, not unlike his *Terminator* films or *Aliens*. The relationship is the one between Jack and Rose, with Rose the protagonist (and Cal as the third point of the triangle). Rose – who narrates – begins the film so enslaved by her class and her loveless relationship with Cal that she's contemplating suicide and ends the film as a strong independent woman renouncing her class and willing to fight both for love and life. Jack, sensitive, handsome, charming and in love with her, remains this way throughout the film.

But if the film doesn't quite succeed as intimate epic, it's because it tries to work as myth. Rose not only carries the burden of character but also a significant part of the action. Jack may save her life emotionally (with his charm and encouragement), but she saves his physically (by socking people in the jaw and bringing out the axe). This is familiar Cameron territory. Rose is an intelligent action woman similar to Sarah Connor and Ripley, two of the most powerful feminist icons in contemporary cinema. In Rose, Cameron is obviously striving for an equally mythic character – but this is seemingly easier when dealing with the future than the past. And it is the past that defeats the director's efforts.

Kate Winslet gives a lovely performance. She's given an old-fashioned movie-star entrance at the beginning – as she gets out of her carriage we see her legs and her hat before her face is finally revealed. She's elegantly dressed, perfectly made up and looks beautiful. As the story develops and her character loosens up, she becomes more and more dishevelled and looks more and more ordinary, albeit attractively so. Yet neither presence nor skill can protect her – nor Leo for that matter – from Cameron's choices with regard to how their characters are written or filmed. Unfortunately most of these choices seem to be informed by old movies.

How Jack looks and acts in the gambling scene immediately recalls one of the Dead

End Kids in a typical Warner Bros movie such as *Angels With Dirty Faces*, where a young kid might grow up to be James Cagney and end up on the wrong side of the law. Cal is strikingly similar to Ballin in *Gilda*: both treat their women as expensive things to be spoilt, abused and controlled. The dialogue is straight out of a pretentious 40s melodrama: a certain painting is apparently by one 'Picasso. He won't amount to much.' 'Freud?' someone asks: 'Who is he? A passenger?' And when Rose tells Jack his drawings are 'rather good; very good actually', the line could just as easily (and perhaps more acceptably) have been something Joan Crawford said to John Garfield (though even in the 40s such a line was already stilted and phoney: 'movie' dialogue).

The film also looks to have been filmed in accordance with old studio practices, particularly MGM's. The first two hours look gorgeously glamorous – as if everything were lit so as elegantly to gash a precipitous cheekbone with the shadow of an eyelash. This brings out the liner's sumptuousness and the finery of its passengers – table-settings shine, fireplaces glow, art-nouveau hairclips glitter – which also serves a narrative function: for 'richness' is an important story element. But applying the same approach to people becomes stultifying. Leo and Kate try to bring some sass and energy to their performances, but the director seems to be paying more attention to the actors stepping on their mark so that their hair is haloed in proper movie-star manner than to bringing life (in rhythm or timing) to the acting.

One assumes the type of dialogue and the mode of filming have been chosen deliberately. In its portentousness and historical allusion, this type of dialogue – which was already mythologised in the movies it originally appeared in – is also an attempt at mythmaking. And the filming is the kind that means to turn people into icons. It's almost as if the film-makers had sought an approach significant and grandiose enough to match the sinking of the *Titanic*. But these diverse efforts at myth-making, operating on so many levels, combine with an already mythic subject matter to ossify everything: the film ends up with an 'importance' and 'significance' it really doesn't need.

The verdict on the film is in, at least from America: a smash. We know the answer to the question the entertainment press has recently been speculating on so insistently: whether or not it makes a vast profit, the most expensive US film to date is at least not sinking ruinously into a sea of red ink.

But is it any good? It is hard to judge whether the budget is on the screen – who's seen a $200 million movie before? But it looks first class and its luxurious expensiveness is a pleasure to watch. Its daunting length is painless. Unlike so many contemporary spectacles, it does not resort to a cheap frenzy of visual jolts: it dares to linger on objects, faces and events and to trust plot, pacing and production values to retain audience attention.

Cameron has succeeded in making a disaster movie in which people and relationships are as important as the excellent effects, if not always as successfully realised. Arguably one of the best big-budget films of the past year, *Titanic* is certainly enjoyable. But it's impressive and depressing in about equal measure: it's of a quality Irwin Allen always aspired to and fell short of, for example, yet to be praising one of Hollywood's most imaginative and proficient film-makers for having made a film better than *The Poseidon Adventure* or *The Towering Inferno* is to have lowered expectations into the realm of the tawdry and the absurd. In this sense *Titanic* is emblematic of the state of contemporary Hollywood film-making. This is particularly apparent in scenes *Titanic* shares with *A Night to Remember*, such as the encounters with the ship's guilt-ridden designer, who waits resigned to his fate, or the attempts by crowds to swamp the remaining lifeboats as the end nears. Cameron's film tries for the same sense of stark terror as the older film, an internalised, gradual awareness of imminent doom, but its scale is too great for such an intimate effect, built on restraint, and subtle turns from character actors sit ill beside the flamboyant ravings of Billy Zane in full cry.

In the twentieth century, speed, movement and action are synonymous with America itself: certainly they were what people all over the world loved US movies for. But US cinema was never just about action: it also had people whose freedom and energy were internationally emulated and stories that enchanted the world. Contemporary US film-making no longer runs to this. Character and stories are now most often the domain of lower-budget films, whatever their quality. Generally (and *only* generally) the only thing big-budget Hollywood currently does well is action and effects – that is, only through action and effects does big-budget Hollywood have anything to say. It is because of its lack of story-telling skills and its execrable character delineation that *Titanic* is emblematic of contemporary Hollywood action/spectacle – it is also because of this that it is not a good film. But it is because Cameron is so peerless a director of action/spectacle that *Titanic* is among the *best* big-budget films of the past year. If the film's lacks seem to be those of contemporary Hollywood in general, its attributes are uniquely its own.

The Matrix (Andy Wachowski, 1999)

Section 8: Action/Spectacle in Review

This selection of reviews offers a partial overview of Hollywood 'blockbuster' cinema of the 90s. This section was originally intended to fill in some of the gaps in the body of the volume. Although it still partly fulfils this function, the process of selection brought out different criteria for inclusion, the most important being that the reviews offer insights on genre and mode. The reviews stand on their own and can be pleasurably dipped into at random. However, if each review offers insight into each film, collectively the reviews offer a revealing commentary on Hollywood cinema in the 1990s. It is no accident that the section begins with Spielberg and ends with Lucas. In between, there is commentary on a range of films varying in quality and popularity. Yet, questions about what films as different as *Dracula, Saving Private Ryan* and *Starship Troopers* are doing on the same list will be answered by comparing the reviews of each film. It should become clear that although the films don't necessarily belong to the same genre (they don't, for example, all share an iconography), they do promise to deliver on similar set of expectations which producers and audiences share and agree upon: i.e. action and spectacle. Read collectively the reviews indicate that these films share a substantial number of characteristics: high production values, striking visuals, a quick pace that speeds up in action sequences, a pattern of structuring narrative around spectacular action set pieces, spectacle is privileged over story and characteristion, a reliance on computer generated imagery and/or special effects. Each review also brings up characteristics that apply to other films. For example, Christopher Frayling notes that *Hook* is structured as an attraction and a ride akin to those found in Disneyland; Cook comments on *Dracula*'s 'hailstorm of visual effects'; Lippman comments on the representation of violence in *Pulp Fiction*. There is also a running argument on the action genre in particular: for example, Atkinson shows how the genre has achieved a critical mass and how the pleasures it offers relate to pulp, James points out how the genre might privilege the producer over the director, and so on. What all these film seem to have in common, what is so characteristic of Action Spectacle, the dominant mode of Hollywood film-making in the 90s, is the attempt to re-spectacularise visual imagery and the representation of motion in order to thrill and awe the audience. We are no longer astonished or terrorised by watching a train arrive at a station. Yet if action/spectacle is an attempt at re-creating the experience of the sublime for millennial microchip culture, it doesn't often succeed. An exploration of what Hollywood action/spectacle attempts to do and how individual films fail and succeed is the subject of these reviews.

HOOK

USA 1991

Director: Steven Spielberg

High-powered lawyer Peter Banning is well-meaning where his wife Moira and children Jack and Maggie are concerned, but business constantly intrudes into his personal life: during his daughter's performance as Wendy during a school production of *Peter Pan*, and before a vital baseball game of Jack's. Peter is still attached to his cellular phone when the family makes a Christmas visit to Granny Wendy in London, on the occasion of her being honoured by the Great Ormond Street Children's Hospital for her work with orphans (of whom Peter is one). During the evening, however, evil forces invade the home, and the Bannings return to find that Jack and Maggie have been spirited away; Captain James Hook has left a challenge for Peter to reclaim his children from Neverland.

Resisting Granny's hints that he is the eternal child, Peter Pan, now grown up, Peter is spirited away in turn by a fairy, Tinkerbell, who drops him in the midst of Hook's cut-throat crew. Hook also scoffs at the idea that this middle-aged man, unable to fly – in fact afraid of heights – could be Peter Pan, and gives Tinkerbell three days to get him in shape for a war that will decide the fate of his children. While Tinkerbell enlists the Lost Boys' help in retraining Peter – with their new leader, Rufio, particularly resistant to accepting him – Hook sets about alienating his children's affections. Maggie refuses to be taken in, but Jack is susceptible to the suggestion that his father doesn't really love him.

Peter at last wins over the Lost Boys by demonstrating how he has not forgotten how to play, besting Rufio in the process. He is dismayed, however, to see how much Hook has made Jack his own son, encouraging him to hit a mighty home run in a baseball game. When he is struck by the returning ball, Peter begins to remember more of his old self. He recalls being rescued as a baby by Tinkerbell – his fear of growing up, because it inevitably meant dying, had driven him from his real mother – and taken to Neverland. He recalls his adventures with Wendy and her brothers, and how he returned for her every spring, until she grew too old, and how he fell in love (to Tinkerbell's dismay) with Wendy's granddaughter, Moira.

Peter then recalls why he wanted to grow up, to become a father, and discovers the happy thought – his children – that enables him to fly again. While Tinkerbell regretfully accepts that now Peter will never be hers, he leads the Lost Boys in an assault on Hook's stronghold. Jack and Maggie are rescued, but Rufio is killed by Hook. Realising that Neverland will always have a hold on him while Hook still lives, Peter is driven into a final duel; he defeats the pirate, and the latter is despatched by the stuffed crocodile that once took his hand. Bidding farewell to the Lost Boys, Peter returns to London, and Moira, with his children.

* * *

For years the fitting image of Tinkerbell – the 1953 cartoon version with blonde pony-tail and nite-club figure, rather than the 1991 live-action version with short-cropped red hair and sassy post-feminist manner – has scattered magic dust over the logos of Walt Disney theme parks. She is our guide to the never-never land of people-movers and roller-coasters, a bit like the character of 'figment' who tells us what imagination is, and, by implication, what its limits are, in the EPCOT pavilion devoted to creativity. This image of Tinkerbell could well have raised the curtain on Steven Spielberg's *Hook*, for the experience of watching it is remarkably similar to the experience of visiting a Disney resort; indeed, the series of set pieces around which the film is structured closely resembles a map of the attractions on offer to vacationers.

SEE London-land, with snow-covered streets, neo-Victorian interiors, Westminster Abbey, the Tower of Big Ben, the rosy red cheeks of the little child-ren: 'London,' says Moira in all seriousness, 'is a magical place for children.' *SEE* Mermaid Lagoon, with its primly clad sirens in – a new one, this – punky colours. *SEE* Pirate-land, with its huge seventeenth-century galleon with skeleton figurehead, its wharfside shops and cafés ('Dick Moby's Whale Burger') and its clock tower in the form of a thirty-foot stuffed crocodile. And *SEE* Neverland, with its wooden skateboard ramp, food-fight area and archery range (not for Red Indians any more – that might upset some of the paying customers – but for streetwise kids from a carefully considered range of ethnic backgrounds, dressed in bamboo and palm-leaf versions of urban Space Invader outfits).

A ticket to *Hook* gets you into all these attractions, complete with reruns of the great moments from *Close Encounters* (craggy island rather than magic mountain), *E.T.* (fairy dust rather than a bicycle to the second star on the right) and *Jaws* (a giant crocodile this time round). Plus other Spielberg trademarks such as doors crashing open to reveal diffused light streaming in from outside; a lot of tears; and transcendental experiences, or conversions, all over the place. It's like the mixture of cartoon and live action shown in the Animation section of the Disney-MGM studio tour in Florida, where fast-talking Robin Williams confesses that he has always wanted to play Peter Pan, turns into a cartoon version of himself, then turns back again to engage in a discussion about Mickey Mouse as corporate symbol.

Above all, *Hook* is a deeply regressive experience, with a hero who retreats from the adult world of portable phones, junk bonds, difficult decisions and fear of flying into another world of theme parks (see above), happy thoughts, moral certainties, imagineering and confidence in letting himself go. The complexities of J.M. Barrie's original, where Peter Pan is described as a 'poor little half and half' – a tragic figure who is both mortal and immortal, and thus condemned to perpetual loneliness – and where a musty atmosphere of Edwardian gloom pervades the proceedings, have been blown away. The boy who *wouldn't* grow up to marry Wendy has become the man who doesn't want to be a grown-up any more; 'To die will be an awfully big adventure' has become the more positive-thinking 'To *live* will be an awfully big adventure.'

This transformation involves updating *Peter Pan* into a post-Freudian piece of New Agery (there's even an arch reference to Tinkerbell as 'a complex Freudian hallucination'), and at the same time scattering the magic dust away from the story and on to the special effects and the kinetic energy. Characters are forever saying head-on things like, 'You promised the children some *real time* here,' or 'You need a mommy very, very badly,' or 'I wish I had a daddy like you,' and there's a lot of primal screaming going on.

Robin Williams' performance is strangely narcissistic throughout, as if he were watching himself being by turns intense, childlike and innocent. He seems much more at home as the yuppie attorney, delivering lines like 'I missed the 60s – I was an accountant,' or, on his introduction to the Lost Boys' camp, 'What is this, a Lord of the Flies pre-school?' The rest of the cast manages surprisingly well to salvage some humanity among the welter of stunts and mechanised attractions; a seven-inch-high Julia Roberts, with fast-fluttering wings, is both sexy and touching; Bob Hoskins mugs away as a Cockney Smee; and Dustin Hoffman, complete with false protruding teeth, waxed moustache, outrageous English accent and costume taken straight from the Disney cartoon version, works hard to steal the show.

Why the film is called *Hook*, though, is never explained. The pirate captain seems to represent the adult world, and those aspects of children's personalities which are self-centred and cunning. But, amid all the schmaltz and idealisation, he never quite manages to put over his point of view. *Hook* should have been the apotheosis of Steven Spielberg: he has been talking about it for years (at one stage, Michael Jackson was to play Peter), and forever telling interviewers that deep down he *is* Peter Pan. Instead, it's a 'filming by numbers' version of a work he has done many times before. And better. After two-and-a-quarter hours, one has to echo the reaction of novelist Anthony Hope (of *The Prisoner of Zenda* fame) to the first night of the stage version of *Peter Pan* in 1904. As the chorus of Beautiful Mothers of London rushed on to adopt the Lost Boys, he was heard to mutter, 'Oh, for an hour of Herod.'

Christopher Frayling

DRACULA
USA 1992
Director: Francis Ford Coppola

Roumania, 1462. Holy Roman knight Vlad the Impaler, known as Dracula, returns victorious from battle with Turkish invaders to find his beloved wife Elisabeta, believing him to be dead, has committed suicide. Bereft, Dracula renounces his faith and becomes a vampire. London, 1897. Young Jonathan Harker is despatched by his firm of estate agents to Translyvania to finalise a deal with Count Dracula, who is acquiring property in England. On seeing a photograph of Jonathan's fiancée Mina Murray, who resembles his dead wife, the Count persuades Jonathan to stay in his castle for a month. It soon becomes clear that the young man is being kept prisoner by the vampire and his female consorts, while Dracula prepares to move the boxes of earth in which they rest to Carfax Abbey. The boxes are transported on board the *Demeter*, and as soon as the ship docks in England, Dracula takes on the body of a wolf and homes in on the mansion of Lucy Westenra, the wealthy friend with whom Mina is staying. Lucy couples with the beast Dracula, who visits her regularly. Her pallor and strange behaviour cause one of her suitors, Dr Jack Seward, who runs the Carfax Lunatic Asylum, to call in a specialist, Dr Van Helsing.

Dracula, in the form of the handsome Prince Vlad, approaches Mina in the street. She rejects him at first, but is gradually seduced by his exotic charm. Meanwhile, Van Helsing arrives in time to save Lucy's life with blood transfusions from her admirers, Seward and Quincey Morris, a Texan, and her fiancé Lord Arthur Holmwood. In Transylvania, Jonathan manages to escape from Dracula's castle and takes refuge in a convent, where the nuns send a message to Mina. She decides to go to him, in spite of her feelings for Vlad, who is devastated. Dracula attacks Lucy violently; she dies, but Van Helsing insists that as a vampire she must be ritually destroyed. He, Seward, Morris and Holmwood go to her crypt, where they drive a stake through her heart and cut off her head. Jonathan and Mina, now married, return to England, where Van Helsing explains that Jonathan, who has not actually tasted vampire blood, is not infected. The three of them go with Morris, Seward and Holmwood to find Dracula's resting place in Carfax Abbey. Mina is secured in Seward's quarters at the asylum while the men search for Dracula.

Dracula as Vlad comes to Mina and they drink each other's blood, pledging eternal love. The others find them and repel the vampire. Van Helsing uses hypnotism on Mina to find out that Dracula is making his way home by sea. The group decide to pursue him by train and destroy him, taking the dying Mina with them. Mina and Van Helsing arrive at the castle first and await the Count, who is racing home in a coach bearing his coffin, with Morris, Seward and Holmwood in pursuit. Dracula's coach arrives as the sun sets. As he emerges from his coffin, Jonathan cuts his throat while Morris stakes his heart. Holding the men at bay with a gun, Mina accompanies the dying Dracula into his castle, where she kisses him before driving a knife into his heart and decapitating him.

*   *   *

The latest in a line of flesh-eating, blood-tasting anti-heroes which includes Hannibal Lecter and Max Cady, Coppola's Dracula is the most baroque incarnation yet of this *fin de siècle* phenomenon. Monsters created by the relentless drive towards 'civilisation', by the constant need to demarcate frontiers between past and future, self and other, these creatures hover around the boundaries between the normal and the unacceptable, threatening to penetrate our defences. They become most active at times of crisis, when, as now, history seems to be running backwards and barbarism looms on a global scale. Where confusion reigns, terror stalks.

Confusion and terror go hand in hand in Coppola's version of Bram Stoker's 1897 novel. The histrionics of Gary Oldman's virtuoso performance as the shape-shifting disaffected Roumanian prince with designs on the English bourgeoisie are matched by a barnstorming *mise en scène* which sacrifices narrative coherence to a patina of allusions. Michael Ballhaus' camerawork is urgent and uneasy, its most frequent trope a hurtling travelling shot which unsettles certainties of time and place. We often cannot tell where we are, who is who, or how and why things happen. The end result lurches between high camp and anxiety dream, between Grand Guignol and Goya's *Sleep of Reason*.

The sense of disorientation goes deeper than this. *Dracula* is, of course, a period costume drama. Much has been made of the film-maker's intention to remain faithful to
Stoker's turn-of-the-century text – to the extent of putting his name above the title.
Screenwriter James Hart cites Leonard Wolf's *The Annotated Dracula* as a primary
source, an open invitation to the buffs to spend many a happy obsessional hour comparing this screen version with its predecessors, many of which are referred to in the
course of Coppola's movie. Nevertheless, authenticity was evidently the last thing on
the film-makers' minds. Yes, they included scenes from the novel which do not appear
in other versions, such as the rings of blue fire encountered by Jonathan Harker as he
approaches Dracula's castle. Yes, they added a prologue to register the fact that Stoker's
Dracula was inspired by a historical figure, Vlad the Impaler. Yes, they used the novel's
diary and letter format as a narrative device. But far from appearing as an Ur-text,
Stoker's *Dracula* fades in and out like a palimpsest, scarcely visible through movie-brat
braggadocio.

Coppola and Hart hit us with a veritable hailstorm of visual effects, spectacular
action sequences and literary, cinematic and artistic references, from Kurosawa to Corman, Beardsley to *Beauty and the Beast*. A fairground atmosphere prevails as we are
moved from one sideshow to another, emerging breathless from a chase finale which
culminates in a homage to *Empire of the Senses* as Winona Ryder's Mina skewers and
decapitates her vampire lover. Pleasurable as all this knowing bravado is, something
is lost. Perhaps unsurprisingly given the influence of Wolf's book, Coppola's movie
comes over less as a new version of Stoker's novel than as an annotated commentary
on it. The relevance of Stoker's themes to 90s audiences is reduced mainly to the trans-
mitting of sexual disease through the bloodstream of young women (Jonathan Harker
escapes contamination because he never actually tastes vampire blood, while Renfield
can be discounted since his obsession is with insects and small animals). Hart's script
makes some attempt to counteract Stoker's misogyny, stressing the independent spirit
of both Mina and Lucy, and portraying Mina as an enlightened New Woman, while
the male characters are by and large buffoons. It is masculine ignorance and fear as
much as feminine weakness and sexual curiosity which allow the invader to enter;
and even though a posse of male heroes traps and destroys Dracula in the end, it is the
dying Mina who delivers the *coup de grâce*, thus sealing the bond between herself and
the threatening Other.

Female sexuality is much in evidence, not least in the costume and decor. The erotic
scene in which Keanu Reeves as Jonathan is swallowed up by a vaginal bed is echoed
in the labial folds and furls of the dresses worn by Mina and Lucy. Costume designer
Eiko Ishioka excels herself with the sexually precocious Lucy, clothing her in a snake-
patterned garment for one scene, a startling crimson nightgown for her encounter
with the wolf/Dracula in the garden, and, after she joins the Undead, a white wedding
dress whose complicated pleats and ruffs uncannily evoke a Noh Theatre ghost. Costume and make-up provide a further link between Dracula and the women. Unlike
the other male characters, the Count in his different incarnations is self-consciously
'dressed', 'made-up' and his hair 'done'. Usually portrayed as a phallic figure, here he
is distinctly feminised and the emphasis is on his orality (it is noticeable, for instance,
that all the erotic sequences feature oral sex). When the ancient vampire first meets

Jonathan he wears a scarlet train extending like a tongue behind him and sports a decorative butterfly wig and long plait. Later, as the exotic Prince Vlad attempting to
seduce Mina, his hair is arranged in dark locks reaching halfway down his back.

A similar ambiguity haunts Dracula's ethnicity. Originating in the 'East', he is a Fu
Manchu for our times, a harbinger of disease and disorder manifesting himself in
creeping mists which threaten miscegenation. In focusing on the love story between
Mina and Prince Vlad, Coppola and Hart have skirted the issue of Orientalism,
attempting to dilute Stoker's racist excesses and the anti-Semitism of Murnau's *Nosferatu*, for example. Yet the problem resurfaces: in the *Arabian Nights* pored over by
Lucy and Mina, or, more chillingly, in the horde of rats into which Dracula dissolves,
an unavoidable reminder of Nazi propaganda films. In the delirium of spectacle and
self-referentiality, it is difficult to know what to make of these darker moments, not
to mention the association of femininity with viral infection. One suspects that the
film-makers would prefer us not to think about it too much.

Pam Cook

DEMOLITION MAN
USA 1993
Director: Marco Brambilla

In the crime-ravaged urban inferno of Los Angeles circa 1997, supercop John Spartan
is coptered in to defuse a hostage situation engineered, as Spartan alone guesses, by
super-villain Simon Phoenix. The two face off in an empty warehouse that Phoenix
has already soaked in gasoline, and in mid-fight, the arch-criminal sets the place
ablaze. Unknown to Spartan, Phoenix's thirty-odd hostages were in the building, and
Spartan stands accused of their manslaughter. Both men are incarcerated in a cryo-
prison, where they will wait out seventy-year sentences while computerised
rehabilitation programmes are drummed into their sleeping brains.

Thirty-five years later, Phoenix is woken for his parole hearing, utters the code word
for his computerised shackles and kills everybody in the room. The futuristic city he
escapes to – San Angeles – is the angelic twin of the 1997 city; the freeways are clear,
nearly everybody wears neo-Buddhist robes, violence is unknown and physical contact of even a sexual nature is taboo. 'Be well' is the interpersonal greeting of choice.
Thus the police are not equipped to deal with homicidal maniacs from the past. To
make things worse, Phoenix seems to possess a thorough foreknowledge of how this
computerised utopia works, a fact that baffles even him. Lenina Huxley, a perky young
policewoman with a love of late twentieth-century trash culture and a yen for even
the mildest excitement, tracks Phoenix's movements and eventually suggests they
thaw Spartan out to deal with the villain.

Once awake and dazed by his new surroundings, Spartan continually tracks and
combats Phoenix until losing him in the city's underground caverns. Soon, the city's
self-appointed mayor/guru Dr Cocteau reveals himself to be the architect of the whole
mess, having engineered Phoenix's freedom and knowledge so that he may find and
assassinate the leader of the homeless underground, Edgar Friendly. Spartan eventu-

ally enters the world beneath the city, meets Friendly, and faces off yet again with Phoenix, returning to the cryo-prison for a final showdown.

*   *   *

High-horsepower action movies are a peculiar breed of mass entertainment, at once dauntingly low-brow, smirkingly self-reflexive and infatuated with haphazard destruction. Having evolved from the gene pool fed by James Bond, Dirty Harry and the *Star Wars* trilogy, and truly taking to land in *The Terminator*, the artillery-expending blockbuster genre has certainly reached some sort of critical mass, if 1993 is any indication. Half of the summer's big Hollywood releases were predicated on comparatively gritty and literate concepts and characterisations (*In The Line Of Fire* and *The Fugitive*), while the other half, most prominently *Cliffhanger* and *Last Action Hero*, were simultaneously preposterous hyperextensions of action-movie aesthetics and self-parodying trashings of the same. *Last Action Hero*, especially is a smoking ruin of Brechtian tropes, disassembling the genre in a fit of bratty cleverness and leaving it in pieces on the floor.

This may seem like a textual dead end, but there are plenty of laughs to be had, as *Demolition Man* also bears out. Less self-parody than a ferociously irreverent comedy (and science-fiction satire) that just happens to entail a lot of *mano-a-mano* gun violence, Sly's newest slice of turkey turns the tables on the *Terminator* films' wholesale-mayhem-from-the-future strategy. Here, the agents of destruction pass from a nightmarish past/present into an absurdly peaceful future, wreaking havoc. *Demolition Man* wears its only-a-movie comic book bravado on its sleeve – in the very first shot of the film, we see the post-Rodney King LA purgatory of 1997 in a wry, swooping helicopter shot that passes *through* the flames engulfing the famous HOLLYWOOD sign.

Of the several credited writers on the film, the recognisable voice of *Heathers* author Daniel Waters is prevalent; one character actually greets another with 'Greetings and salutations', a quote from the earlier film. Presumably thanks to Waters, the movie is chock-a-block with hilarious present-mocking futurisms, from the empty LA freeways, the oldies radio stations (and lounge singers) playing ad jingles as if they were yesterday's Top 40 hits, and the President Schwarzenegger Memorial Library, to someone answering a phone with, 'If you'd prefer an automated response to your call, push "one" now.'

Given the goofy wit of the film's script, the actors either rise to the occasion or, in the case of Stallone, simply lurch about dimly. Phoenix is as pure a comic book villain as any dreamed up by Marvel Comics, and Snipes chews each matte painting and neo-modernist set like the damned on holiday. Comedian Denis Leary, as the irascible nonconformist Friendly, is a brilliant bit of casting, digging into his trademarked firecracker routine to fire off some pro-vice *bon mots* at San Angeles' utopian new-ageism. Though imbued with all the personality of a lump of coal, Stallone manages occasionally to find the right moment amid the firefighting and explosions, as when he hungrily digs into an illegal rat burger, or presents Sandra Bullock, his ersatz partner in the twenty-first century, with a sweater he knitted in one night, thanks to the rehab programming he got in cryo-prison.

Frankly, *Demolition Man* is, like nearly all films of its genre not directed by James

Cameron or John McTiernan, an enjoyable mess. Its plot makes little sense (Friendly is hardly formidable enough a threat to San Angeles to warrant Cocteau's excavation of one-man shitstorm Snipes), and its action sequences inevitably become repetitious and crisscrossed with narrative errors. It floats thanks to its consistency, and the gutsiness of its humour – how many other films would dare to re-enact and somersault the Rodney King beating scenario? Here, of course, it's seven wimpy, white future cops well versed in etiquette, trying to take in a single black man, and he kicks their asses. On the one hand, this may seem to excuse the LAPD's use of excessive force; on the other, this is the moviest of movies and there's nothing wrong with a little payback.

Michael Atkinson

PULP FICTION
USA 1994
Director: Quentin Tarantino

Honey Bunny and her boyfriend Pumpkin sit in a diner. Pumpkin persuades her that the only way for them to make a living is by holding up restaurants; they decide to start there and then. Two hitmen, Vincent and Jules, drive to an assignment for their boss Marsellus; Vincent tells Jules that Marsellus has asked him to take his wife Mia out for the night. Jules and Vincent burst into an apartment where three boys are eating breakfast, take a briefcase, which apparently belongs to Marsellus, and kill two of the boys. In an empty bar, Marsellus pays a boxer, Butch, to lose an upcoming title fight. Vincent and Jules turn up, having swapped their suits for T-shirts and shorts. Vincent buys some heroin from his dealer. That evening, he takes Mia out to a gimmicky restaurant. When they return Mia, who has been snorting cocaine all night, finds Vincent's heroin. Thinking it is cocaine, she takes it and overdoses. Vincent takes her to his dealer's house and they manage to bring her back to life with an adrenaline injection. Mia and Vincent decide not to tell Marsellus what has happened.

The scene changes. A small boy is introduced to a Captain Koons, a Vietnam friend of his father's, who has come to give him his dead father's watch. The little boy is Butch, who, as an adult, wakes with a start just before his prize-fight. Butch wins the fight and escapes with his money to a motel where his girlfriend Fabienne is waiting for him. The next morning, Butch discovers that Fabienne has left his father's watch in his apartment, and decides to go back for it. Entering the apartment, he disturbs Vincent, who is sitting on the toilet. Butch kills him with his own gun, takes his watch and drives off. Seeing Marsellus in the road, he tries to run him down; both survive, and Marsellus chases Butch into a pawn shop. The owner points a gun at both of them, ties them up and, with a friend, Zed, rapes Marsellus. Butch manages to escape but decides to go back and rescue Marsellus. Marsellus allows him to leave town with his money as long as he promises not to return. Butch drives off on Zed's motorbike to collect Fabienne.

The scene flashes back to Jules and Vincent in the apartment where they kill the two boys. There is another young man hiding in the bathroom; he bursts out firing at the two men, and misses. They shoot him, and Jules vows that after this job he will give up being a hit man. They take the remaining boy hostage but in the car Vincent accidentally kills him. Covered in blood, they drive to the house of a friend, Jimmy, and elicit the help of the 'Wolf'. He instructs them on how to clean up the mess, puts them in Jimmy's casual clothes and disposes of the car and the body. Jules and Vincent go for breakfast in the diner, just as Honey Bunny and Pumpkin announce their stick-up. Jules talks them out of taking the mysterious briefcase he has for Marsellus, and persuades them to leave quietly.

*   *   *

It looks like a tribute to Quentin Tarantino's fast rise to fame that he has managed to draw quite such a varied crowd of names for *Pulp Fiction*. And yet, when you examine those names, they are mostly those of actors in search of a hit. *Pulp Fiction* is full of five-minute culture jokes; could this be another one? Possibly, for several of the cast appear to be playing warped versions of characters for which they are known. Bruce Willis' tough guy Butch may be a *Die Hard*sman, but this time round, Butch is a little bit stupid and has a nasty temper. Rosanna Arquette's crazy lady from *After Hours* has turned into a junkie's housewife, utterly absorbed in the piercings on her body. Harvey Keitel reprises his role in the *Nikita* remake *The Assassin*, as the icy, mute killer, who cleans up after dead bodies and gets rid of the living ones. Only this time, the grim-faced Wolf has absurd touches of Regular Guy about him. He chats about coffee, and his clean-up operation does not involve acid baths but soapy sponges and hose-downs. Some of the actors are not even playing out their own former roles in this rag-bag of film references: to take just Tarantino's own work, Honey Bunny and Pumpkin, who open and close the film, are straight out of *True Romance*, while the hitmen Jules and Vincent could have been in *Reservoir Dogs*.

It is a remarkable achievement that the film manages to hold all these people together through four different storylines. Perhaps because we get to know him best, the link seems to be John Travolta's Vincent. Flashy Vincent is what the disco-loving street boy Tony Manero would have grown up to be after *Saturday Night Fever*. And he still needs to sort himself out. Vincent has enough sense not to let himself sleep with Marsellus's wife, Mia, when he gets the opportunity, but is stupid enough to leave his gun lying around while he goes to the bathroom. We see him shoot heroin and we see him on the lavatory, and Vincent therefore becomes vulnerable. But like everyone else here, he has little regard for human life, and when he accidentally shoots his hostage's head off, he worries more about his suit than about what he has done.

Violence is still Tarantino's watchword, and *Pulp Fiction* abounds with other nasty, casual deaths. No one is immune: even Vincent, the hero of sorts, dies with an undignified snap of the fingers. Life in the 90s, Tarantino seems to be saying, is speedy and worthless. The people on the screen are, as the film's title makes plain, characters from trash novels. They are drug dealers, killers, crime lords, spoilt ladies, prize boxers, S&M rapists. Everyone is on the run, off their heads, or on the wrong side of the law. And yet in a way they could be us, too. If Tarantino has anything to say, it seems to be that there is no morality or justice in the patterns of life and death. Instead, the nihilist argument continues, there is trivia.

For if we are not supposed to empathise with the characters themselves, we cannot help recognising the junk culture world they inhabit: a world filled with ridiculous

TV programmes, gimmicky restaurants where the waiters dress up as film stars and steaks are named after directors, and powerful drugs that demand their own place in a daily timetable. Trash is not just the written word, it is all around. And here it is, endlessly recycled in the endless conversations of Tarantino's pulp protagonists.

In the car, Vincent and Jules are engrossed in the French names for hamburgers. As the camera follows them towards the apartment of boys they are about to kill, they talk about foot massages. When Butch gets to the motel in which he is meeting Fabienne before they flee with his winnings, she starts chatting about the fatness of her stomach. This is the kind of stuff most of us actually do spend much of our time talking about, and it puts us on a level of understanding with the characters. The effect is strangely subtle in a film that is all about crude gestures. Mia, herself a bizarre mixture of spoilt child and wise woman, remarks that Marsellus' henchmen are worse than a sewing circle when it comes to gossip. And suddenly the killers have been emasculated.

True Romance seemed to become less Quentin Tarantino and more its director Tony Scott every time it lapsed into sentimentality, so it is hardly surprising that Tarantino imposes a sizeable emotional distance between the audience and the characters. When Butch dreams about Captain Koons (a hilarious cameo by Christopher Walken) giving him his father's watch, a sentimental episode from a thousand TV movies becomes more ludicrous and disgusting by the minute. And even though each section of the film ends with a moment of collaboration – between Vincent and Mia, Marsellus and Butch and finally Jules, Pumpkin and Honey Bunny – the sense of shame that could bring about an attempt at a heartfelt moment is subsumed by the characters' self-interest. In the same way, it would be an effort to feel sentimental over the film's one big emotional transformation. Samuel L. Jackson's Jules is an extraordinary character, with touches of Robert Mitchum's preaching murderer in *The Night of the Hunter*. He goes about his killing business with religious fervour, spouting Ezekiel at his terrified victims as if to justify his acts. And what changes his mind about his work? Not a crisis of conscience but a realisation of his own mortality. More self-preservation: the philosophical new Jules is as hard and cold as the old one. He resists the temptation to kill Pumpkin, not because he has found mercy, but because he has made a decision to stop killing.

Butch is the nearest we might get to a sentimentalist – he has a girl he loves and enough heart to go back and rescue his arch-enemy from the rapists. But Butch is not nice either. In Tarantino's movie reference library, Butch is more loudmouth Ralph Meeker in *Kiss Me Deadly* than sappy Fred MacMurray in *Double Indemnity*.

Tarantino sees such things and laughs, and makes us laugh, too. But it is not simply the nervous laughter of voyeurs relieved that these horrible things are happening to someone else and not to them. There are plenty of brilliantly funny moments, and it is to Tarantino's credit that he has managed to work modern, junk, and retro culture into his script with such ease. Some of the comedy is less engaging: there is occasionally too much slapstick screaming; the odd, knowing *Wayne's World*-style joke, in which the characters almost turn to the camera and start acting to us rather than to each other, seems out of place. We have to believe that they believe in what is happening or everything falls apart.

Like *Reservoir Dogs*, this is stylishly shot in neo-cartoon style, with massive, distorting close-ups offset by attractively angled shots. The effect, again, is of a hard, closed, rather linear world. But in some ways, there is more to *Pulp Fiction* than to the first film. For one thing, there are a few women in it and a broader spectrum of characters. For another, by allowing just a few chinks in its dispassionate armour, mostly through Travolta's oddly affable Vincent Vega, it is easier to like rather than just admire.

Amanda Lipman

THE SPECIALIST
USA 1994
Director: Luis Llosa

Ray Quick and Ned Trent are US demolition experts assigned to assassinate a South American drugs bigwig by blowing up a bridge as he drives over it. When the approaching vehicle is acknowledged to contain children, Quick tries to stop the explosion. Trent prevents him. After the explosion, they are permanently estranged.

Years later, Quick is repeatedly asked by May Munro over the phone to help her kill a Cuban drug lord who murdered her father. Living in seclusion, in a waterfront compound rigged to explode if it is penetrated, Quick vacillates. He finally agrees to help only after Munro – who's positioned herself as girlfriend of the drug lord's son – vows to do it herself. Soon we realise that Trent, who is now in the pay of the drug lord, has set Munro to ferret out Quick. Trent can use his employer's resources to eliminate Quick, as soon as he begins offing the drug lord's men.

Munro and Quick make love, and this apparently muddies Munro's resolve. She then seems to have been caught in one of Quick's explosions – she wasn't, and she uses her apparent death to break her connection to both Trent and the drug lord's son. Quick meets her surreptitiously, but the two are cornered in a hotel room by Trent and his men. Quick escapes (he rigs a series of explosions that dumps the whole hotel suite into the ocean), and Munro is used by Trent as bait to get Quick out into the open again. They escape yet again, leading Trent to Quick's dockyard compound, where everything explodes. Eventually, Quick offs Trent and the two lovers drive off together.

*   *   *

Quentin Tarantino is right – we love pulp, the crustier and sillier the better. Pulp is by definition yesterday's trash, garnished with nostalgic kitsch. Contemporary B-movies and fiction won't be real pulp until decades hence, and Tarantino's *Pulp Fiction* is too knowing to be mistaken for the real thing. True pulp is most often badly conceived, crudely executed and has little to recommend it beyond the allure of juvenile lust and the smell of ripe cheese. It brings us down a peg or two, it throws raw porterhouse into our inner psychopath's rusty cage and, best of all, it never minds if we don't think very highly of it. Like a cheap whore, it prefers that we simply do our dirty business and be on our way.

More than any other recent film, *The Specialist* deserves the title Pulp Fiction. Sloppy, adolescent and proud of it, the movie rarely tries to be witty, and never important. It seems allergic to narrative logic as we've come to know it in Hollywood films. Based on John Shirley's series of paperback thrillers – which *are* pulp by now – *The Specialist* is all attitude, nudity and pyrotechnics, with acting that stretches from somnambulism to eye-popping *grand mal*. But the film's connection with its source material is vital. It places what might otherwise be yet another action film in a context that glories in its own triviality. Like many films based on comics, *The Specialist* is borne from the baby-boomer childhood of the 70s – it's a movie for the kids we were when there seemed to be nothing but time to ponder the equities of superheroes, breakfast cereal, Bugs Bunny quips, old horror movies and board games. Like Most Hollywood movies, it's of a specific time and place, and if you cannot connect with the cultural circuits it pulses along – if you've never read a *Specialist* or *Executioner* or *Doc Savage* paperback – then you're unlikely to recognise the film's Ghost of Trash Culture Past.

All the same, perhaps the more enlightened reading of director Llosa's first shot at the big time (he'd previously directed *Sniper*) would be as blinkered, time-wasting idiocy. It is poorly judged, thoughtless and often boring. Even the languorous sex scenes garner unintentional laughs. The average audience's primary concern will be for Sly's ageing physique; the veins bulge so alarmingly in his shoulders and neck we begin to imagine eventual Cronenbergian implosions. At the very least, a loved one should tell him to ease off with the free weights.

But there's a great deal of pulpy pleasure to be had. There's oodles of 70s Latin disco offsetting the laconic 90s baloney. In one scene, in the back of a hushed church, Stallone hikes up Stone's skirt and discovers a gun in her garter. In another, a waterfront explosion results in a rain of flaming crabs. As sweaty drug lord Joe Leon, Rod Steiger uses a preposterous Cuban accent like a small gauge shotgun, while Eric Roberts seethes lispily as his son. Still, the real star of the movie is Woods, who has returned to portraying weasels after an inexplicable daytrip as leading man. Nobody can exude wormy, dead-eyed rage like Woods, and in scene after scene he takes wolf-sized bites out of an otherwise mundane action scenario.

The Specialist is indeed a movie of junky incidental treats. The bulk of it is enervating – Stallone has become an anti-actor, while Stone fleshes out a role that is tellingly reminiscent of the vapid blonde sluts she played before *Basic Instinct*. As Hollywood product, Llosa's movie is a botch, but as an artefact of our pulpiest urges, a high-rent condo bursting with cheap cultural effluvia, it is sometimes sublime.

Michael Atkinson

BAD BOYS
USA 1995
Director: Michael Bay

Porsche-driving bachelor Mike Lowrey and his married buddy Marcus Burnett are black narcotics cops in Miami. When one million dollars worth of heroin captured in evidence is stolen from their station house, Mike asks his friend Max Logan, a high-class hooker, to look out for any new big spenders in town. Lois Fields, a madame, puts her on to Eddie Dominguez, who turns out to be a former cop and the driver for the robbery gang. Max persuades her friend Julie to go with her. While Max is partying with Eddie, who has helped himself to one of the dope packages from the robbery, Julie goes to the bathroom. On her return, she sees the robbery gang – led by the crazed Fouchet – shoot Eddie and Max. Julie escapes via the roof.

Wanting revenge, Mike goes to find Lois, but she's already dead. Meanwhile Marcus is trying to access Dominguez's old cop file on the computer. His boss Captain Howard gets a call from Julie, saying she will only talk to Mike. At Howard's insistence, Marcus pretends to be Mike. He goes to Julie's apartment but she is suspicious. Only when Fouchet's hoods arrive does she agree to go along, taking her two dogs with her. As 'Mike', Marcus brings her to Mike's apartment.

That night Marcus's wife Theresa kicks him out of their bedroom, but Howard offers Marcus to continue the deception. After Julie identifies Fouchet's henchman Noah from mugshots, Marcus and Mike visit Noah's favourite haunt, Club Hell. Julie follows, armed with one of Mike's guns, and tries to shoot Fouchet but misses. Mike, Marcus and Julie then make their getaway in a truck full of ether. Noah pursues them onto a road under repair where Mike unloads the barrels of ether and sets them aflame, killing Noah. A helicopter television news crew films the result.

Two of Fouchet's men are arrested outside Marcus' home and give up Fouchet's name. Mike, Marcus and Julie are spotted watching Fouchet's boat, and are followed back to Mike's apartment building. During a gun battle in the lobby, the gang kidnap Julie. Marcus persuades a computer hacker felon to access Dominguez's file and the cops discover that their receptionist is his former lover. She gives Mike a car phone number which they track to an airport hangar where a major drug deal is about to occur. Mike, Marcus and two Latino colleagues attack the heavily protected site, rescuing Julie, blowing up the drugs, a huge cash pay-off and a private jet before pursuing Fouchet to his doom in a final car chase across the airfield.

*   *   *

Those who regard a director's credit as the most crucial piece of information about a film will be interested to know that the promotional credits sheet for *Bad Boys* contains no reference to the director at all. He is credited on the film print itself, fleetingly, but even there the actual authorship of *Bad Boys* is clearly denied him. For this is a Don Simpson and Jerry Bruckheimer film, branded by the production duo who defined a certain kind of 80s action movie with *Top Gun* and *Beverly Hills Cop*, as well as a particular image of the bodybuilt, Tao-reading Hollywood production exec who was perpetually 'ready to go'.

That might be the first question that an audience asks of an action movie: is it ready to go? The immediate answer for *Bad Boys* is undoubtedly yes. All of the gunfights, car chases and explosions that one would expect are there, unobtrusively directed by Michael Bay in the requisite rock-video style and edited as much for punch and easy laughs as ever. They were also there when the duo came a cropper with the hugely expensive car-racing flop *Days of Thunder*. *Bad Boys* is more like *Beverly Hills Cop*, and so it relies, for its main strength, on the ideological double-whammy of slick African-American humour and a near-fetishistic reverence for destructive mayhem, as if the two go naturally together.

The plot simply requires us to dip into the lifestyles on view and to enjoy the almost Shakespearean cuckoldry humour while waiting for the next burst of gunfire. Both the action heroics and the sexual banter are well managed by Will Smith (of *Fresh Prince of Bel Air* fame) and Martin Lawrence (star of the spoof US talkshow *Martin* and host of *Russell Simmons' Def Comedy Jam*). They work in a similar but sufficiently different vein to that of the *Lethal Weapon* pairing Mel Gibson and Danny Glover but in a more subtle key than Eddie Murphy's. The obvious contrast between Smith's character, Mike Lowrey, a smoothie with a private income and a beautiful apartment, and Lawrence's character Marcus, a working-class married man with a suspicious wife, is nicely shaded by their role-reversal when Marcus has to pretend to be Mike. Obsessed as it is with male sexual performance, their patter is often edgy and tense. Some of this tension cannot resolve itself because the affect-free white girl Julie Mott who comes between them isn't allowed to have a meaningful or physical relationship with either of them. She is the object of frustration for both of them, yet she remains somehow unattainable. Clearly, American mainstream action movies are still not ready to go on miscegenation any more than they were in the days of *Beverly Hills Cop*. On the other hand the vigilante cop ethics required of the Hollywood action hero might nowadays be more palatably expressed by black characters than white as there's not much chance of these cops moonlighting with the militia. It is also refreshing that the villain is French rather than English with Tcheky Karyo reprising his more psychotic moments from *Nikita*. Otherwise *Bad Boys* is as nasty, thrilling, sexist, sexy, dumb, sharp and reprehensible as you want it to be – any number of qualifying adjectives will do because the experience it provides is so infuriatingly, enjoyably and successfully all-encompassing an entertainment.

Nick James

BATMAN FOREVER
USA 1995
Director: Joel Schumacher

Harvey Two-Face, a former District Attorney, had one side of his face disfigured by a courtroom mishap and blames Batman. Two-Face tosses a security guard out of a skyscraper window in Gotham City, but Batman thwarts this attempt to trap him.

Batman is the alter ego of Bruce Wayne, owner of Wayne Enterprises, which employs a scientist named Edward Nygma. Wayne is approached by Nygma to consider a device that hijacks human brain waves and channels them into the mind of the device's wearer. Wayne rejects the invention as inhumane. Clandestinely, Nygma tests the machine on his reluctant manager and accidentally upends his own sanity. He returns home, a place plastered with photos of Bruce Wayne, and resolves to exact revenge on his former employer.

Wayne meets and falls for a beautiful criminal psychologist, Dr Chase Meridian, whose main pursuit is Batman. Meridian accompanies Wayne to a glittering circus event. A family of aerialists, the Graysons, are entertaining the crowd when Two-Face arrives, threatening to blow up the circus. Wayne fights the thugs, and the Graysons join in. Two-Face causes three of the Graysons to fall to their deaths. The remaining member, Dick, removes the bomb. He is put under Wayne's guardianship. The young aerialist bonds with Wayne's faithful butler, Alfred, and soon stumbles into the Batcave. After a clandestine spin in the Batmobile, Dick confronts Wayne and insists they become partners. Wayne/Batman refuses.

Nygma assumes a super-criminal identity as the Riddler and approaches Two-Face with a plan to uncover Batman's identity. As E. Nygma, an urbane entrepreneur closely modelled on Wayne, he sells a version of his device to thousands of customers. Among the invited guests at his launch party for the device are Wayne and Meridian. The Riddler's scheme is to submit each guest to his invention and from their brain waves determine who is Batman. Two-Face grows impatient with the scheme, however, and brings in the heavy artillery, only to be scuppered by Batman with Dick's help.

The Riddler figures out that Wayne is Batman. With Two-Face, he invades Wayne's mansion, destroys the Batcave and kidnaps Meridian. Grayson adopts the identity of Robin and Batman agrees that they become partners. The two home in on the villains and save the day.

* * *

Director Joel Schumacher – auteur of such disposable classics as *The Lost Boys* and *Flatliners* – doesn't traffic in the same grim whimsy as Tim Burton, the original visionary behind this popular franchise, but when it comes to camp values his *Batman Forever* far exceeds the first and second instalments. It's a fusion of old-school Hollywood spectaculars, Kenneth Anger-inflected fetishism, and all the hardware studio money can buy.

A pouty Val Kilmer plays the billionaire depressive who undergoes a radical personality change once he slips on his form-enhancing rubber suit (one version features nipples that virtually snap to attention). Less opaque than Michael Keaton, his predecessor in the role, Kilmer essays a more sensual and benevolent creature of the night, his lips occasionally curling into an actual smile. Yet, although more accessible, Kilmer's Batman is no more distinct a character. He is still closer to a smudged sketch than bone and gristle.

This decidedly prettier Batman is in keeping with a general mellowing. The second movie – directed, like the first, by Burton – frightened away profitable product tie-in deals; somehow the whip-wielding Catwoman, psychotic Penguin, and too dark knight didn't fit tidily enough on hamburger wrappers. Enter Schumacher, a talent for hire who's never dived too deep, even in his Dystopia Lite fantasy of Los Angeles, *Falling Down.* This most unlikely of action directors (also know for *Car Wash* and *D.C. Cab*) steers the third Batman movie into safer, more lucrative waters. Yet he's also engineered the most gaudily camp spectacle to hit screens since *Wigstock: The Movie.*

Crammed with provocative quips and not-so-*double entendres, Batman Forever* proves how mainstream camp has become – so much so that most critics have sidestepped the issue. Maybe it's because the camp impulse has been so fully absorbed into the popular stream? Why else ignore the wisecrack about biker bars? Or the Riddler's fixation with Bruce Wayne? Or the outrageous attention to male genitalia both in costume and visual cues? When Robin first emerges in his vermilion costume, Batman not only gives him a studied looking-over, he stops to fix his gaze on his comrade's bright red package.

Given that in *Batman Forever*, the text is all about subtext, it's no surprise that no real story emerges. Batman chases Two-Face, the Riddler chases Batman, Dr Meridian chases Bruce Wayne, and so on. It's all a lot of bat-and-mouse. While tangy repartee helps to fill the cavernous void, it's really too bad that Schumacher has no feel for action. The post-production design is fabulous – neon greens and fuchsia push through the shadows, the costumes wouldn't look out of place at a Vegas cotillion, and the Riddler's secret weapon looks exactly like an enormous Deco blender – but Schumacher's *mise en scène* is as cluttered as a rummage sale, his direction as inert as a panel strip.

The one intriguing narrative glimmer in *Batman Forever* is how certain male power brokers lead very divided lives, squiring beautiful women in public (Nicole Kidman as Dr Meridian) while in private they swing with the boys – in this case a surprisingly game Chris O'Donnell as Robin, a turbo-charged Jim Carrey as the Riddler and Tommy Lee Jones doing yet another of his psychotics. Although Jones' Two-Face is the only character whose two-dimensionality is telegraphed by his name (and his neatly cleaved face), he's not the only one endowed with a split personality. It's no wonder. After all, the story of the double life is one that Hollywood knows full well, on screen and off, confidentially or not.

Manohla Dargis

DIE HARD WITH A VENGEANCE
USA 1995
Director: John McTiernan

Summer in New York City. Bonwit Teller's, the department store on 5th Avenue, blows up. The police receive a phone call from someone playing a deadly game of Simon Says. He demands to speak to John McClane. McClane is separated from his wife Holly, on suspension from the police and hungover. Simon orders McClane to the corner of 138th and Amsterdam or there will be another big bang. In Harlem, Zeus, a proprietor of an electronics store, sees McClane wearing a sandwich-board stating 'I hate niggers'. A gang of black youths is standing nearby. Zeus goes to confront McClane but ends up saving him.

Simon is not happy. He makes Zeus accompany McClane on the next part of the game. They have to answer a phone on 72nd and Broadway or another bomb will blow up. The pair make it only to be given a half-hour to answer a phone at the Wall Street subway station. This occasions a car chase through Central Park. Zeus arrives first but the phone is busy. He harasses a man into hanging up only to have a policeman draw a gun on him. He finally answers the phone but Simon realises that McClane is not there and detonates the bomb. McClane is in the train, finds the bomb in the nick of time and throws it away but the detonation derails the subway car. McClane is then met by government agents who identify Simon as Peter Gruber, whose brother, Hans, McClane threw off a skyscraper in Los Angeles.

Simon tells the police that there is a bomb in one of New York's 446 primary schools that will detonate at 3pm. While the city's resources are channelled into finding the bomb, Simon robs the Federal Reserve Bank of New York of $140 billion in gold. McClane and Zeus figure this out only to arrive after the loot has gone. In pursuit of another riddle, Zeus goes to Yankee Stadium where Simon's assassins decide not to kill him because McClane isn't there. Meanwhile, McClane tracks Simon's truck convoy through the tunnels of an aqueduct. McClane and Zeus reunite on the highway when McClane is spewed out of a water tunnel. They follow the villains on to a ship. Simon captures Zeus and forces McClane's surrender. They are tied to a huge bomb. Back in New York City, the police find the bomb in the school that Zeus' nephews attend. Zeus and McClane extricate themselves and, at the Canadian border, destroy Simon's helicopter. The bomb in the school proves fake. John McClane lives to call his wife.

*   *   *

After a touristy montage of New York summer scene which lasts barely through the credits, *Die Hard with a Vengeance* opens with an unexpectedly prompt bang as Bonwit Teller's blows up. From those first few minutes, the film delivers the delights promised by the big-budget action genre – spectacular stunts, thrilling car chases, big explosions, suspenseful shoot-'em-ups – all depicted with the best production values money can buy. There is more of all this than in any of the previous *Die Hard* films, and most of it is bigger, but not better.

There are several reasons though why *Die Hard with a Vengeance* is a disappointment. The major one is that the film is barely recognisable as a sequel. If the title, the name of the hero and that of the villain were changed, there could be little to connect it to the previous *Die Hard* films. The central concept of these was 'lone cop fighting to free loved ones from an enclosed space in which they are held for ransom by a greedy madman'. Here, however, John McClane has a sidekick, Samuel L. Jackson's Zeus; his loved ones are not in danger (albeit by the end of the film, Zeus's are); and the plot takes us not only through most of New York but also practically into Canada. These changes are fundamental. They don't affect genre expectations but they do deny the audience the pleasure generally expected from sequels.

I miss the recurring supporting cast of the previous two films – William Atherton, Sheila McCarthy and particularly Bonnie Bodelia. This is not only because this hyperactive film could have used the calm and understated emotionality Bodelia brought to the role of Holly. It was only after watching *Die Hard with a Vengeance* that I realised how important Holly was to the very structure of the films. Her role in the *Die Hard* films is analogous to that of women in the western. She represents order, stability, family. McClane's attempt to save her is an attempt to overturn the moral and social chaos imposed by the villain. She not only symbolises the utopian value the hero attempts to restore, but also provides the moral context for the hero's derring-do. It is because he fights for her, for what she represents, that he is allowed to kill. Because of her, we are allowed to see McClane express love, anxiety, fear – emotions whose expression is denied the villain. Holly is both the motivation for the hero's extraordinary deeds and the source of the melodrama.

Die Hard with a Vengeance makes no attempt to replace the moral and emotional context for bangs and bloodshed which Holly previously provided. Perhaps this is why it seems such a cynical thrill machine, particularly in light of the Oklahoma bombing – too many deaths and too little emotional residue. The film falls short in other areas as well: the script has as many happy coincidences (McClane being spewed out of the tunnel as Zeus happens to drive past) as plot holes (several aspects of the end are still not clear to me); the editing is often clumsy (the alternation between Zeus and McClane and Zeus' kids at the end); and the extensive use of hand-held camera is an enervating addition to the film's general frenzy. It is as if McTiernan hasn't quite shaken off *The Last Action Hero*. Whenever his direction attempts more, it produces a kind of nervous elephantiasis.

What saves *Die Hard with a Vengeance* from the charmlessness of *Last Action Hero* is the actors. With the exception of Jeremy Irons – who hasn't quite figured out when to add camp relish to an inflection and when to simply throw a line away – the cast is excellent. Genre is often not considered when evaluating acting. But different genres call for different styles of performance. Action requires actors who can read lines and move their bodies with equal nonchalance and breezy agility. Willis is so superb at this I even forgive him for looking slightly less hunky in his vest than he usually does. The banter between Jackson and Willis, witty exchanges on questions of race and power, is perhaps the best thing about the film.

Good acting, however, is not essential to action cinema. Good action is. *Die Hard with a Vengeance* delivers more than the bare essentials. The scene where water gets released in the underground tunnel is imaginative and exciting. The revelation of the slogan McClane is wearing in Harlem and the revelation that a man has been chopped in half later in the film both demonstrate visual wit. The stunts throughout are spectacular. Yet the film's pace is too furious. The action scenes don't achieve the effects they should because the director hasn't set them up properly. A better pace would have generated a bigger payoff.

Speed, last summer's hit action film, is a measure of how *Die Hard with a Vengeance* falls short. Jan De Bont, the director of *Speed* and cinematographer of *Die Hard*, seems to have absorbed more from his collaboration with McTiernan on *Die Hard* than McTiernan himself. *Speed* is not only the better action film, it is arguably a better *Die Hard* film than *Die Hard with a Vengeance*.

José Arroyo

GOLDENEYE
United Kingdom/USA 1995
Director: Martin Campbell

James Bond (Secret Agent 007) is on a mission with Alec Trevelyan (006) to blow up a Soviet chemical weapons facility. 006 is caught by General Ourumov and 007 is forced to choose between completing the mission or saving his friend. Before he is shot, 006 encourages Bond to blow up the base. Bond does so and escapes.

We next see Bond nine years later on the road to Monaco. Inside his Aston Martin, a young British woman is trying to evaluate him psychologically for his job; on the road, a beautiful woman races him with her red sports car. That evening Bond meets the other driver, Xenia Onatopp, at the casino. He flirts with her and beats her at baccarat. She leaves with an admiral whom she later kills during sex. The next day, she and General Ourumov steal a stealth helicopter, return to Russia and there blow up a base in Siberia to gain sole access to GoldenEye, a secret satellite electronic-pulse weapon. Only two people, both computer experts, survive the destruction of the base: Natalya Simonova and Boris Grishenko.

Bond's boss 'M' sends him to Russia. He meets a former KGB agent who directs him to the plot's organisers. Bond avoids getting killed by Onatopp, but is then captured by the mastermind, Trevelyan, who is still alive. Natalya, betrayed by Boris, is strapped with Bond into the helicopter which is primed to self-destruct. They escape only to be arrested. In captivity, they meet the Russian Defence Minister and tell him that Ourumov is a traitor but Ourumov shoots the Minister and kidnaps Natalya. Bond chases after them through the streets of St Petersburg in a tank. The villains board a train but Bond derails it and shoots Ourumov; the others escape. Natalya pinpoints the location of Trevelyan's headquarters in Cuba. Trevelyan intends to disable every electrical device in London. Bond and Natalya infiltrate the base and destroy it, eliminating Trevelyan and Onatopp.

*   *   *

The Bond films are such an institution that their producers know if they don't screw up they've got a guaranteed audience. We want to like most movies we pay to see but we already know the Bond formula – it has already earned our good will – so our pleasure revolves around seeing how the film-makers execute their turn. *GoldenEye* doesn't blow it.

In *GoldenEye*, the usually spectacular pre-credits sequence must also present a new star as Bond. We first see Pierce Brosnan running, bungee-jumping from an incredible height and sneaking into a military facility to blow it up. The scene has all the integral elements of the series: great scale, witty repartee, a sense of duty and spectacular stunts. When Bond free-falls after his aeroplane, the very notion is so ridiculously Bond the audience I saw it with burst into applause.

The Bond films are a fantasy bred from the Cold War (and from the need to produce films that could compete with television). Part of the fantasy was that the appearance of the Iron Curtain created new sites of conflict as well as new types of heroism. Since the battle was international and covert, the hero's manhood could be tested in luxury hotels and resorts all over the world rather than in grimy battlefields. The skills required were no longer merely physical and moral but also social, intellectual and sexual. Another part of the fantasy was that Great Britain still had a role to play as a major power in this conflict.

One would think that the fall of the Soviet Union and the decline of Britain as an international power would have affected the potency of these fantasies, but seemingly they haven't. Perhaps we've seen the Bond films so often and for so long that we understand *GoldenEye* in relation to the history of Bond films rather than feel the need to relate it to a broader history through some notion of realism. If anything, the fall of the former Soviet Union has allowed Western film-makers to represent Russia in ways they would not have dared before *glasnost*. *GoldenEye*'s credit sequence, like all the

Bond films, has semi-naked girls dancing. Except this time they are doing it on a giant hammer and sickle while Communist icons collapse. The audacity of the sequence springs from seeing such powerful symbols reduced to mere camp props. What bothered me most is that *GoldenEye* pulls this off so well that it didn't bother me at all.

GoldenEye follows the Bond formula well – all the familiar characters are back and the gadgets are demonstrated. The film offers luxury, beautiful women, a strong villain and an elegant hero in exotic locales. Set pieces bookend the film: there is a good car chase and the rest offers a fine mixture of wit and action. However, *GoldenEye*'s greatest success, especially in the light of how *The Living Daylights* and *Licence to Kill* failed, is in modernising Bond.

It seems that though the Bond series need pay little attention to history, a greater degree of verisimilitude in its portrayal of contemporary sexual mores is deemed essential. If not in the avant-garde of the 60s Playboy ethos, the Connery Bonds were certainly in tune with it; the Dalton Bonds attempted to catch up with the times. *GoldenEye* does not attempt to change Bond by making him a New(ish) Man as the Dalton Bonds did. Instead the film nods slightly towards the present by changing the attitudes of those around him. Miss Moneypenny jokes with him about construing his advances as sexual harassment. 'M' is now a working mother who tells Bond he is a sexist, misogynist dinosaur. The film positions Bond as beleaguered by powerful women ('M', his psychological evaluator, Onatopp) even though Bond himself seems not to have a problem with female authority.

There is likely to be some debate about the effectiveness of Brosnan as Bond, but a large measure of *GoldenEye*'s success is due to him. He's arguably as handsome as any of the previous Bonds and he's a much better actor than George Lazenby. He doesn't read all of his lines as if they were in quotation marks as Roger Moore did, or seem embarrassed to be playing the role like Timothy Dalton. Brosnan is the fittest Bond we've had since early Sean Connery. He is elegant and moves well. The moment when he's running over everything in sight with his tank and takes time to rearrange his tie is quintessential Bond. Inevitably, all new Bonds are compared to Connery. Both he and Brosnan give the impression that there is a mystery behind the martinis and the guns. Dalton had that too but there was stiffness in his characterisation that reduced mystery to distance or blankness. With Dalton one didn't want to resolve that mystery. With Brosnan, as with Connery, one does.

Director Martin Campbell (whose credits include *Edge of Darkness* and *No Escape*) can be credited for his staging of the film's action and humour. At a time when so many villains in American action films signify their villainy through their Britishness it is also a pleasure to have a British hero in a big-budget movie. I do have one serious gripe: that despite all the spectacle the only thing one would miss by watching the film on video is the scale. Now scale in itself is reason enough to see a film in the cinema, but I resented the amount of close-ups; the feeling that the action seemed to take place on only one plane, that all the possibilities of staging on a big screen were reduced to maximise the limitations of a small one. Limited use of screen space is one element which prevents *GoldenEye* from being what some other Bond films were – a particular kind of great cinema.

José Arroyo

HEAT
USA 1995
Director: Michael Mann

Neil McCauley and his crew, Chris Shiherlis, Michael Cheritto and Trejo, plan the armed robbery of a security van carrying bearer bonds; the job goes perfectly, except that a new recruit to the crew, Waingro, shoots a guard. Afterwards, McCauley tries to kill Waingro, but he escapes. Vincent Hanna, a homicide cop whose third marriage is falling apart because of his devotion to his job, examines the scene of the crime and admires the professionalism of the job; the only clue is that one of the robbers was over-heard calling a security guard 'Slick'. McCauley's associate Nate arranges to sell the bearer bonds back to their original owner, Van Zant, but the meeting in a deserted drive-in turns out to be an ambush; McCauley and his crew kill Van Zant's men and escape.

A chance lead from the brother of one of Hanna's informers identifies Cheritto as the man who calls people Slick. Hanna puts Cheritto under surveillance and starts tracking the crew around Los Angeles as they prepare their next heist. Meanwhile McCauley, who prides himself on his lack of attachments, has met and fallen in love with Eady, a graphic designer who knows nothing about his criminal career, and with whom he plans to leave for New Zealand after one last job. While burgling a metal depository, however, McCauley realises that they are being watched and calls the job off; because they have not stolen anything yet, Hanna doesn't arrest them. Even though they know the police are on to them, the crew decides to carry out one final bank robbery.

Following him one night, Hanna stops McCauley, takes him for a cup of coffee and tries to warn him off. The same night, the crew all shake off their tails, except for Trejo. The crew goes ahead without him, and the bank robbery they have planned goes smoothly; but after a tip-off, the police arrive as the robbers are leaving. A gun battle ensues, in which Cheritto is killed and Shiherlis wounded. Aiming to settle scores before he leaves town on a plane arranged by Nate, McCauley traces the tip-off to Trejo, who has been tortured into betraying the plan by Waingro, who has been recruited by Van Zant to get revenge on McCauley. After tracking down and killing Van Zant, McCauley persuades Eady to leave with him that night. But, learning that Waingro is holed up in a hotel near the airport, he can't resist having a go. Although the hotel is staked out by the police, McCauley manages to kill Waingro, but Hanna spots him on his way out of the hotel, chases him across the airport runways and shoots him down. Hanna holds McCauley's hand as he dies.

*   *   *

After a journey into the eighteenth-century wilderness for *The Last of the Mohicans*, Michael Mann returns to the urban terrain of his television series *Miami Vice* and *Crime Story* and his features *Manhunter* and *Thief* with a film which can be read as a compendium of his works to date. Like James Caan's safe-cracker, Frank, in 1981's *Thief* (released in this country as *Violent Streets*), Neil McCauley is single-mindedly devoted to his profession ('What are you?' Hanna asks him, 'A monk?'), and only loses control of his own destiny when he tries to buy himself what Hanna, when he confronts him in the coffee shop, dismisses as 'a regular-type life'. Vincent Hanna, meanwhile, is a variation on William Petersen's Will Graham from *Manhunter* in his talent for putting himself in the shoes of his prey and seeing what they see, and in the way this leaves him closer to those he is pursuing than those he is protecting.

In one breathtaking sequence in *Heat* which evokes the voyeuristic, hall-of-mirrors feel of *Manhunter*, Hanna and his men watch McCauley's crew scouting out a refinery. When they have gone, Hanna stands exactly where they stood, trying to guess what they were looking at – before realising that they were looking at *him*, and that McCauley has now lured him into the open. The camera then pulls back to show McCauley taking his picture. Hanna can ultimately catch McCauley because they are alike. (Mann suggests this early on with near identical shots of Hanna picking up his gun from the table before he goes to work, and McCauley putting his down when he gets home.) Both have their matching crews, and the presence of Wes Studi, the formidable Magua from *The Last of the Mohicans*, as Hanna's right-hand man Casals, alerts us to *Heat*'s echo of that film, as the bands of modern-day Mohicans and Hurons track each other across the jungle that is Los Angeles.

Mann reinvents LA here with the same visionary gaze he turned on Miami in *Miami Vice*, Las Vegas in *Crime Story* and Atlanta in *Manhunter*. From the 'dead-tech, postmodernist' home where Hanna's marriage falls apart, to McCauley's beach-side glass box, bathed in blue light (just like Graham's home in *Manhunter*), to the red-and-white-checked concrete cubes by the runway where McCauley dies, there's not a boring building in the film. Mann is the best director of architecture since Antonioni. In fact, few film-makers at work today can rival Mann's control of every detail of the film-making process – perhaps this is why his films are so infrequent – from the fluent but unostentatious camera movements (worthy, as David Thomson has pointed out, of Max Ophüls), to the precise, almost David Mamet-like dialogue, to the expertly chosen soundtrack, which manages to make artists as diverse as Moby and György Ligeti sound like they belong on the same record.

David Thomson has singled out another Mann trademark, his peerless use of vivid supporting players, and *Heat* certainly doesn't disappoint in this respect. Mann discovers compelling new sides of Jon Voight (Nate, who could be Jack Palance's younger brother), Val Kilmer (blond, pony-tailed, puffy-faced and petulant as the safe-cracker Shiherlis) and Tom Sizemore, typecast as a cartoon psychopath in the likes of *Natural Born Killers* and *Devil in a Blue Dress*, but here reinvented as the solid, grey-haired foot soldier, Cheritto. Tom Noonan, the serial killer from *Manhunter*, has a great cameo, bearded like an orthodox priest, as the source who tips McCauley off about the bank job, while Ted Levine – the killer in *Manhunter*'s de facto sequel, *The Silence of the Lambs*, and a veteran of *Crime Story* – turns up balding and moustachioed as one of Hanna's men. Mann also takes the trouble to populate his man's world with interesting women: Diane Venora, barely glimpsed since *Bird*, as Justine Hanna; Natalie Portman of *Léon* as her suicidal daughter; Ashley Judd, finally fulfilling the promise of *Ruby In Paradise*, as Charlene Shiherlis. Only *NYPD Blue*'s Amy Brenneman, in the pivotal role of Eady, fails to make much of an impression.

The real casting coup, of course, lies in the first pairing of De Niro and Pacino (they were father and son in *The Godfather Part II*, but never shared a scene). The first half of *Heat* plays absorbingly off the mounting tension about when the two will meet. Hanna first sees McCauley's Satanic image through a heat-vision viewfinder while staking out the metal depository. McCauley gets his look at Hanna through a tele-photo lens. When it finally arrives, two hours in, their single scene together (bar the final shoot-out) is all the more highly charged for the banality of the setting, in a cof-fee shop. Rewardingly, the confrontation seems to have the same significance for the actors as it does for the characters: two driven professionals, frequently compared to each other and both at the peak of their powers, finally get the chance to size each other up at close range. In the same way that McCauley and Hanna's duel inspires each to greater feats of ingenuity, so the actors bring out the best in each other. Pacino is on edge here, with an alarming habit of suddenly shouting his words, but such is his auth-ority that he makes it seem like the character's mannerism rather than the actor's; Hanna is not the loose cannon of cop-movie cliché, but a man who *pretends* to be when he needs to intimidate people, whether an informer or his wife's lover. De Niro, mean-while, rises to the challenge with his most compelling work since *The King of Comedy*. Thankfully free of tics, his McCauley is so ruthlessly controlled that he barely moves his head: his eyes do all the work. If *Heat* were a play, you could imagine De Niro and Pacino swapping the roles every night, like Olivier and Richardson in *Othello*.

'All I am is what I'm going after,' says Hanna near the end of his quest, a motto that could serve as well for McCauley, or for any of Mann's protagonists. In Mann's uni-verse, as in that of Howard Hawks, professionalism is all that counts; but, unlike Hawks, Mann shows the cost of such a code in widows and wrecked marriages. In fact, for a cop movie, *Heat* seems unusually suffused with an awareness of death. Hanna's wife Justine, who, like her husband, always wears black, keeps telling him that he is walking dead through life. When McCauley and Hanna meet, they compare their dreams – and both have been dreaming of death, of time running out. (For Mann and his leads, all into their fifties, this seems to carry a real weight.) And, in the film's only superfluous scene, Waingro announces himself as the Grim Reaper before murdering a prostitute – leaving Hanna, who, in his wife's haunting words 'lives among the remains of dead people', to pick up the pieces.

Of all the directors in America today who are set on keeping film noir alive, Mann seems the most willing to invest the genre with real characters and morality, and the most reluctant to fall back on cliché. (Which doesn't mean he fails to deliver on the set pieces: the bank robbery here, which spirals into a pitched battle on the streets of downtown LA that's as ferocious as anything in *The Last of the Mohicans*, will surely stand as one of the great failed-heist sequences.) For those who cherish *Thief, Man-hunter* and *Mohicans*, and for those who believe that Martin Scorsese's post-*King of Comedy* output has slipped into a sort of flashy self-parody identified by Gilbert Adair as 'Scors*ese*', as in journalese or legalese, *Heat*, placed by the accident of its British release schedule within a month of *Casino*, another, more vigorously hyped three-hour De Niro crime story, only serves to bolster the case for Michael Mann as the key American auteur of the last ten years.

John Wrathall

SUDDEN DEATH
USA 1995
Director: Peter Hyams

After planting a series of bombs in and around Pittsburgh's Civil Arena stadium, Joshua Foss' terrorist gang kidnap the US Vice President and assorted local dignitaries in the VIP lounge during an ice-hockey game between the Pittsburgh Penguins and the Chicago Blackhawks. The gang holds the VIPs hostage and threatens to kill a number of them at the end of each period of play unless over £1 billion in frozen foreign government accounts is electronically transferred to them.

Stadium fire-safety officer Darren McCord is also attending the game with his two young children, Emily and Tyler. Emily is kidnapped and taken hostage after she walks in on one of the terrorists. McCord goes after the terrorist and battles him successfully in the stadium kitchen. He then rushes to the nearest security guard who also turns out to be a terrorist. A further fight in the kitchen ends with McCord interrogating the villain using a hot plate before killing him. Aware now of the gang's plans, McCord starts defusing the bombs. Meanwhile, the authorities' attempts to storm the stadium are thwarted. As the game continues, McCord is chased through the stadium, taking refuge on the rink, where he disguises himself as the goalkeeper and makes a crucial save. He then kills another villain in the dressing room.

Meanwhile as the Penguins score in the closing seconds, the game goes to a 'sudden death' play-off – which delays Foss's final murders. With a home-made stun bomb McCord climbs up the outside of the stadium's huge dome roof. Killing the guard stationed there, he swings down into the stadium, throws his bomb through the VIP lounge window and then follows through himself, shooting as he goes. With all of his team dead, Foss grabs Emily and makes for the roof and his getaway helicopter. McCord follows, pushes Emily safely aside and shoots the chopper's pilot from below while hanging in mid-air from the chopper's rope ladder. He falls safely onto the domed part of the open roof and catches Foss's eye as the chopper slowly plunges tail first through it to explode in the centre of the now empty stadium.

*   *   *

Sudden Death sets itself the strictly limited task of accommodating Jean-Claude Van Damme within the modern lone warrior format first perfected in *Hard* and since much imitated by the likes of *Under Siege, On Deadly Ground* and *Cliffhanger*. The conventions of the sub-genre are now so obviously foregrounded that comedy has become as much a requirement as action. With a mature variant such as this movie, *Under Siege 2* or *Die Hard with a Vengeance*, one of the main sources of audience pleasure is to share in the film-makers' gleeful sense of contrivance as they force their heroes through the same set of dangerous hoops as before. Contrivance thus becomes something to celebrate rather than to disguise.

Contrived convention number one is that a group of terrorists should attempt to take over a key location. Number two is that the ever-resourceful hero has to be isolated in some way from the authorities so that he can wage an increasingly spectacular (and ludicrous) one-man guerrilla war against them. Number three is that the terrorist leader should be witty, highly articulate, irredeemably cruel and driven by selfish rather than political goals. And number four is that this Manichean struggle should climax with a major stunt set piece in which the villain is killed. Narrative closure and the moral and physical superiority of the hero are thus asserted, typically with a huge explosion and/or the bad guy falling from a great height.

Sudden Death proficiently covers all four conventions and shows genuine panache in its handling of its many action set pieces. The use of the Pittsburgh Civic Arena (producer Howard Baldwin is the owner of the Penguins' team; his wife Karen Baldwin came up with the original story) makes for a suitably spectacular finale when McCord swings down through its distinctive opening roof like a latter day Tarzan. The stadium here almost becomes a character in its own right. That the ice hockey game goes on throughout the crisis allows the director Peter Hyams (*Narrow Margin, Stay Tuned, Timecop*) to exploit the hard knock physicality of that sport, both as an effective form of cross-cutting punctuation and as a rhythmic way of racking up the tension. Although the opening scenes, which set up the story's premise, are awkwardly presented, once the game starts, the plot shifts into a high gear which doesn't let up until the final big explosion.

Presenting the battle of wits between McCord and Foss as a game gives a tightly knit sense of closure to the narrative: McCord has to defuse the bombs and save his daughter and the Vice President, whereas Foss has to secure the transfer of the funds, all by the end of the match. As a computer-game format it's obviously ready made, but more importantly as a film narrative it has a directness and an economy which gain greatly from its unities of time and place. Asking for credibility is futile in this kind of scenario, where the aim is to offer the entertainingly incredible. So McCord bounds around the arena, dispatches sundry villains and defuses assorted bombs and then, in the comedy highlight, actually finds himself playing in goal for the home side. The screenplay's playful sense of humour is also much in evidence in the pivotal fight sequence which delivers the absurd spectacle of McCord kicking his way through a kitchen while dealing with an assassin dressed up as a giant penguin. This kind of crisply choreographed unarmed combat is what Van Damme does best and Hyams handles it with so much manic, fast-cutting relish that it almost thumps its way through the screen. In the acting rather than action stakes, Powers Boothe also delivers the goods with a smoothly sinuous performance which, again typically for the sub-genre, puts the accent on black comedy ('He needs a doctor!' 'Not any more!').

Paradoxically it's Van Damme's very lack of range as an actor, the sheer blank simplicity of his screen personality, which makes him so indispensable as an action hero. In the dullish *Nowhere to Run* his athletic style was cramped by a numbing relationship with Rosanna Arquette and in the disastrous *Street Fighter* he was too often sidelined by dull talk and ragged plot exposition. *Timecop*, which Peter Hyams also directed, was a much stronger vehicle and, here again, recognising that his star's acting limitations are also his strength, the director gives only the minimum of lip service to character while pushing the action for all its worth.

A less astute director would waste valuable time eliciting thoughtful reactions from his star to such clichéd plot points as the threat to his character McCord's child Emily. Hyams realises that, as an actor, Van Damme is a child's idea of what a grown-up should be: brave, loyal, steadfast and true. Fundamentally, the heroes of this sub-genre are no different at the end of their movies than they are at the start. The only difference is they've killed sundry bad guys and asserted, yet again, their moral and physical superiority to the world at large. The continuing voracious appetite for such warriors implies much about the real 90s worlds of work, the community and law enforcement.

It's also symbolically apt that this latest example of lone heroics should be set in a sports stadium. Violence as a ritualised spectator sport is the concept at the heart of the lone warrior sub-genre. The insistence on violence as theatre strongly recalls the gladiatorial contests of Ancient Rome. The Romans had bread and circuses: the modern audience has Dolph Lundgren, Steven Seagal and Jean-Claude Van Damme. And, to invert the same analogy, the likes of Alan Rickman, Jeremy Irons and Powers Boothe will always get a big thumbs-up so long as they amuse us on the way to their screen deaths. Not for nothing do the villains here smuggle their bombs into the stadium inside huge bags of popcorn.

Tom Tunney

INDEPENDENCE DAY
USA 1996
Director: Roland Emmerich

July 2. Radio signals buzzing across monitors in the USA prove to be emanating from a massive spaceship. As government agencies try to communicate with the ship, and a half dozen smaller vessels that have taken up positions across the world, a New York cable executive, David Levinson, discovers that the signal is actually a countdown. David and his father, Julius, drive to Washington DC to pass the information to David's former wife, Constance, who gave up on her marriage for a job with the President. Meanwhile, a fighter pilot, Captain Hiller, takes leave of his fiancée and her son in order to 'kick E.T.'s butt', while Russell Casse, a former Vietnam pilot turned alcoholic crop-duster with three kids, explains to anyone who will listen how he was once abducted by aliens.

July 3. The smaller alien ships begin to attack the earth. The President and most of his staff, along with David and his father, escape the White House just before it is blown up. They travel to Area 51 in Nevada, where, since the 50s, government scientists have been studying a space ship identical to those in the invading force. The President launches an unsuccessful nuclear attack. David discovers a way to disarm the invaders' defence system with a computer virus. He and Steven, who has gunned down one of the aliens in a dogfight, navigate the older space craft to the mother ship in order to plant the virus. A convoy of survivors arrive in Roswell, including the pilot's girlfriend, her son and the wounded First Lady, who then dies.

July 4. Steven and David hack into the alien computer system, disarming its defence shields. The US launches a successful air strike on the extraterrestrials. They spread the word via morse code to the rest of the world's armies, all of whom are then able to join in the battle. The invading forces are routed, leaving the world's survivors to carry on the business of rebuilding the earth.

*   *   *

Blame *The X-Files*. Or perhaps give thanks, as do so many of the television faithful. Whatever the genesis of *Independence Day*, it's more than likely that without Mulder and Scully this unrepentantly slam-bam extravaganza wouldn't exist – neither as the season's most eagerly awaited box-office phenomenon, nor as a gateway into the renewed uneasy collective dream of extraterrestrial invasion. A truly scary extraterrestrial alien invasion, that is, with superior hardware and intellect and none of the pieties that make for so many warm-and-fuzzy *Star Treks*, not to mention *E.T. The Extra-Terrestrial*.

Less the new science fiction than old-fashioned hokum, *Independence Day* is an SF disaster film self-consciously cut from the same movie mouldiness that made for such unforgettable 50s titles as *The War of the Worlds* and *Invaders from Mars*. The message is: think back to the future, with tongue lightly in cheek. Directed by Roland Emmerich, who established his SF credentials with *Moon 44* and *Stargate*, the film opens with a quick trip to the moon, then cuts to an earthbound lab. As a technician putts golf balls, Michael Stipe chirps on the radio, 'It's the end of the world as we know it and I feel fine.' On cue, a radio signal shivers across the lab's monitors. There's excitement, followed by alarm, then panic after spaceships begin cruising the skies. Heads of states convene; the masses scramble.

A waiting game stretched over three days, *Independence Day* switches between long shots (aliens looming) and close-ups (humans cringing). Emmerich may be no Steven Spielberg or George Lucas (never mind Stanley Kubrick), but he knows that even the biggest mousetrap needs mice to keep things interesting. Here, the mice are numerous and multiculturally equalised – Will Smith as Steven, a black fighter pilot; Jeff Goldblum as a Jewish cybergenius called David; and Bill Pullman, blanded out as the WASP President.

The good news is that Hollywood can still make good, solid, goose-bump movies where neat effects keep time with story, characters and loads of good cheer. Doomsday aside, *Independence Day* is consistently, weirdly, upbeat in mood, a gloss on the same vibrations that end *Dr. Strangelove*, but without the venom. Emmerich doesn't have Kubrick's wit, style or intellectual reach, but he does have a feel for epic moviemaking. If nothing else, *Independence Day* fulfills the primal promise of the movies: to deliver the audience out of the everyday and into the sensational, be it into Valhalla or ruin.

Emmerich and his producer/co-writer, Dean Devlin, tweak convention, but they're far too smart to dump it altogether. The film works its most ticklish fun exercising the gee-whiz principle: as in, gee-whiz, what if we glued this thingamajig to that thingamabob. It's something that works best when the odds are laughably impossible, as when half a dozen spaceships hang over the world's major cities promising destruction and all that stands between life and death are three extravagantly capable, impeccably fit American men with good hair.

Independence Day may be goofy, but it's not dumb. It barely cheats at story level and it hints at life beyond the frame. If only Emmerich could turn suggestion into substance. Unlike the directors of so many blockbusters, he knows that what makes a movie are its people; unlike Spielberg he doesn't spend time shading them in. *Close Encounters of the Third Kind* takes a few knocks in this film, yet what makes that movie memorable isn't just any close encounter, but one with Richard Dreyfuss.

Emmerich's film rarely climbs to the same woozy heights as a *Star Wars* or an *E.T.*, but it has necessary downtime and loads of action. It even has some terrific set pieces: most memorably a procession of RV's crossing the desert like covered wagons. What it doesn't have is an emphatic pulse, the kind that forces hearts into throats and keeps them there. The problem is partly logistical, the headaches of effects and extras, and partly inspirational; the film never shakes the B-movie tag.

In the end, this may be the key to the film's success. Firmly located between art and trash, virtuosity and insignificance, *Independence Day*'s success is in being bigger but never better than its audience. Its mediocrity is its greatest triumph. This may be the most cheerful movie about the apocalypse ever. Faced with the end, there's barely one character in the film who sheds a tear. Most simply swallow fear and turn towards danger. Like the audience, they know that it will all be over, soon.

Manohla Dargis

CHAIN REACTION
USA 1996
Director: Andrew Davis

Chicago, Illinois. A team of dedicated scientists, led by Dr. Alistair Barkley, has succeeded in finding a cheap, clean and safe new source of energy. The process – known as sonoluminescence – involves the extraction of hydrogen from water using high-frequency sound waves. Barkley congratulates machinist Eddie Kasalivich (who hit upon the all-important frequency) and physicist Lily Sinclair. Paul Shannon, head of the foundation funding the project, advises against going public. Eddie gallantly escorts the drunken Lily home. Returning for his motorcycle, he finds Barkley has been murdered, his assistant, Lu Chen, has vanished and a bomb is set to go off. Eddie speeds away, pursued by a fireball that levels eight city blocks.

FBI Agent Ford orders a wiretap of all the project workers. Suspicion falls on Lily when she receives a fax, supposedly from Chen. When a satellite transmitter and £50,000 are found in Eddie's flat, Eddie and Lily hide out with Maggie, an old friend who works in an observatory. The FBI tracks Shannon to the checkpoint of C-Systems, a secret research complex. Inside, Shannon argues with his associate Lyman Collier. We learn that Shannon ordered Barkley's murder at the behest of various defence contractors and big business interests. Collier insists that Eddie and Lily should take the fall.

The FBI traces them to Maggie's, but the policeman sent to apprehend them is shot dead. Confused, Eddie and Lily escape across a frozen lake on an ice-boat. Lily catches a chill, so they stop at an unoccupied house. Attacked by two hired thugs, they escape, having pocketed an I.D. card from C-Systems. Eddie sends a coded message to Shannon to meet them in a museum. Shannon brings some heavies and, during a struggle, Lily is abducted. Eddie tracks her to C-Systems headquarters, where she – and the missing Chen – have been put to work rerunning the original experiment. Eddie stabilises the hydrogen generator and downloads the C-Systems mainframe onto the FBI computer. Next day, he bargains with Collier: the correct frequency in exchange for his and Lily's life. When Collier refuses, Eddie shuts down the system. When C-Systems boot it up again, there's a huge explosion from which Eddie and Lily are rescued, but Shannon, having shot Collier, manages to sneak away.

*   *   *

The title *Chain Reaction* is pretty meaningless, but (like *Cliffhanger* or *Sudden Death*) it accurately portrays the kind of entertainment on offer: abstract thrills devoid of any psychic kick. Connoisseurs insist that the big new action movies represent pure cinema – as if decent characterisation and a plausible social context were intrusive literary elements. When one watches something as elegantly contrived as Jan de Bont's *Speed*, which raises its formalism to virtually a meta-physical principle, one is *almost* convinced. *Chain Reaction* is, however, a counter-argument for the surviving humanists among us, being not so much directed by the reliably pile-driving Andrew Davis as superintended by technocrats.

Davis belongs to a paradoxical breed of Hollywood auteur: he conforms so selflessly to the corporate style that it becomes unmistakably his own. There isn't a whisper of private obsession anywhere in his work, but perhaps no-one else delivers suspense with such scrupulous efficiency. Davis can't be called a virile director like Howard Hawks; nor is he a euphoric high-tech wizard like Steven Spielberg used to be. Rather, one imagines him as a consummate *apparatchik*, endlessly checking the logistics of each stunt and storyboarding every shot to within an inch of its life. I'm far from trying to discredit this scientific type of film-making – one need only compare the hypertense control of Davis' *Under Siege* to its flabby sequel (directed by Geoff Murphy) to appreciate its advantages. But cardiovascular stimulation should not be mistaken for emotional involvement: on this level, Davis' professionalism counts for zilch.

Even his best movie, *The Fugitive*, has little effectiveness beyond its obvious kinaesthetic splendour. It hurtles along from crisis to crisis as inexorably as a row of collapsing dominoes; but you aren't spooked by it afterwards. Davis' straight-arrow approach (and a peculiarly clean-minded script by Jeb Stuart and David Twohy) irons out all the paranoiac, twisty potential of the wrong-man-in-jeopardy plot – as if audiences would find that a tedious distraction from the stunts. It's only too evident, then, why Davis was hired to direct *Chain Reaction*: the screenplay (by J.F. Lawton and Michael Bortman) is a fairly cynical retread of the innocents-on-the-lam formula; and if slick excitement minus friction and ambiguity equals box-office gold, then Davis is your man.

Chain Reaction bears all the hallmarks of his industrial, degree-zero style. There are those grandiloquent but strangely anodyne aerial views (of a power dam, an observatory or a city at night) which imply the vantage point of some remote technological deity. There are the favoured Davis locales for a chase (marble staircases, a museum corridor), strictly functional in getting the harried protagonists from A to B. There are the unusual forms of transport (an ice-boat) and architecture (a drawbridge), chosen more for their novelty value than for any poetic suggestiveness. And, of course, loud percussive sounds thump your innards periodically – not too mercifully varied by those millennial fanfares which once greeted apparitions of the Holy Virgin and now accompany the hero and heroine as they are lifted to safety.

Davis keeps the ball rolling without beauty, mystery or real menace. In *The Fugitive*, it was a bit disappointing how the one-armed villain, so potently malevolent in the old television series, was explained away rationally (something to do with a phoney drugs patent). *Chain Reaction* makes an analogous error in tipping us off too early about Paul Shannon. The bad guys, who want to monopolise the new miracle source of energy, are apparently a consortium of industrialists, munitions dealers and CIA-operatives, but really it's anybody's guess. It's puzzling why these hazy plutocrats spend so much time trying to frame poor Eddie (Keanu Reeves), as he's the only one who knows the magic frequency they are all presumably after. But maybe they're not too bright anyway, since our plucky blue-collar hero just ambles unnoticed into their clandestine headquarters and spots their nefarious plans neatly laid out in plain sight.

Yet I don't suppose anyone cares about the plot holes any more than the film-makers genuinely care about alternative energy sources. One attends this sort of claptrap for the delights of overscaled technological barbarism; and indeed the exploding mega-tonnage in the opening and closing sequences is shot and edited to knock you out of your seat. The actors merely connect the dots between these twin apocalypses. Yet a few of them come off better than you'd expect. Rachel Weisz has a nice, purring presence as Lily; Brian Cox does his turn of soft-spoken Southern malignancy to perfection in the part of Collier. And while it's a minority opinion by now, I *like* Keanu Reeves. He may not have the customary musculature of an action hero, but his youth, freshness and vague exoticism make him atypically interesting alongside such inelastic warriors as Steven Seagal. In some hard-to-define way, Reeves' gaucheness and inexpressivity cut across the grain of this machine-tooled movie and humanise it a little.

Peter Matthews

THE LONG KISS GOODNIGHT
USA 1996
Director: Renny Harlin

Samantha Caine is a school teacher in a small New England town with an eight-year-old daughter named Caitlin and a boyfriend, Hal. When Sam was only two months pregnant with Caitlin she was found with severe amnesia and almost no identification. A chance discovery of some of her old possessions by a sleazy detective agency run by Mitch Henessey, promises to provide a few clues. At the same time, Sam's appearance in a minor news item is seen by a one-eyed convict, who recognises her and subsequently breaks out of jail.

A car accident sets off memory flashes of Sam's previous personality: a woman named Charly. She discovers a new aptitude with knives, and when the convict attacks her at home, she kills him with astonishing defensive skills. Sam and Mitch set off to find out who she was. She leaves Caitlin a key and charm bracelet – one of the few things found on her eight years ago. Gradually, it is revealed that Sam is really Charly Baltimore, a top CIA assassin who was about to kill a man named Daedalus (who is now working for the CIA) when she had a near-fatal encounter with the convict and another man named Timothy (also now working for the CIA).

In the present, Timothy, Daedalus and CIA head Perkins all want Sam killed. Although Nathan, Charly's old mentor, tries to help her, Mitch's interference gets him and Sam captured and Nathan killed. However, tortured under freezing water, Sam recovers her memory and skills, enabling her to kill Daedalus, save Mitch and escape. Reverting to hard-nut Charly's personality, she realises she needs the bracelet left at home. It holds a key to a box containing passports and money stashed years ago. While Charly retrieves the key, Caitlin is kidnapped by Timothy. He suggests an exchange: Charly for the kid.

Tracking down Caitlin, Charly and Mitch also uncover the CIA's plan to set off a truck-bomb at a parade and make it look like an Arab hostage did it. This would force Congress to increase their funding. After a series of struggles and escapes, Caitlin accidentally hides in the truck, and is almost blown up with the bomb, but Charly and Mitch manage to save her and kill Timothy (who is Caitlin's real father, but who would have let her die). Charly settles down to a new life with Caitlin and Hal, while Mitch finds brief fame on television.

*   *   *

Those who survived viewing *Cut-Throat Island* will be shocked to learn that *The Long Kiss Goodnight*, the latest adventure by actor Geena Davis and her director/husband Renny Harlin is a superbly entertaining action movie, perhaps the best of this year's many shoot-'em-ups. Granted, the plot is far from original, borrowing substantially from James Cameron's *True Lies* in particular. Moreover, it demonstrates not a flicker of interest in being anything more profound than a polished piece of genre manipulation and entertainment, as was the case with Harlin's best films so far, *Cliffhanger* and *Die Hard 2*. However, it has a clarity of purpose that makes it impervious to glibly dismissive criticisms.

Most of the credit for its integrated slickness must go to the screenwriter, Shane Black (writer of *Lethal Weapon*, *The Last Boy Scout* and *Last Action Hero*). For *The Long Kiss Goodnight*, Black was reputedly paid $4 million, the highest price yet shelled out for a script – money well spent compared to the sums the industry lavishes on the likes of Joe Eszterhas for his dreadful pap. The plot revolves around a former-CIA assassin Charly Baltimore (Davis) who has suffered amnesia and become a mellow, cookie-baking citizen, Samantha Caine. She gets her memory back with the help of Mitch Henessey (Samuel L. Jackson), a black private detective and a few traumatic experiences. It's all quite ridiculous of course, but Black and Harlin make sure the whole thing runs with nanosecond precision – not a detail is wasted or a plot point left unexplained.

Like *True Lies*, the film plays off domestic stability and boredom against the excitement and peril of the spy's life which ultimately intersect and conflict. There's a clever scene in which Samantha, slowly chopping a carrot, feels the urge to speed up. Her new-found skill with a knife, she concludes, means she must have been a chef. Inevitably, events lead up to a progeny-in-peril climax. No surprises there, but the one really interesting plot twist, as in *True Lies*, is the use of a female protagonist, this time not playing mere back-up to any gun-toting he-husband. In fact, the film plays cute games with this reversal: Jackson's Mitch, captured by the baddies a second time, takes his leave of Davis' Sam/Charly, saying he'll be just downstairs waiting for her to rescue him again. And as in Black's *Lethal Weapon*, the two leads banter about their ethnicity, but there's an extra twist played here on the usual buddy-movie romance moves when the possibility of real sex and miscegenation is raised. There is also a nicely judged tweaking of the old Cold War dialectics that have provided the narrative impetus for so many spy movies: in this, the baddies are not Russians, or Arabs or drug barons, but the CIA itself, staging things in order to blackmail Congress into increasing its funding.

This sort of film's success hinges crucially on its leads, and the two here are richly charismatic. Davis, shot with loving flattery, makes a noble screen amazon, six feet of tawny grace whether balancing a knife by its point on her fingertip or executing the perfect snowplow on ice skates. She even looks better in a white vest than Bruce Willis. But Jackson, wearing a ridiculous furry green flatcap and nasty check trousers, steals the show, injecting more aggression, sardonic wit and complexity into what is basically the black second-banana role that Danny Glover developed in *Lethal Weapon* and Jackson himself honed in *Die Hard with a Vengeance*. Several of his moments are especially memorable: thrown out of the car by Charly, Mitch lies prostrate on the road and smokes a cigarette as the traffic careens around him, the camera craning languorously away; or when he makes a blues narration of his own actions to a Muddy Waters riff while preparing for a confrontation. Apparently, an earlier version of the film had his character die at the end. Test screening audiences – understandably – were so distraught by this that the film had to be reshot to keep him alive.

Finally, it's a testament to *The Long Kiss Goodnight*'s strength as a story, that one comes away from it remembering these aspects more vividly than the spectacular effects, stunts and editing (which are all, indeed, spectacular). All the technical elements are subordinated to the business of keeping the viewer interested in what will happen next to the characters, and that is a rare control on priorities in a genre so often afflicted these days with 'postmodern' jokiness (there's a little here too, but not too much) and spectacle for spectacle's sake. You can forget *Cut-Throat Island* now, all is forgiven.

Leslie Felperin

AIR FORCE ONE
USA 1997
Director: Wolfgang Petersen

James Marshall, the President of the United States, is on his way back home from Moscow aboard the presidential jet, *Air Force One*. Six Russian journalists are also aboard, ostensibly to interview the President. On a signal from a sympathetic US

Secret Service agent, the Russians hijack the plane. It seems the President himself has escaped in a special emergency pod. Ivan Korshunov, the leader of the terrorists, establishes contact with the White House. He tells Vice President Kathryn Bennett that unless his leader, the extreme nationalist General Radek, is released from a Moscow prison, he will kill the passengers one by one. He makes it clear that he has the President's wife and child in captivity.

Marshall is actually lurking in the hold. Using his mobile phone, he establishes contact with the White House. He tells the Vice President not to negotiate despite the execution of hostages. Meanwhile, he picks off one of the terrorists, sheds the plane's extra fuel, and eventually helps most of the hostages to escape using parachutes. However, Ivan is still holding his wife and daughter. Rather than see either killed, Marshall instructs Moscow to release General Radek. He and Ivan fight it out and eventually Ivan is throttled by parachute cords. Marshall rings Moscow just in time to prevent Radek getting away.

The plane has become damaged and is rapidly losing altitude. Needing to evacuate, Marshall allows his wife and daughter to leave first. He escapes only in the nick of time. *Air Force One* crashes into the sea, killing the renegade Secret Service agent who is still aboard.

* * *

Wolfgang Petersen has a knack for making popular, big-budget thrillers which combine spectacle with at least a degree of plausibility and intelligence. *In the Line of Fire* not only elicited a fine performance from Clint Eastwood as the greying Secret Service agent, but also wittily satirised Washington DC, while getting under the skin of its political assassin villain. *Outbreak* was miscast (Dustin Hoffman isn't a natural action hero) but it tapped into the anxiety surrounding the Ebola virus, worked well as a study in small-town hysteria, and boasted some bravura camerawork from Michael Ballhaus.

In theory, *Air Force One* must have seemed like another ideal vehicle for the German émigré director. The film's action is largely confined to the interior of a hi-tech flying fortress but, as he showed in his brilliant U-boat drama *Das Boot*, Petersen relishes stoking up the tension in constricted spaces. He also usually avoids the most obvious stereotypes. Early on here, as first a renegade fascist general is arrested by US and Russian joint forces, and then as President Marshall makes a rousing Abe Lincoln-style speech in Moscow about human rights, it looks as if he is attempting to move beyond old Cold War caricatures of the Russians. But as soon as Gary Oldman comes into view sporting a ridiculous goatee it becomes apparent that the evil empire is still evil as far as Hollywood is concerned.

Action pics aren't under any obligation to be politically accurate. Even so, Andrew W. Marlowe's screenplay seems deeply muddled. The terrorist boss ostensibly comes from Kazakhstan and yet he warbles on tremulously about Mother Russia. By rights, as a nationalist, he ought to hate the old Communist regime, but a tear still comes to his eyes when he hears his imprisoned comrades singing 'The Internationale'. Oldman plays him as a virtual pantomime figure, a sort of cross between Count Dracula and a KGB agent. President Marshall is an equally implausible creation. Harrison Ford, one of the few contemporary stars with the gravitas of a James Stewart or a Henry Fonda, starts off in solemn, self-righteous fashion, but quickly reverts to an Indiana Jones type when his wife and daughter are put in danger. Just in case his sudden muscular heroics seem incongruous for a man in late middle-age, we're tossed a line of dialogue about his medal-winning exploits in Vietnam.

After Tim Burton's mercilessly iconoclastic *Mars Attacks!* it's well-nigh impossible to take US generals and politicians sitting in the Oval Office seriously. It doesn't help that Glenn Close's one-dimensional Vice President, forced to negotiate with the terrorists, and Dean Stockwell's hawkish Defense Secretary look as if they have strayed out of Burton's movie. They're so stern-faced that they seem comic. Marlowe's screenplay throws in occasional intentionally self-parodic moments. Ford's gung-ho performance and Oldman's rent-a-Russian mugging are certainly tongue-in-cheek, but on the whole, this is played very straight, with little of the knowing humour of, say, *Last Action Hero.* Stripped of its old-fashioned Cold War gloss, it is essentially an airborne *Die Hard.* And like *Die Hard,* it stands or falls by its action sequences.

There is plenty of noisy spectacle. Once again, Ballhaus' cinematography is fluid and arresting. We prowl up and down the corridors of the plane, and explore its every hidden recess. A near crash landing is handled with tremendous, giddy *élan,* as are the refuelling and parachuting sequences. But Ford's advice to the Vice President – 'if you give a mouse a cookie, it'll want a glass of milk' – seems to have been given to the filmmakers themselves. The inflationary logic of action pics demands that every time they mount a stunt, they must immediately try to trump it. As a result, the effects become ever more exaggerated and all contact is lost with the characters. Dialogue is reduced to a few clunking soundbites of the 'nobody does this to America!' variety. Outside the Manichean struggle between the US President and the Russian terrorist, the other actors are largely ignored. Jürgen Prochnow is wasted as General Radek (we see him being kidnapped by the commandos and walking down a long prison corridor, but he isn't even allowed so much as to speak). William H. Macy, the venal car salesman in *Fargo,* shows a touching, labrador-like loyalty to the President as a patriotic army major, but is likewise underused. Petersen never really explores the relationship between the hostages and their captors. At times, it seems as if he is taking his cue from Jerry Goldsmith's overblown score. He certainly doesn't skimp on spectacle, but the sheer, pummelling bombast of the film-making is ultimately more enervating than exhilarating. Only the most undiscriminating of boys' own action-adventure fans are likely to be satisfied with it.

Geoffrey Macnab

THE PEACEMAKER
USA 1997
Director: Mimi Leder

In Russia's Ural Mountains, two trains collide, producing a nuclear explosion. Amid the confusion this causes, a number of nuclear warheads are smuggled out of Russia by a small group of profiteers led by rogue soldier Alexsander Kodoroff. The American response to the crisis is headed by nuclear scientist Julia Kelly and military agent

Col. Thomas Devoe, who has doubts concerning both Kelly's gender and inexperience. Kelly and Devoe fly to Vienna to meet Dimitri Vertikoff, a Russian friend of Devoe's, who gives them vital information but is killed by Kodoroff's associates. Kodoroff's gang is tracked down to a small road near the Iranian border, where Devoe leads a mission to ambush and capture them.

In the battle that follows, Kodoroff and most of his gang are killed, but one escapes with a single warhead. He delivers this to Dusan Gavrich, a Bosnian politician about to attend a summit conference in New York. Once a believer in democratic processes, Gavrich has been pushed towards violent revenge by the death of his wife and child in Sarajevo and what he sees as Western complicity in the bloodshed in Bosnia. By the time Kelly and Devoe have identified him and traced his movements, both Gavrich and the bomb he now carries have eluded them. He plans to detonate the bomb at the UN, thereby focusing world attention on the situation in Bosnia. After a desperate chase through the streets of New York, Kelly and Devoe corner the wounded Gavrich in a church. Before dying, he primes the bomb to explode, but Kelly saves the day and earns Devoe's respect by defusing it.

*   *   *

This is an impossible, and therefore fascinating, film. What it wants to be is a politically subtle action thriller, but its chosen genre simply has no room for the moral complexity to which it aspires, resulting in a deeply fractured text. An audience that allows itself to enjoy action thrillers, to relish their spectacle, tension and expense, always has to leave its ideological sensitivities at home – unless, of course, it's an audience so reactionary as to positively relish the naked racism of, say, *True Lies*. Certain films of the genre invite that amnesia either by being spectacularly naïve (my favourite example of this tendency is *Rambo III*'s version of Afghanistan) or so complex and fanciful it's impossible to grasp what the politics on offer actually are (*Mission Impossible*).

The Peacemaker refuses to take either option, striving instead to blend the thick-ear pleasures of explosions and chases with a sincere attempt to address the recent and current tragedies of Eastern Europe. The ambiguities of that project are nicely captured in its title: who or what precisely is 'the peacemaker'? The United States? The United Nations? Clooney's all-American hero? The despairing Bosnian Gavrich? The nuclear device which he intends to use for his desperate purpose? Juggling all these possibilities while still pushing the required generic buttons puts an insupportable strain on the film, but even if it can't hope to succeed, its noble failure demands a certain degree of respect.

The real strength of the film lies outside its top-line stars, though both are on reasonable form. Clooney is even more scrumptious in army gear than he was in Batman drag, and looks increasingly set to be a key male star of mainstream Hollywood's next decade, while Kidman does what she can with the now clichéd role of the gorgeous-yet-brainy female lead. Their sparring has an occasional zinginess that suggests they'd make an outstanding team in a romantic comedy. Here, though, both are outclassed by the little-known Marcel Iures in the pivotal role of Dusan Gavrich. His character is saddled with a degree of stereotyping – he has soulfully suffering eyes and is given to playing moodily classical piano – but in general he delivers an affecting performance that gives the film real weight. It's rare indeed for a Hollywood film to concede that a 'terrorist' determined to blow the heart out of a US city might, in fact, be someone with complex motivations well beyond the simplistic model of 'evil' usually wheeled on in films of this type. Yet this raises a generic problem, for if the usual villain figure is for once treated with dignity and even sympathy, who is the gung-ho hero going to kick around the screen?

The part of Clooney's punchbag and all-round slimebag is occupied by Kodoroff, suggesting that though the intractable messiness of the Bosnian situation precludes demonising Dusan, there will always be a reliably diabolical Russian to hunt down and destroy. Even here, though, *The Peacemaker* distances itself from a purely moronic Cold War mentality by counterposing Kodoroff with the avuncular, likeable Vertikoff, whose brutal killing is intended to legitimate much of the US-instigated mayhem that follows.

Mimi Leder, in charge of her first film after impressing Steven Spielberg with her work directing *ER*, shows no sign of nerves on being entrusted with such a block-buster. Indeed, the film's supple visual dynamism should lay to rest forever those tired industry truisms about women's inability to handle action pictures, with the vertiginous fight over a gorge at the Iranian border and the panic-inducing editing of the climactic New York pursuit constituting two especially impressive sequences.

The tensions between visceral pleasure and political responsibility make this a schizophrenic film – Kidman's attempts to map out the convolutions of Balkan politics are more than once rudely disrupted by another car chase or military alert, while the way the script scatters names like Chechnya and Azerbaijan may alienate some insular US audiences, leaving them impatient for imperialist fisticuffs. Nonetheless, *The Peacemaker* is at least trying to widen the remit of action cinema, to inject a little complication into a traditionally reductive genre and, as such, stands as one of the most intriguing Hollywood films of the year.

Andy Medhurst

STARSHIP TROOPERS
USA 1997
Director: Paul Verhoeven

At some point in the distant future, democracy on Earth has been replaced by military rule. The planet prepares for war against the Bugs, an alien arachnid race. In Buenos Aires, four high school friends prepare to do their part: outstanding student Carmen hopes to become a starship captain; Johnny, her boyfriend, enlists in the infantry; computer whiz Carl is assigned to military intelligence; and Dizzy, a girl Johnny has spurned, follows him into the infantry. Johnny nearly quits boot camp when his blunder causes a death.

The Bugs launch a surprise attack on Earth, destroying Buenos Aires, and Johnny rejoins the infantry for the assault on Klendathu, the Bugs' home planet. Carmen has become a rising starship officer, breaking off her relationship with Johnny along the way and teaming up with Zander, a fellow officer, instead. She saves her ship from destruction during the disastrous invasion of Klendathu, which results in heavy casualties and full-scale retreat. Faced with evidence that the Bug race is intelligent, Earth generals – including Carl, who has become a leading strategist – resolve to attack the outer reaches of the Bug empire first.

In an extended series of battles, human forces begin to turn the tide. Johnny proves himself in combat and rises to the rank of lieutenant. Dizzy finally gets Johnny into bed, but is killed soon thereafter. In a daring mission, Zander and Carmen rescue Johnny and the dying Dizzy. A climactic battle ensues in which Zander is killed, but he, Carmen, Johnny and Carl are all instrumental in capturing a Brain Bug, an arachnid mastermind. The war goes on, but humanity has seized a dramatic advantage as the three friends are reunited.

*   *   *

Featuring astonishing special effects and some of the most harrowing battle scenes in movie history, *Starship Troopers* is the crowning achievement of Paul Verhoeven's filmmaking career to date. It also offers an opportunity to rethink his peculiar genius. For all his love of virile spectacle and evident desire to engage a mass audience, Verhoeven retains an inscrutable ironic streak that constantly threatens to undermine his quest for commercial success. Despite the artery-constricting pace and remarkably fluid photography, *Starship Troopers* may strike many viewers as a chilly, off-putting work, lacking the reassuring moral certitude and myth-informed sentimentality of a Lucas or Spielberg epic. It also offers a curious mixture of genres, half World War II guts-and-glory, half *Melrose Place*. While the fearsome Bugs (special effects artist Phil Tippett far outdoes his *Jurassic Park* work here) will please the crowds, rather more unnerving is *Starship Troopers'* presentation of the fascist-flavoured utopia, based on Robert A. Heinlein's original novel.

In *Starship*'s future, the twentieth century is remembered as an age when 'social scientists brought our world to the brink of chaos', and the generals seized the reins, as Michael Ironside's history teacher-cum-infantry lieutenant informs his charges. Inspired by the philosophy of Ayn Rand and others, Heinlein's 'utopia' may have been a deadly earnest prescription, but for Verhoeven it becomes an aesthetic and ideological field of play. As in *RoboCop* (and, less effectively, *Total Recall*), he constructs a half-ironic future landscape, a densely textured mix of historical imagery, Swiftian satire, and, most importantly, movie allusions.

This is a world where male and female soldiers fight, shower and bunk together with comradely nonchalance; where battlefield nuclear weapons and psychic powers have become nearly commonplace; where a murderer convicted in the morning will be executed that night on live television. Nonconformity, along with racial and ethnic divisions, has been swept away by a hegemonic Anglo-American monoculture. As usual, Verhoeven wants to play both ironist and devil's advocate. He maintains a plausible sardonic distance, while doing little to discourage viewers who may find the film's orderly universe appealing.

It's also a universe crowded with free-floating fragments of earlier fictions. In a broadcast called *Why We Fight* (the title of a World War II US-produced propaganda series), citizens proclaim, 'I'm doing my part!' and 'The only good bug is a dead bug!' A tough-as-nails infantry officer defending an impossible position rallies his troops by hollering: 'Come on, you apes! You want to live forever?' *Starship Troopers* clearly follows the pattern of numerous war pictures: a group of civilians is moulded into a warrior band and tested in the crucible of combat where some are killed and others hardened. Furthermore, the film echoes assorted World War II events: from the Bugs' sneak attack (Pearl Harbor), via the disastrous invasion and pell-mell retreat from Klendathu (Dunkirk) and the series of strategic peripheral attacks (island hopping in the Pacific), to the decisive turning point (D-Day).

But if classic war films offer unambiguous good guys and bad guys, Verhoeven here pulls an almost moral bait-and-switch. Of course, we'll root for the human race against a teeming hive of insects. But the humans in this film look and act more like the Nazis than the Allies. As Carl, the intelligence officer, Neil Patrick Harris boasts the wardrobe and insouciant smirk of a youthful *Ubersturmführer*. Moreover, we are told at first that the Bugs have no personalities and no civilisation, but the discovery of the caste of Brain Bugs scotches all such theories. For all the movie's humans know, there are arachnid poets greater than Milton.

Furthermore, if you understand the movie as an elaborate confidence game to illustrate the untrustworthy yet irresistible nature of narrative, its implausibly superficial characters (and no-star cast, drawn largely from US prime-time soaps) begin to make sense. With his Aryan cast for whom we're meant to root, Verhoeven seems to be commenting on the power of popular dramatic forms to mask noxious ideologies. As the relentlessly gung-ho Johnny, Casper Van Dien is less a handsome hunk than a 50s comic-book illustration of one, with his squarish, dimpled jaw and Popeye biceps. Boasting supermodel eyebrows, startling electric-blue eyes, and an infinitesimally upturned nose, Denise Richards, as the faithless Carmen, can muster only two expressions: happy and sad. Verhoeven seems to be simultaneously ridiculing this style of vapid, televisual melodrama and celebrating its power.

Add the parodic snippets of interactive television interspersed throughout the film – in which adorable tots play with live ammunition or stomp insects on suburban streets ('Know Your Foe!') – and the whole enterprise feels closer to Buñuel than to George Lucas. Like Fritz Lang and Ernst Lubitsch before him, Verhoeven is a European director who has learned to translate his artistic concerns into the Hollywood idiom. Verhoeven also lived under Nazi occupation as a small child in Amsterdam, and it's tempting to read *Starship Troopers* as a fable in which that occupation never ended. But it's not entirely clear what that child brought from that experience, in growing into the most duplicitous and diabolical mainstream film-maker since another tormented expatriate, Alfred Hitchcock. Verhoeven seems both hypnotised and horrified by the mass audience, imprisoned by his own need to attract a crowd and then feel superior to it. The results are fascinating, but when will the crowd, and the conjurer, grow tired of the game?

Andrew O'Hehir

SAVING PRIVATE RYAN
USA 1998
Director: Steven Spielberg

On D-Day, 1944, Captain Miller loses most of his men during an assault on Omaha beach. Afterwards, he is singled out for a special mission at the behest of the US chief of staff: three out of four Ryan brothers have been killed in the same week and the surviving Ryan, who is behind enemy lines, must be saved. Miller chooses six of his men, including Privates Reiben and Mellish, plus an interpreter, Corporal Upham. Reaching a town held by US airborne troops, the squad locates another Private Ryan. Miller loses one man to a sniper.

The next day, a wounded soldier tells them that Ryan has been sent to the town of Ramelle to guard a bridge against counterattack. En route, they attack a German machine-gun post, losing another man. The only surviving German soldier surrenders. They are about to kill him when Upham persuades Miller to let the man go. Enraged by the futility of their mission, Reiben threatens to desert. They finally track down Ryan outside Ramelle, but he refuses to leave his comrades. Miller decides to stay and help defend the bridge.

German tanks attack. Upham, paralysed by fear, fails to save Mellish from being killed by the same German soldier they spared earlier. After heavy losses, Miller retreats across the bridge, but US planes arrive just in time. The bridge is held, but Miller dies of his wounds. Upham captures the German soldier who killed Mellish and shoots him. The only other survivors are Ryan and Reiben. In the present, the elderly Ryan looks down at Miller's grave, and hopes that his life has proved worth saving.

*   *   *

Like *Schindler's List*, *Saving Private Ryan* ends in the present day, with a survivor of appalling carnage during World War II contemplating a memorial to the man who saved him. The saviour this time is Tom Hanks' Captain Miller, who in the aftermath of D-Day is sent behind German lines on a mission to rescue Private Ryan, an American soldier whose three brothers have all been killed in action in the same week. Miller's quixotic mission, to save one symbolic American soldier while thousands die around him, inevitably recalls Schindler's struggle to save a thousand out of the six million. In fact, the same tagline could do for both films: 'Whoever saves one life, saves the world entire.'

Unlike *Schindler's List*, which was based on fact (by way of Thomas Keneally's novel, *Schindler's Ark*), *Saving Private Ryan* is the invention of screenwriter Robert Rodat (whose best-known work hitherto was as co-writer of *Fly Away Home*). Unusually for Spielberg, it's not a project he initiated himself. But by choosing it he seems to be grasping the opportunity to revisit *Schindler's List*, only this time liberated from the ideological baggage which any Holocaust film must carry.

Working once again with the Polish-born cinematographer Janusz Kaminski, Spielberg abandons his usual emphatically storyboarded style in favour of a more urgent, handheld approach, with desaturated colour emulating the look of World War II colour newsreels. From the staggering twenty-five-minute opening sequence on Omaha beach during which Miller's troops are shot to pieces as they struggle to disembark from landing craft, the violence has the terrifying immediacy of the ghetto-clearance scenes in *Schindler's List*. But this time there's no equivalent of the little girl in red, the one sentimental spot of colour in a monochrome world. Apart from John Williams' sparingly used music, the climactic, *deus ex machina* appearance of US bombers roaring overhead, and the moment before the final battle when the rumble of approaching German tanks conjures up a memory of *Jurassic Park*, *Saving Private Ryan* is conspicuously free of overt Spielberg touches.

It's meaningless for critics to write of 'realism' in war movies, as most of us have no idea what war really looks like. But the action sequences in *Saving Private Ryan* are extraordinary: utterly believable, horrifyingly graphic in their depiction of death and injury, but somehow matter of fact, so that the worst atrocities are glimpsed out of the corner of one's eye, and the choreography never shows. For sheer gut-wrenching immediacy, the only war film that's comparable is *Come and See*, Elem Klimov's gruelling 1985 account of Nazi massacres in Belarus, which Spielberg would surely have watched while doing research for *Schindler's List*, if not before. One trick in particular recalls Klimov: at the height of the fighting, first on Omaha beach, then again at the very end in the devastated town of Ramelle, as the US soldiers defend a bridge from ferocious Panzer attack, Spielberg fades out the sound and replaces it with the roar inside the shellshocked Miller's head as all hell breaks loose around him.

The unselfconscious directness of Spielberg's *mise en scène* is matched by Robert Rodat's solidly constructed, unsensationalist script. Although the futility of Miller's mission – losing several men in order to save one – is pointed out by the squad's resident malcontent, Edward Burns' Private Reiben, this isn't a film about the insanity of war. Spielberg's war may be hell, but it has a point. Holding the bridge at Ramelle in the film's climactic battle will, we are told, help the Allies get to Berlin more quickly. (While contemporaries like Francis Ford Coppola, Brian De Palma and Oliver Stone have made films about Vietnam, Spielberg has preferred the more clear-cut moral universe of World War II. This is his fourth film about that war, not counting the *Indiana Jones* trilogy with its Nazi villains.)

In between the breathtaking action sequences, Rodat subtly sketches in the character and background of Miller and his seven men, including dependable NCO (Tom Sizemore's Horvath), Brooklyn cynic (Reiben) and sensitive medic (Giovanni Ribisi's Wade). They may sound like stock characters on paper, but it's to the credit of Rodat's writing and some very astute casting that only one of them ever seems like a scriptwriter's contrivance: Private Jackson (Barry Pepper), a superhumanly gifted sniper from the Deep South who prays out loud as he squints down his telescopic sight.

In *Apollo 13*, Hanks never seemed totally convincing as a man of action. But here he is perfectly cast as an ordinary man doing the best he can in impossible circumstances, and gradually losing his grip. The revelation of Miller's peacetime origins, the subject of much speculation among the other soldiers, is brilliantly timed to provide one of the film's most compelling moments. The film's key character isn't Miller, however, or Matt Damon's Private Ryan, but Corporal Upham. An interpreter seconded to Miller's squad after the landing at Omaha, Upham is the character closest to the audience and to Spielberg himself: he knows about war, and can quote Tennyson's 'The Charge of the Light Brigade', but he has never seen action. Played by Jeremy Davies, the incestuous teenager from *Spanking the Monkey*, Upham is bright, but nervous and clumsy. From the start he is set up as the innocent who – in time-honoured war-movie tradition – will surely come into his own under fire. There's a running joke about the squad's favourite expression, 'FUBAR', an acronym which he understands only when he has experienced the situation it describes first hand (to reveal it here would spoil the joke).

Upham also represents the squad's conscience. When they storm a machine-gun post behind lines, the other soldiers, enraged by the death of their comrade Wade during the assault, are about to kill the only surviving German soldier. Upham is appalled. After talking to the German, who pleads for his life by reeling off every American pop-culture reference he can think of, Upham persuades Miller to spare him. As they cannot take the prisoner with them on their mission, they have to let him go. Later, during the final battle in Ramelle, Upham is paralysed by fear. Spielberg keeps playing on our expectations that he will snap out of it and do something heroic. But he never does. In fact, in the film's most agonising scene, Upham fails to come to the rescue of Mellish, one of his comrades, as a German soldier slowly, almost tenderly, stabs him to death, telling him it's easier just to give in and die than to keep on fighting. Mellish isn't just any old GI: he's the squad's only Jew, earlier seen defiantly waving a Star of David in the faces of German prisoners of war. The man who kills him turns out to be the same German Upham saved earlier. Only at the very end of the film does Upham finally take action, recapturing the German and shooting him in cold blood. But it's hardly an act of redemption.

All this, in the light of *Schindler's List*, can hardly be coincidental. But what exactly is Spielberg trying to tell us here? That it's all right to kill prisoners of war? Or that American intellectuals like Upham, through their sympathy with the Germans as civilised human beings, somehow condoned the Holocaust? It's open to interpretation. But that itself is a breakthrough in a Spielberg film. The fact that he refrains from telling us what to think, even after setting us up for manipulation, is the ultimate proof – if any more were needed after this magnificent film – that he has come of age as an artist.

John Wrathall

THE MATRIX
USA/Australia 1999
Director: Andy Wachowski

Menial office worker Thomas Anderson operates by night as computer hacker Neo. Warnings from unknown girl Trinity fail to prevent his detection by law-enforcement agent Smith, who demands Neo help capture notorious subversive Morpheus. Refusing to co-operate, Neo is released. Trinity takes him to meet Morpheus, leader of the struggle against the Matrix, an artificial intelligence that controls the world. Morpheus explains that the planet's long-derelict citizens are trapped in the illusion of 1999 (really the distant past) until converted into food and energy to power the Matrix itself.

Joining Morpheus' team, Neo endures an agonising awakening process. Although his body is on a life-support system, a mental projection of his digital self roams the Matrix's simulation of the everyday. He can also be programmed with phenomenal skills. Morpheus is convinced they have found in Neo the fabled leader, The One, who can rescue the planet. Betrayed by fellow crew-member, Cypher, Morpheus is captured by Smith, desperate to prise from him the location of Zion, the last stronghold of humanity. Rushing to the rescue, Neo and Trinity battle enormous odds to save him. As Matrix forces close in, Smith traps Neo and shoots him down. But when Trinity declares her love to Neo's body his digital self is miraculously resurrected. He blows Smith apart and returns to his body just in time to thwart the Matrix invaders. Embracing Trinity and accepting his role as The One, he prepares to revitalise a dormant world.

*   *   *

The Wachowski Brothers wrote and sold the script for *The Matrix* before they made their first film, the mesmerising crime thriller *Bound*. They have since reported that between comic-book conception (a spin-off from their work at Marvel on the *Hellraiser* stories) and production go-ahead, 'the script that nobody understands' underwent considerable fine-tuning, thanks to studio insistence on explanatory dialogue. Even so, for a breathlessly vertiginous first quarter *The Matrix* scorns offering any rationale behind its attention-grabbing assaults and chases, leaving only its peevish spokesperson to mutter legitimate protests on our behalf ('This is insane! Why is it happening to me? What did *I* do?') until reasonably concluding he must be half-asleep. At which point, naturally, he falls into the grasp of Morpheus.

The Wachowskis are good at names, as they demonstrated with the title and main trio of *Bound*: Corky (buoyant), Violet (clinging) and Caesar (dictatorial). Conjuring up a flock of evocations – Cypher, Tank, Switch, Apoc, Mouse – for *The Matrix*, they invest the film's gradually uncovered crusade with a rich blend of messianic implications blatantly signalled by warrior priestess Trinity. Her unifying presence links – and exchanges – the powers of Morpheus the dream-master with those of the long-sought saviour Neo (note the anagram) who is at once the New Man (as in, by useful coincidence, Neo-Tokyo, subsumed by *Akira*) and the neophyte disciple.

More squarely, the film is an ironic rereading of *Logan's Run* (1976), with a nod to *Soylent Green* (1973) and more than a dash of *Zardoz* (1973). The Wachowskis unveil a seedy utopia where mankind is preserved, protected and endlessly recycled by its own mega-computer. The alternative to this artificial stasis is, as usual, well beyond the wit of mortal proles. Necessarily, *The Matrix* ends much where it started, its newborn visionary poised – like Logan or *2001*'s Starchild or *THX 1138*'s hero or even like Luke Skywalker (prime exponent of the 'Why me?' syndrome) – on the brink of literally unimaginable new benefits. Away from the meddlesome tyranny of the machine, the superhero will be in charge. There's always One.

The prospect is less than reassuring and the Wachowskis don't hide their misgivings. Played by Keanu Reeves with a certain gloomy helplessness, Neo gives a good impression of being incapable of original thought (he is, after all, as programmed as any Matrix slave) and little sign of inspiring social reform. But two voices speak loudly and persuasively on behalf of the Matrix: the traitorous terrorist Cypher celebrates it for colourful comforts unmatched by the drab post-apocalyptic real world; and the fearsome man-in-black humanoid, Agent Smith (not quite Winston Smith, but the Wachowskis, recognising an affinity, have mischievously appended a Room 101) spells out its evolutionary task by dismissing humans as 'a plague – and we are the cure'. The same dispassionate logic was prologue to *The Terminator* and more recently at the core of *Virus*.

But if the Wachowskis claim no originality of message, they are startling innovators of method. As with *Bound*, the film is a feast of unexpected fidgets and perspectives, punctuated by trademark overhead shots and teasing detail and detour, such as the squeal of washed windows as Neo is reprimanded by his boss, or the White Rabbit subtext culminating in a glimpse of *Night of the Lepus* (1972) on a television. Just as in *Bound*, telephones play a vital role, while the fetishistic use of shades and black leather tells yet another story, encompassing Smith's chipped lens and Neo's triumphal final outfit. Primarily, *The Matrix* is a wonderland of tricks and stunts, light years from Kansas, combining computerised slow-motion with the extravagant choreography of martial-arts movies to create a broadside of astonishing images. As Neo turns cartwheels, blazing away behind wildly exploding decor, it seems clear that the Wachowskis have discovered a gleeful utopia of their own.

Philip Strick

STAR WARS EPISODE I THE PHANTOM MENACE
USA 1999
Director: George Lucas

The Galactic Republic is in jeopardy. Two Jedi knights, Qui-Gon Jinn and his apprentice Obi-Wan Kenobi, are sent to the distant planet of Naboo to negotiate a dispute between the planet's leaders and the nefarious heads of the Trade Federation. Qui-Gon and Obi-Wan are ambushed and barely survive: the Federation's blockade is a cover for an invasion of Naboo, sponsored by a shadowy Sith master, or dark Jedi.

Landing on the planet, Qui-Gon and Obi-Wan befriend Jar Jar Binks, a member of the Gunga species. The invasion is successful, but Qui-Gon and Obi-Wan help Naboo's Queen Amidala escape. While escaping, the droid R2-D2 saves their ship from destruction, but needing repairs, they stop on the trade planet of Tatooine. Meanwhile the Sith lord sends his apprentice Darth Maul after Amidala.

On Tatooine, Qui-Gon meets a slave boy named Anakin Skywalker whom he identifies immediately as a born Jedi. Qui-Gon wins the boy's freedom – and spare parts for the ship – by betting against Anakin's master on a pod race which Anakin wins over his archrival. As the group leaves Tatooine, Darth Maul appears and duels with Qui-Gon. On the Republic's central planet, Amidala learns the Galactic Senate will not help Naboo. The Jedi Council is disturbed to hear a new Sith is at large, but refuses to let Qui-Gon train Anakin as a Jedi Knight, despite Qui-Gon's contention that Anakin is 'the chosen one who will bring balance to the Force'. Yoda believes Anakin is potentially vulnerable to the Dark Side.

Amidala decides to go back to Naboo to mount an insurrection against the Federation. Qui-Gon, Obi-Wan, Jar Jar and Anakin go with her. On Naboo, she convinces the Gunga to mount an assault, drawing droid forces away from the city, while her band sneak into the palace to capture the Federation's viceroy. Just as the Gunga are losing the battle, Anakin pilots a ship that destroys the Federation's command vessel. Darth Maul kills Qui-Gon in a light-sabre duel, but is then killed by Obi-Wan, who takes Anakin as his apprentice after Naboo is liberated.

*   *   *

Any film that begins with a seven-word title and then includes the words 'taxation' and 'debate' in its first five seconds is either a deadly historical epic about the American Revolution or is taking its audience for granted. I'm tempted to suggest *Star Wars Episode I The Phantom Menace* fits both of these criteria, but George Lucas' allegories are so muddled it's impossible to make sense of them. Start with a distinctive New World lust for ancient traditions of aristocracy and order, toss in a misguided effort at multiculturalism and season with the Aryan myth of racial purity, and you've got a murky, talky prequel that emphasises all the series' weakest elements rather than its strongest ones.

In the last year or two, film-makers have finally reached the point of diminishing returns with computer-generated effects. It's now possible for films to spend vast sums on effects and still look laughably cheap (see, for instance, *The Mummy*). *The Phantom Menace* doesn't have that problem precisely, but almost nothing in it is based on photographing actual human beings in their environments. Every shot is such a complex technical achievement, so full of droids, aliens, spacecraft or gargantuan structures, that the movie itself takes on the hazy, ugly look of software. Even if this is deliberate, it doesn't work – the excessively electric-blue skies and green fields of the planet Naboo may be meant to remind us that we are not on earth, but what they really make us aware of is that what we're seeing isn't real.

Lucas has never been much of a visual stylist (at least, not since the days of *THX 1138*, 1970), but the characteristic cleanliness and contrast of his compositions – the brilliant, antiseptic white of the stormtroopers' uniforms, the lustrous blue-black of Darth Vader's helmet – have been abandoned here in favour of meaningless clutter. Certainly some of this film's grand set pieces are impressive. The great battle between the benevolent, amphibious Gunga and the Federation's droids, lightly echoing the Agincourt scene from Olivier's *Henry V* (1944), is marvellous to behold in a *Jurassic Park* way. The vast, ovoid interior of the Galactic Senate, with its regimented rows of desks curving away into infinity, is a splendid visual joke about the inefficacy of politics on a grand scale. But Lucas' imagery often seems rooted in nothing particular. Naboo's capital looks like the Babylon of D.W. Griffith's *Intolerance* (1916) just because it *can*, not because it should. Compared with the visual wit and imagination of such 90s science-fiction epics as *The Matrix* and *Starship Troopers*, *The Phantom Menace*'s aesthetic seems leaden and outdated.

In a laboured quest to recapture some of the first trilogy's (sorry, the *second* trilogy's) humour, Lucas and his enormous team of collaborators have created many cartoonish new species. The Gunga character Jar Jar Binks, with his rubbery platypus face, joke-Caribbean accent and jive walk right out of a 70s blaxploitation movie (with bell-bottom trousers to match) may amuse small children, but many adults will find *The Phantom Menace*'s quasi-racial typing patronising at best. When you consider that the Trade Federation leaders speak in hackneyed Fu Manchu accents and the elephant-insect character who owns the slave Anakin Skywalker resembles a traditional caricature of the hook-nosed Jewish trader, the whole picture becomes much more disturbing. Of course I don't believe Lucas has any consciously racist agenda; what's involved here are multiple failures of common sense, good taste and imagination. You have to wonder whether he has spent so long in an alternative universe – both the one inside his own head and the one in Marin County – that he can't tell the difference between a sensitive depiction of cultural difference and offensive stereotypes.

But the biggest problem with *The Phantom Menace* is that it lacks narrative coherence. Lucas' intrusive use of diagonal and horizontal optical wipes only reinforces the sense that this movie is all stitches and no fabric. Logically, this wants to be the story of Obi-Wan Kenobi's early relationship with Anakin Skywalker (soon to become Darth Vader), but the two scarcely exchange a word until the movie's final scenes. Qui-Gon Jinn is arguably the central character, with Liam Neeson supplying the requisite combination of Zen gnosticism and kung-fu athleticism. But we learn nothing about his life, and his relationship with Obi-Wan adds up to little more than a lot of graceful tandem swordplay. As Obi-Wan Ewan McGregor is one of several outstanding actors given virtually nothing to do. Another is Pernilla August as Anakin's mother. We're told she and Anakin are passionately attached (and it's hinted that his love for his mother will be his downfall), but their scenes together are bland and generic and she surrenders him to Qui-Gon without a murmur.

Indeed, the film's extended sojourn on Tatooine mostly serves to set up Anakin's pod race, which may thrill younger viewers who haven't grown tired of Lucas' careening point-of-view shots, but doesn't really advance the story. Similar galactic-bazaar locations have been presented with equal vigour in earlier films, and we don't learn anything about Anakin's childhood we couldn't grasp quickly in a brief flashback. Beyond our general sympathy for David over Goliath, it's also not clear why we should care much about Naboo. As its Queen Amidala, Natalie Portman looks smashing in a series of Japanese-influenced getups and hairdos (did she escape with her hairdresser?) but neither she nor anyone else has anything like an adult emotional life. I understand the series' prepubescent asexuality is part of its appeal, but it might be nice to feel some sense of evolution or possibility. Lucas' narrative's mystical long arc – the conflict between the Jedi and the Sith, the Force and the Dark Side – isn't foregrounded until Qui-Gon brings Anakin before the Jedi Council. The whole Jedi concept – a eugenic warrior caste guided by pure spirit and shaped by elite training – is so troubling it calls the entire political dimension of Lucas' universe into question. His desire to combine a faith in democracy with idealised systems of royalty, nobility and knighthood is almost comically American. But the *Star Wars* notion of democracy is no better than a fuzzy abstraction, a cover story for the mystical Manichaeanism of the Jedi, who, by all appearances, are a masculine cult of chastity and purity straight out of Wagner's *Parsifal*. Like the great Teutonic composer, Lucas has tapped into a tremendously powerful Jungian current of pantheistic myth. However one interprets it, this

Index